EVERYDAY POSTSOCIALISM IN EASTERN EUROPE

CENTRAL EUROPEAN STUDIES

The demise of the Communist Bloc and more recent conflicts in the Balkans and Ukraine have exposed the need for greater understanding of the broad stretch of Europe that lies between Germany and Russia. The Central European Studies series enriches our knowledge of the region by producing scholarly work of the highest quality. Since its founding, this has been one of the only English-language series devoted primarily to the lands and peoples of the Habsburg Empire, its successor states, and those areas lying along its immediate periphery. Salient issues such as democratization, censorship, competing national narratives, and the aspirations and treatment of national minorities bear evidence to the continuity between the region's past and present.

SERIES EDITORS

Howard Louthan, University of Minnesota
Daniel L. Unowsky, University of Memphis
Dominique Reill, University of Miami
Paul Hanebrink, Rutgers University
Maureen Healy, Lewis & Clark College
Nancy M. Wingfield, Northern Illinois University

OTHER TITLES IN THIS SERIES

Limiting Privilege: Upward Mobility Within Higher Education in Socialist Poland
Agata Zysiak

Women, Nationalism, and Social Networks in the Habsburg Monarchy, 1848–1918
Marta Verginella

Imagining Slovene Socialist Modernity:
The Urban Redesign of Ljubljana's Beloved Trnovo Neighborhood, 1951–1989
Veronica E. Aplenc

Combating the Hydra: Violence and Resistance in the Habsburg Empire, 1500–1900
Stephan Steiner

Przemyśl, Poland: A Multiethnic City During and After a Fortress, 1867–1939
John E. Fahey

Transleithanian Paradise: A History of the Budapest Jewish Community, 1738–1938
Howard N. Lupovitch

Finding Order in Diversity: Religious Toleration in the Habsburg Empire, 1792–1848
Scott Berg

EVERYDAY POSTSOCIALISM IN EASTERN EUROPE

History Doesn't Travel in One Direction

Edited by
Jill Massino and
Markus Wien

Purdue University Press · West Lafayette, Indiana

Copyright 2024 by Purdue University. All rights reserved.

Cataloging-in-Publication Data is available from the Library of Congress.
978-1-61249-969-7 (hardback)
978-1-61249-970-3 (paperback)
978-1-61249-971-0 (epub)
978-1-61249-972-7 (epdf)

Cover image courtesy of Hajdu Tamás

For Sofia and Sebastian
For Martin and Sabina

CONTENTS

FOREWORD

Mapping Heres and Theres

CRISTOFER SCARBORO

IT's A TRICKY THING TO WRITE A FOREWORD FOR A VOLUME ENTITLED *EVeryday Postsocialism in Eastern Europe*. Forewords imply beginnings—looking to the future from the clean page of the present. Forewords imply, well, *forward* movement and clear directions. We are *here* and are going *there*. As the chapters in this volume make clear, beginnings and heres and theres are muddy and complicated things in Eastern Europe. They are muddy and complicated everywhere, but Eastern Europeans seem to be more attuned to this fact than most—this is perhaps the most important thing we can learn by delving into Eastern European studies. History does not travel in one direction.

As Victor Petrov notes, very few people in the East understand 1989 as a clean break with the socialist past, but, every semester, my students are shocked that Bulgarians call the events of that year "the changes," *promenite*. The ambiguity of the term—*changes from what to what?*—offends their need for clarity. So too does the lack of judgment: any verdict on whether the changes were *good* or *not*. The students, with their American sense of history, assume the changes were for the better.

This volume serves as a bracing corrective to these assumptions. The "flowering of human rights" promised by the collapse of communism (a movement that, as Joanna Wawryzniak pointedly notes, had antecedents in the communist period) are often plowed under in the transition to liberal democratic capitalism. A resurgent Catholic Church in Poland, hand in glove with the formerly anticommunist opposition (now firmly in power as the Law and Justice Party), has positioned itself firmly *against* LGBTQ rights (see Agnieska Kościańska's chapter). Hungary, under the leadership of the proudly illiberal Viktor Orbán, has erected barrier after barrier between his vision of a Christian, ethnically Magyar, and heteronormative nation and those that "don't fit" (see Renkin). Events after 1989, seen from 20,000 feet, are perhaps best viewed as a "hollowing out" of alternative visions of globalization—moving from socialist networks and visions of political economy to liberal democratic capitalist ones (again, as

Aninna Gagiyova notes, with antecedents in the socialist era).[1] Privatization and global-ization (with a capitalist face) has meant the loss of worker autonomy and the closing of sugar plants (Klipa) and the demonization and expulsion of formerly fraternal social-ist students and workers (Apostolova). The "revolutionary year" saw the entrenchment of party elites across the supposed rupture of the collapse of communism (Horváth).

Orienting self and society in this world of "time out of joint" are exercises in coping with uncertain futures and searching for usable pasts in the misty reaches of time (again with its antecedents under state socialism—see Petrov). Romanians living abroad—forming a "diaspora at home"—have sought to shape a "normal country" in the face of, I suppose, the *abnormality* of the transition present and/or the state socialist past (Gh-erghina and Farcas). It was not only East German children suffering feelings of "loss, disappointment, and disillusionment" in the face of the changes (Kind-Kovács). Ironi-cally or not, this is the same language I increasingly hear from my students as they think about their place in history. In the intervening three decades since 1989, the valences have shifted. Orbán's illiberalism has given him something of a star turn on Fox News' *Tucker Carlson Today* (at one point the most highly viewed cable news program in the United States), highlighted by the documentary "Hungary vs. Soros: A Fight for Civi-lization."[2] Close observation of Eastern Europe allows us to rethink understandings of normalcy and abnormality in the seemingly timeless global present. With apologies for self-indulgence, I want to use this foreword to think a bit about why we study Eastern Europe and what we can learn from its asynchronicity and ambivalence.

My students are a product of a reading of history born out of the end of the Cold War closely entwined with the *Bildungsroman* of my generation and our expectations for the future. In the United States the collapse of communism was understood as an epochal event—ushering in what the first George Bush claimed was a "new world order."[3] His-tory and ideology, frozen by the Cold War, were flowing again after 1989—we could see change unfolding at dizzying speed. Communism, as an alternative form of modernity and the great challenger to liberal democratic capitalism as an ideological vision of the good life, was seemingly consigned to the dustbin of history. One teleological history leading to communism as the final stage of human social evolution was replaced by an-other promising a historical endpoint realized in full freedom and growing prosperity. The history of Eastern Europe—"derailed" according to Ivan Berend—was returning to its tracks.[4] In his New Year's address as the world moved from 1989 to 1990, the first postcommunist president of Czechoslovakia, Václav Havel, joyfully proclaimed, "Peo-ple, your government has returned to you!"[5] We didn't ask where it had been.

Instead, we were told that there was no going back—the old social contracts were (as much as possible) rendered null and void. Margaret Thatcher confidently declared that "there were no alternatives" to the Western model. Perhaps more prosaically, she also declared that "there was no such thing as society, only individuals and interests."[6] This was couched at the time as creating "normal societies" in the postcommunist eastern half of the continent (and the connection to the project of "normalization" after 1968 in Czechoslovakia—a society Havel acidly understood as "refrigerator socialism"—was either unnoticed or left unsaid). The new world—the new normal—was to be a slightly boring world of shared global values and tastes. The unique tributaries of social development joined together in a common flow until they reached the mighty ocean at the end of history's shore.[7] Eastern Europeans were to "rejoin" what Gorbachev, embodying fully the spirit of the age, called "our common European home."[8] A little-known State Department functionary, Francis Fukuyama, became a star by announcing that we had arrived at the "end of history." The good society, or at least the very best we could do, was cooked down to a simple formula: "liberal democracy in the political sphere; easy access to VCRs in the economic."[9] This was couched as a *universal* history—larded with Hegel to give it a philosophical heft—which promised a single destination for all human society: liberal democratic capitalism. Not everyone was there yet, but arrival for *all* was certain. What a time to be alive!

Many of us—those coming of age in what was soon to be called post–Cold War America—believed this. History itself had fulfilled its function. The triumph of the American way of life seemed poured in concrete—we had turned Faulkner inside out: the past *was* past and dead. History was quickly moving in one direction toward its obsolescence. I was a history major in the early 1990s, captivated by the epochal changes unfolding around me, worried about missing out, and (giving myself too much credit) fretful about the white bread suburban future promised to me at the end of history. Fukuyama warned that the end of history would be boring, and I was bored. And I promised that, as I graduated, I would find somewhere that history mattered (before it disappeared).

Eastern Europe, for good or ill, seemed just that kind of space in the mid-1990s. In college, I spent much of my free time reading stories of the triumph of democracy mixed with lurid and gory stories of the wars in Yugoslavia. These are wars that are often left out of accounts of the end of the state socialist system (and they ask us to think again about the nature of state violence in the past thirty years in Eastern Europe). When I was a sophomore, my father gave me a copy of Rebecca West's *Black Lamb and Grey Falcon*, a traveler's account of interwar Yugoslavia, for summer reading, and its dedication: "to my friends in Yugoslavia, who are all now dead or enslaved," seemed all too current and kept me up at night. West's project to "show the past side by side with the present it created"[10] seemed like something to dedicate one's life to. In the Balkans this still seemed possible. (I do want to note here, parenthetically, that this was before I had read and absorbed the works of Said and Todorova—the orientalism involved in the creation of my twenty-year-old Balkan fever dream was fully uninvestigated at the time). I told everyone who would listen that when I graduated, I wanted to go to Serbia (then in the midst of its genocidal civil war). Being less brave than I thought myself to be, I got a job teaching English in Haskovo, Bulgaria.

As you might suspect, I became a historian because I fell in love with Bulgaria. Most Bulgarians find this pretty funny, as I was there during what was called the *Videnovo vreme*: from 1996 to 1997.[11] This was a time of triple-digit inflation. A time of $800 million "bailouts" from the International Monetary Fund. This was a time when my school closed for the winter—for almost three months—because it could not afford the heating bills. This was a time of packs of semi-feral, hungry dogs in the streets. I loved it— this is the part that my Bulgarian friends find either uproariously funny or legitimately insane—and my time there, and the questions it raised, have indeed been something to dedicate my life to. What I loved most was that Bulgaria *was*, in fact, a place where one *could* see the past side by side with the present it created. You could still see the vague outlines of alternative modernities and unburied pasts. The packs of dogs were alternatively blamed on the communist past and/or the capitalist present (sometimes by the same people). My friends were only too happy to talk about the legacy of communism (for good or ill), the development of national identity, and the role of shifting borders. Nothing was settled. History in Bulgaria seemed alive and meaningful—one's reading of it was constitutive of one's identity (including, of course, my own).

I was not at all unique in this experience. Eastern Europe in the 1990s was littered with Americans traveling to the "exotic" postcommunist world to find themselves. To experience the revolution. To live the transition from communism to capitalism and to see the "return of liberty" for themselves. To see time stop (or restart) and see the end of history arrive. In the moment, it seemed as if everyone my age was writing a novel while discovering themselves in Prague. Eastern Europe served as something of a fun house mirror for those of us traveling from "normal" liberal democratic capitalist societies. We came to define ourselves against the reflected outlines of Borat and imagined countries like Molvania, "a land untouched by modern dentistry."[12] Reports on Eastern Europe have continued in the long tradition of (self-) orientalization and the heavy burden of historical backwardness. "Rivers of blood" (in this case the Danube and its historical baggage) turning into rivers of hope (future ascension into the European Union).[13] Witold Szabłowski's *Dancing Bears: True Stories of People Nostalgic for Life under Tyranny* uses the hairy metaphor of retired dancing bears at Belitsa nature preserve in southwestern Bulgaria—a place where "bears are taught to live in freedom"—without noting that they are learning these lessons in a deeply artificial environment. Nor does he seriously ask why people might be nostalgic for a world undone.[14] John Feffer's *Aftershock* is subtitled a journey into Eastern Europe's broken dreams—tellingly the journey is divided into two sections: "Stepping Backward" and "Leaping Forward."[15] The transition after 1989 seemed destined to carry Eastern Europeans into a new (brighter?!) era.

But the step back was painful—and it employed the loss of futures promised. And the "transition has now lasted more than three decades." The thirtieth anniversary of the collapse of communism has produced a range of work detailing the Eastern European understandings of the time of transition—little of which confirms what those writing from the West anticipated. In Kristen Ghodsee and Mitchell Orenstein's recent book *Taking Stock of Shock*, the through line for all of this is: "The irony is that the transition to liberal democracy and free markets was largely achieved through undemocratic means and failed to generate widespread prosperity."[16] Their work outlines a series of Eastern European crises: gross income inequality, a mortality crisis, a fertility crisis, and an outmigration crisis (and in her book *Why Women Have Better Sex under Socialism*, Ghodsee outlines a crisis in sexual pleasure and personal autonomy).

Public opinion surveys reveal striking ambivalence about the transition to liberal democratic capitalism. Typical is the Pew Center's study published in October 2019, "European Public Opinion Three Decades since the Fall of Communism."[17] In every country in Eastern Europe—with the notable exception of Poland—approval of the shift to a multiparty electoral system and a free market economy has decreased significantly since 1989: 76 percent of Bulgarians approved of multiparty electoral systems in 1991 (when the Pew Center first began polling)—today it's 54 percent. Similarly, approval for a free-market economy in Bulgaria has declined from 73 percent to 55 percent. Barely half of Bulgarians today approve of these changes—and only 32 percent say the transition has improved their standards of living. In parts of the former Soviet Union approval is even harder to find. Only 43 percent of Russians approve of multiparty elections; fewer still—38 percent—approve of the free market. Even the "success stories" of Central and Eastern Europe—Poland, the former German Democratic Republic (GDR), and the Czech Republic—range from 15 to 25 percent *disapproval* of free-market liberal democracy. Overall, across all of Eastern Europe, only 41 percent believe that the collapse of communism has benefited "ordinary people" a "great deal or a fair amount"—56 percent believe that ordinary people have benefited "not too much or not at all."[18]

It is true, and the Pew study notes, that the young and better educated are more supportive of the changes undertaken since 1989. Those who didn't grow up under communism are less likely to bemoan its passing. These are, however, precisely the people that are leaving Eastern Europe in droves (Lenin would say that they are voting with their feet). As Tim Judah notes in his recent article "Bye-Bye Balkans: A Region in Critical Demographic Decline," current projections indicate that Bulgaria will have 38.6 percent fewer people by 2050 than it did in 1990. Bulgaria's population has already declined in real numbers from around 9 million in 1989 to fewer than 7 million today. These numbers are broadly true across the region—Moldova has already lost over a third of its population since 1991.[19]

Again, even the "winners" in transition are in the midst of a demographic crisis: Poland projects to have 15 percent fewer people in 2050; Hungary 20 percent fewer.[20] Stories abound in the European press of Polish plumbers (and Russian oligarchs) in London; teenagers from Ukraine sex-trafficked to Germany; and Romanian taxi drivers in Paris. According to the Institute of Population and People at the Bulgarian Academy of Sciences, there are now officially over 500 so-called ghost villages in the country.[21] These are villages that existed in 1989 but now no longer do; 1989 created new landscapes and subjects. Sofia, at least parts of Sofia, have been completely transformed (my friends in Sofia note that the city must have the highest number of malls per capita in Europe). So has Haskovo, the city where I first began teaching. In 1996 it had 80,000 people; the most recent census, conducted in 2021, lists it as having fewer than 40,000 people. During my last visit there (in December 2021) I couldn't find a place to buy a toothbrush after 7:00 p.m.

Eastern European politics and public opinion have not been kind to Fukuyama's thesis. A quick look at Bulgarian parliamentary elections since the collapse of communism reveal two major trends. The first is a cratering of political participation. Since elections for the constitutional assembly in 1990, which saw 91 percent voter participation, the number has settled at around half of eligible voters. This is perhaps to be expected in a world without politics (or a world without ideological debate). Bulgarian voter participation rates are more or less equivalent to rates in other states in transition.[22] Eastern European voter participation quickly found itself within the expected range of established European democracies—though Bulgaria, along with France and Portugal, finds itself at the lower end of this spectrum. Of course, much of this decline comes from the euphoria and hangover brought on by the arrival of liberal democratic practices. It is hard to imagine a scenario where 95 percent turnout rates are normalized. Even in the "Western democracies" turnout has declined significantly since 1989. France fell from 68.9 percent in 1993 to 48.7 percent in 2022; Great Britain from 77.7 percent in 1992 to 67.3 percent in 2019; Italy from 87.4 percent in 1992 to 73.01 percent in 2018; Portugal from 67.8 percent in 1990 to 51.5 percent in 2022. During this time voter participation rates were only stable in Germany, the Netherlands, and Spain. Democracy at the end of history seems to result in a declining interest in democratic practices.

The second major trend in the transition politics has been the striking rise of what might be called "savior candidates"—those from outside the political system, come to rescue the Bulgarian people from the political class and the chaos that has emerged in their wake. You can see this in the precipitous rise and fall of ephemeral personality-driven parties that have erupted with regularity over the course of the past thirty years. Since the changes, Bulgarians have elected their former czar (a man with no political experience and who had not been in the country since 1946) as prime minister in 2001—he won 43 percent of the vote in a field of five parties in what had to be understood as a "plague on both your houses" election. Most recently, the country has seen the rise of the popular late-night television show personality Slavi Trifonov. And, as in much of Europe, Bulgarians have seen the rise of ugly nationalist parties (most importantly the Ataka Party, led by Volen Siderov, a role now being taken by the Vuzrazhdane [Revival] Party). The Bulgarian political system has lurched from crisis to crisis—since April 2021 the country has held five national elections (with a sixth scheduled for June 2024).

Timothy Garton Ash's famous offhand comment that the transition from one system to another took "ten years in Poland, Hungary ten months, East Germany ten weeks," and Czechoslovakia "ten days" has revealed itself in thirty years of equivocal transition.[23] Time has not moved uniformly in any direction; sharp breaks with the past reveal themselves to be anything but. The carnival of revolution has left something of a long hangover.[24] Most horrifically, the Russian invasion of Ukraine has covered all of this in a shroud of tragedy and pathos-filled conversations of missed opportunities and roads not taken. Timothy Garton Ash's newest work asks if it is "time for a new liberation?"[25] And Fukuyama is in the *New York Times* promoting his newest book, *Liberalism and Its Discontents*, which predicts (hopes?) that the war in Ukraine will "revive the spirit of 1989."[26]

So what was this spirit of 1989? We were promised that the collapse of communism represented the dawning of a new historical era—the triumph of liberalism and human rights, democratic practices, and capitalist economic principles. If not an ideal, the changes ushered in by the collapse of communism were understood as "the best that we could do," ending what Tony Judt has called the "200-year promise of radical progress."[27] This volume demonstrates that the promises of radical progress were put to bed while there was still much work to be done. The eerie familiarity of the social crisis in Eastern Europe when viewed from the other side of the ruins of the Berlin Wall speaks to the painful limits of the promised new world order. In Eastern Europe we can see that time does not move in one direction, and that alternative futures, thought buried, can spring to life.

NOTES

1. See also, James Mark, Bogdan C. Iacob, Tobias Rupprecht, and Ljubica Spaskovska, *1989: A Global History of Eastern Europe* (Cambridge: Cambridge University Press, 2019).
2. Benjamin Novak and Michael M. Grynbaum, "Conservative Fellow Travelers: Tucker Carlson Drops In on Viktor Orban," *New York Times*, August 7, 2021, https://www.nytimes.com/2021/08/07/world/europe/tucker-carlson-hungary.html; Viktória Serdült, "Tucker Carlson Has Become Obsessed with Hungary. Here's What He

Doesn't Understand," *Politico*, February 1, 2022, https://www.politico.com/news /magazine/2022/02/01/tucker-carlson-hungary-orban-00004149.

3. George Bush, "Address Before a Joint Session of the Congress on the Persian Gulf Crisis and the Federal Budget Deficit. September 11, 1990," George H. W. Bush Presidential Library, https://bush41library.tamu.edu/archives/public-papers/2217.

4. Ivan Berend, *History Derailed: Central and Eastern Europe in the Long Nineteenth Century* (Berkeley: University of California Press, 2005).

5. President Václav Havel, "Havel's New Year's Address to the Nation, 1990," *Making the History of 1989*, Item #111, http://old.hrad.cz/president/Havel/speeches/1990/0101 _uk.html.

6. Margaret Thatcher, "There is no alternative" (from a speech to the Conservative Women's Conference, May 21, 1980), Margaret Thatcher Foundation, https://www.margaret thatcher.org/document/104368; Thatcher, "There is no such thing as society" (from an interview for *Woman's Own*, September 23, 1987), Margaret Thatcher Foundation, https://www.margaretthatcher.org/document/106689.

7. Jacob Mikanowski, "Goodbye to Eastern Europe," *Los Angeles Review of Books*, January 27, 2017, https://lareviewofbooks.org/article/goodbye-eastern-europe/.

8. Speech by Mikhail Gorbachev to the Council of Europe in Strasbourg, "Europe as a Common Home," Wilson Center Digital Archive, July 6, 1989, https://digitalarchive .wilsoncenter.org/document/speech-mikhail-gorbachev-council-europe-strasbourg -europe-common-home.

9. Francis Fukuyama, "The End of History?" *National Interest* 16 (Summer 1989): 3–18.

10. Rebecca West, *Black Lamb and Grey Falcon: A Journey through Yugoslavia*, repr. ed. (New York: Penguin Classics, 2007).

11. *Videnovo vreme*, the time of Zhan Videnov as prime minister of Bulgaria (February 1995–January 1997) and a period of hyperinflation and economic crisis. The very definition of "disaster capitalism."

12. Santo Cilauro, Tom Gleisner, and Rob Sitch, *Molvania: A Land Untouched by Modern Dentistry* (New York: Overlook Press, 2005).

13. Richard Bernstein, "The Danube Transformed: From River of Blood to River of Hope," *New York Times*, August 1, 2003; Bernstein, "Vienna's Grandeur Fails to Mask a Sense of Loss," *New York Times*, August 3, 2003; Bernstein, "East on the Danube: Hungary's Tragic Century," *New York Times*, August 9, 2003; "Down the River to the Sullen Balkans," *New York Times*, August 19, 2003; Bernstein, "A Declining City's Past, A Dislocated Writer's Memory," *New York Times*, September 1, 2003; Bernstein, "Romania Survives, but It Falls Behind in Europe," *New York Times*, September 21, 2003. These articles were all connected to the decision to admit Bulgaria and Romania into the European Union.

14. Witold Szabłowski, *Dancing Bears: True Stories of People Nostalgic for Life under Tyranny* (New York: Penguin Books, 2014).

15. John Feffer, *Aftershocks: A Journey into Eastern Europe's Broken Dreams* (London: Zed Books, 2017).

16. Kristin Ghodsee and Mitchell A. Orenstein, *Taking Stock of Shock: Social Consequences of the 1989 Revolutions* (Oxford: Oxford University Press, 2021), 197.

17. Richard Wike et al., *European Public Opinion Three Decades after the Fall of Communism*, Pew Research Center, October 15, 2019, https://www.pewresearch.org/global/2019/10/15/european-public-opinion-three-decades-after-the-fall-of-communism.

18. Wike et al., *European Public Opinion.*

19. Tim Judah, "Bye-Bye Balkans: A Region in Critical Decline," *Balkan Insight*, October 24, 2019, https://balkaninsight.com/2019/10/14/bye-bye-balkans-a-region-in-critical-demographic-decline/.

20. Judah, "Bye-Bye Balkans."

21. Ivan Bakalov and Nevena Borisova, "Ghost Villages and the Slow Death of Rural Bulgaria," *Equal Times*, October 21, 2013, https://www.equaltimes.org/ghost-villages-and-the-slow-death#.Xah0buhKjD5.

22. Slovakia saw voter participation fall from 95 percent in 1990 to 65 percent in 2020 (bottoming out at 55 percent in 2006). This mirrors almost exactly Czech participation during those years. Most dramatically, Romania's voter turnout fell from 86 percent in 1990 to 32 percent in 2020. Hungary and Poland are the only postcommunist states whose turnout rates remained stable, both beginning and ending in the 60 percent range (though this stability depends more on the fact that turnout rate in these countries started out lower than in their fellow Eastern European states).

23. Timothy Garton Ash, *The Magic Lantern: The Revolution of '89 Witnessed in Warsaw, Budapest, Berlin and Prague*, repr. ed. (London: Vintage, 1999), 78.

24. Padraic Kenney, *A Carnival of Revolution: Central Europe* (Princeton, NJ: Princeton University Press, 2003).

25. Timothy Garton Ash, "Time for a New Liberation?" *New York Review of Books*, no. 16, Oct. 24, 2019.

26. Jennifer Schuessler, "Francis Fukuyama Predicted the End of History: It's Back (Again)," *New York Times*, May 10, 2022. See Francis Fukuyama, *Liberalism and Its Discontents* (New York: Farrar, Straus and Giroux, 2022).

27. Tony Judt, *Ill Fares the Land* (New York: Penguin, 2010), 139.

ACKNOWLEDGMENTS

THE INSPIRATION FOR THIS VOLUME EMERGED OUT OF A ROUNDTABLE Jill organized on "The Contours of Real Existing Postsocialism" for the Association of East European, Eurasian, and Slavic Studies Conference (ASEEES) in 2019. The roundtable sparked a lively and thought-provoking discussion among panelists and the audience, and the chair, Ulf Brunnbauer, suggested a sequel panel for ASEEES 2020—an event forestalled by the outbreak of the COVID-19 pandemic. Housebound and unable to conduct archival research, Jill decided to jump the gun and prepare an actual book on the topic, recruiting Markus as coeditor. What follows is the fruit of this labor and that of our sixteen authors, with whom it has been a pleasure and privilege to work. We thank them as well as the two anonymous reviewers for their careful reading of the texts and their detailed feedback. Finally, the book would not have found a welcoming home without the sustained support of Purdue University Press, particularly its editor, Justin Race, and the editorial board of the Central European Studies series, and would not have come together so seamlessly without the indefatigable efforts of production manager, Katherine Purple.

EVERYDAY POSTSOCIALISM IN EASTERN EUROPE: CONTINUITIES, RUPTURES, AND ALTERNATIVE TEMPORALITIES

JILL MASSINO AND MARKUS WIEN

MUCH ATTENTION HAS BEEN DEVOTED TO THE RISE OF POPULISM AND illiberal democracy in Eastern Europe.[1] The advent of (right-wing) populist rule, especially in states once considered leaders in democratization such as Poland and Hungary, signifies a dramatic departure from the hopeful and (allegedly) liberal climate of the 1990s and early 2000s.[2] While a worrying development, support for populism in the region is not wholly irrational. It is, at least in part, an expression of people's disappointment and frustration after years of deindustrialization, privatization, and declining social entitlements and purchasing power. This leaner and meaner capitalism, which differed considerably from the social democratic economies of some Western states, was presented by neoliberal policymakers as the only way forward—"the only alternative"—effectively precluding other paths and, by extension, other outcomes.[3] In privileging economic liberalization and global integration over democratic consolidation and material security, the collateral damage of economic transformation, such as precarity and rising poverty rates, was minimized, even justified. Meanwhile, elite corruption and creeping authoritarianism, though officially criticized, were tolerated.[4]

Despite these negative outcomes, neoliberal policymakers and their advocates (the emerging business class, including former communist elites, and some intellectuals) remained firmly committed to rapid economic change, while those unable to integrate into the new system were dismissed as having "adaptation problems." Accordingly, popular disenchantment with the nature of transformation is rooted not only in material concerns, but in policymakers' seeming abandonment of large swaths of the population and apparent disregard for the indignities and trauma people have experienced. It is also rooted in the (often accurate) perception that marketization rewards cronyism and favoritism rather than merit and diligence.

Dissatisfaction with governance was a continuity with the previous (communist) period, and a far cry from what East Europeans anticipated when they envisaged postsocialism. It is no wonder, then, that populists have successfully instrumentalized the failed promises of economic and, by extension, political liberalism—exemplified in the 2008 global financial crisis—to woo voters. To be sure, marketization modernized East European states, diversifying the economy, facilitating access to a range of goods and services, and increasing trade and foreign investment. Moreover, it broadened occupational opportunities and mobility, which improved the lives of many. However, it also widened social inequalities and facilitated corruption.[5] The appeal of populism, then, is rooted—at least in part—in the lack of social justice and viable centrist options. It is also rooted in the populist promise to reconstitute the social fabric, torn asunder by neoliberalism, through redistributionist measures and the restoration of national greatness.[6] Thus, for some East Europeans who feel betrayed by (liberal) democratic leaders, many of whom have lost loved ones to greener pastures in the West, it seems that *populism is the only alternative.*

Yet, while democratic backsliding and the increased appeal of exclusionary solutions make it appear that Eastern Europe is moving backward, this is only part of the picture. And this volume is not about populism, but about people. It is about how a range of individuals have been affected by, responded to, and more generally made sense of the manifold changes over the last three decades—populism being one among many. More fundamentally, it is about how people look forward *and* backward to understand and navigate change—as well as continuity. The fact that the socialist past remains salient, albeit in different ways than populists might have us believe, and that postsocialist normality remains elusive for many, illustrates that history does not travel in one direction.

The multidirectionality of history serves as the point of departure in this volume. It is premised on the belief that understanding the complexities of postsocialism requires examining it from diverse vantage points and multiple perspectives; in short, through the prism of "real existing postsocialism." Granting nonelites center stage, the featured authors illustrate that major systemic ruptures were not necessarily momentous events for ordinary individuals, and that continuities from the pre-1989 period (and even the presocialist period) shape people's understandings of, attitudes toward, and behaviors in the present.[7]

The volume is inspired by and complements studies of transition that have emerged over the past three decades, in particular pathbreaking anthropological and sociological work from the 1990s and early 2000s, which, through qualitative and ground-level approaches, complicated quantitative and macro-level analyses. It is also influenced by studies that have examined specific groups—laborers, rural populations, women, ethnic and sexual minorities—and analyzed the period through particular themes or paradigms such as East-West convergence, economic shock, and deindustrialization.[8] Finally, it builds upon scholarship on postsocialist memory, specifically vernacular memories of postsocialism.[9] By showcasing the lived experiences and recollections of ordinary people, it challenges dominant narratives of transition, in particular the anticommunist narrative mobilized by elites to justify political and economic policies. This narrative excludes views critical of postsocialism—not to mention supportive of socialism—disparaging those who express them as nostalgics with "dependent mentalities." Marginalized—or wholly excised—from hegemonic narratives of postsocialism, people's "discursive dispossession" often reinforces their social dispossession.[10] In featuring some of these neglected voices, then, this volume seeks to restore discursive agency and, in the process, provide a rich and variegated portrait of postsocialist memory. At the same time, the authors critique the past-oriented script of populists who, by appealing to dispossessed groups, reinforce existing exclusions—and create new ones—targeting ethnic and sexual minorities and (non-European) foreigners as impediments to national growth and glory.[11]

In adopting "postsocialism" as our frame of analysis we acknowledge that it is a freighted and contentious designation to which scholars have ascribed different temporal parameters or discarded altogether, preferring the teleological "transition" (or more hopeful "democratic transition"). However, it is precisely because "postsocialism" also evokes the pre-1989 period that we believe it is most suited and resonant for analyzing East Europeans' everyday lives. Rather than delineating particular temporal parameters per se, in this volume "postsocialism" refers to ideas, policies, and practices that have characterized (and continue to characterize) the region and its people. During the Cold War, East European states sought to transform politics, the economy, and society according to Marxist-Leninist principles, national adaptations notwithstanding. As a result, East European populations often experienced and negotiated state policies in similar ways. Just as there were shared experiences of the socialist project, so too there have been shared experiences of the postsocialist project: deindustrialization, privatization, and declining social rights; the ambiguities of democratization, EU integration, and globalization. Finally, "postsocialist" challenges the linearity often associated with transition, underscoring socialist legacies, which are visible on multiple levels, from styles of political leadership, corruption, and institutional dysfunction to social relations, everyday forms of managing, and yearnings for normality.

As a corollary, this volume problematizes 1989 as an epochal event, suggesting alternative and, indeed, multiple temporalities. Among these temporalities are those advanced by former dissidents and political elites (domestic and foreign alike) who have presented—and thus sought to naturalize—1989 as a definitive rupture, as well as those advanced by populists such as Viktor Orbán and Jarosław Kaczyński who have strategically revised the conventional narrative, emphasizing 2008 as the salient break.[12] Peddling the "unfinished revolution" narrative, populists attribute economic woes to liberal elites who, they argue, through reckless privatization schemes and collusion with the former communist *nomenklatura* betrayed the democratic promises of 1989—and thus ordinary East Europeans.[13] New leftists, too, have challenged triumphalist narratives, arguing that rather than a victory, 1989 ushered in an era of suffering and sacrifice, especially for the working class.[14] At the same time, since the 2010s, civic activists, ordinary individuals, and (some) politicians have redeployed 1989 to counter populist and authoritarian tendencies, mobilizing it as a symbol of the democratic values they (or their parents) fought for decades ago and to which they still aspire.[15]

Arguing for multiple temporalities is not to deny that the revolutions of 1989 were not momentous, exhilarating, and even frightening, but that what mattered, what was life-changing for some East Europeans, happened months, years, or perhaps even a decade or more later (or a decade before). For instance, due to variations within socialist economies and governance, change, including engagements with other parts of the world, often began well before the fall of the Wall, as demonstrated in recent scholarship that analyzes postwar Eastern Europe's global entanglements.[16] Indeed, some East Europeans experienced substantive change before 1989 (with the introduction of market mechanisms into the Polish and Hungarian economies, the advent of the Solidarity movement, or *glasnost* and *perestroika*, for example) or later (with EU accession in the early 2000s and the global financial crisis of 2008). For some there was not one definitive rupture, but multiple ruptures. It is these diverse, quotidian, and local ruptures that are among the focal points in this volume.

Meanwhile, although the collapse of communist dictatorships and the opening of markets to Western goods was welcomed by nearly all East Europeans, with the lucky few experiencing Helmut Kohl's promise of "flourishing landscapes," these coexisted with barren fields, some of which remain uncultivated to this day. These barren fields are both literal and figurative, apparent in the crumbling industries that dot the region and in the outlook of some East Europeans, whose hopes have been dashed by political ineptitude and economic uncertainty, further exacerbated by the aftershocks of the global financial crisis. Accordingly, transition was experienced unevenly, ambiguously, and in some cases negligibly, underscoring why interpretations of it continue to be contested.

Although the volume analyzes "barren fields," it also examines efforts at recultivation, and in this respect literal and figurative connotations also apply, as individuals, concerned with labor precarity and rising inflation in urban areas, have returned to the countryside as a form of homesteading. Recultivation is also apparent in the resourceful ways people have managed uncertainty through informal networks and in efforts to weed out corruption, both in their daily practices and popular mobilization. People also cultivate memories of the past, which can serve as sources of sustenance in troubled times. In some cases, these are nostalgic recollections of a carefree youth and a more predictable time; in other cases, they are lamentations over lost social entitlements and friendships. Often, however, they are a varied mix, yielding diverse views of the past that embody the romanticized and the mundane, the joyous and sorrowful.

Like "real existing socialism," the term used to differentiate socialism as envisaged by theorists and as lived by ordinary people, "real existing postsocialism" sheds light on the (often considerable) gulf between ideal and reality; between the promises of liberal democracy and market capitalism on the one hand and people's actual experiences of them on the other. This disconnect is largely related to the unexpected features of postsocialism: widening social inequalities, institutional dysfunction, and corruption. While characteristic of the socialist period as well—and even earlier periods— this was not what people anticipated as they imagined their lives and societies after 1989. Accordingly, this gulf is the product of the idealized portraits of liberal democracy and market capitalism nourished by communist-era dissidents and promoted by foreign and domestic experts (and other elites) *and* the idealized aspirations that ordinary people, in turn, had cultivated based on these aforementioned portraits. They are also a product of idealized visions of Western life people had been nourishing for decades under socialism.

Exploring the transformation from the perspective of "real existing postsocialism" also illuminates the different, often starkly divergent ways this period has been narrated. Writing thirty years after socialism's collapse, historian Paul Betts contended, "Like all revolutions, 1989 brought in its train a mixed bag of dreams and disappointments, stark ruptures and stubborn continuities. But its legacy has largely been written as a bright story of liberalism triumphant, with comparatively less attention towards some of the grey and even darker tones of the inheritance."[17] By foregrounding people's reflections and perspectives, it is these gray and even darker tones (and the brighter ones, too) we seek to draw attention to. More generally, we aim to validate people's lived experiences both before and after 1989 and, thereby, complicate elite representations of both past and present. These latter representations, fashioned by a host of actors—politicians, former dissidents and intellectuals, entrepreneurs and business moguls, and nationalists and religious figures, among others—portray the communist past as an aberration in their country's historical trajectory. Emphasizing the criminal and dictatorial aspects of socialism has been a useful foil for policymakers of various stripes, enabling them to justify austerity measures and socially conservative and exclusionary policies. These Manichean portraits of socialism are, in turn, widely disseminated in public forums, constituting *the* collective memory of the socialist past. In such a climate those who present more nuanced portraits of the past are marginalized—or even vilified as apologists for totalitarianism.[18]

By elucidating the varied effects of the transition, this volume complicates such selective and instrumentalist representations. Moreover, it goes beyond crude divisions of postsocialist society into "winners" and "losers." Rather than assess whether postsocialism was a success or a failure, we shed light on how it has played out in various spheres, analyzing the degree to which recent developments represent a departure from the socialist era or a blending of different aspects of it. More fundamentally, the alterative narratives featured here offer insight into the local particularities and unintended consequences of "real existing liberal democracy and capitalism," consequences that often depart from preconceived notions and expectations—and also bear a striking resemblance to (perhaps even a continuity with) previous socialist practices.

CONTINUITIES AND RUPTURES

The collapse of state socialism ushered in dramatic change, most notably in the political and economic systems that emerged. While welcomed by many, these changes were also a source of concern due to rising inflation and unemployment. As East Europeans were faced with adapting, floundering, or simply getting by, some began questioning the hopes and aspirations they had associated with liberal democracy, in particular its capacity to guarantee economic stability, let alone increased standards of living. As corruption continued apace and precarity compromised the democratic promise, public trust declined and individuals devised ways of managing the system, drawing on both old and new practices. Such continuities bring into sharp relief the fluidity, elasticity, and, for some, irrelevance of conventional temporal benchmarks and larger systemic changes. Alongside practices, people's perspectives have been framed by their pre-1989 experiences. Of particular interest in this volume, then, is how perspectives and practices from socialism have informed and framed people's perspectives and practices during postsocialism.

Alongside examining continuities, our volume explores discontinuities. The impact of major systemic breaks, including the dissolution of economic rights (guaranteed work) and reduction in social rights (subsidized childcare, healthcare, travel, and housing), as well as the privatization of enterprises and public services (health care, utilities) have fundamentally altered the social contract and feelings of belonging. These systemic ruptures have been unevenly felt, however, as their impact is dependent on numerous factors such as age, gender, location, socioeconomic status, ethnic identity, ability, and sexual orientation. In some cases, change has facilitated professional advancement, civic engagement, mobility, and a future-oriented perspective; in other cases, it has negatively affected individuals' livelihoods and agency, prompting them to look back fondly to the socialist past. This is especially true of many industrial laborers who, under the current postindustrial climate, are no longer valued. As Joanna Wawrzyniak and Ondřej Klípa (chapters 1 and 2) demonstrate, these laborers yearn not only for a stable income and professional validation, but also for the social networks and sense of community they had enjoyed under socialism.[19] Similarly, young people, as Friederike Kind-Kovács illustrates in her study of East Germany's transitional generation, experienced change acutely and rapidly. Indeed, youths often experienced multiple transitions—economic, political, personal, and familial—which decisively shaped their memories of the socialist and postsocialist periods, as well as their identities as (East) German adults.

People also experienced change at different periods. Factories did not shut their doors overnight and social entitlements did not end in January 1990. Rupture was thus a varied, contextual, gradual, and subjective process. In this respect, we might speak of smaller ruptures that individuals experienced incrementally, which, when taken as a whole, culminate in a larger, more definitive rupture. Reproductive and LGBTQ rights are cases in point. For instance, since 1993, Polish women's bodily control has been under attack by church and state, and Poland currently has one of the most restrictive abortion laws in the world. Meanwhile, as illustrated by Corina Doboş (chapter 8), Romanian doctors in public hospitals are increasingly refusing to perform abortions (which are legal on demand up to fourteen weeks of pregnancy) on the basis of "ethical norms." Combined with lack of subsidies for contraceptives, such practices undermine women's reproductive rights and signify, on the one hand, a dramatic departure from the 1990s and early 2000s when Romanian women, regardless of socioeconomic status, enjoyed increased reproductive freedom, and, on the other, an apparent return to the more repressive pronatalist climate under Nicolae Ceauşescu. Meanwhile, with the consolidation of populist rule in Hungary and Poland, LGBTQ individuals, who in the 1990s and early 2000s embraced opportunities for free association and open expression of their gender identity and sexual orientation, have experienced discursive and physical violence (as discussed by Agnieszka Kościańska and Hadley Renkin). Indeed, as Renkin illustrates (chapter 5), Orbán's heteronationalist Hungary, despite being a European Union (EU) member, flouts EU antidiscrimination legislation and denies sexual minorities a host of civil liberties (from the right to legal marriage and adoption to officially changing their gender). These legislative moves constitute not only discontinuity, but a reversal from the earlier transition when East European governments, in anticipation of EU accession, passed a raft of laws that safeguarded minorities' and women's rights. Indeed, such reversals are evocative of a more repressive era in Cold War Europe, when people's intimate lives were subject to restrictive legislation and state surveillance. Meanwhile, for LGBTQ individuals, women of reproductive age, and, for that matter, anyone else who feels insecure or unsafe in a country that is sliding into illiberalism, it has produced existential ruptures.

Another major rupture is emigration. While East Europeans began immigrating to various parts of Western Europe and North America in the 1990s, this process accelerated in the 2000s, when most East European states were admitted to the EU. Indeed, according to the United Nations, in 2018 the ten fastest-shrinking populations in the world were in Eastern Europe.[20] Among those experiencing the highest emigration growth rates are Romania and Bulgaria, the latter having lost a staggering one-fifth of its population since 1989. Emigration has often expanded East Europeans' educational and professional opportunities, increasing their social mobility and standard of living. For young people frustrated with pervasive corruption, crumbling public services, and low salaries, and eager to experience other parts of the world and live "normally," studying or working abroad is a sensible and appealing alternative. As Ivan Krastev and Stephen Holmes assert, "Why should a young Pole or Hungarian wait for his country to one day be like Germany, when he can start working and raising a family in Germany tomorrow?"[21] At the same time, experiences in the West have not been rosy for all. Blue-collar migrants, including caregivers and agricultural workers, have experienced exploitative labor conditions, including sexual abuse.[22] Mass emigration has also affected East European societies, producing not only a brain drain but a care drain, as hospitals and care facilities face shortages of critical workers such as doctors and nurses. Moreover, East European states have smaller labor pools on which to draw and thus to tax, resulting in scaled-back social entitlements and stagnant pensions and child allowances, among other social expenditures. Meanwhile, for those left behind, particularly children in the care of extended family or neighbors, these physical ruptures are emotional and psychological, a reality typically unacknowledged in macro-level studies. At the same time, migrants send remittances back home, which increase household consumption levels and generally improve the overall standard of living. In addition, some return home to apply newly minted skills and innovative ideas in the hopes of effecting positive change. Finally, as Sergiu Gherghina and Raluca Farcas demonstrate (chapter 13), migrants seek to effect political change in their countries of origin through voting, popular mobilization, and efforts to influence the electoral choices of friends and family.

Yet, the West is not simply a physical destination but an existential one. Rather than leave for greener pastures abroad, many East Europeans aspire to Western (European) norms, including political transparency, respect for the rule of law, rising living standards, and a reliable safety net; in short, "to live normally." While alignment with

European norms and laws was, at least initially, a means whereby states in the region could attain legal and economic convergence with Western countries, as well as enjoy the free flow of goods, services, and ideas, convergence has fallen short of popular expectations.[23] What's more, for some EU membership has meant job loss (see Wawrzyniak, Klípa, and Gagyiova) and the termination of essential services and subsidies for low-income and vulnerable populations (Doboş). This, in turn, has produced disappointment and resentment. More generally, the impact of Europeanization has been ambiguous, and East Europeans' attitudes toward it, while generally supportive, are also ambivalent due to the divergence between postsocialist expectations and realities.

The transnational focus of this volume offers insight into convergence as well as divergence. While divergence (from the West) is evident in some states' efforts to undermine minority, women's, and LGBTQ rights and to tamper with judicial, press, and reproductive freedom, it is also evident in their relationship to countries outside of Europe, particularly the Global South. Here the story is less ambiguous, characterized primarily by rupture with more progressive pre-1989 policies.[24] As socialist regimes collapsed, so too did the internationalist ethos and solidarities they had cultivated during the Cold War. On the basis of ideological, political, and economic expedience (i.e., the need to align with European values, distance themselves from communism, and balance the budget), postsocialist states began purging "friends" from the Global South who had worked and studied in their countries prior to 1989. In essence, as postsocialist governments narrowed their gaze toward the European continent, their view of globalization also narrowed, with the result that their focus shifted from people to goods. Raia Apastolova (chapter 6) explores how this about-face was experienced by African nationals targeted for expulsion from Bulgaria after 1989, including the discursive and physical violence they faced. Accordingly, while postsocialism facilitated mobility for some, it forestalled it for others. It also enabled more open expressions of racism and xenophobia. When placed in the longer period of postsocialism, such expulsions appear as a prelude to the xenophobic discourses and policies of Hungary's and Poland's populist governments during the 2015 refugee "crisis." Europeanization thus became a powerful and flexible rhetorical tool after 1989, used variously to achieve European Union membership (and benefit from its concomitant structural funds), decry the "cultural colonization" of Brussels, and reverse the conventional East-West relationship by redefining the contours of European civilization.[25]

CHAPTER ORGANIZATION

Analyzing how political, institutional, and economic policies bear upon people's experiences and memories, the following chapters explore ruptures and continuities, ambiguities and contradictions, and advances and reversals, underscoring the multidirectionality of change in the region. The authors analyze the transition from various perspectives—industrial laborers and entrepreneurs; women, young people, and sexual minorities; professional and amateur historians; and former party members, diaspora populations, and foreign students—and with respect to various topics: cultures of labor, the moral economy, and educational policies; sexual identity and reproductive health; and social mobilization and migration. Collectively, the chapters provide an interdisciplinary and ground-level approach to postsocialism, incorporating insights from history, anthropology, economics, international relations, and gender and LGBTQ studies, and they draw on a range of qualitative sources including oral histories, speeches, magazine interviews, autobiographies, and blog posts.

The volume is divided into five parts, each addressing a different aspect of "real existing postsocialism." Part I, "Socioeconomic Transformations," examines blue- and white-collar workers' memories of postsocialism in Poland, the Czech Republic, and Hungary. Drawing extensively on oral histories, these ground-level views of deindustrialization and privatization challenge hegemonic portraits of the transition, illuminating people's ambiguous experiences of economic change. As the authors argue, 1989 was not perceived as a turning point by all, particularly Hungarians and Poles, who had experienced market elements prior to the collapse of socialism. For them, along with the Czech workers featured here, rupture began in the late 1990s and early 2000s with the influx of foreign companies, a process that decisively affected their occupational trajectories. These chapters thus demonstrate the complex ways neoliberalism and Europeanization have shaped people's self-identities, work cultures, political choices, and more generally their attitudes toward the transition.

In chapter 1, Joanna Wawrzyniak illuminates local memories of the transition, focusing on Polish engineers and skilled laborers whose enterprises were privatized and sold to multinationals after 1989. For the engineers she interviewed, 1989 did not signify a definitive rupture, as already in the 1970s their enterprises had contracted with foreign firms, facilitating engagement with the global marketplace and global actors well before the 1990s. Discontinuities, however, are more apparent in the case of laborers, especially female laborers, as they were among the first to be let go during the shock therapy of the early 1990s. As such, these individuals regarded the early transition as a decisive break that dramatically altered the course of their lives.

Ondřej Klípa, in chapter 2, similarly draws on the recollections of industrial employees, namely sugar plant workers in the Czech Republic, analyzing how economic change affected their daily lives, political allegiances, and local culture. While the featured workers weathered privatization and the eventual closure of their plant relatively well due to generous severance packages and reintegration into other areas of the economy, many nonetheless embrace Euroskeptic and populist politics. Klípa interprets workers' provincialism as reactions to their devaluation as laborers, loss of community, and exclusion from the dominant narrative of the transition. In their mind, Europeanization, which for them includes British businessmen, Brussels bureaucrats, and Prague policymakers, is antinational and antiworker.

In chapter 3, Annina Gagiyova analyzes the trajectories of small business owners in Hungary, which, like Poland, introduced market mechanisms well before 1989. Participants in the "second economy" who emerged in the 1980s to satisfy consumer demand, these socialist entrepreneurs anticipated a seamless and successful transition to full capitalism after 1989. Yet, as Gagiyova demonstrates, their hopes were soon dashed as the Hungarian state privileged large-scale foreign investors over smaller domestic businesses, the latter of whom were burdened with high taxes. Such measures, combined with the increased popularity of (foreign) hypermarkets, left entrepreneurs struggling to make ends meet, and many were forced to close their businesses in the early 2000s. Consequently, they expressed disillusionment with economic change in Hungary after 1989.

Part II, "The Politics of Exclusion," explores the ambiguous experiences of sexual minorities and (non-Western) foreigners in Poland, Hungary, and Bulgaria since the collapse of socialism. In all three states, transition entailed instituting new rights and civil liberties, among them freedom of association and expression, including the right to express one's gender identity and sexual orientation. Yet, transition also involved a definitive break with socialist multiculturalism, dramatically expressed in the administrative expulsion of African students from Bulgaria after 1989 and the racial violence perpetrated against them by ordinary Bulgarians. Meanwhile, reassertion of national identity in Poland and Hungary was expressed through the promotion of traditional (i.e., religious and heteronormative) values by right-wing groups, members of the Catholic Church, and some policymakers and ordinary citizens. Consequently, Hungarians and Poles who had welcomed the open climate of the 1990s have experienced existential threats by their own states—despite the fact they are required, by European law, to protect them. These chapters thus illuminate the unanticipated, contradictory, and adverse outcomes of postsocialism for LGBTQ individuals and non-European foreign nationals, among others.

In chapter 4, Agnieszka Kościańska analyzes LGBTQ individuals' ambiguous experiences of both socialism and postsocialism in Poland. While LGBTQ people are now able to speak and organize freely, right-wing and populist parties, along with the conservative wing of the Catholic Church and conservative civic groups, have attempted to undermine sexual minorities' civil rights, presenting them as threats to children, morality, and the Polish nation. Consequently, some LGBTQ individuals feel that their invisibility under socialism ironically gave them a sense of freedom they currently no longer enjoy, even though they had previously been subjected to discrimination, violence, and state surveillance. As such, Kościańska concludes that the story of LGBTQ rights and individuals' experiences in Poland has been characterized not simply by progress and convergence with the West, but also by ambiguities and, more recently, reversals.

In chapter 5, Hadley Renkin explores how gender identity and intimate politics have been instrumentalized for nationalist purposes in postsocialist Hungary—and the tragic implications of this process for sexual minorities and women. This is largely a story of rupture and regression, graphically evident during the Budapest Pride March in 2007, when participants were violently attacked by ultra-nationalists. Such everyday assaults on sexual minorities have been fueled—and are legislatively paralleled—by the policies of Prime Minister Viktor Orbán and his party, Fidesz. Orbán's "heteronationalist" project has undermined postsocialism's original promise of increased social and political equality and inclusion, including opportunities for diverse expressions of identity, community, and gendered and sexual belonging. Orbán's attack extends to gender, which he characterizes as an ideology and which he has banned as an official category of identification and area of study in Hungary. As Renkin emphasizes, such reversals have shattered people's lives, their sense of security, and their expectations for the future direction of their country.

In chapter 6, Raia Apostalova analyzes the expulsion of African nationals from Bulgaria in the 1990s, a practice that constituted a dramatic rupture from the socialist internationalism promoted by the regime from the 1960s through the 1980s. This policy change was both ideological and financial: after 1989, political leaders of varying stripes sought to distance themselves from the previous regime, including discontinuing programs for foreign students, who were presented as residues of the socialist past and a financial drain on an economy already heavily in debt. By placing the financial burden of their education on foreign students themselves, the government insidiously sought to deter them from coming to Bulgaria altogether. These administrative expulsions were accompanied by increased racism, as some Bulgarians expressed contempt for the students' perceived privileged position under communism by verbally and physically attacking them. For foreign nationals who had cultivated friendships and earned their degrees in Bulgaria, such outcomes were felt as a painful rupture. More significantly, Bulgaria's efforts to "return to Europe" paradoxically entailed embracing nativism and enforcing exclusionary policies, an approach expanded by populist regimes (via anti-immigrant discourses and measures) not only in Hungary, Poland, and Bulgaria, but also Romania and Serbia.

Part III, "Something Old, Something New," examines postsocialism through the lens of reproductive and sexual policies, practices, and beliefs in Romania. As the authors illustrate, the transition to market capitalism and liberal democracy, including the introduction of new rights such as freedom of the press, association, and religion, have been both liberating and constraining. Despite the fact that Romania has one of the highest teen pregnancy, abortion, and STI rates in the EU, there is no mandatory sex education curriculum in schools. Moreover, some parents, along with conservative groups, are opposed to such a curriculum and reluctant to broach the topic with their children. Young people thus rely on friends, the media, and NGOs to learn about sexual health and hygiene, underscoring the importance of a free press and association. Meanwhile, and relatedly, women's reproductive freedom and health is being undermined by lack of access to affordable contraceptives, disinformation, and medical professionals who refuse to perform abortions in public hospitals on ethical grounds. Given such realities, some women and teenage girls resort to desperate measures to control their fertility in a manner tragically evocative of the Ceauşescu period. The chapters in this section are thus stories of discontinuities and continuities; progress and reversal.

In chapter 7, Beatrice Scutaru and Luciana Jinga offer a multilevel view of sex education in Romania's public school system. Highlighting young people's perspectives and experiences of sex and sex education (including adults' recollections of their experiences as young people), the authors give voice to those who have been marginalized in debates about mandatory sex education. They also explore how policymakers, parents, and NGOs, on various parts of the political spectrum, have positioned themselves within these debates and sought to either expand or restrict access to sex education. Yet, as the authors contend, while adults debate, youth suffer, as lack of obligatory, universal, and effective sex education curricula in Romania is responsible for high rates—among the highest in the EU—of teen pregnancy, STIs, and school dropout, especially among rural populations.

In chapter 8, Corina Doboş examines how the combined influence of conservativism, neoliberalism, and misinformation has undermined women's reproductive rights in postsocialist Romania—with dire consequences for low-income women. While reproductive rights expanded dramatically after 1989 with the decriminalization of abortion, introduction of family planning services, and the subsidization of contraceptives for low-income groups, by the late 2000s after Romania's accession to the EU, this situation changed due to underfunding (by the Romanian Ministry of Health) and doctors' refusals, on ethical grounds, to perform abortions in public hospitals. Consequently, economically vulnerable women have resorted to desperate measures—as they did under socialism—to control their fertility, with hauntingly familiar outcomes. While suffering the combined effects of austerity and the de facto restriction of their reproductive rights, women who seek abortions now also face overt criticism by the Orthodox Church and neoconservative groups, the latter of which are, as in Poland, new to the postsocialist climate, representing a rupture.

Part IV, "Origin Stories," examines the politics of (re)fashioning one's adversary, the self, and the nation in (East) Germany, the Czech Republic, Bulgaria, and Hungary.

The authors argue that the flux and uncertainty of the early transition provided fertile ground for new beginnings but also reinventions, rationalizations, and resurrections. Some individuals, for the purpose of security and personal enrichment in the new liberal-democratic order, sought to distance themselves from their socialist past, while others embraced it. Meanwhile, some looked to the distant past, evoking episodes of national glory and grandeur. Forging a flattering "origin story" thus served the authors' personal interests as well as the nation's, functioning as a type of sustenance during a time of crisis and uncertainty.

In chapter 9, Till Hilmar uses the persona of the "turncoat" to illuminate how people apprehended and assessed work, value, and community in (East) Germany and the Czech Republic after 1989. Regarded as an opportunistic individual who enjoyed special privileges due to their position in the communist system, the "turncoat" met a different fate in each country. In the Czech Republic, turncoats (typically former technocrats and firm insiders) took advantage of their social networks, translating their political capital into economic capital, signifying continuity. In Germany, by contrast, there was minimal elite reproduction, as (West) Germans assumed positions in previously state-owned enterprises. Thus, the turncoat had fewer opportunities for reinvention and adaptation to the new system, signifying rupture.

In chapter 10, Victor Petrov explores how Bulgarian history has been reimagined since 1989 by both professional historians and amateurs, analyzing its widespread currency among the Bulgarian public. While focusing on different episodes in Bulgarian history, these "origin stories" highlight Bulgaria's contributions to modern European statehood, Orthodox Christianity, Slavic culture, and world civilization. Claiming to offer "authentic" narratives of Bulgarian history, as opposed to the ideologically inflected ones of the communist era, Petrov demonstrates that these "historians" ironically reproduce the same nationalist narratives advanced by scholars under communism. Popularized by an open publishing market and leaders of varying political stripes, the featured authors attract an impressive following on social media, television, and in bookstores. The appeal of such stories, Petrov argues, lies in Bulgarians' need of a glorious past during a gloomy present.

In chapter 11, Sándor Horváth analyzes the interpretive strategies used by former members of the Hungarian communist party to narrate their past after 1989. While some claimed that party membership was necessary for securing a job in their field and for professional advancement, others, especially those who joined the party in the late 1950s and 1960s, claimed commitment to social equality, portraying themselves as Marxist reformists and part of the new left. By highlighting such motives, they positioned themselves as socially committed citizens rather than opportunistic supporters of a dictatorial regime. In so doing, former party members justified their retention in educational and administrative posts after 1989. Meanwhile, other former party members, by drawing on the social networks they had developed under communism, translated their political capital into economic capital, ensuring a smooth transition to the business world after 1989. Both instances, Horváth argues, illustrate the utility of Communist Party membership in facilitating individuals' privileged status both before and after 1989, reflecting continuity.

Part V, "Home Is Where the Heart Is," examines the significance (East) Germans and Romanians ascribe to their places of birth, which they conceptualize as both a geographical space and a state of mind. The authors argue that although the transition produced physical rupture from their country of origin (in the form of the dissolution of it or departure from it), Germans' and Romanians' connection to it remains strong. In the case of (East) Germans this connection is manifested in memories of the pre- and immediate post-1989 period, while for Romanians this connection is manifested in current relationships and political engagement.

In chapter 12, Friederike Kind-Kovács analyzes youths' memories of *die Wende* (the Changes) in the former East Germany to illuminate how political and economic ruptures affected central aspects of young people's lives: the family, schooling, and leisure. As Kind-Kovács demonstrates, youth, a demographic typically neglected in studies of the East German transition, acutely felt the changes of the period, especially because the very people they typically turned to for guidance—their parents—struggled themselves to cope with uncertainty. For youths who remained in the East after unification, there were few continuities, as caregivers and teachers lost their jobs and socialist youth organizations were disbanded. Meanwhile, young people who moved westward felt this rupture even more dramatically, particularly those who were dubbed "Ossis" by classmates and made to feel inferior. Their feelings of grief, longing, and displacement continue to linger in their memories of this period decades later.

In chapter 13, Sergiu Gherghina and Raluca Farcas examine the Romanian diaspora's engagement in politics and popular mobilization back home. Compelled to leave Romania due to declining living standards, corruption, and government incompetence, the individuals featured in this chapter are committed to democratic principles and seek to effect change by voting—and encouraging family and friends to vote—for particular candidates and through popular mobilization. Their aim is to improve the political and economic situation and, ideally, return to Romania one day. Given their large number, the diaspora has proven to be a potent political force in Romanian politics, determining the outcome of two presidential elections. That said, the diaspora's support of populist candidates in more recent legislative elections may indicate a worrying trend.[26]

NOTES

1. See the articles in the "Critical Forum on Global Populisms," *Slavic Review* 76, no. S1 (2017). Our use of *populism* in this introduction refers to its right-wing variant.

2. Michael Bernhard, "Democratic Backsliding in Poland and Hungary," *Slavic Review* 80, no. 3 (Fall 2021): 585–607.

3. By neoliberal policymakers we mean state officials who pursued economic reform according to the Washington Consensus model. With the financial support of international organizations such as the International Monetary Fund (IMF), World Bank, and the European Bank for Reconstruction and Development (EBRD), these policymakers initiated a host of reforms, including the privatization of enterprises, lifting of price controls, trade liberalization, promotion of foreign direct investment (FDI), and curtailment of social rights. This model was implemented to different degrees and at different stages between the 1990s and early 2000s in the countries of the former Eastern Bloc. While economically liberal, these policymakers were not necessarily progressive in their cultural politics, as some embraced social conservatism and nationalism. To add another layer of complexity, in certain instances socialist or leftist-identified parties, such as the Social Democratic Party (PSD) in Romania, blended redistributionist policies with neoliberal ones, while at the same time promoting social conservatism in an effort to attract a wide range of constituents.

4. See Dorothee Bohle and Béla Greskovits, "Staring through the Mocking Glass: Three Misperceptions of the East-West Divide since 1989," in *The Legacy of Division: East and West after 1989*, ed. Ferenc Laczó and Luka Lisjak Gabrijelčič (Budapest: Central European University Press, 2020), 11–19.

5. On the ambiguous impact of neoliberalism in Eastern Europe, see Philipp Ther, *Europe since 1989: A History* (Princeton, NJ: Princeton University Press, 2016); Kristen Ghodsee and Mitchell Orenstein, *Taking Stock of Shock: Social Consequences of the 1989 Revolutions* (Oxford: Oxford University Press, 2021); and Veronika Pehe and Joanna Wawrzyniak, eds., *Remembering the Neoliberal Turn: Economic Change and Collective Memory in Eastern Europe after 1989* (New York: Routledge, 2023).

6. For the Hungarian case, see Eszter Bartha, "A Loss of Collective Consciousness? Working Class Images of Socialism and Capitalism in Two Generations in Post-1989 Hungary," in *Erinnerung des Umbruchs, Umbruch der Erinnerung*, ed. Till Hilmar, Hanna Haag, and Julian Göpffahrt (Wiesbaden: Springer VS, 2024).

7. Our understanding of elites includes political (ruling) elites, as well as economic and cultural elites who have particular influence in the discursive and/or political realm.

8. Katherine Verdery, *What Was Socialism? And What Comes Next?* (Princeton, NJ: Princeton University Press, 1996); Gerald Creed, *Domesticating Revolution: From Socialist Reform to Ambivalent Transition in a Bulgarian Village* (University Park: Penn

State University Press, 1998); Roman Frydman, Kenneth Murphy, and Andrzej Rapaczyński, eds., *Capitalism with a Comrade's Face: Studies in Postcommunist Transition* (Budapest: Central European University Press, 1998); Gil Eyal, Ivan Szelény, and Eleanor Townsley, *Making Capitalism without Capitalists: Class Formation and Elite Struggles in Post-Communist Central Europe* (London: Verso, 1998); Michael Burawoy and Katherine Verdery, eds., *Uncertain Transitions: Ethnographies of Change in the Postsocialist World* (Lanham, MD: Rowman and Littlefield, 1999); Daphne Berdahl, Matti Bunzl, and Martha Lampland, eds., *Altering States: Ethnographies of Transition in Eastern Europe and the Former Soviet Union* (Ann Arbor: University of Michigan Press, 2000); David Kideckel, *Getting By in Postsocialist Romania: Labor, the Body, and Working Class Culture* (Bloomington: Indiana University Press, 2008); Chris Hann, ed., *Postsocialism: Ideals, Ideologies, and Practices in Eurasia* (London: Routledge, 2002); Michal Kopeček and Piotr Wciślik, eds., *Thinking through Transition: Liberal Democracy, Authoritarian Pasts, and Intellectual History in East Central Europe after 1989* (Budapest: Central European University Press, 2015); Ivan Krastev and Stephen Holmes, *The Light That Failed: Why the West Is Losing the Fight for Democracy* (New York: Pegasus Books, 2020); Laczó and Gabrijelčič, eds., *The Legacy of Division*; and Ghodsee and Orenstein, *Taking Stock of Shock*.

9. See Daphne Berdahl, *Where the World Ended: Reunification and Identity in the German Borderland* (Berkeley: University of California Press, 1999); James Mark, *The Unfinished Revolution: Making Sense of the Communist Past in Central Eastern Europe* (New Haven, CT: Yale University Press, 2011); Michael Bernhard and Jan Kubik, eds., *Twenty Years after Communism: The Politics of Memory and Commemoration* (Oxford: Oxford University Press, 2014); Maya Nadkarni, *Remains of Socialism: Memory and the Futures of the Past in Postsocialist Hungary* (Ithaca, NY: Cornell University Press, 2020); and Pehe and Wawrzyniak, eds., *Remembering the Neoliberal Turn*.

10. Pierre Bourdieu, *Language and Symbolic Power* (Cambridge, MA: Harvard University Press, 1991).

11. For an analysis of assaults on gender in Poland, see Elżbieta Korolczuk, "'Worse than communism and Nazism put together': War on Gender in Poland," in *Anti-Gender Campaigns in Europe: Mobilizing against Equality*, ed. Roman Kuhar and David Paternotte (London: Rowman & Littlefield, 2017): 175–94.

12. Holly Case, "The Great Substitution," in *The Legacy of Division*, ed. Laczó and Gabrijelčič, 111–22.

13. Presenting themselves as champions of democracy, populists are in fact adversaries of it, as they seek to dismantle the checks and balances fundamental to democracy and repopulate the judicial system and media outlets with party loyalists. Moreover, their redistributionist measures coexist with neoliberal policies, and in spite of their rabid anti-immigration polices and racializing discourse, they are more than willing to support FDI and employ non-European laborers if it sustains their power and privilege.

14. James Mark, Muriel Blaive, Adam Hudek, Anna Saunders, and Stanislav Tyszka, "1989 after 1989: Remembering the End of State Socialism in East Central Europe," in *Thinking Through Transition,* ed. Kopeček and Wciślik, 474–75.

15. See Bogdan C. Iacob, James Mark, and Tobias Rupprecht, "The Struggle over 1989: The Rise and Contestation of Eastern European Populism," in *The Legacy of Division,* ed. Laczó and Gabrijelčič, 123–33.

16. See, for example, James Mark, Bogdan Iacob, Tobias Rupprecht, and Ljubica Spaskovska, *1989: A Global History of Eastern Europe* (Cambridge: Cambridge University Press, 2019).

17. Paul Betts, "1989 at Thirty: A Recast Legacy," *Past and Present,* no. 244 (Aug. 2019): 274.

18. See Veronika Pehe, "Totalitarianism as Defensive Memory of the Transformation: Unpacking a Czech Mnemonic Conflict," in *Erinnerung des Umbruchs,* ed. Hilmar, Haag, and Göpffahrt.

19. For the Croatian case, see Chiara Bonfiglioli, "Post-Socialist Deindustrialization and Its Gendered Structure of Feeling: The Devaluation of Women's Work in the Croatian Garment Industry," *Labor History* 61, no. 1 (2020): 36–47.

20. Aamna Mohdin, "The Fastest Shrinking Countries on Earth Are in Eastern Europe," *Quartz,* January 24, 2018, https://qz.com/1187819country-rankingworlds-fastest-shrinking-countries-are-in-eastern-europe/.

21. Krastev and Holmes, *The Light That Failed.*

22. Lorenzo Tondo and Annie Kelly, "'Terrible Conditions': Police Uncover Abuse and Exploitation on Farms in Sicily," *Guardian,* October 31, 2017; and Manuela Boatcă, "[Thou Shalt] Honour the Asparagus!: Romanian Agricultural Labour in Germany during the COVID-19 Season," *LeftEast,* May 11, 2020; https://lefteast.org/thou-shalt-honour-the-asparagus%EF%BB%BF-romanian-agricultural-labour-in-germany-during-the-covid-19-season/.

23. For an illuminating and comprehensive analysis of East-West convergence and its discontents after 1989, see Laczó and Gabrijelčič, eds., *The Legacy of Division.*

24. For an extensive discussion of this process, see chapters 3 and 6 in Mark et al., *1989.*

25. According to populist leaders such as Viktor Orbán, Hungary as a heteronormative, Christian, and white state epitomizes "authentic European values," in contrast to the West, which is characterized by cosmopolitan values.

26. At the same time, it should be noted that during the 2020 parliamentary elections, a considerable portion of the diaspora population campaigned and voted for the Alliance of the Union of Romanians (AUR), a right-wing populist party that espouses exclusionary nationalism and promotes the (heterosexual) family and Christian values, indicating increased disenchantment with Romanian politics, in particular liberal and centrist parties. As a result, AUR became the fourth largest party in the Romanian Parliament. See Luminita Pirvu, "Cum au pierdut PNL și USR 'glonțul de argint' în bătălia pentru

Diaspora. Rareș Bogdan: AUR poate să ia în diaspora undeva la 50% din voturi," *Hot-News.ro,* March 12, 2023, https://www.hotnews.ro/stiri-politic-26133000-fotografia -momentului-diaspora-cum-sunt-primiti-politicieni.htm.

BIBLIOGRAPHY

Bartha, Eszter. "A Loss of Collective Consciousness? Working-Class Images of Socialism and Capitalism in Two Generations in Post-1989 Hungary." In *Erinnerung des Umbruchs, Umbruch der Erinnerung,* edited by Till Hilmar, Hanna Haag, and Julian Göpffahrt. Wiesbaden: Springer VS, 2024.

Berdahl, Daphne. *Where the World Ended: Reunification and Identity in the German Borderland.* Berkeley: University of California Press, 1999.

Berdahl, Daphne, Matti Bunzl, and Martha Lampland, eds. *Altering States: Ethnographies of Transition in Eastern Europe and the Former Soviet Union.* Ann Arbor: University of Michigan Press, 2000.

Bernhard, Michael. "Democratic Backsliding in Poland and Hungary." *Slavic Review* 80, no. 3 (Fall 2021): 585–607.

Bernhard, Michael, and Jan Kubik, eds. *Twenty Years after Communism: The Politics of Memory and Commemoration.* Oxford: Oxford University Press, 2014.

Betts, Paul. "1989 at Thirty: A Recast Legacy." *Past and Present,* no. 244 (Aug. 2019): 271–305.

Boatcă, Manuela. "[Thou Shalt] Honour the Asparagus!: Romanian Agricultural Labour in Germany during the COVID-19 Season." *LeftEast,* May 11, 2020. https://lefteast.org/thou -shalt-honour-the-asparagus%EF%BB%BF-romanian-agricultural-labour-in-germany -during-the-covid-19-season/.

Bohle, Dorothee, and Béla Greskovits. "Staring through the Mocking Glass: Three Misperceptions of the East-West Divide since 1989." In *The Legacy of Division: East and West after 1989,* edited by Ferenc Laczó and Luka Lisjak Gabrijelčič. Budapest: Central European University Press, 2020.

Bonfiglioli, Chiara. "Post-Socialist Deindustrialization and Its Gendered Structure of Feeling: The Devaluation of Women's Work in the Croatian Garment Industry." *Labor History* 61, no. 1 (2020): 36–47.

Bourdieu, Pierre. *Language and Symbolic Power.* Cambridge, MA: Harvard University Press, 1991.

Burawoy, Michael, and Katherine Verdery, eds. *Uncertain Transitions: Ethnographies of Change in the Postsocialist World.* Lanham, MD: Rowman and Littlefield, 1999.

Case, Holly. "The Great Substitution." In *The Legacy of Division,* edited by Ferenc Laczó and Luka Lisjac Gabrijelčič. Budapest: Central European University Press, 111–22.

Creed, Gerald. *Domesticating Revolution: From Socialist Reform to Ambivalent Transition in a Bulgarian Village.* University Park: Penn State University Press, 1998.

"Critical Forum on Global Populisms." *Slavic Review* 76, no. S1 (2017).

Eyal, Gil, Ivan Szelény, and Eleanor Townsley. *Making Capitalism without Capitalists: Class Formation and Elite Struggles in Post-Communist Central Europe.* London: Verso, 1998.

Frydman, Roman, Kenneth Murphy, and Andrzej Rapaczyński, eds. *Capitalism with a Comrade's Face: Studies in Postcommunist Transition.* Budapest: Central European University Press, 1998.

Ghodsee, Kristen, and Mitchell Orenstein. *Taking Stock of Shock: Social Consequences of the 1989 Revolutions.* Oxford: Oxford University Press, 2021.

Hann, Chris, ed. *Postsocialism: Ideals, Ideologies, and Practices in Eurasia.* London: Routledge, 2002.

Kideckel, David. *Getting By in Postsocialist Romania: Labor, the Body, and Working-Class Culture.* Bloomington: Indiana University Press, 2008.

Kopeček, Michal, and Piotr Wciślik, eds. *Thinking through Transition: Liberal Democracy, Authoritarian Pasts, and Intellectual History in East Central Europe after 1989.* Budapest: Central European University Press, 2015.

Korolczuk, Elżbieta. "'Worse than communism and Nazism put together': War on Gender in Poland." In *Anti-Gender Campaigns in Europe: Mobilizing against Equality,* edited by Roman Kuhar and David Paternotte. London: Rowman & Littlefield, 2017: 175–94.

Krastev, Ivan, and Stephen Holmes. *The Light That Failed: Why the West Is Losing the Fight for Democracy.* New York: Pegasus Books, 2020.

Mark, James. *The Unfinished Revolution: Making Sense of the Communist Past in Central Eastern Europe.* New Haven, CT: Yale University Press, 2011.

Mark, James, Bogdan Iacob, Tobias Rupprecht, and Ljubica Spaskovska. *1989: A Global History of Eastern Europe.* Cambridge: Cambridge University Press, 2019.

Mohdin, Aamna. "The Fastest Shrinking Countries on Earth Are in Eastern Europe." *Quartz,* January 24, 2018. https://qz.com/1187819/country-rankingworlds-fastest-shrinking-countries-are-in-eastern-europe/.

Nadkarni, Maya. *Remains of Socialism: Memory and the Futures of the Past in Postsocialist Hungary.* Ithaca, NY: Cornell University Press, 2020.

Pehe, Veronika. "Totalitarianism as Defensive Memory of the Transformation: Unpacking a Czech Mnemonic Conflict." In *Erinnerung des Umbruchs, Umbruch der Erinnerung,* edited by Till Hilmar, Hanna Haag, and Julian Göpffahrt. Wiesbaden: Springer VS, 2024.

Pehe, Veronika, and Joanna Wawrzyniak, eds. *Remembering the Neoliberal Turn: Economic Change and Collective Memory in Eastern Europe after 1989.* New York: Routledge, 2023.

Ther, Philipp. *Europe since 1989: A History.* Princeton, NJ: Princeton University Press, 2016.

Tondo, Lorenzo, and Annie Kelly. "'Terrible Conditions': Police Uncover Abuse and Exploitation on Farms in Sicily." *Guardian,* October 31, 2017.

Verdery, Katherine. *What Was Socialism? And What Comes Next?* Princeton, NJ: Princeton University Press, 1996.

PART I

SOCIOECONOMIC TRANSFORMATIONS

1

"PEOPLE KNEW THEY WOULDN'T HAVE TO SCRAPE DRY CHOCOLATE IF THEY CALLED ME IN"

Industry, Subjectivity, and the Long Transformation

JOANNA WAWRZYNIAK

INTRODUCTION

RECENTLY, THERE HAS BEEN A WAVE OF NEW RESEARCH ON THE HISTORY of the transformation in East-Central Europe that contextualizes this turbulent period in larger patterns of cultural and socioeconomic developments. It proposes alternative periodization(s) of transformation by pointing to the 1970s, rather than to 1989–1991, as the beginning of accelerated socioeconomic change. In this way, the post-1989 period is analyzed with respect to earlier *and* later developments of globalization, democratization, and the Europeanization of culture. By complementing the earlier focus on political history, this new research invites us to rethink the recent past in terms of "the long 1990s," a fluid category used universally to refer to the period in which the Washington Consensus and neoliberal policies were established, technocratic governance expanded, and dictatorships withdrew—at least temporarily.[1]

This long view of recent history, which has informed transnational studies of East-Central Europe, is rarely appreciated, if even noticed, in hegemonic interpretations of Eastern Europe. In the Baltic states and in the Visegrád Group, constituted by the Czech Republic, Hungary, Poland, and Slovakia, neoliberal and right-wing populist interpretations of the causes and course of the transition from communism to capitalism, dictatorship to democracy, and accession to NATO and the European Union (EU) are still governed by the anticommunist paradigm. The former views the transition as a necessary and welcome change, the latter feeds on dissatisfaction with the neoliberal turn, including austerity measures, rising inequality, and outmigration. Although liberals and populists in those countries tend to clash over political symbols such as the role of particular politicians in the transition process or the meaning(s) of transition agreements, they both draw on the ideology of anticommunism. This paradigm has influenced how recent history has been represented in the public sphere, including in journalistic accounts, history classes, and history museums.[2]

In this chapter I discuss possible ways of narrating recent history that incorporate both longer patterns of socioeconomic change and the subjective, local experience of the transformation without becoming entrapped in "the anticommunist politics of history." I also demonstrate how oral history, by illuminating how different actors remember the 1990s, challenges old narratives and enriches our understanding of the transition. A return to narratives of transformation "from below" illuminates the different paths historical interpretations take, despite the hegemony of an anticommunist memory regime.

My analysis is influenced by a current discussion in memory studies about the so-called "mnemonic agonism," an approach that repoliticizes the past and the relation of the past to the present and which relies on radical (as opposed to consensual) multiperspectivity to weaken the hegemonic memory regimes developed by political elites.[3] It highlights the perspectives of political, social, and cultural actors heretofore marginalized in the public sphere and examines the controversies, as well as differences, in values, meanings, and emotions. Although memory studies scholars have been rethinking the political ideas of Chantal Mouffe in different ways, the agonistic approach is broadly understood as a way to question official discourses and explore alternative historical narratives.[4]

Thus far, the main conceptual and practical insights on agonistic oral history have been advanced by Chris Reynolds, historian and co-curator of an exhibition at the Ulster Museum in 2018, which featured testimonies of thirty activists who participated in the civil rights movement in Northern Ireland in 1968, at the onset of the Troubles. Comprised of oral history accounts, the exhibition depicted the legacy of the Troubles as part of the Northern Irish peace process. Instead of offering one single interpretation of 1968, the exhibition invited visitors to draw their own views of how this period should be remembered, thereby encouraging recognition of the complexities of memory in a divided and politically fraught society. In addition to the display of conflicting perspectives and emphasis on alternative narratives of the Troubles, agonism was articulated by displaying them against the new background of international history that went beyond the standard interpretations of Northern Ireland in 1968.[5]

This chapter relies on agonistic insights derived from an oral history project on the memories of transformation and deindustrialization in Poland. Between 2010 and 2016, I led a team of researchers who conducted over 130 life story interviews with the employees of twelve industrial sites that were modernized in the 1970s and later privatized and sold to multinationals in the 1990s.[6] Relating to a critical strand of literature on postsocialism in Poland on the one hand and to a wider context of labor transformations under global capitalism on the other, our research supplemented earlier studies of the transformation owing to its focus on how postsocialism and industrial reorganization were remembered by workers two decades after the "shock therapy" of the 1990s.[7]

The featured postsocialist factories—heavy and light branches of industry, including a steel works, cement plant, car factory, tire factory, paper mill, as well as enterprises that produced food, cigarettes, chemicals, and pharmaceuticals—did not collapse after 1989, but stayed in operation in the reframed setting of the multinationals that purchased them. Although all these industries experienced severe downsizing as part of the privatization and restructuring process, the global position of their new owners (among them PepsiCo, Heineken, ArcelorMittal, Philips, Michelin, Daewoo, Nestlé, to name a few) meant they were privileged over many other industries that were disbanded. Most of our interviewees remained employed until their retirement, while others changed jobs or went on to collect various forms of severance pay. This collection of interviews not only provides a comparative basis for understanding how diverse actors, including management, trade unions, and various blue-collar and white-collar workers were affected by privatization, but also expands the temporal parameters of the transformation to encompass longer patterns of economic and social history.

Drawing on oral histories from this project, I showcase three instances that challenge hegemonic interpretations of the transformation. By analyzing the memories of engineers and other qualified technical workers who already worked within the global economy in the 1970s, I complicate the notion of 1989 as an anticommunist breakthrough, underscoring the diverse temporalities that characterized the transformation in Poland. Additionally, by analyzing different memories of privatization, I reconstruct grassroots, agonistic views of the mass redundancies of the 1990s, which were key experiences of the neoliberal turn in Poland (with the unemployment rate around 16 percent in the mid-1990s). Finally, the chapter reflects on the countermemory of a Communist Party member whose views challenge hegemonic, anticommunist interpretations of recent history. More generally, the oral histories featured here demonstrate how social actors mobilized their own resources to act; how they understood the results of their actions; and how they reflected on their agency under late socialism and during early postsocialism.

TEMPORALITY, OR WHY THE 1970S MATTER

The diverse temporalities of the transformation are understudied; however, their reconstruction could enhance our understanding of why social groups clash over the meanings of the recent past. Temporalities are neither neutral nor natural, but powerful tools for naturalizing social worlds and social change for social actors.[8] They also have distinct implications for the ways in which groups and individuals engage with the past. Therefore, a discussion of when the transformation began does not make much sense unless we ask: for whom? In our project, one of the most coherent groups whose narratives suggest the need for alternative periodizations of the transformation were engineers and other qualified workers who were later employed in postsocialist factories. If we understand the transformation as a convergence, or at least an entanglement, between capitalist and socialist types of production, the engineers' life stories reveal how this process had started (for them) in the 1970s. The recollections I refer to in the following pages derive mainly from interviews conducted with former employees of a car producer, Fabryka Samochodów Osobowych (FSO), and a chocolate factory, Wedel, in Warsaw, but we have observed similar stories in other factories in our sample. However, it is difficult to say if those stories are representative beyond our sample; the factories we studied had a specific and privileged trajectory: modernized in the 1970s, they ended up in the hands of large multinationals in the 1990s.

Part of the postwar baby boom generation, the featured workers completed their schooling and higher education by the late 1960s and early 1970s, and the accelerated industrialization of the 1970s enabled them to acquire skills necessary for working in socialist industry. During the 1970s Polish industries also adopted new modes of production and explored markets in the Global South. At the time, the Polish state relied on Western loans to boost industrial development, resulting in an increase in foreign debt from $1 billion to $24 billion between 1970 and 1980. The state continued buying Western licenses for industrial production, which increased access to consumer durables such as cars and supported technological modernization. This process also promoted détente in Europe and facilitated Poland's engagement in the global economy.[9] While goods produced in Polish factories as a result of those technology transfers were not competitive in Western markets, they were attractive to the domestic (Polish) market and to developing economies of the Global South. Young Polish engineers and qualified workers at these factories thus became a privileged group, trained by workers from leading Western companies that sold their (often outdated) technologies to Poland. In addition to acquiring technical knowledge, the engineers traveled within and outside of Europe and learned foreign languages. They negotiated contracts, supervised production, and trained subcontractors in countries throughout Europe, Asia, Africa, and Latin America. In our interviews, they spoke with enthusiasm and fascination about the 1970s, referring to it as a period of great personal adventure. They shared numerous stories about observing strikes in Italy, throngs of people in factories in Bulgaria, negotiations of contracts in the UK, learning how to operate a new machine in Scandinavia, sending cars to Mexico, opening production lines in Libya, or getting stuck without family contacts in China. "We drew a lot of satisfaction from belonging to the elite staff," recalled a process engineer in a car plant.[10] Another added: "Work was very interesting. More and more duties, more and more money, I dare say. . . . And a sense of self-improvement: I had to learn English, I completed two post-graduate study programs."[11]

Participating in the circulation of knowledge and building industry were not the only factors that shaped workers' memories of late socialism. Another important layer was the sense of being locally needed and useful. Beginning in the late 1970s, the Polish state could not afford to update technologies and production. Thus, the skills of local staff were essential in keeping factories running. On the one hand, the constant rush during production was a source of frustration for our interviewees. The level of stress was high as nothing worked properly, and there were many, often fatal, accidents in the factories. Sometimes their superiors, themselves threatened by the police, added to this atmosphere of tension, often blaming the engineers for accidents or broken production lines. On the other hand, the engineers and high-skilled blue-collar workers created affective bonds with each other and the factories, to which they devoted their time, ambitions, and energy. The "gendered structure of feelings" of those predominantly male workers rested on the conviction that they were, in fact, the ones who ran the factories under difficult working conditions.[12] One of the electricians in the chocolate factory told us about how essential his skills were for fixing an Italian generator:

> Several such fixes and I was on good terms with the managers and foremen—they never wanted anyone else to do the job. It was a new generator, but it did break down. And you've got to fix it fast, because otherwise chocolate dries up. People knew they wouldn't have to scrape dry chocolate if they called me in, for I was the fastest on the job. . . . I had worked there for several decades; I loved it and I was appreciated.[13]

When the factories were sold to multinationals in the 1990s, the engineers were, as a whole, not negatively affected by downsizing as they already possessed skills necessary for surviving in the capitalist system. If they were laid off, they could find a new job or start their own business. Or they could emigrate and find work abroad.

Meanwhile, those still employed in the factories could enroll in training programs and improve their skills. In many respects, the transition was better: the secret police no longer surveilled them and they were not forced to attend compulsory courses on Marxism-Leninism. Nor were they bombarded with propaganda about "the Communist Party's leading role," the "economic plans," or "the internal enemies." Moreover, safety standards improved, production lines worked smoothly, and salaries increased. Nonetheless their experiences and narratives of this period display significant discrepancies from one another.

On the one hand, they acknowledged that their lobbying for foreign investments enabled them to connect with the global economy, which they were already quite familiar with. This was related by those in advanced managerial positions, on executive boards, and even those who took part in negotiations about privatization schemes for their factories. Thus, some managed to make impressive careers afterward. For instance, Jan (b. 1946), a physicist who implemented production lines in a tire factory in Olsztyn, Poland in the 1970s (on the license of American Uniroyal), organized production in Libya in the 1980s. After the Olsztyn factory was bought by Michelin in the 1990s, he became its CEO and was later relocated to the company headquarters in France.[14]

Additionally, Lucyna (b. 1947), an engineer and economist employed at the Wedel chocolate factory, held several managerial positions in the 1980s and helped open FritoLay factories in Poland and Russia.[15] For well-educated, competent, and ambitious women such as Lucyna the transformation opened up possibilities previously unthinkable in the patriarchal world of masculinist socialist industry. These women not only effectively adapted to, but thrived in the new system, as Jill Massino argued observing women in similar careers in Romania.[16]

At the same time, some of the engineers and other specialists, particularly those who did not secure careers in privatized companies, lamented their shrinking agency as they could no longer influence the course of events. The skills upon which they had built their status in socialist factories, including the resourceful ways they compensated for shortages in production, repaired broken machines, or even designed new ones, were devalued under postsocialism.[17] This sense of loss was articulated with reference to both the self and the nation, as they emphasized that the factories were no longer "theirs." Because the factories were sold to multinationals, they were no longer Polish, which undermined the engineers' sense of national pride. The sense of local community was gone, too. It was bad enough to no longer produce Polish goods; it was even worse to be forced to adjust to foreign superiors and different organizational cultures. Workers felt they were being treated as inferiors simply because they were Poles, which they found frustrating and offensive. A woman employed in a paper mill recalled with bitterness the negotiations with an Austrian company about restructuring: "They kept repeating that 'in Eastern Europe teaching is needed, you need training.' I remember a colleague who, at some point, could not put up with it anymore so she took out a ruler and map and showed them that Warsaw and Vienna are almost equally eastern."[18]

This widening social divide between individuals who once belonged to the same stratum of workers explains why some had negative perspectives on the transformation. Though privileged when compared with blue-collar workers, many engineers felt the Western companies treated them in a patronizing manner, minimizing their skills and experience. Yet, even though they were frustrated with foreign organizational cultures, this well-educated group of workers kept their jobs and often experienced upward mobility. The stories of engineers and technical staff employed in privatized factories illustrate that the 1970s mattered for this generation, in part because of their encounters with the global economy. Thereafter, they experienced a gradual opening up of their workplaces and their careers to foreign contacts, practices, and technologies.

While some were enthusiastic about privatization, others were more ambivalent; meanwhile others were indignant. For this latter group, the 1990s signified neither "the end" of the old world nor "the beginning" of a new one. Instead, the 1990s became another challenge that individuals with transferable skills had to face. Sociological research on the conversion of cultural and social capital into economic capital reveals that the Polish intelligentsia generally managed to do well under postsocialism.[19] However, oral histories with Polish engineers point to continuities in their professional roles rather than abrupt conversions of cultural and social capital that were acquired over several decades. Even though their perceptions of agency after 1989 varied, the engineers maintained or enhanced their material status, drawing on and expanding the resources amassed well before then. This stands in stark contrast to biographies of shop floor workers who were laid off in the 1990s and whose entire world dissolved in less than a decade.

AGONISM, OR HOW DOWNSIZING MATTERS

Another way to analyze the transformation is to juxtapose narratives expressing different values and emotions. Our project enables us to compare accounts of the same processes from different perspectives: by individuals who differed from each other in the way they witnessed or experienced those processes, often according to social status, gender, age, skill level, and/or other identifiers. Among the various episodes conveyed to us, the most salient were those that revolved around downsizing in the 1990s. Interviews with two managers, Magda (b. 1950) and Jan (b. 1952), both employed at the same paper mill in Świecie, a small town in northern Poland, illustrate this well. The paper mill was built during the late 1960s and early 1970s and became the main local employer, offering work for inhabitants of the surrounding villages, as well as for industrial laborers throughout Poland. As a result, between 1961 and 1988 the town's population almost doubled—from 13,000 to 25,000. Like other socialist factories, the paper mill became a center of communal life through formal and informal hierarchies, clientelist networks involving the reciprocal exchange of favors between the management and workers, and organized social welfare, including state-sponsored holidays, sports facilities, childcare centers, health care facilities, and the distribution of consumer goods. By the 1980s, the factory had become the largest producer of cellulose and paper in East-Central Europe; however, it struggled with problems common in shortage economies: decrepit machines, scarcity of materials, and lack of access to new markets. Privatization occurred over a relatively long period, and a deal with Austrian Mondi was finalized only in 1997. The factory was downsized several times, with the most severe layoffs occurring alongside the reorganization of production in the late 1990s. In 2003, the factory, renamed Frantschach Świecie S.A., numbered around 1,000 workers, less than a quarter of those employed in 1989.

Mass redundancies were a recurrent topic of all fourteen interviews we conducted in Świecie. However, Magda's and Jan's stories bear striking contrasts, even though neither of them had been laid off. On the contrary, they were both successful in advancing their careers until their retirement in the late 2010s. Yet, while Magda described restructuring, including learning new technologies and languages, as a painful process of "survival" that her generation suffered, Jan spoke of it as an adventure that modernized the community by reorienting it toward market principles. Magda noted:

> When the firm got privatized and went public, our age group was stripped of its sense of dignity. We always said we were a lost generation, for we had been denied an opportunity to learn foreign languages. I knew colleagues who were full of practical knowledge but could not share it because of the language barrier. Then there appeared a group of very young people, straight from college, whose advantage over us was that they were able to say beautifully [in English] "how do you do?"[20]

Jan, meanwhile, framed his story differently:

> I managed to learn English "just in time." I had started rather late, in 1990, but very intensively. In 1992, I was sent to Japan for two months for a state-owned enterprise management training program. In a group of twenty of various trades, we learned the theory and practice of business management. I covered two modules: strategic management and finance and investment.[21]

While talking about the mass redundancies Magda had witnessed and Jan had initiated as a manager, each conveyed fundamentally different values and emotions. As Magda reflected:

Later on, it got better, but in the '90s, that turn, it was really bad. On your way to work, you met women in tears. Tears, and tears, and tears. One is sobbing right here; another is crying over there. Then your family member loses their job. And you feel bad because you have a job. And what will you do? You, a member of a supervisory board? Won't you arrange something for your sister, for your cousin? I saw genuine despair. Those women sacked on the spot. Downsizing in Świecie, where there were no longer any jobs for women.... But the worst thing was that it came with no warning: you worked the night shift and then at dawn you were dismissed. I remember the tears in an inventory department: the women came to the office in the morning and were told to go back home. On the spot. The next day they came to collect their possessions.[22]

Meanwhile, Jan displayed a different sentiment:

During the first year we offered special severance pay to those who would accept "voluntary termination" and agree to go. About two or three hundred went like that. Then, unavoidable collective layoffs started. They were very well prepared. We hired reputable consultants from Hay Group and they helped us prepare a detailed plan on how to downsize as painlessly as possible, with much support to the laid off: psychological support, when they were told they had to go; support in the process of retraining; and obviously financial support: the severance pay was equal to one annual salary.... I am sure it was tough for them at the time, but perhaps, from a distance, they found some justification and understanding that it was worth it for the benefit of their children or even grandchildren, that this was for future generations. I sincerely hope so.[23]

The difference between Magda's and Jan's stories lay in their views on their responsibility vis-à-vis communal life and how they acted to influence the course of events. Magda depicted her situation as a personal struggle for survival as she was a single mother with dependent children. However, she also saw it as her duty to help other women, to save them from being laid off. For Jan, the 1990s meant unlimited possibilities of developing his career, though he also felt responsible for the factory, which could not survive under the harsh conditions of shock therapy unless workers were let go. Their attitudes reflect essentialist gender sensitivities and affectual bonds. In her narrative, Magda appears compassionate and caring, and she sees the factory in familial terms. Jan, meanwhile, distances himself from personal relationships and cloaks his actions behind the professionalism of a global management consulting firm. In sum, while Magda's responsibilities are with the people, Jan's are with the system and the factory.

Although it is tempting to generalize about the broader gendered implications of the above reflections, in other interviews we conducted we found female managers who were not particularly compassionate toward their staff, as well as men who expressed concern about weakening communal bonds. For instance, the aforementioned Lucyna conveyed a bitter story of how she overworked her employees—as well as herself— to such an extent that her American boss asked her to slow down and stop coming to work on weekends. Meanwhile, several senior-level male employees were quite emotional about the loss of the factory world, relating instances when they tried to soften the blow of restructuring. The differing views of Jan and Magda, rather than being gendered per se, instead offer windows onto two dominant modes of remembering—and justifying—actions during the transition: the "there was no alternative" future-oriented approach and the "moral economy" past-oriented approach. The former is characterized by rational economic calculations, a neoliberal work ethic, and managerial technocracy. It emphasizes modernization, technological development, a strong position within the global marketplace, improvements in organization (e.g., the physical appearance and safety of the workplace), as well as the prosperity of future generations and benefits for the local community and the country in general.

By contrast, the past-oriented mode (of remembering the transition) placed the disintegration of community values at its core. Concern revolved around not only loss of employment, but the erosion of former ways of life and the rise in mutual distrust. The detrimental effect of the "cuts" on both employment and social bonds can be understood through the lens of Karl Polanyi's concept of "disembeddedness," as employed in an analysis of the transformation of Polish and Croatian shipyards.[24] While disembeddedness can refer to loss of social control over the economic process of production and distribution, it can also refer to the "moral economy," in which communities oppose the effects of the "rational economy" within their social worlds. Accordingly, they defend— or lament—the waning of their collective identities, which are based on reciprocity and decision-making grounded primarily in community-based considerations.[25] Rather than looking forward, as with those who adhere to the "there was no alternative" approach, supporters of the "moral economy" approach dwell on feelings of collective deprivation and nostalgically reference the "good old times" from the socialist past, when people had time to cherish one another.[26] This mode of remembrance was evident in Magda's story and some of the engineers' accounts discussed in the previous section. It was also typical of shop floor workers whose stories stressed values such as reciprocity, fairness, stability, security, relative equality, sociability, and control over one's life. Some of our interviewees also lamented the dashed hopes of the transformation and expressed nostalgia for unrealized alternatives. Those included workers' share options and, in general, more social democratic and nationally oriented models of economic development. This "moral economy" perspective revealed the gulf between vague expectations that the collapse of the communist system would bring "normality" by increasing living standards and reducing the party's control over the workplaces, and the economic reality, which produced immense levels of stress, insecurity, and feelings of powerlessness.

COUNTERMEMORY, OR HOW A COMMUNIST PARTY MEMBER REMEMBERS

Another way to discuss alternative memories of transformation is to look at counternarratives that directly question the hegemonic myths of the transformation. For three decades now, Polish politics has been divided into two opposite camps: liberal-leaning and conservative-populist. Although they differ in many fundamental respects, they both originated in dissident milieus that organized themselves in support of workers' protests in the 1970s and later transformed into the Solidarity movement. In 1976, workers' strikes, brutally quashed by the communist government, took place in Radom, a medium-size town in central Poland situated 100 kilometers south of Warsaw. This event consequently led to the founding of the Workers' Defense Committee (Komitet Obrony Robotników; KOR) and other initiatives by the Polish opposition. After the collapse of communism, it became the core founding myth of postsocialist Poland.

In 2014, we interviewed employees of a privatized tobacco factory in Radom, among them Michał, a former party member whose anti-Solidarity story differed from those presented in public memory forums such as history textbooks and commemorative rituals. Michał was born into a poor peasant family in Lower Silesia in the late 1940s. After graduating from high school in 1967, he moved to Radom to complete his education at a two-year vocational teacher training center, specializing in art education. He met his future wife there, married, had two daughters, and was offered a job as a graphic designer (*plastyk*), where he was responsible for party propaganda in the tobacco factory and decorating for celebratory events such as May Day rallies and marches. During that time, Michał also supplemented his income with private catering jobs.

One of the first significant episodes of his narrative is the workers' protests of 1976. He describes the violence on the streets, the looting of shops, the beating of the factory's director, and, upon his return home, his crying children because of tear gas and a burning bus outside of his place:

I ran the tub full of water, secured all the doors with rolled blankets; we were afraid the place would go up in flames, there was so much smoke all around; tears rolled. It was 1976. And I shall never see that monument [to the workers] here as anything else but a monument to the memory of firebrands and troublemakers, because I know how it was.[27]

With a certain satisfaction, he rounds out this episode by noting that he earned extra money for decorating the local stadium with party slogans condemning the protests.

In the late 1970s, Michał ran a workers' club at the factory, where he organized sports and dancing events, and, because of his knowledge of Western rock and pop music, he became widely popular. This seemed to be the reason why, in 1980, he was offered a party propaganda job to run the factory's broadcasting facility, which he willingly accepted and where he kept condemning the Solidarity movement. He recalled: "As a radio operator I gave the only voice to the other side; Solidarity had no advantage. The party was all fed up with it, so they let me into the broadcasting." This facilitated his promotion to secretary of the factory committee, which he was courageous to accept given Solidarity's popularity among workers. Michał lost his job at the radio station upon the introduction of martial law in 1981. For some time, he was excluded from the factory, probably so as not to cause further tensions, and was given a behind-the-scenes position in the party regional committee, though he wished to return to the factory. In the 1980s, he was elected to the factory workers' council, but came into conflict with both the party and Solidarity members. In 1989, at a local party meeting, Michał reluctantly opted for the changes: "If these gentlemen—and, mind you, I was earlier the main critic of Michnik and Kuroń—if they wish to take responsibility for the shit and squalor we now have, well, let them suit themselves."

Later developments were not so favorable for Michał, as power was now in the hands of the local representatives of Solidarity. Even though Michał was allowed to play music on the factory radio for the next four years, Solidarity increasingly isolated him, and he realized he would be among the first to be laid off as the country adopted shock therapy measures. In 1996, eighteen years before Michał's legal retirement age, he was laid off after the factory came under French ownership. Since then, Michał has run his own home decorating business, drawing on resources from his past: his decorative skills and his connections, often with former party members and police, who advertise his services among themselves. Nonetheless, the family's financial security rests on his wife, who successfully transitioned from receptionist to sales manager at the same tobacco factory. Although some women, due to their greater flexibility and determination, adapted more successfully than men to the capitalist job market, which often produced resentment in their male partners, Michał did not mention any tension between him and his wife.

There are two interesting layers to this interview. One is Michał's view of both economic systems he lived and worked in. Contrary to many stories, the way Michał describes the factory—and life under communism more generally—is far from nostalgic. Unlike others, he emphasized low wages, poor organization, drunkenness, and theft. Yet, his view of the post-1990 period is equally bitter. Here he turns to Darwinian logic, namely the survival of the fittest, to explain how the world is organized. He noted:

I have worked for illusions and I'm fed up with it. As a party comrade, as a gig organizer, as a graphic designer: all for illusions. . . . I can't openly admit it without spitting on myself, so let me put it this way: they all kept stealing. Socialism would be great, if people were honest. That's impossible. Capitalism is built on one solid principle: on the recognition, on the axiom, that greed is the basic human trait. One always rakes toward, never away, from oneself.[28]

Despite the disconnect between expectations and reality, the other interesting—and astonishing—layer of Michał's narrative is that he describes his life as a success story. He does so by stressing that he and his wife made the "right choices" in the past. This was most visible when he described the way they raised their two daughters, namely to encourage their financial independence: "The most important thing in life we managed to do is that we brought up our children in such a way they now do not need anything from me; from us." (At the time of the interview, one of his daughters ran a firm with her husband in Poznań and had worked as an accountant in a Danish firm; the other obtained her PhD in geophysics and combined her salary with that of her husband, an IT manager at an American firm in Warsaw.) Michał is proud that he convinced his daughters to acquire languages and higher education in science. "We kept saying: do not repeat your parents' mistakes; learn mathematics. No one is going to rewrite mathematics for you, as they did history, literature and all that."

Michał also measures his family's success by the fact that his daughters did not need to emigrate for economic reasons: "And anyway, you know, it's bloody important. At my age, in my circle I can say: my children are in Poland; my grandchildren are in Poland." He makes this a key point in his interview when comparing his relative success to that of his neighbor, a retired militia officer: "And from six to four he got his parking lot security job, good luck to him. . . . But he visits his grandson somewhere in Germany . . . and for me it is not more than three hours along the highway to Poznan; and I've got the other grandson in Warsaw."

Michał's life trajectory encompasses both aspects of the transformation: "from above," which forced him out of his main workplace, and "from below," namely the ability to use his skills under capitalism. It is also the story of the gradual collapse of two patrons—Lenin and Ford. Michał speaks of the lost illusions of communist ideology and the downsizing of industry that cost him a job. Yet, despite his loss of faith in ideology, he nonetheless draws on competencies he acquired during socialism: skill, networks, drive, and adaptability. His children's stories, meanwhile, serve to normalize his biography in a society that publicly nurses the myths of Solidarity and silences those of former communists. In this way, Michał's recollections fill in the gap left by the official politics of history.

CONCLUSIONS

As the personal, postindustrial narratives discussed in this chapter demonstrate, attempts at historicizing the transformation must be attentive to longer socioeconomic changes, rather than identifying 1989 as a decisive breakthrough. Those shifts have different, sometimes overlapping, temporalities than political ones do, and an analysis of them should account for differences across sectors and professions. This chapter highlighted the life stories of engineers, for whom encounters with the global economy started in the 1970s. Moreover, by analyzing factory managers' perceptions of mass redundancies, as well as the narrative of a former Communist Party member, the chapter demonstrated how broadening our perspective and incorporating diverse memories—with their varied agencies and trajectories—can provide a more complex, albeit at times conflicting, history of socialism and postsocialism. Such an agonistic approach, which advocates illuminating controversies and tensions in the perception of past events and articulating unknown, silenced, or repressed stories, is particularly needed in the public spaces of Eastern Europe, which are still characterized by anticommunist, and thus oversimplified, interpretations of recent history.

NOTES

1. James Mark, Bogdan C. Iacob, Tobias Rupprecht, and Ljubica Spaskovska, *1989: A Global History of Eastern Europe* (Cambridge: Cambridge University Press, 2019); and Philipp Ther, Ulf Brunnbauer, Piotr Filipkowski, Andrew Hodges, Stefano Petrungaro, and Peter Wegenschimmel, *In den Stürmen der Transformation: Zwei Werften zwischen Sozialismus und EU* (Berlin: Suhrkamp Verlag, 2022).

2. Michael Bernhard and Jan Kubik, eds., *Twenty Years after Communism: The Politics of Memory and Commemoration* (Oxford: Oxford University Press, 2014); James Krapfl, "Passing the Torch, Despite Bananas: The Twentieth Anniversary Commemorations of 1989 in Central Europe," *Remembrance and Solidarity* 3 (2014): 63–102; and Zoltan Dujisin, "A History of Post-Communist Remembrance: From Memory Politics to the Emergence of a Field of Anticommunism," *Theory and Society* 50 (2021): 65–96.

3. Anna Cento Bull and Hans Lauge Hansen, "On Agonistic Memory," *Memory Studies* 9, no. 4 (2016): 390–404; and Stefan Berger and Wulf Kansteiner, *Agonistic Memory and the Legacy of 20th Century Wars in Europe* (Cham: Palgrave Macmillan, 2021).

4. See, for instance, Chantal Mouffe, "Deliberative Democracy or Agonistic Pluralism?" *Social Research* 66, no. 3 (1999): 745–58.

5. Chris Reynolds, "The Symbiosis of Oral History and Agonistic Memory: Voices of '68 and the Legacy of the Past in Northern Ireland," *Journal of the British Academy* 9, no.

3 (2021): 73–94; and Chris Reynolds and Anna C. Bull, "Uses of Oral History in Museums: A Tool for Agonism and Dissonance or Promoting a Linear Narrative?" *Museum and Society* 19, no. 3 (2021): 283–300.

6. We used the narrative biographical approach, soliciting life stories. All interviews were audio recorded and archived in the oral history center in Warsaw (Dom Spotkań z Historia). A documentary book with twenty-seven accounts about life under socialism and the transformation to capitalism was published in Aleksandra Leyk and Joanna Wawrzyniak, *Cięcia: Historia mówiona transformacji* (Warszawa: Wydawnictwo Krytyki Politycznej, 2020).

7. In Poland, the rapid macroeconomic reforms designed to liberalize the economy were introduced at the beginning of the 1990s by the finance minister, Leszek Balcerowicz, and his team of experts. Drafted according to the principles of the Washington Consensus, it aimed at liberalization of prices, mass-scale privatization, trade liberalization, and stabilization by tight fiscal policy and austerity measures. The consequences of this "shock therapy" for the shrinking social world of industry have been described in numerous monographs, including: Elizabeth C. Dunn, *Privatizing Poland: Baby Food, Big Business, and the Remaking of Labor* (Ithaca, NY: Cornell University Press, 2004); Kaja Kaźmierska and Katarzyna Waniek, eds., *Telling the Great Change: The Processes of the Systemic Transformation in Poland in Biographical Perspective* (Łódź: Wydawnictwa Uniwersytetu Łódzkiego, 2020); Adam Mrozowicki, *Coping with Social Change: Life Strategies of Workers in Poland's New Capitalism* (Leuven: Leuven University Press, 2011); David Ost, *The Defeat of Solidarity: Anger and Politics in Postcommunist Europe* (Ithaca, NY: Cornell University Press, 2005); Kinga Pozniak, *Nowa Huta: Generations of Change in a Model Socialist Town* (Pittsburgh: Pittsburgh University Press, 2014); Aleksandra Sznajder Lee, *Transnational Capitalism in East Central Europe's Heavy Industry: From Flagship Enterprises to Subsidiaries* (Ann Arbor: University of Michigan Press, 2016); and Vera Trappmann, *Fallen Heroes in Global Capitalism: Workers and the Restructuring of the Polish Steel Industry* (Basingstoke: Palgrave Macmillan, 2013).

8. Jacques Ranciére, "In What Time Do We Live?" *Política común* 4 (2013).

9. Aleksandra Komornicka, "Socialist Poland's Opening towards the West, 1970–1980" (PhD diss., European University Institute, Florence, 2021), 133.

10. Leyk and Wawrzyniak, *Cięcia*, 344.

11. Leyk and Wawrzyniak, *Cięcia*, 365.

12. See Chiara Bonfiglioli, "Post-Socialist Deindustrialization and Its Gendered Structure of Feeling: The Devaluation of Women's Work in the Croatian Garment Industry," *Labor History* 61, no. 1 (2020): 36–47.

13. Leyk and Wawrzyniak, *Cięcia*, 108.

14. Leyk and Wawrzyniak, *Cięcia*, 287–313.

15. Leyk and Wawrzyniak, *Cięcia*, 137–53.

16. Jill Massino, "'The Lost Years': Gender, Citizenship, and Economic Change in Romania during the Long '90s," *Remembering the Neoliberal Turn: Collective Memory and Economic Transformation in Eastern Europe after 1989*, ed. Veronika Pehe and Joanna Wawrzyniak (London: Routledge, 2023).

17. See Elizabeth's Dunn's account of female workers who experienced a similar devaluation of their skills in Dunn, *Privatizing Poland*.

18. Leyk and Wawrzyniak, *Cięcia*, 198.

19. Tomasz Zarycki, *Kapitał kulturowy: Inteligencja w Polsce i Rosji* (Warszawa: Wydawnictwa Uniwersytetu Warszawskiego, 2008).

20. Leyk and Wawrzyniak, *Cięcia*, 201.

21. Leyk and Wawrzyniak, *Cięcia*, 185.

22. Leyk and Wawrzyniak, *Cięcia*, 202.

23. Leyk and Wawrzyniak, *Cięcia*, 190.

24. Das Werftenkollektiv, in *In den Stürmen der Transformation*, Ther et al.; Karl Polanyi, *The Great Transformation* (New York: Farrar & Rinehart, 1944).

25. E. P. Thompson, "The Moral Economy of the English Crowd in the Eighteenth Century," *Past and Present* 50 (1971): 76–136; and Tim Strangleman, "Deindustrialization and the Historical Sociological Imagination: Making Sense of Work and Industrial Change," *Sociology* 51, no. 2 (2016).

26. Joanna Wawrzyniak, "'Hard Times but Our Own': Post-Socialist Nostalgia and the Transformation of Industrial Life in Poland," *Zeithistorische Forschungen/Studies in Contemporary History* 18 (2021), 73–92.

27. Dom Spotkań z Historią, Archiwum Historii Mówionej (DSH AHM), IS_3_0010, audio recording.

28. Dom Spotkań z Historią, Archiwum Historii Mówione.

BIBLIOGRAPHY

Berger, Stefan, and Wulf Kansteiner. *Agonistic Memory and the Legacy of 20th Century Wars in Europe*. Cham: Palgrave Macmillan, 2021.

Bernhard, Michael, and Jan Kubik, eds. *Twenty Years after Communism: The Politics of Memory and Commemoration*. Oxford: Oxford University Press, 2014.

Bonfiglioli, Chiara. "Post-Socialist Deindustrialization and Its Gendered Structure of Feeling: The Devaluation of Women's Work in the Croatian Garment Industry." *Labor History* 61, no. 1 (2020): 36–47.

Bull, Anna Cento, and Hans Lauge Hansen. "On Agonistic Memory." *Memory Studies* 9, no. 4 (2016): 390–404.

Dujisin, Zoltan. "A History of Post-Communist Remembrance: From Memory Politics to the Emergence of a Field of Anticommunism." *Theory and Society* 50 (2021): 65–96.

Dunn, Elizabeth C. *Privatizing Poland: Baby Food, Big Business, and the Remaking of Labor.* Ithaca, NY: Cornell University Press, 2004.

Kaźmierska, Kaja, and Katarzyna Waniek, eds. *Telling the Great Change: The Processes of the Systemic Transformation in Poland in Biographical Perspective.* Łódź: Wydawnictwa Uniwersytetu Łódzkiego, 2020.

Komornicka, Aleksandra. "Socialist Poland's Opening towards the West, 1970–1980." PhD diss., European University Institute, Florence, 2021.

Krapfl, James. "Passing the Torch, Despite Bananas: The Twentieth Anniversary Commemorations of 1989 in Central Europe." *Remembrance and Solidarity* 3 (2014): 63–102.

Leyk, Aleksandra, and Joanna Wawrzyniak. *Cięcia: Historia mówiona transformacji.* Warszawa: Wydawnictwo Krytyki Politycznej, 2020.

Mark, James, Bogdan C. Iacob, Tobias Rupprecht, and Ljubica Spaskovska. *1989: A Global History of Eastern Europe.* Cambridge: Cambridge University Press, 2019.

Massino, Jill. "'The Lost Years': Gender, Citizenship, and Economic Change in Romania during the Long '90s." In *Remembering the Neoliberal Turn: Collective Memory and Economic Transformation in Eastern Europe after 1989*, edited by Veronika Pehe and Joanna Wawrzyniak. London: Routledge, 2023.

Mouffe, Chantal. "Deliberative Democracy or Agonistic Pluralism?" *Social Research* 66, no. 3 (1999): 745–58.

Mrozowicki, Adam. *Coping with Social Change: Life Strategies of Workers in Poland's New Capitalism.* Leuven: Leuven University Press, 2011.

Ost, David. *The Defeat of Solidarity: Anger and Politics in Postcommunist Europe.* Ithaca, NY: Cornell University Press, 2005.

Polanyi, Karl. *The Great Transformation.* New York: Farrar & Rinehart, 1944.

Pozniak, Kinga. *Nowa Huta: Generations of Change in a Model Socialist Town.* Pittsburgh: Pittsburgh University Press, 2014.

Ranciére, Jacques. "In What Time Do We Live?" *Política común* 4 (2013).

Reynolds, Chris. "The Symbiosis of Oral History and Agonistic Memory: Voices of '68 and the Legacy of the Past in Northern Ireland." *Journal of the British Academy* 9, no. 3 (2021): 73–94.

Reynolds, Chris, and Anna C. Bull. "Uses of Oral History in Museums: A Tool for Agonism and Dissonance or Promoting a Linear Narrative?" *Museum and Society* 19, no. 3 (2021): 283–300.

Strangleman, Tim. "Deindustrialization and the Historical Sociological Imagination: Making Sense of Work and Industrial Change." *Sociology* 51, no. 2 (2016).

Sznajder Lee, Aleksandra. *Transnational Capitalism in East Central Europe's Heavy Industry: From Flagship Enterprises to Subsidiaries.* Ann Arbor: University of Michigan Press, 2016.

Ther, Philipp, Ulf Brunnbauer, Piotr Filipkowski, Andrew Hodges, Stefano Petrungaro, and Peter Wegenschimmel. *In den Stürmen der Transformation: Zwei Werften zwischen Sozialismus und EU.* Berlin: Suhrkamp Verlag, 2022.

Thompson, E. P. "The Moral Economy of the English Crowd in the Eighteenth Century." *Past and Present* 50 (1971): 76–136.

Trappmann, Vera. *Fallen Heroes in Global Capitalism: Workers and the Restructuring of the Polish Steel Industry.* Basingstoke: Palgrave Macmillan, 2013.

Wawrzyniak, Joanna. "'Hard Times but Our Own': Post-Socialist Nostalgia and the Transformation of Industrial Life in Poland." *Zeithistorische Forschungen/Studies in Contemporary History* 18 (2021), 73–92.

Zarycki, Tomasz. *Kapitał kulturowy: Inteligencja w Polsce i Rosji.* Warszawa: Wydawnictwa Uniwersytetu Warszawskiego, 2008.

2

HOW FOREIGNERS DESTROYED OUR FACTORY

Repressed Memories of a Czech Flagship Sugar Plant [1]

ONDŘEJ KLÍPA

"I KNOW THE YOUNGSTERS HERE ALL VOTE FOR OKAMURA OUT OF SPITE," SAID Jaroslav, one of the longest-serving (former) workers of a sugar plant in the East Bohemian town of Hrochův Týnec.[2] Jaroslav was referring to Tomio Okamura, a politician of Czech-Japanese-Korean descent and the leader of a Czech far-right nationalist movement that received almost 10 percent of the vote in the 2021 parliamentary elections. It is hard to say whether Jaroslav is right since Okamura's party did not score above the national average in Hrochův Týnec and the nearby municipalities. Nevertheless, at least some of the locals—old and young alike—still believe they have a reason for grievance against broadly defined "foreigners."

In this chapter I analyze the nexus between deindustrialization, transnational capital, and nationalist populism in postsocialist Czechia. I draw on archival materials related to the sugar plant's operation during socialism, media reports, government documents, and six in-depth interviews I conducted with former plant employees (both women and men of various ages). My approach is influenced by Eszter Bartha, who analyzed the changing position of workers in postcommunist East Germany and Hungary from their perspective. In the Hungarian case, declining industrial sectors, disrupted working communities, and the economic vulnerability of individual employees led to a growth in the popularity of ethnocentric political radicalism that "seemed to offer the only means to express social criticism."[3] By examining Euroskeptic, nationalist, and anti-elite sentiment among Czech workers who, unlike Bartha's Hungarian narrators, did not suffer economic hardship and whose industrial branch successfully survived postcommunist transformation, I highlight the noneconomic factors shaping workers' political attitudes. In particular, I am concerned with the disintegration of their professional identities and the exclusion of their specific community of memory, or, as Eviatar Zerubavel puts it, their "mnemonic community," from the dominant historical narrative.[4] The repression of the workers' collective memory may help explain why the sugar plant—built explicitly to showcase socialist internationalism in the economic sphere, and especially Czechoslovak-Polish friendship—so easily became a hotbed of xenophobia and anti-European nationalism.

THE DISASTER

From 1969 to 2008, the town of Hrochův Týnec, home today to some 2,100 inhabitants, was the site of the last sugar plant in Bohemia. In 1970, construction on its "twin" plant was completed in Moravia. Both plants were built as "turnkey projects" (constructed as completed products) by Polish construction companies. The Poles not only provided the necessary equipment and machinery, but also furnished construction materials, including sand and cement. Out of fifty Czech sugar plants, these two were the most expansive and remained so into the 1990s, when large-scale privatization began changing the trajectories of state-owned enterprises. This included the plant in Hrochův Týnec, which was purchased three times after 1989, the last owner being a French-British company—Eastern Sugar.[5] While under the ownership of Cukrspol, the plant reached its highest production rate (in 2001); since the plant's acquisition by Eastern Sugar production rates have plummeted.[6] According to the plant's former employees, the French-British owner made immediate changes to the managerial style, treating workers as anonymous and expendable items—in contrast to the previous owner—and launched intensive cost-cutting measures. To demonstrate their worth, workers were required to pass a series of cognitive tests. As Karel, one of the employees, explained: "There was a picture of a transmission with four gears, and we had to point in the direction the vehicle would move when the gears were rotated. That was not difficult for me at all, but I was fired anyway because my position was simply cancelled. Many of our female colleagues had trouble with the task despite being good at their jobs. The tests contained nothing about making sugar!"[7]

The plant's doom, however, was sealed by much more radical decisions in the following years. By coincidence, soon after the Czech Republic and other postcommunist states entered the European Union (EU) in 2004, Brussels (the EU "capital") was forced to reform its sugar policy, which had been in place for about forty years. Increased sugar production in developing countries, especially Brazil and India, had put the commodity's global prices under pressure. As such, the EU's import tariffs and subsidies for local producers faced growing criticism from the World Trade Organization (WTO), which regarded EU policy as discriminatory toward poorer members. As a result, in mid-2006, the EU began subsidizing Europe's sugar production, though even before the reform all member states had been given national quotas limiting the amount of sugar they could produce. Later, however, the EU announced its aim to cut overall sugar production by at least five million tons by 2010. As an incentive, every company that chose to stop production and hand its share of the national quota over to Brussels was eligible for financial compensation from EU funds (730 euros per ton of sugar).[8]

Eastern Sugar was the only sugar plant owner in the Czech Republic that chose to cease production.[9] As all former employees noted with marked bitterness, the transnational company opted to shut down its (recently acquired) assets, but only "in the East" (i.e., its three Czech plants, a plant in Slovakia, and one in Hungary). Notably, factories in the company's home countries of the UK and France were not affected.[10] Moreover, the company sought the highest EU compensation possible, which required leveling the entire factory (and removing all underground installations) to ensure production could not resume in the future. Undeterred by employee protests and despite the best efforts of a handful of Czech civil servants and politicians, the factory was demolished in 2008.[11] In exchange for surrendering the production quota for its three Czech plants (102,000 tons per year), Eastern Sugar received some 60 million euros.

At the end of 2006, to commemorate the factory's final processed crop, the managerial staff and rank and file employees came together for a symbolic "funeral." Accompanied by a brass band, they marched with an allegorical coffin (a large, modified sugar bag) to an "altar" that had been erected in front of the factory's main entrance and decorated with flower wreaths, candles, and an "obituary." The text read: "Betrayed by foreign owners, discriminated against by EU policy, abandoned by money-grubbers in Brussels and Prague, I was fatally shot by the invisible hand of the market. I died after almost 40 years of hard, sweet labour." And so, after 137 years (the town's first sugar plant had been built in 1871 and was demolished in 1982), Hrochův Týnec lost its characteristic skyline with sugar-plant chimney.

Yet, not only were locals deprived of a visual symbol of their town, they were also robbed of the centerpiece of their social life. During socialism, the plant had employed about 380 full-time workers, numbers that increased during the fall sugar campaigns by another 500 temporary laborers. Most of the core workforce, as well as many of the "campaign workers" (usually pensioners), were from Hrochův Týnec or the nearby village of Čaňkovice. It is therefore hardly an exaggeration to say that nearly every adult from both communities worked in the refinery or had a neighbor or family member who worked there. Petr, a resident of Čaňkovice and one of the last employees to retire from the factory, recalled in an interview: "Almost the entire village met there every day. Now we miss that because there's no other place where we can all see each other, have a chat, and hear about what's new from the neighbors." Indeed, my respondents repeatedly mentioned that all the refinery's staff was "like one big family." As Daphne Berdahl wrote about former East Germany, "The workplace was not only the center of everyday sociality, it was a symbolic space of community and national belonging."[12] Likewise, the sugar plant in Hrochův Týnec served in many capacities long after 1989, from providing welfare entitlements (subsidized housing, collective vacations, summer camps for children, etc.) to organizing leisure activities, sports teams, and events for its community of workers.[13]

The demolition of this immense, relatively new factory, along with two smaller sugar refineries in 2008, attracted a fair amount of national media attention. Pictures of the demolition can still be found online, often accompanied by comments from angry readers and interviews complaining about global capital and corrupt politicians "in Prague," "foreigners" (sometimes identified as the "French"), Brussels, and the EU in general.[14] In a newspaper article entitled "French goodbye. Adieu, sucrerie Hrochův Týnec" an anonymous reader commented: "'The Big Václav' [meaning the former Euroskeptic Czech president Václav Klaus] and I did not want into the EU. We suspected that this is going to be just another COMECON. The only difference now is that everything is no longer ordered behind the scenes, but 'democratically.' The EU will soon wipe us out with its goods."[15] Although it is not clear if this and similar comments were made by the former factory workers, the sense of being subject to decisions made "about us, without us" was quite palpable in my interviews as well.

In many ways, this story resembles that of the blue-collar workers in postsocialist (East) Germany and Hungary analyzed by Bartha. Each of the groups she studied— both Germans and Hungarians—"recalled the collegiality and intensive community life under socialism with a sense of loss."[16] But only in the Hungarian case were the "workers susceptible to nationalistic-populist 'catchwords' which operate with a concrete enemy picture: 'foreign,' 'exploiting capital,' 'multinational enterprises,' which 'take the profit out of the country,' etc."[17] As Jan Veleba, former president of the Agricultural Chamber of the Czech Republic, stated at a debate in the Czech Senate in March 2007: "[The decision to close the Hrochův Týnec sugar plant] is the first practical and visible example illustrating at whose expense common agricultural policy reform will be conducted. At the expense of new [EU member] countries because sugar production is restricted [only] in the Czech Republic, Slovakia, and Hungary."[18] Thus, many former workers in Hrochův Týnec, as well as likeminded people who backed them in public debates, may have believed that "corrupt" political elites "sold the country to foreign interests."[19] As Jaroslav bluntly put it, "You know what? Fu**ing Praguers! I know you come from Prague . . . don't take it personally. But they cheated us and had been plotting to for a long time. [A Czech] minister came down to meet us, he had his coffee and then left as quickly as he could. No one asked the [workers] what they thought. No one was interested in our opinion."

THE GOLDEN PARACHUTE

An important element of Bartha's argument about the rise of nationalism among blue-collar workers is missing in the Czech case. She observed that typically the nationalist-populist "longing for a strong state, order, and an autocratic government" is confused with the "vision of greater social and material equality."[20] Bartha draws on the works of Don Kalb and Gábor Halmai who contend that "right-wing populism offers a panacea for the insecurity of the world and the everyday struggle to make a decent living."[21] These economic concerns seem less important for the Czech sugar plant workers, however.

In 2007, when most workers in Hrochův Týnec were dismissed, the factory employed only 150, and over 70 percent of the redundant workforce found other work immediately—an unusual success story in the context of economic transformation in the Czech Republic and Eastern Europe more generally.[22] Unlike other discharged employees in the region, the workers in Hrochův Týnec were relatively well positioned as they possessed experience and skill, ensuring their smooth transition to another sugar plant or in other nearby factories. In addition, thanks to a favorably negotiated collective agreement, all workers were compensated with eleven to sixteen monthly salaries, a rather extraordinary move for a private company in the Czech Republic. This enabled some to set up small businesses (one of my respondents opened a little pub) or to enter early retirement.[23] A substantial severance pay—as a share of the total sum paid to Eastern Sugar—was also provided to the local sugar beet producers who lost their primary customers. Unlike their colleagues in Slovakia and Hungary, who received 20 percent and 27 percent respectively, the Czech government negotiated 30 percent for all Eastern Sugar's local producers. Although Eastern Sugar's decision to close and bulldoze the plant was unexpected and "contrary to accepted principles of morality," as Czech deputy minister of agriculture Stanislav Kozák put it, in purely economic terms the story of Hrochův Týnec does not conform to the early 1990s scenario of plundering capitalists (mostly homeland business tycoons) that simply do not care.[24]

Surprisingly, in economic terms the entire sugar industry was doing well, too, though the number of factories was small and the staff continued to dwindle. The other two major sugar plant owners in the Czech Republic (Austrian and French-German companies) continued modernizing their equipment and entered the period following 2017, when the EU's sugar policy was (once again) deregulated and fully liberalized, in a highly competitive climate. Right after deregulation (the campaign of 2017–2018),

Czech sugar production reached its highest rate since 1965. But whereas back then there had been seventy-six sugar plants, in 2017 there were only seven. The largest Czech sugar refinery can currently process almost four times as many sugar beets per day as the factory in Hrochův Týnec could after it was put into operation.[25]

NO SENTIMENTS FOR THE FACTORY

What frustration then, if not purely economic, could have produced such xenophobic and antiestablishment sentiments in the population some thirteen years after the plant's demolition? Before answering this question, it is important to discuss the striking lack of nostalgia—as a sentiment of loss and displacement—in interviews with former factory workers. In Bartha's Hungarian interviews, "the narrators always contrasted the 'glorious old times' with the reality of today."[26] My narrators were careful not to mention any pre-1989 "golden age" or celebrate the era of state socialism in any respect. Their stance was closer to that of the East German workers who, in Bartha's words, refused "the narrative of decline" and who "sought to give an objective and depersonalized account of their factory's transition from planned economy to integration into the global capitalist system, refusing to be 'nostalgic' about the paternalistic enterprise."[27] But, unlike Bartha's East German respondents who were generally happy with their employer's postsocialist development, the workers in Hrochův Týnec experienced traumatizing treatment at the hands of the transnational company, against which they actively protested despite the generous payoff.

And yet, the workers I interviewed and whose interviews I read in the media insist they do not mourn the factory. I asked Petr, a former worker, whether he would have preferred to preserve some of the emblematic elements of the plant (the chimney, the sugar silo) over its total destruction. He fiercely refused. Instead of feeling sentimental, he, as well as the other respondents, maintained that their objection to the refinery's complete demolition was rooted wholly in economic and pragmatic arguments, namely that the facilities should have been used for other, profitable businesses. Nor did they hesitate to underline that the plant had been modernized by their private owners, including Eastern Sugar, quite recently. In addition to significantly renovating and expanding the factory in 1995 (building a new sugar silo, the most visible object on the skyline aside from the chimney) and again in 1998 (in commemoration of its thirtieth anniversary), the owners constantly upgraded equipment until shortly before the plant was shut down. "Everything inside was stainless steel and shiny," Jaroslav recalled. Thus, to many the demolition looked like a blatantly wasted investment.

Economic "common sense" arguments were also raised within the broader context of "national interests." For instance, my respondents expressed concern that by closing its three Czech refineries Eastern Sugar would make the Czech Republic a net sugar importer.[28] That argument was presented both as a humiliation of the national tradition of sugar production (especially in the interwar period as it played a crucial role for the nascent Czechoslovak state, whose share in European sugar export was 57 percent) and as an economic risk due to the volatility of the commodity's price on the world market.[29] Additionally, former plant workers asserted that, in comparison with "Western Europe," their factory had manufactured sugar at a fraction of the cost, and their region offered much more suitable natural conditions for growing sugar beets (soil fertility). In sum, the demolition of their sugar plant was presented primarily as economic nonsense.

In his emotional and nostalgic memoirs of a different sugar plant that had been demolished in the Czech town of Mnichovo Hradiště, Jan Hozák of the National Technical Museum in Prague repeatedly proclaimed, "It is surely very strange to cling to an old factory," which is, in reality, "quite an ugly object." Yet he closes his article poetically, asking readers to allow him to express how much he misses the old sugar plant.[30] Former workers in Hrochův Týnec are far more reluctant to show emotional ties to their factory. Whereas Hozák mourned a 130-year-old building erected during a legendary era when Czech industry was blossoming, the factory in Hrochův Týnec was "too young," with none of the red bricks or architectural aesthetic of *Gründerzeit* capitalism.[31]

A book cataloguing a "lost Czech industrial heritage" provides another telling example of this. Published in 2009 and entitled *What We Have Torn Down*, the book carefully documents many cases where industrial objects were bulldozed to the ground. Among other things, it points a finger at the widespread public ignorance of the post-1989 neoliberal era.[32] Although the book lists the dismantling of two of Eastern Sugar's smaller and more historic refineries, the case of the plant in Hrochův Týnec, broadly covered by the media, is completely left out. Without any delimitation of the timespan in focus, the authors tacitly assert that objects built during state socialism are simply not worthy of being called the nation's "industrial heritage." It seems the "boring" grey concrete, of which most of the late state socialist factories are built, intersects with the stereotype of post-1968 communist Czechoslovakia as one of the least popular periods in the mainstream historical narrative.

NO NOSTALGIA FOR THE COMMUNIST PAST

It is arguable that many former sugar plant workers do not want to be associated with "communist times" at all, though their symbolic social status (not necessarily corresponding to material wealth) back then was far higher than it is today. Although sugar production did not enjoy as much of the political spotlight as heavy industry, it was an important sector with easily quantifiable—and thus demonstrable—output. In the period of "real existing socialism" in the 1970s and 1980s, increased production of "white gold" (a notorious cliché coined for sugar in the interwar period and later used excessively in communist media) served as one of the regime's legitimizing tools.

The Hrochův Týnec sugar plant was in a position clearly far ahead of other factories in the sector. At the time of the communist takeover in 1948, there were about 90 sugar refineries in Czechoslovakia. By 1989, only four new ones had been erected: one in the 1950s and three more in the following decade. Of those, one was in Slovakia while the two Polish-built factories were located in Moravia and Bohemia. Not only were they unprecedently large—Hrochův Týnec alone replaced six local factories—but they were highly advanced, the latter two in particular. Specialized Polish companies had recently acquired a wealth of experience building similar sugar plants in China, Spain, Yugoslavia, Egypt, Iraq, Morocco, Turkey, Sweden, and Korea, and had become decidedly competitive in both East and West.[33] Indeed, the next generation of technology did not enter Czech sugar manufacturing until the post-1989 "capitalist era." During the aforementioned Senate debate on the fate of the Hrochův Týnec sugar plant, Deputy Minister Stanislav Kozák argued against the factory's demolition, contending: "[The sugar plant] was equipped with state-of-the-art technology. It was the most modern factory of its kind before privatization."[34] A symbolic "seal of quality" and proof of the refinery's national import was made by an official visit of Communist Party secretary-general (and later Czechoslovak president) Gustáv Husák to Hrochův Týnec in 1972, soon after the plant's opening. Yet, though the tiny town has never since been honored by such a prominent and high-ranking visitor, my narrators did not appear to yearn for it. On the contrary, when recounting the dismal fate of their sugar plant, they entirely failed to mention anything about its "glorious" past under state socialism.

I have spent the last few years collecting dozens of photographs that document the history of the refinery from its construction to its final bulldozing. When I showed them to my narrators, most of whom had never seen any of the images before, the "ice" between stranger and local cracked, and I witnessed a flood of fond memories and powerful emotions that bound the narrators to every aspect of the bygone factory, including—and perhaps most of all—to its older period. This was one of the occasions when the struggle to harmonize one's own personal experience with the demands of professional identity and honor came vividly into focus. On the one hand, the former factory workers remember both the "happy times" they enjoyed during state socialism or, more precisely, in the "pre-Eastern Sugar" period, as well as the dismal end of their factory in the era of global capitalism.[35] On the other hand, their identity as proud sugar makers (often going back generations) compels them to acknowledge and celebrate the wonders of Czech sugar production today, despite the increasing redundancy of its laborers. This paradox was palpable in Milan's remarks about the sugar plant he now works in. He spoke with a sense of both pride and sorrow for the fading future of sugar makers:

"Everything there is automatic, it's all been digitized, we have the best computers. . . . What used to take ten people to do can now be done by one!"

It is illustrative that the only narrator who freely shared with me her outright nostalgic and—as the factory workers together with the aforementioned Mr. Hozák might call it— "irrational" emotions for the factory was a woman who did not work in the sugar plant at all. She recalled missing certain sweet smells, the night lights, and the characteristic, ever-present hum of the plant in action, which created sensory scenes for most of her life.

THE STIGMA OF "NORMALIZATION"

Undoubtedly, it will always be difficult to reconcile one's own traumatized professional experience with positive developments in that profession or industry. However, it is even harder in present-day Czech society for those who lived their happiest years during late socialism. Stanislav Holubec analyzed how Czech media outlets in the 1990s portrayed the final two decades under state socialism, or "normalization" as it is often called. All that was perceived by the communist authorities as successful was questioned by the post-1989 media and depicted as a fraud. Indeed, it was impossible to accept that anything of genuine value could have been produced under the mantle of normalization, let alone with direct assistance from the regime.[36] Although the situation nowadays is more nuanced, especially with regard to partly rehabilitated Czechoslovak normalization-era architecture and design, industry under state socialism is still burdened with fairly negative associations, and it is considered by many to be ugly, wasteful, inefficient, and detrimental to the environment.[37] This last complaint in particular, which was frequently expressed by dissident circles in the 1980s and, unsurprisingly, highlighted by the media in the 1990s, received a new impetus in the twenty-first century.[38] While an earlier generation protested air and soil pollution from pesticides and chemicals, nowadays the greatest outcry is against climate change caused by greenhouse gas emissions. In popular opinion, both are caused by the factories erected during late socialism. And indeed, Czech brown coal power plants belong to some of Europe's largest carbon dioxide producers and are at the center of heated public debates.

Thus, the former factory workers from Hrochův Týnec may feel they could be "compromised" by their role in normalization and the portrayal of that period in the dominant collective memory. Moreover, for both my narrators and the Hungarian workers in Bartha's study, "decent work, skills and diligence used to be central to the construction of their identity."[39] Yet the significant features ascribed to the period of normalization are at odds with the values of the "diligent professional." Therefore, to express overt nostalgia means to admit one has failed to keep up with the modern world and enjoy its prosperity. As Bartha notes, the "winners" of the postcommunist transition exert immense pressure. The blue-collar industrial workers of state socialism were identified "with the failed regime as neoliberal economists increasingly saw them as 'unfit' for training, competition, and integration into the capitalist market economy."[40] But the former employees from Hrochův Týnec do not want to be seen as "losers," "remnants of the past," or "scrap labor." Quite the contrary, it seems they wish to be part of the future-oriented "success story" that dates back to their precommunist local (and family) sugar-making tradition. After all, unlike the Hungarian laborers, most of them never suffered economically.

Solid financial compensation for the jobs they lost, combined with the dominant historical narrative regarding normalization, make it quite difficult for workers from Hrochův Týnec to defend any "alternative" over the current liberal-capitalist regime. Yet their frustration has not vanished. After their heyday of fame and glory, the workers experienced declining public respect and recognition for their profession, ironically despite their industry's growth. This fall from grace was capped with the humiliating destruction of their factory, a symbol of the workers' identity and professional honor. It is unsurprising, therefore, that, similar to their Hungarian colleagues, at least some of the workers believed the culprit to be vaguely defined "foreigners" or "Brussels" (and, to some extent "Prague"). Unlike Hungarian laborers, however, a nostalgic longing for the "golden days" is lacking or perhaps intentionally downplayed.

FORGOTTEN FOREIGNERS

Aside from the fact that systematically marginalizing certain collective memories can deepen the deprivation of the "mnemonic community" in focus, it also discourages more nuanced voices from taking part in public debate regarding normalization-era industrial development in general. In the case of the sugar plant in Hrochův Týnec, lesser-known but important facts could have shed additional light on that theme. For instance, I did not discover a single comment (not to mention analysis) in the media or in any of my interviews that would place the refinery in a broader historical and political context. It should be noted that it was the communists who, in building the new plant, resurrected the local sugar production industry, which had been "in the red" since the 1920s—long before the Communist Party of Czechoslovakia ever took power.[41] Indeed, a critical debate, without oversimplified labels, on the sugar plant's "communist" past would also mean acknowledging the share of Western cutting-edge technology in its arsenal of equipment. As archival sources reveal, the plant was literally stuffed with "capitalist" machinery—from Austria, Italy, Britain, France, and Denmark, to mention a few—or machinery made under Western licenses.[42]

Moreover, silencing the "subversive" memory in the studied case means wiping out the role of the Polish construction workers who built the refinery. When the plant's workers wrote their "obituary" commemorating all the important events in the life of the factory, the Poles were not mentioned. And I have found no mention of the Poles in subsequent media comments on the matter either. If anything, they appear only as a brief footnote ("built by a Polish company"). In my interviews, the Polish builders were acknowledged—usually without further details—only when I asked about them directly.

Yet, they played a much larger role than just "the people who built a plant to repay Polish bilateral trade debt," as Miroslav, another of my narrators, put it. It is well documented in archival materials that building the Hrochův Týnec plant opened a completely new chapter in Czechoslovak–Polish cooperation. The Czechs were particularly impressed with the speed and discipline of the Polish workers. One of the opening pages of the plant's chronicle, which was kept by the staff themselves from the laying of the cornerstone up until the year 2000, reads: "The Poles take full advantage of their working time to maximize their performance, and it is their habitual discipline and obedience to their supervisors which helps them to achieve it. There is no answering back, and they would never dream of not fulfilling an order."[43] A few days after construction was completed and the plant was handed over to Czechoslovak personnel, a Czech journalist described the tremendous speed with which the Poles worked in undisguised astonishment. "It is like something straight out of a fairy tale," he wrote, comparing the two years it took Polish construction workers to build Hrochův Týnec with the five years it took Czechoslovak companies to erect a sugar refinery of equal proportions in the Slovak town of Dunajská Streda.[44] When Hrochův Týnec's twin plant in Hrušovany was finished by the Poles shortly thereafter, the director of the national enterprise to which the new plant belonged declared, in farewell to the Polish crew, that "the speed of construction is without precedent in the sugar production industry" and that the plant had been built in "record-breaking time."[45]

The reason for such "miraculous" performance by the Poles was simple. Polish companies in Czechoslovakia operated on de facto market conditions. Warsaw had negotiated a "market" price for the project, but it had to be completed on time. Had the construction been prolonged, serious financial penalties would have been imposed. Warsaw, therefore, was compelled to prioritize all the supplies for the foreign project over its own domestic construction plans in order to meet the deadline. Because the Polish construction firms (under the umbrella of companies like CEKOP and later Budimex) specialized in building complete turnkey industrial compounds abroad and were already very experienced in both "capitalist" and "socialist" environments, they had no difficulties fulfilling their obligations in Hrochův Týnec.

Since the Hrochův Týnec sugar plant was Czechoslovakia's first experience with a large turnkey industrial project carried out by a foreign company *and* also very successful, the Poles got the green light for similar commissions. They soon became essential builders on the most expensive industrial project in Czechoslovakia—the new energy grid powered nearly exclusively by brown coal power plants. By 1980, Polish firms had already completed about 100 huge industrial turnkey projects in Czechoslovakia such as chemical plants, glass factories, paper mills, cooling plants, ironworks, and so on.[46] To the satisfaction of both countries, Czechoslovakia became the world's largest importer of Polish construction services. It was undoubtedly the most intensive and fruitful long-term partnership between the two states in the modern era, and it all started in the nearly forgotten, and now defunct, factory in Hrochův Týnec.

Furthermore, the Poles in Hrochův Týnec had a profound impact on the life of the sleepy town. At the peak of construction, there were around 2,500 Polish workers living there, more than doubling the local population. As is revealed by the plant's chronicle, many of the workers were housed by local families, even contributing to the household budget.[47] They made friends and some even married local Czechs. And they remained in contact long after construction was complete, coming for maintenance visits, swapping company timeshares, and visiting the families they once boarded with. No wonder that in 1995, several years after the transition, the sugar plant's management asked the same Polish company (Chemadex Warsaw) to construct their new sugar silo. Given the significance of the Polish-built sugar plant for both the local community and the Czechoslovak state, it is quite understandable that the communist government named it "the plant of Polish–Czechoslovak friendship."

The near complete erasure of this international partnership from how the plant is remembered today may also be partly due to the emphasis placed on this relationship under socialism. Similar to how the former factory workers are ashamed to be associated with the previous "backwater" regime, they do not want to subscribe to any of its discredited ideas, including socialist internationalism or—in the vernacular of many Slavic languages—"*druzhba*" (meaning "friendship").[48] On January 25, 1990, in one of his first international speeches, Czechoslovak president Václav Havel addressed the Polish Parliament thus: "'*Druzhba*'—the formal, top-down, orchestrated, false friendship of the Warsaw Pact and COMECON–is departing along with its totalitarian systems."[49]

However, it was primarily the experience of the brutal destruction of the sugar plant that engendered the perception of "foreigners" as predators and annihilators among former plant workers and other like-minded people. Polish builders simply do not fit into such an image. One can only wonder, then, whether highlighting the Poles in public discourse, without whom the factory never would have existed, would challenge the prevailing nationalist perception. Would it then make it more difficult to "vote for Okamura," the frontman of Czech xenophobic populists?

CONCLUSION

With respect to (dis)continuity, a key theme of this volume, my case portrays friction between continuity of the studied industrial sector on one hand and rupture experienced in the "microhistory" of a factory and the professional lives of its workers on the other. However, from the perspective of the workers, the rupture does not accord with conventional historical periodization. Specific temporal benchmarks—underlining the advent of the new factory owner (Eastern Sugar) in 2001 over the regime change in 1989—reveal how the experience of rank-and-file workers might differ from the nation's "elite" temporal perception.

Moreover, the aloofness of those who rule/own "us" (workers) is another element that, in the eyes of the sugar plant workers, clearly connects the periods of "real existing postsocialism" with its socialist predecessor. Whereas the principle "about us, without us" was inherent in the authoritarian nature of the latter, the ignorance and disdain of the former comes from the belief that "money is the answer for everything."

While it is certainly praiseworthy that the sugar plant's final owner—and its bearer of doom—compensated the workers financially, it was surely not enough to alleviate the resentment caused by the inevitable downfall of their professional status or the stigma of being "scrap labor" and the "losers" of capitalism.[50] It seems they yearn neither for the media attention and flashy honors, nor for the presidential visits in black limousines. Rather, they yearn for more responsible and considerate handling of the fundamentals that bind workers to their industrial tradition and anchor them in their professional identity. Likewise, opening up the hegemonic narrative (in the media, public history institutions, by local authorities, etc.) of the late state socialist regime to a critical discussion devoid of ideology might be another remedy. Otherwise, the former factory workers of Hrochův Týnec—and others like them—will never be able to freely express their understandable "feeling of loss and displacement" without being accused of supporting an "evil" regime, and the role of the Polish builders—"the other foreigners"—in the story of the sugar plant will remain forgotten.

NOTES

1. This work was supported by the Czech Science Foundation (grant number 19–12941S). I thank Helena Stoklasová for providing me with a significant part of the archival documents and helping me with field research.
2. To protect their anonymity, the names of all interviewees quoted in this chapter have been changed.
3. Eszter Bartha, "Transforming Labour: From the Workers' State to the Post-Socialist

Re-Organization of Industry and Workplace Communities," *Jahrbuch für Wirtschafts-geschichte* 58, no. 2 (2017): 413–38.

4. Eviatar Zerubavel, *Time Maps: Collective Memory and the Social Shape of the Past* (Chicago: University of Chicago Press, 2003), 4.

5. This was the joint venture of the two well-known companies Générale Sucrière and Tate & Lyle, who sought to acquire sugar factories across postcommunist Europe.

6. Helena Stoklasová, "Konec cukrovaru v Hrochově Týnci očima jeho zaměstnanců," *Listy cukrovarnické a řepařské* 126, nos. 9–10 (September–October 2010): 332–35.

7. For a similar approach, see Elizabeth C. Dunn, *Privatizing Poland: Baby Food, Big Business, and the Remaking of Labor* (Ithaca, NY: Cornell University Press, 2015).

8. Stoklasová, "Konec cukrovaru," 334.

9. At that time, there were eleven sugar plants owned by three big international companies and three small domestic owners in Czechia.

10. See, for instance, the speech by the Czech deputy minister of agriculture Stanislav Kozák: "I am surprised that the main producers of sugar in the EU have not launched the reform [i.e., decreasing the production rates] yet. I mean France and Germany. The same holds true for Denmark, the UK, the Netherlands, and Belgium." *Senát Parlamentu České republiky: Reforma společné zemědělské politiky. Seminář*, March 6, 2007, https://www.senat.cz/xqw/xervlet/pssenat/htmlhled?action=doc&value=39965.

11. *Senát Parlamentu.*

12. Daphne Berdahl, "'(N)Ostalgie' for the present: Memory, longing, and East German things," *Ethnos* 64, no. 2 (1999): 194.

13. The plant had its own volleyball, tennis, table tennis, chess, football, ice hockey, bowling, and indoor football teams.

14. Tomáš Krejčiřík, "Lihovar v Kojetíně koupili Francouzi," *Přerovský deník*, February 14, 2012, https://prerovsky.denik.cz/zpravy_region/lihovar-v-kojetine-koupili-francouzi20120214.html; and Adam Šůra, "Ten barák musí pryč," *Respekt*, July 4, 2008, https://www.respekt.cz/tydenik/2008/28/ten-barak-musi-pryc.

15. Miloš Pekař, "Francouzské sbohem: Adieu, sucrerie Hrochuv Tynec!" *Chrudimský deník*, December 14, 2007, https://chrudimsky.denik.cz/podnikani/cukrovartyne c20071213.html.

16. Bartha, "Transforming Labour," 435.

17. Bartha, "Transforming Labour," 436.

18. *Senát Parlamentu.*

19. Bartha, "Transforming Labour," 433.

20. Bartha, "Transforming Labour," 437.

21. Bartha, "Transforming Labour," 425.

22. "Lidé z cukrovaru teď hledají práci," *Chrudimský deník*, April 10, 2007, https://chru dimsky.denik.cz/podnikani/cukrovar_lidi20070410.html.

23. I did not find any serious complaints about the economic impact of the plant's destruction except that some people had to travel farther to their workplace. Milan, another narrator, grumbled about the fifty-kilometer drive he makes to his new job (in another sugar plant) every day. The refinery in Hrochův Týnec was a mere few hundred meters from his doorstep.

24. For more details on Slovakia and Hungary see Ilona Németh, ed., *Eastern Sugar* (Žilina: Absynt, 2021).

25. Výroba cukrovky a cukru na území České republiky. *Listy cukrovarnické a řepařské*, 2012, http://www.cukr-listy.cz/lc-statistika.html; Michal Bureš, "Kdo vlastní české cukrovary?" *Finance.cz*, October 22, 2021, https://www.finance.cz/498046-vlastnici-cukrovaru/.

26. Svetlana Boym, *The Future of Nostalgia* (New York: Basic Books, 2001); and Bartha, "Transforming Labour," 439.

27. Bartha, "Transforming Labour," 428–29.

28. This was unfounded, however. The Czech Republic had already been a net sugar importer in the 1990s due to cheaper sugar prices abroad, but local Czech production satisfied domestic demand. Nowadays, despite having fewer sugar plants, local production not only exceeds domestic demand by 35 percent, but in 2020, Czech sugar exports were almost double its imports. Bureš, "Kdo vlastní."

29. Karel Duffek, "Zamyšlení: Český cukrovarnický průmysl—historie a současnost," in *Prameny a studie 47: Cukrovarnictví, cukrovary a cukrovarníci* (Praha: Národní zemědělské museum, 2011), 24–31.

30. Jan Hozák, "Proměny cukrovaru v Mnichově Hradišti aneb nekrolog za jednu fabriku," in *Prameny a studie 47 Cukrovarnictví, cukrovary a cukrovarníci* (Praha: Národní zemědělské muzeum, 2011), 177–83.

31. Speaking specifically of industrial ruins, Andreas Huyssen adds, "We are nostalgic for the ruins of modernity because they still seem to hold a promise that has vanished from our own age: the promise of an alternative future." Andreas Huyssen, "Nostalgia for Ruins," *Grey Room*, no. 23 (MIT Press Stable, Spring 2006): 6–21.

32. Benjamin Fragner and Jan Zikmund, eds., *Co jsme si zbořili: Bilance mizející průmyslové éry / deset let* (Praha: ČVUT, 2009), 14.

33. Zygmunt Makomaski, *Polskie cukrownie za granicą* (Toruń: Adam Marszałek, 2007).

34. *Senát Parlamentu.*

35. The former factory workers apparently preferred a different political periodization than the dominant "before and after 1989 (the Velvet Revolution)." This is obvious from the plant's chronicle in which there is virtually no mention of the revolution. One can deduce political transformation only from the list of collective tour destinations (Western states such as France, Switzerland, Austria, the Netherlands, etc., first appeared in 1990 and after) and the company's modified legal status (from 1992). See *Kronika*

nového cukrovaru v Hrochově Týnci–závodu polsko-československého přátelství: Založeno při převzetí cukrovaru dne 17. října 1969, 47. For similarly "subversive" periodizations among blue-collar workers in postcommunist Serbia, see Rory Archer, "'It was better when it was worse': Blue-Collar Narratives of the Recent Past in Belgrade," *Social History* 43, no. 1 (2018): 30–55.

36. Stanislav Holubec, *Ještě nejsme za vodou: Obrazy druhých a historická paměť v období postkomunistické transformace* (Praha: Scriptorium, 2015), 135.

37. Pavel Karous and Sabina Jankovičová, eds., *Aliens and Herons: A Guide to Fine Art in the Public Space in the Era of Normalisation in Czechoslovakia (1968–1989)* (Řevnice: Arbor Vitae, 2013); and Lada Hubatová-Vacková and Cyril Říha, eds., *Husákovo 3+1. Bytová kultura 70. Let* (Praha: UMPRUM, 2018). The first book was preceded by a documentary film on Czech TV, the second by a highly visited exhibition. A similar event was the exhibition *No Demolitions! Forms of Brutalism in Prague*, organized by the National Gallery Prague in 2020.

38. Holubec, *Ještě nejsme za vodou*, 135.

39. Bartha, "Transforming Labour," 430.

40. Bartha, "Transforming Labour," 417.

41. Vlastislav Smutný, "První cukrovar v Hrochově Týnci," *Listy cukrovarnické a řepařské* 126, nos. 9–10 (September–October 2010): 336–39.

42. Cf. *Kronika*, 12. Nevertheless, even highly advanced technology in sugar plants did not prevent Czechoslovakia from significantly lagging behind more efficient Western European sugar production, especially due to a lack of adequate agricultural methods and harvesting machines. Duffek, "Zamyšlení," 25.

43. *Kronika*, 6.

44. Jozef Inovecký, "Príčina nie je v socializme," *Roľnícke noviny*, October 22, 1969, 3.

45. Moravský zemský archiv v Brně, coll. Jihomoravské cukrovary, n.p., inv. No. 1628/257, "Dopis F. Junáka J. Domagalovi," Uherské Hradiště, January 28, 1972.

46. C.f. Edward Marek, *Zatrudnienie pracowników polskich za granicą* (Warsaw: Instytut pracy i spraw socjalnych, 1991), 40.

47. *Kronika*, 10.

48. I analyze socialist internationalism and its meaning in state socialism elsewhere. Ondřej Klípa, "Disenchanting Socialist Internationalism: Polish Workers in Czechoslovakia and East Germany, 1962–91," *Journal of Contemporary History* 57, no. 2 (2021): 1–24.

49. Václav Havel, *Projev prezidenta CSSR Václava Havla v polském Sejmu a Senátu* (Varšava, 25. ledna 1990), https://www.cvce.eu/content/publication/2006/3/27/d639c9ab-79ce-41d9-8767-4a9bd804ec35/publishable_cs.pdf.

50. Bartha, "Transforming Labour," 417.

BIBLIOGRAPHY

Archer, Rory. "'It was better when it was worse': Blue-Collar Narratives of the Recent Past in Belgrade." *Social History* 43, no. 1 (2018): 30–55.

Bartha, Eszter. "Transforming Labour: From the Workers' State to the Post-Socialist Re-Organization of Industry and Workplace Communities." *Jahrbuch für Wirtschaftsgeschichte* 58, no. 2 (2017): 413–38.

Berdahl, Daphne. "'(N)Ostalgie' for the Present: Memory, Longing, and East German Things." *Ethnos* 64, no. 2 (1999), 192–211.

Boym, Svetlana. *The Future of Nostalgia*. New York: Basic Books, 2001.

Bureš, Michal. "Kdo vlastní české cukrovary?" *Finance.cz*. October 22, 2021, https://www.finance.cz/498046-vlastnici-cukrovaru/.

Duffek, Karel. "Zamyšlení: Český cukrovarnický průmysl—historie a současnost." In *Prameny a studie 47: Cukrovarnictví, cukrovary a cukrovarníci*. Praha: Národní zemědělské museum, 2011.

Dunn, Elizabeth C. *Privatizing Poland: Baby Food, Big Business, and the Remaking of Labor*. Ithaca, NY: Cornell University Press, 2015.

Fragner, Benjamin, and Jan Zikmund, eds. *Co jsme si zbořili: Bilance mizející průmyslové éry / deset let*. Praha: ČVUT, 2009.

Havel, Václav. *Projev prezidenta CSSR Václava Havla v polském Sejmu a Senátu*. Varšava, 25. ledna 1990. https://www.cvce.eu/content/publication/2006/3/27/d639c9ab-79ce-41d9-8767-4a9bd804ec35/publishable_cs.pdf

Holubec, Stanislav. *Ještě nejsme za vodou: Obrazy druhých a historická paměť v období postkomunistické transformace*. Praha: Scriptorium, 2015.

Hozák, Jan. "Proměny cukrovaru v Mnichově Hradišti aneb nekrolog za jednu fabriku." In *Prameny a studie 47 Cukrovarnictví, cukrovary a cukrovarníci*. Praha: Národní zemědělské muzeum, 2011.

Hubatová-Vacková, Lada, and Cyril Říha, eds. *Husákovo 3+1. Bytová kultura 70. Let*. Praha: UMPRUM, 2018.

Huyssen, Andreas. "Nostalgia for Ruins." *Grey Room* 23 (Spring 2006): 6–21.

Inovecký, Jozef. "Príčina nie je v socializme." *Roľnícke noviny*, October 22, 1969, 3.

Karous, Pavel, and Sabina Jankovičová, eds. *Aliens and Herons: A Guide to Fine Art in the Public Space in the Era of Normalisation in Czechoslovakia (1968–1989)*. Řevnice: Arbor Vitae, 2013.

Klípa, Ondřej. "Disenchanting Socialist Internationalism: Polish Workers in Czechoslovakia and East Germany, 1962–91." *Journal of Contemporary History* 57, no. 2 (2021): 1–24.

Krejčiřík, Tomáš. "Lihovar v Kojetíně koupili Francouzi." *Přerovský deník*, February 14, 2012, https://prerovsky.denik.cz/zpravy_region/lihovar-v-kojetine-koupili-francouzi20120214.html.

Makomaski, Zygmunt. *Polskie cukrownie za granicą*. Toruń: Adam Marszałek, 2007.

Marek, Edward. *Zatrudnienie pracowników polskich za granicą*. Warsaw: Instytut pracy i spraw socjalnych, 1991.

Németh, Ilona, ed. *Eastern Sugar*. Žilina: Absynt, 2021.

Pekař, Miloš. "Francouzské sbohem: Adieu, sucrerie Hrochuv Tynec!" *Chrudimský deník*, December 14, 2007, https://chrudimsky.denik.cz/podnikani/cukrovartynec20071213.html.

Smutný, Vlastislav. "První cukrovar v Hrochově Týnci." *Listy cukrovarnické a řepařské* 126, nos. 9–10 (September–October 2010): 336–39.

Stoklasová, Helena. "Konec cukrovaru v Hrochově Týnci očima jeho zaměstnanců." *Listy cukrovarnické a řepařské* 126, nos. 9–10 (September–October 2010): 332–35.

Šůra, Adam. "Ten barák musí pryč." *Respekt*, July 4, 2008, https://www.respekt.cz/tydenik/2008/28/ten-barak-musi-pryc.

Zerubavel, Eviatar. *Time Maps: Collective Memory and the Social Shape of the Past*. Chicago: University of Chicago Press, 2003.

3

FROM RISK TO RISKY

Hungary's Second Economy and Its
Transition to the Market after 1989

ANNINA GAGYIOVA

COMPARED TO MOST STATES IN THE EASTERN BLOC, HUNGARY EMBRACED far-reaching economic reforms at the beginning of the 1980s, introducing market elements into the socialist economy. A central component of this process was the legalization of individual economic activity outside the state sector and within the so-called "second economy." As a result, the number of high-quality shops and services expanded, and consumers had access to boutique clothing stores, ice cream parlors, computer software, and taxi services. Legalization of private economic activity enabled the regime to deal with supply problems, which had become endemic to the planned economy, as well as satisfy—at least to some extent—consumer demand. However, the systemic ruptures that occurred in 1989, when Hungary transitioned to a liberal economy, significantly affected the second economy. Private shop owners and service providers, who previously had little or no competition, were now faced with harsh neoliberal measures and the influx of multinationals into the country.

This chapter examines how entrepreneurs, specifically small shop owners, transitioned from the state socialist command economy to a market economy. It focuses on their expectations and realities, highlighting the challenges they experienced under postsocialism. Employing an everyday life approach, I draw on oral history interviews and socialist and Western media, including documentary films.[1] Consumer and (small-scale) business practices serve as rich sites for illuminating the ruptures and continuities between socialism and postsocialism, and for problematizing the notion of 1989 as a caesura. As Márk Áron Éber has claimed, "regime change in Hungary is not a shift between two universally definable distinct systems of 'socialism' and 'capitalism,' but part of a long-term historical process in which social relations in Hungary are embedded in the processes of the modern capitalist world system and are an integral part of it. Neither the characteristics of capitalist modernisation prior to socialism nor the socialist period and post-socialist development can be understood without placing these elements in the context of the wider system."[2] Accordingly, postsocialism cannot be understood without acknowledging the legacies of socialism. By analyzing the tensions between ordinary Hungarians' expectations and realities, I demonstrate that history does not travel in one direction toward some "end of history." Instead, the transformation to democracy and market capitalism was a bumpy and sometimes arduous journey, characterized by starts and stops and advances and retreats.

PRIVATIZING THE PLANNED ECONOMY

Due to hikes in oil prices during the 1970s, Hungary's economy, like many others, faced serious challenges. To avert defaulting on its debt, Hungary joined the International Monetary Fund (IMF) and World Bank in 1982, enabling it to take out loans, though at the cost of implementing austerity measures.[3] In the context of mounting crisis at the beginning of the 1980s, reform economists also pushed for an expansion of the private sector, introducing two distinct employment cultures into socialist society.[4] Dubbed "the second economy," this was the most groundbreaking economic policy since the New Economic Mechanism (NEM) of 1968, when Hungary instituted "goulash communism," blending planned and market economy elements.[5] According to sociologist Endre Sík, the second economy was "perhaps the most important economic policy of the Kádárist experiment," facilitating economic activity beyond the state framework.[6] While presented as an opportunity to improve one's economic situation, the very need for a second economy underscored the command economy's failure to respond to increasingly diverse and sophisticated consumer demands; in essence, the Hungarian state's inability to fulfil its central promise of improving living standards, or as Judit Bodnár puts it, "provisioning responsibility."

The legalization of the informal sector led to an increase in the already sizable number of private entrepreneurs, composed mainly of small-scale traders, artisans, and service providers. These self-employed workers were referred to as *maszek* in everyday parlance, an abbreviation of *magánszektor* (private sector), which comedian Dezső Kellér coined in the 1950s. Based on mostly positive consumer experiences, the term also came to mean something "extraordinary" or "first class." Throughout the 1960s and 1970s, the number of *maszeks* remained stable at around 80,000 to 100,000.[7] While *maszeks* worked primarily in the private sector, the majority of Hungarian workers combined low-income jobs in the first economy—which were tied to social welfare entitlements—with consumer-oriented jobs in the second economy. Hungarians largely welcomed the possibility of working in the private sector as the additional income could offset price hikes and help them maintain—or even enhance—their quality of life.[8] The story of Gizella Szabó, who worked in the Gobelin Cooperative in Budapest for thirty years, illustrates well the economic opportunities available to ordinary Hungarians from 1980 onward. Szabó chose to work an additional twenty hours a week, increasing her overall income to 9,000 forints—a quarter more than the average skilled industrial worker earned at the time. With these extra earnings, Szabó was able to purchase the small holiday cottage she had always dreamed of. Unsurprisingly, she expressed support for the state's integration of market incentives into the planned economy:

> Life is better in Hungary than in other socialist countries. The shops are full, and we can afford to go shopping in them because we have the chance to work hard and earn it. In Hungary, the difference is that nobody is doomed to be poor. That is because everybody who is willing can work hard and make more money. If someone is poor, it's the person's own fault.[9]

While diligence was a feature of socialist economies as well, in this case it is the result of individual initiative, rather than state directive. Thus, it was no longer the paternalistic state that ensured the "socialist good life," but rather individuals who took advantage of the possibilities provided by the state. The connection between individual initiative and personal enrichment reflected the logic of the market economy. Accordingly, participants in Hungary's second economy experienced market-like conditions before 1989 and, therefore, should have been well equipped (with respect to social, cultural, and economic capital) to navigate the challenges of the postsocialist transformation. While most countries in the region had more catching up to do, Poland, where limited privatization was already underway during the late 1970s, shared similar features with Hungary.[10]

As unemployment remained practically nonexistent in Hungary until the 1980s, secure workplaces in the first economy provided a social and economic safety net unknown to market societies. Indeed, engagements in the first and second economy provided great benefits to workers without the risk of losing one's first job and being wholly dependent on market conditions.[11] As Judit Bodnár wrote: "The lukewarm context of this low-risk economy, a moderate entrepreneurialism saturated by the petit bourgeois spirit of security so characteristic of the Kádár era, seemed to hold out a unique opportunity."[12]

While this was true for the entire socialist workforce in Hungary, entrepreneurs solely engaged in the second economy experienced slightly different challenges:

establishing one's own firm was more capital-intensive and required a range of skills to navigate the low-risk market sphere. This comprised an array of different areas, including computer software development, repair services, construction, tourist accommodation, taxi services, restaurants, and boutiques—to name some of the most important ones.[13] Emőke (born in 1945) was representative of this entrepreneurial stratum in socialist Hungary.[14] A divorced mother of two who entered the florist business after completing high school and studies at a technical university, Emőke was drawn to the second economy for the promise of increased earning potential. Thus, in 1978, after years of working for a state florist, she decided to become a *maszek*, opening a flower shop in front of the Cinkotai cemetery in Budapest. At the time, Emőke was the only florist there, but that changed two years later when one state store and two *maszek* stores opened nearby. Here, the market, sheltered by socialist conditions, generated a competitive environment, which Emőke was forced to navigate on her own. While *maszek* flower shops used their access to the wholesale flower market to their advantage, responding swiftly to customers' requests, state shops relied on what the official state buyer purchased for them. As products and services offered by the second economy were usually more expensive, Emőke recalled that it was important "to build personal relationships in order to have more customers. It was not dependent on whether a shop was state or privately owned but on its range of goods, who the seller was and the kind of relationships they had with the customer."[15] Indeed, the higher quality goods and more reliable services offered by private entrepreneurs were even acknowledged in official discourse. *Maszeks*, as the magazine *Műszaki Élet* (*Technical Life*) wrote, complemented the state sector and were "designed to improve the well-being of the population."[16]

Such "well-being" was only achieved by maintaining and then later expanding the second economy, whose flexibility and earning potential came with a price for its participants. For example, Emőke kept her shop open from 8 a.m. to 6 p.m., purchasing flowers from the wholesale market, which opened at 3 a.m. As she emphasized: "I earned more here than in my state job, but I also worked more, Saturdays and Sundays included. I basically had no break, and I did it all by myself—so I did not need to pay anyone a salary."[17] Succeeding in the second economy thus typically required working longer hours per day and additional days per week. Hungarian consumers who relied on and enjoyed the increased variety of goods and services viewed *maszeks* as role models because of their work ethic. The relationship between state-owned and privately owned shops is illustrated by a cartoon published in the satirical magazine *Ludas Matyi* in 1987, in which two shops are depicted on a busy Budapest street. One is named Közért—everyday parlance for grocery store, which translates as "for the public"—and the other is named Magamért, which means "for myself," a play on socialist and market conditions respectively (see Figure 3.1). While the latter keeps its doors

Figure 3.1. "Közért-Magamért, our company's advertising," *Ludas Matyi* 28, July 15, 1987.

open with an overflowing display of fruit and vegetables, the state-owned shop's shutters are already closed.[18] The cartoon is also an allusion to the reality that the economy is increasingly being driven by self-interest, rather than the collective good, thus anticipating the transformation to a market economy.

The economic and political uncertainties of the 1980s, paired with the burgeoning second economy, created possibilities for unprecedented growth among entrepreneurial-minded individuals. Along with independent shops and services, a new type of entrepreneur emerged from this mixed economy: small-scale producers of agrarian and industrial products, which required capital-intensive equipment. In 1983, filmmaker Pál Schiffer explored this topic in the documentary *Földi Paradicsom*. The film's title is a play on words, translating as "Paradise on Earth" and "Field Tomato," and features the story of the Kerekes family in southern Szentes, who are presented as an exemplar of the risk-taking professionals that emerged in late socialist Hungary. The film examines how the Kerekes family built up their tomato-growing business by using greenhouses, which required an investment of over a million forints and the support of seasonal workers.[19] Sociologists Ivan Szelenyi and Robert Manchin have estimated that 2 to 5 percent of all families were entrepreneurial in socialist Hungary, among them dozens of families who pursued investments of between ten and a hundred million forints (the equivalent of $250,000 and $2.5 million). Unfortunately, exact numbers on investments and turnover within the second economy are almost impossible to obtain due to the widespread practice of disguising income from tax authorities. Thus, the typical annual income, as well as the actual wealth, of entrepreneurs is unknown.[20] However, as a result of their conspicuous consumption they were increasingly perceived as rich by the general populace. Moreover, they began to form an alternative society, challenging the socialist elite, which was largely comprised of members of the *nomenklatura*.[21] As one of the reviewers of *Földi Paradicsom* put it in the most prominent daily newspaper, *Népszabadság* (*People's Freedom*): "All public opinion agrees that the *maszek* world under socialism would be paradise on earth itself."[22]

While during the 1980s entrepreneurs' incomes were increasing, up to a third of the population was living at or below the minimum living wage and were continuously concerned with their material circumstances. These people had neither the necessary qualifications nor resources to secure work in the second economy and were thus particularly sensitive to growing socioeconomic differences.[23] Already in 1980, finance minister Lajos Faluvégi anticipated that rising income inequality among laborers might pose a threat to social cohesion. Yet, by prioritizing living standards over the egalitarian promises of socialism, he recognized that the second economy was necessary, though not necessarily sufficient, for the survival of the worker's state. For Faluvégi only a growing private sector, along with a differentiated system of salaries, could promote economic growth.[24]

By the early 1980s, the state had retreated from its self-proclaimed promise of improving the living standards of the population, placing this responsibility instead on participants in the second economy. In 1984, the party issued the new paradigm of "equality of opportunities," placing the onus on individuals to capitalize on the welfare framework provided by the state.[25] This silent, yet tectonic shift in party ideology signified a dramatically different understanding of the relationship between state and citizen. The state went from being the (supposedly) all-mighty entity capable of creating a "new man" in the service of the collective, to a mere shadow of itself. Thus, General Secretary János Kádár encouraged entrepreneurs to earn—and consume—as much as they wanted as long as they continued to work honorably (e.g., not engage in bribing, price gauging, speculation, and tax evasion).[26]

After yearly peaks in the inflation rate, popular mood fell to an all-time low when, in 1988, the government announced the introduction of a value-added tax (VAT), as well as income taxes, being the first country in the bloc to do so.[27] This was rooted in the need to establish a unified tax regime for the second economy and to curtail black marketeering. While the VAT affected the consumption practices of most Hungarians, the tax reform was disproportionately felt by those at lower income brackets as inflation reached 18 percent by 1988.

The tax reform also affected the *maszeks*. As Emőke recalled:

The only disadvantage was that the taxes—well into 1992—were not based on the actual turnover but based on an estimate. It was dependent on what the state official from the tax agency worked out for me. At the time we did not yet operate with a cash register and we were not obliged to give receipts. This is why I had to pay taxes of 79,000 Forint per year, which equaled the price of a middle-class car. It was a huge amount. One had to economize very cleverly.[28]

The high tax rates were based on the assumption—often unfounded—that *maszeks* were underreporting their incomes to avoid taxation and were thus considerably better off than the average worker. Moreover, the tax rate was calculated by an individual tax official, creating possibilities for corruption.

The success and popularity of the second economy influenced people's understanding of the market economy.[29] As Johanna Bockman has demonstrated, the market and competition were constitutive of the socialist experience in Hungary and Yugoslavia, especially during late socialism.[30] According to István Benczes, such experiments had begun with the NEM in 1968, which he identified as a "critical juncture" for the country's economic trajectory.[31] As Hungarians objected to the widening inequalities created by a mixed economy, they quite ironically believed that the full transition to a market economy would facilitate greater equality.[32] As a result, market capitalism came to be understood in positive terms in Hungary, rather than being a potential cause of social inequality.[33] Pointing to the historical exceptionality of the second economy due to its symbiotic relationship with the planned economy, Krisztina Fehérváry observed that:

> Success of second-economy endeavors, combined with the inefficiencies and sometimes outright absurdities wrought by centralized economic control, had convinced much of the population that shifting to a decentralized market economy would usher in Western-style prosperity—maybe not immediately, but fairly quickly.[34]

While many Hungarians believed that "normalcy" in consumption practices (understood as Western levels of consumption) would emerge once Hungary transitioned to a full market economy, *maszeks'* perspectives were distinctly different.[35] Péter, a well-connected economist who worked at the National Bank during socialism, recalled that *maszeks* feared what might happen as the country transitioned to full-fledged capitalism. In particular, they worried about the competition that a free market would bring.[36] Emőke, by contrast, believed that political change would positively affect market developments and improve the situation of entrepreneurs, especially with respect to the taxation system.[37] And, indeed, her business weathered the transition without problems—at least during the earlier years.

FROM *MASZEK* TO ENTREPRENEUR: BUSINESS AFTER 1989

The dissolution of socialist rule in 1989 and the subsequent transition to a full market economy turned *maszeks* into capitalist entrepreneurs (*vállalkozók*).[38] Products of the "small transformation" that had taken place during late socialism, they thus constituted part of an already existing private sector.[39] Given that elements of privatization already existed in Hungary before 1989, the first democratic government under Prime Minister József Antall, as well as the population more generally, anticipated a smooth economic transition.[40] In particular, they were optimistic that full capitalism would facilitate social equality.[41] While privatization produced unemployment, some laborers became entrepreneurs, setting up small shops that did not require much capital or expertise.[42] Although demand for goods and services declined steadily after 1990— and hindered production on the Hungarian market—there were no longer shortages of materials.[43] Meanwhile, those in the private sector enjoyed, at least during the early period of the transition, more possibilities for competition as they could purchase materials on the open market.

The initial blow for those who had been involved in the private sector before 1989 came in 1990, when the first democratic government required the use of cashier machines. Entrepreneurs responded by protesting in the streets and temporarily pausing operations and service activities. As a newspaper article in the region of Fejér noted, entrepreneurs were especially unhappy about the high cost of the cashier machines (around 1,600 German marks) and the bureaucratic burden associated with them. They also felt that being forced to issue receipts for even the smallest sums was absurd. However, legislators showed little compassion for the entrepreneurs, noting, "The cash register is expensive, which is how most shopkeepers defend themselves, while they drive Western cars costing between 8,000 and 10,000 German marks."[44] This statement echoed popular resentments that had built up during late socialism in response to *maszeks'* conspicuous consumption.[45]

As the private sector increased its market share in the 1990s (from 18 percent of the GDP in 1990 to 80 percent in 2000), its participants grew accustomed to what Judit Bodnár calls a "high risk realm of economic activity."[46] In contrast to the mixed economy of late socialism, where employment in the command economy cushioned individuals through a host of entitlements, entrepreneurs in the market economy needed to carefully navigate the challenges of the new system to maintain their livelihoods.[47] The unpredictability of market capitalism (e.g., changes in tax rates, laws, prices, inflation, and cyclical factors) rendered the future uncertain.[48] Entrepreneurs tried to cope with this uncertainty through training and educational initiatives, which they believed would make them more competitive.[49] Emőke thus completed another round of studies in the florist field in 1997, followed by a master's certificate in 2000. Her decision to augment her skills, despite having acquired the necessary qualifications under socialism, reflect her "flexibility" as a capitalist worker. As Elizabeth Dunn has asserted about the Alima-Gerber baby food factory in Poland, the introduction of capitalism demanded that workers become "self-regulating selves," capable of successfully navigating postsocialist work conditions. Such workers "flexibly alter their bundles of skills and manage their careers, but they also become the bearers of risk, thus shifting the burden of risk from the state to the individual."[50] Although Emőke tried to comply with the neoliberal ethos, she did not view work under postsocialism as empowering, but instead found it challenging and risky.

In contrast to pre-1989, the state silently withdrew support from the private sector that it was once so dependent on for securing the socialist good life.[51] The democratic governments of the 1990s introduced tax policies, which from the point of view of entrepreneurs discouraged individual economic activity by making it virtually impossible to compete on the free market.[52] Yet, while small-scale entrepreneurs struggled to survive, multinational corporations thrived, thanks to tax exemptions and public subsidies.[53] This was not unique to Hungary, but rather a general trend throughout the region with the aim of attracting foreign investment and competing in the global economy.

In such a climate, entrepreneurs were forced to disguise their earnings and buck the system if they wanted to stay in business.[54] Anthropologist Maya Nadkarni, in analyzing the dilemmas created by the postsocialist state, referred to "abnormal economic behavior" that "complicated the question of personal responsibility and agency: the idea that being a citizen requires a sense of public citizenship."[55] Hungarian citizens thus developed a dysfunctional relationship with the state, which they felt was not acting in their best interests. In essence, state-directed policies that favored corporations undermined the moral economy that entrepreneurs had been accustomed to under socialism.

Already during the 1990s, then, the fragmented domestic private sector was poorly positioned for competing with the products and services offered by multinational companies that could rely on state-of-the-art technology and expertise.[56] As small and mid-sized companies faced difficulties accumulating capital for further investment, wealth was unevenly distributed.[57] Such a development was in fact supported by many Hungarians, who, according to Jonathan Kelley and Krzysztof Zagorski, "accepted much more inequality than Westerners think proper" at a time "when objective inequalities often grow rapidly and are perceived as such."[58]

THE MULTINATIONALS ARE COMING! THE NEOLIBERAL TURN

When the Federation of Young Democrats (Fidesz–Fiatal Demokraták Szövetsége–Magyar Polgári Szövetség) under Prime Minister Viktor Orbán formed a new government in 1998, Hungary entered what sociologist Besnik Pula called a "heightened globalization period," which lasted an entire decade.[59] The period was characterized by increased inflow of international capital (in the form of foreign direct investment [FDI]) and the assumption of strategic positions in banking, utilities, retail, telecom, and energy by foreign multinationals.[60] These financial flows coincided with further economic and political integration in the form of NATO and European Union (EU) accession (in 1999 and 2004, respectively). The influx of foreign capital also facilitated a process of concentration in the retail sector, changing the landscape of a heretofore largely decentralized retail sector consisting of many small shops.[61] With Tesco, Auchan, and Ikea in immediate proximity, Hungarian consumers had never been so close to Western consumption patterns. And, with growth in real incomes reaching the 1990 level only in 2001, Hungarians had the opportunity to shop at these places.[62]

For Emőke the arrival of the "multis," as they were called in everyday parlance, threatened her earning possibilities. Once small supermarkets and specialized shops had been dominant; now the multis, which included French, Austrian, and British hypermarkets selling food and nonfood items, opened in large retail spaces located in industrial zones at the edges of the city. Emőke recalled the difficulties faced by independent florists as the newly established hypermarkets also sold fresh flowers.[63] Péter also emphasized the increasing difficulties for *maszeks* at the beginning of the 2000s, when the service and construction sectors were thriving.[64] Already in 1999, the economic weekly *Figyelő* (*Watchdog*) raised concerns about competition within the retail sector, noting that local supermarkets were suffering losses, while smaller shops, catering to neighborhood communities, had so far noticed only a marginal decline.[65]

The advent of hypermarkets and shopping malls transformed shopping practices in unprecedented ways, and consumers never felt so close to Western abundance. A wide selection of products was now available within arm's reach and within one place. In addition to reasonable prices, consumers appreciated the freedom of choice and quality of products at hypermarkets.[66] In contrast to the socialist period, the amount of goods in one's shopping cart was limited only by one's personal budget, not by what was on store shelves. By the end of 2000, hypermarkets became such an established part of the Hungarian shopping experience that the widely read daily, *Népszabadság*, announced their triumph over conventional shops: rather than a semiweekly, female-dominated practice, shopping was depicted as a weekend outing for the entire family. Even though a vehicle was necessary for much hypermarket shopping, people found a way to make it possible by relying on friends and family members who owned a car or on microbuses. In addition, elderly people and others on fixed incomes traveled far distances to make use of special offers, stocking up on a month's worth of supplies.

While hypermarkets became ubiquitous throughout the region during the 2000s, they were especially popular in the Czech Republic, where 29 percent of consumers chose them as their primary place for shopping in 2001.[67] Indeed, the vogue for hypermarkets prompted Vít Klusák and Filip Remunda to produce a documentary entitled *Czech Dream* about a hypermarket supposedly slated to open on the outskirts of Prague. By launching a massive advertising campaign beforehand, the film ridiculed Western consumerism with slogans like "don't come" and "don't spend." Despite the discouraging messages, Klusák and Remunda still managed to attract over 3,000 curious customers to the opening event who, once they realized they had been duped, reacted with a range of emotions from laughter and smirking to anger and cursing the government.[68] This social experiment implicitly addressed former Czech dissident Václav Havel's distinction between "living within a lie" and "living in truth," underscoring the similarity between "post-totalitarian" society and postsocialist society.[69] The filmmakers offer a self-critical stand on how marketing and advertising essentially create consumer desire.

The arrival of multinational hypermarkets with competitive prices and extensive marketing signified a crucial turning point for independent traders—more significant than the political transformation—illustrating that the early 2000s, rather than 1989, was a major point of rupture for some. Specialized small businesses, from florists to

shoe shops, especially suffered in this economic climate. An article in *Népszabadság* ti-
tled "Shoes from the Shoe Shop," which referred to a well-known advertisement campaign from the 1950s, claimed that within the Visegrád region, Hungarians were the
least likely to buy from specialized stores.[70] While Hungarians still liked to purchase
home electronics, furniture, and clothing from specialty shops, and shoes and under-
wear either in open markets or the street, all other shops that sold items that were also
available at hypermarkets suffered.[71] This had serious consequences for the city center
of Budapest and other large cities in Hungary, reshaping the geographies of urban reference points in mostly disadvantageous ways. As a result, many central shopping areas suffered neglect, with attractive shops moving into newly constructed shopping
malls and leaving empty retail spaces behind. Shoddy shops were soon established in
their place, negatively affecting the aesthetics of once-upscale areas. Emőke remembers
clearly that it was "with the arrival of the multinationals, when the private sector started
to go downhill."[72] Though of inferior quality, flowers were much cheaper at the hypermarket and she was unable to compete with them: in 2007, after almost thirty years in
business, Emőke closed her florist shop.

CONCLUSION

Compared with other countries in the bloc, Hungary, with its mixed economy, was considered well poised for weathering the changes brought by the full adoption of market
capitalism. As such, Hungarians entered the economic transition with a particular set
of expectations, largely informed by the workings of the second economy. Indeed, they
believed that full marketization and privatization would reduce the socioeconomic differences that had emerged as a result of the second economy. However, reality did not
match expectations, and participants in the second economy, especially *maszeks* with
small-scale businesses and services, experienced massive changes during the transition
to a pluralist system and a market economy.

Foreign direct investment and state support of multinationals rendered many small
and mid-sized businesses superfluous. To be sure, all Hungarian governments of the
1990s, regardless of political affiliation, engaged in an almost frantic search for FDI
while discriminating against domestic entrepreneurs, especially small and mid-sized
companies. Hence, former participants of the second economy, once a source of hope
for a smooth transition to capitalism, came to the rude awakening that the new democratic governments would not support them.

With respect to the central theme of this volume, namely the bidirectionality of
history, during the 1990s and early 2000s, many previously successful *maszeks* looked
back to the pre-1989 period, when they had done relatively well and had anticipated

doing better under market capitalism. While under socialism they found it challenging to deal with an omnipresent and often unpredictable state, dealing with the retreat of the state in the 1990s was even more challenging, as they had no shelter from the storm of neoliberalism and the torrent of multinational firms that set up shop in the country. As this chapter has shown, the real turning point for participants of the domestic private sector was not 1989 but rather the end of the 1990s. As such, focusing on the experiences of ordinary citizens suggests the need for alternative periodizations of postsocialism that capture the local particularities and unintended consequences of change. It is therefore perhaps more productive to emphasize different meanings through the lenses of everyday life. As Martin Müller contends, "socialism is no longer the prime reference point for people in Eastern Europe and the former Soviet Union, but rather one among many, including neoliberalism, nationalism, consumption, Europeanisation and globalisation."[73] Indeed, events after 1989 did not turn out to be the "end of history." Nor did they move along a linear and predictable development toward the imagined utopia of market democracy. This was as true for the transformative years of the 1990s as it is today.

NOTES

1. Alf Lüdtke and William Templer, *The History of Everyday Life: Reconstructing Historical Experiences and Ways of Life* (Princeton, NJ: Princeton University Press, 1995), 6. All interviews were conducted by the author via video call February 15–18, 2021.
   Regarding the use of oral history interviews, I am aware of interviews being a reconstruction by narrators and interviewers alike and other methodological challenges of creating retrospective evidence. However, in the (near) absence of other historical sources on the workings of the second economy on an individual level, I consider oral testimonies a way of recovering a part of everyday history that would otherwise remain unknown.

2. Márk Áron Éber, Ágnes Gagyi, Tamás Gerőcs, Csaba Jelinek, and András Pinkasz, "1989: Szempontok a rendszerváltás globális politikai gazdaságtanához," *Fordulat* 21, no. 1 (2014): 10–63.

3. Richard Phillips, Jeffrey Henderson, László Andor, and David Hulme, "Usurping Social Policy: Neoliberalism and Economic Governance in Hungary," *Journal of Social Policy* 35, no. 4 (2006): 588.

4. Ágnes Gagyi, "'Coloniality of Power' in East Central Europe: External Penetration as Internal Force in Post-Socialist Hungarian Politics," *Journal of World-Systems Research* 22, no. 2 (August 2016): 66.

5. Heino Nyyssönen, "Salami Reconstructed: 'Goulash Communism' and Political Culture

in Hungary," *Cahiers du Monde russe* 47, no. 1–2 (2006): 153–72. The Hungarian socialist leadership introduced the New Economic Mechanism in 1968, which merged market elements with centralized planning. Unprecedented within the Socialist Bloc, it opened up avenues for limited competition within the socialist framework by allowing firms a degree of independence in matters of production and price formation. Furthermore, wage incentives were based on profit instead of quantitative outcomes to encourage the production of goods consumers actually wanted to buy, both domestically and internationally. The economic decentralization process gained new momentum at the beginning of the 1980s when, during a severe debt crisis, the Hungarian state settled on legalizing the private sector, resulting in a dynamically growing second economy.

6. Endre Sík, "From Second Economy to Informal Economy," *Journal of Public Policy* 12, no. 2 (1992): 169.

7. Tibor Valuch, *Magyarország társadalomtörténete a XX: század második felében* (Budapest: Osiris K, 2005), 171.

8. On the issue of rising consumer prices, see Annina Gagyiova, *Vom Gulasch zum Kühlschrank: Privater Konsum zwischen Eigensinn und Herrschaftssicherung* (Wiesbaden: Harrassowitz, 2020), 134–52.

9. Cited from Jackson Diehl, "Moonlighting on the Danube," *Washington Post*, March 24, 1986. See also Krisztina Fehérváry, *Politics in Color and Concrete: Socialist Materialities and the Middle Class in Hungary* (Bloomington: Indiana University Press, 2013), 138.

10. Kálmán Mizsei, "Privatisation in Eastern Europe: A Comparative Study of Poland and Hungary," *Soviet Studies* 44, no. 2 (1992): 283–96.

11. On the notion of risk see Judit Bodnaŕ, *Fin de Millénaire Budapest: Metamorphoses of Urban Life* (Minneapolis: University of Minnesota Press, 2001), 123.

12. Bodnaŕ, *Fin de Millénaire Budapest*, 125.

13. József Böröcz and Alejandro Portes, "The Informal Sector under Capitalism and State Socialism: A Preliminary Comparison," *Social Justice* 15, no. 3/4 (1988): 20.

14. Emőke, interview by author, Budapest, February 18, 2021.

15. Emőke, interview by author, Budapest, February 18, 2021.

16. Mária A. Varga, "Jaj, de maszek," *Műszaki Élet*, September 15, 1983, 6.

17. Emőke, interview by author, Budapest, February 18, 2021.

18. "Közért–Magamért, our company's advertising," *Ludas Matyi* 28, July 15, 1987.

19. *Földi Paradicsom*, directed by Pál Schiffer (Budapest: Malfim-Studio Hunnia, 1984).

20. Ákos Róna-Tas, *The Great Surprise of the Small Transformation: The Demise of Communism and the Rise of the Private Sector in Hungary* (Ann Arbor: University of Michigan Press, 1997), 53; and Tibor Valuch, *Magyar hétköznapok: Fejezetek a mindennapi élet történetéből a második világháborútól az ezredfordulóig* (Budapest: Napvilág Kiadó, 2013), 46.

21. Valuch, "Magyar Hétköznapok," 120; and Annina Gagyiova, "Socialism without Future: Consumption as a Marker of Growing Social Difference in 1980s Hungary," in *Consumption and Advertising in Eastern Europe and Russia in the Twentieth Century*, ed. Magdalena Eriksroed-Burger, Heidi Hein-Kircher, and Julia Malitska (Cham: Springer International, 2023), 181–204.

22. Ervin Gyertyán, "Két Dokumentumfilm. Nyugodjak békében, Földi paradicsom," *Népszabadság* 251, October 25, 1984, 7.

23. Lynne A. Haney, *Inventing the Needy: Gender and the Politics of Welfare in Hungary* (Berkeley: University of California Press, 2002), 166; and "Living Conditions and Public Opinion," February 15, 1984, HU OSA 420-2-3; Records of the Hungarian Institute for Public Opinion Research TK/MKI: Open Publications, OSA at CEU, Budapest. See also Rudolf Andorka, "A valóságos társadalmi egyenlőtlenségek és a közvélemény," *Társadalmi Szemle* 42, no. 10 (1987): 35–47.

24. Pénzűgyminiszter: Elterjesztés a Gazdaságpolitikai Bizottsághoz. A magas jövedelmüek helyzete és a vagyonképződés szabályozásáról, Pénzügyminiszterium 1-0034/1980. TÜK, MOL 288/ff15./393.

25. Bradley Graham, "It's Now OK with the Party to Acquire Riches in Hungary," *Washington Post*, March 29, 1985.

26. Cited in Tibor Valuch, "Everyday Life," in *Social History of Hungary from the Reform Era to the End of the Twentieth Century*, ed. Gábor Gyáni, György Kövér and Tibor Valuch (New York: Social Science Monographs, 2004), 627.

27. Kay Withers, "Hungarians Grow Increasingly Unhappy over State Plans for Personal Tax, VAT," *Toronto Globe and Mail*, October 22, 1987.

28. Emőke, interview by author, Budapest, February 18, 2021.

29. Bodnár, *Fin de Millenaire Budapest*, 490.

30. Johanna Bockman, *Markets in the Name of Socialism: The Left-Wing Origins of Neoliberalism* (Stanford: Stanford University Press, 2011).

31. István Benczes, "From Goulash Communism to Goulash Populism: The Unwanted Legacy of Hungarian Reform Socialism," *Post-Communist Economies* 28, no. 2 (April 2, 2016): 146–66.

32. Chris M. Hann, ed., *Market Economy and Civil Society in Hungary* (London: Frank Cass, 1990).

33. Bodnár, *Fin de Millenaire Budapest*, 490.

34. Fehérváry, *Politics in Color and Concrete*, 154; and Bodnár, *Fin de Millenaire Budapest*, 507–9.

35. Maya Nadkarni, *Remains of Socialism: Memory and the Futures of the Past in Postsocialist Hungary* (Ithaca, NY: Cornell University Press, 2020), 206.

36. Péter, interview by author, Budapest, February 15, 2021.

37. Emőke, interview by author, Budapest, February 18, 2021.

38. Sík, "Second Economy," 160.

39. Róna-Tas, *The Great Surprise*.

40. Nadkarni, *Remains of Socialism*, 21, 423–24.

41. Bodnár, *Fin de Millenaire Budapest*, 508; and Fehérváry, *Color and Concrete*, 154.

42. Béla Tomka, *Austerities and Aspirations: A Comparative History of Growth, Consumption, and Quality of Life in East Central Europe since 1945* (New York: Central European University Press, 2020), 287.

43. Tomka, *Austerities and Aspirations*, 280; Sík, "Second Economy," 160.

44. K. L.-H., J. Cs.-P., "Felemás az első maszek-strájk," in *Fejer Megyei Hírlap*, January 23, 1990, 1/3.

45. See Gagyiova, *Vom Gulasch zum Kühlschrank*, 202–6. During this time, vandalism of expensive cars, presumably owned by well-off participants of the second economy, occurred frequently, underscoring growing social tensions.

46. Tomka, *Austerities and Aspirations*, 280; Bodnár, *Fin de Millenaire Budapest*, 490.

47. Tomka, *Austerities and Aspirations*, 280; Bodnár, *Fin de Millenaire Budapest*, 490.

48. Tomka, *Austerities and Aspirations*, 274.

49. Fehérváry, *Color and Concrete*, 168.

50. Elizabeth C. Dunn, *Privatizing Poland: Baby Food, Big Business, and the Remaking of Labor, Culture and Society after Socialism* (Ithaca, NY: Cornell University Press, 2004), 22.

51. Dunn, *Privatizing Poland*, 172; and Péter, interview by author, Budapest, February 15, 2021.

52. Dunn, *Privatizing Poland*, 172; and Nadkarni, *Remains of Socialism*, 418–20.

53. Jagdish N. Bhagwati, *Free Trade Today* (Princeton, NJ: Princeton University Press, 2003), 59. The race-to-the-bottom thesis has been contested by Nina Bandelj, *From Communists to Foreign Capitalists: The Social Foundations of Foreign Direct Investment in Postsocialist Europe* (Princeton, NJ: Princeton University Press, 2011). For Hungary see Gábor Scheiring, *Retreat of Liberal Democracy: Authoritarian Capitalism and the Accumulative State in Hungary* (Basingstoke: Palgrave Macmillan, 2020).

54. Bodnár, *Fin de Millenaire Budapest*, 512.

55. Nadkarni, *Remains of Socialism*, 419.

56. Jan Drahokoupil, "From National Capitalisms to Foreign-Led Growth: The Moment of Convergence in Central and Eastern Europe," in *Dollarization, Euroization and Financial Instability: Central and Eastern European Countries between Stagnation and Financial Crisis?* ed. Joachim Becker and Rudy Weissenbacher (Weimar b. Marburg: Metropolis Verlag, 2007), 87–108.

57. Scheiring, *Retreat of Liberal Democracy*.

58. Jonathan Kelley and Krzysztof Zagorski, "Economic Change and the Legitimation of Inequality: The Transition from Socialism to the Free Market in Central-East Europe," *Research in Social Stratification and Mobility* 22 (2004): 319–64.

59. Besnik Pula, *Globalization under and after Socialism: The Evolution of Transnational Capital in Central and Eastern Europe, Emerging Frontiers in the Global Economy* (Stanford: Stanford University Press, 2018), 152.

60. Gagyi, "'Coloniality of Power.'".

61. Tomka, *Austerities and Aspirations*, 287.

62. Tomka, *Austerities and Aspirations*, 286.

63. Emőke, interview by author, Budapest, February 18, 2021.

64. Péter, interview by author, Budapest, February 15, 2021.

65. "Súlycsoportmérkőzés," *Figyelő*, May 6, 1999, 35.

66. Ernő Bajai and Annamária Horváth, "A hipermarketek győzelme: Széles választék, eltérő árstratégiák," *Népszabadság*, November 16, 2000, 32.

67. Mária A. Varga, "Igényesek a magyar vásárlók," *Népszabadság*, April 18, 2002, 32. Those figures for Hungary are 15 percent, for Poland 12 percent, and for Slovakia 8 percent.

68. *Czech Dream*, directed by Vít Klusák and Filip Remunda (Česká televize, 2004). I am grateful to Muriel Blaive for drawing my attention to the film.

69. Václav Havel, *The Power of the Powerless*, trans. Paul R. Wilson (London: Vintage, 2018).

70. See Gagyiova, *Vom Gulasch zum Kühlschrank*, 176–94.

71. Mária A. Varga, "Cipőt a Cipőboltból. Szaküzletek és hipermarketek versenye," *Népszabadság*, April 18, 2002, 32.

72. Emőke, interview by author, Budapest, February 18, 2021.

73. Martin Müller, "Goodbye, Postsocialism!" *Europe-Asia Studies* 71, no. 4 (April 21, 2019): 533–50.

BIBLIOGRAPHY

Andorka, Rudolf. "A valóságos társadalmi egyenlőtlenségek és a közvélemény." *Társadalmi Szemle* 42, no. 10 (1987): 35–47.

Bajai, Ernő, and Annamária Horváth. "A hipermarketek győzelme: Széles választék, eltérő árstratégiák." *Népszabadság*, November 16, 2000, 32.

Bandelj, Nina. *From Communists to Foreign Capitalists: The Social Foundations of Foreign Direct Investment in Postsocialist Europe.* Princeton, NJ: Princeton University Press, 2011.

Benczes, István. "From Goulash Communism to Goulash Populism: The Unwanted Legacy of Hungarian Reform Socialism." *Post-Communist Economies* 28, no. 2 (April 2, 2016): 146–66.

Bhagwati, Jagdish N. *Free Trade Today.* Princeton, NJ: Princeton University Press, 2003.

Bockman, Johanna. *Markets in the Name of Socialism: The Left-Wing Origins of Neoliberalism.* Stanford: Stanford University Press, 2011.

Bodnár, Judit. *Fin de Millénaire Budapest: Metamorphoses of Urban Life.* Minneapolis: University of Minnesota Press, 2001, 123.

Böröcz, József, and Alejandro Portes. "The Informal Sector under Capitalism and State Socialism: A Preliminary Comparison." *Social Justice* 15, nos. 3–4 (1988): 20.

Czech Dream, directed by Vít Klusák and Filip Remunda (Česká televize, 2004).

Diehl, Jackson. "Moonlighting on the Danube." *Washington Post*, March 24, 1986.

Drahokoupil, Jan. "From National Capitalisms to Foreign-Led Growth: The Moment of Convergence in Central and Eastern Europe." In *Dollarization, Euroization and Financial Instability. Central and Eastern European Countries between Stagnation and Financial Crisis?,* edited by Joachim Becker and Rudy Weissenbacher, 87–108. Weimar b. Marburg: Metropolis Verlag, 2007.

Dunn, Elizabeth C. *Privatizing Poland: Baby Food, Big Business, and the Remaking of Labor, Culture and Society after Socialism.* Ithaca, NY: Cornell University Press, 2004.

Éber, Márk Áron, Ágnes Gagyi, Tamás Gerőcs, Csaba Jelinek, and András Pinkasz. "1989: Szempontok a rendszerváltás globális politikai gazdaságtanához." *Fordulat* 21, no. 1 (2014): 10–63.

Fehérváry, Krisztina. *Politics in Color and Concrete: Socialist Materialities and the Middle Class in Hungary.* Bloomington: Indiana University Press, 2013.

Földi Paradicsom. Pál Schiffer, director. Budapest: Malfim-Studio Hunnia, 1984.

Gagyi, Ágnes. "'Coloniality of Power' in East Central Europe: External Penetration as Internal Force in Post-Socialist Hungarian Politics." *Journal of World-Systems Research* 22, no. 2 (August 2016): 349–72.

Gagyiova, Annina. "Socialism without Future: Consumption as a Marker of Growing Social Difference in 1980s Hungary." In *Consumption and Advertising in Eastern Europe and Russia in the Twentieth Century,* edited by Magdalena Eriksroed-Burger, et al., 181–204. Cham: Springer International, 2023.

Gagyiova, Annina. *Vom Gulasch zum Kühlschrank: Privater Konsum zwischen Eigensinn und Herrschaftssicherung.* Wiesbaden: Harrassowitz, 2020.

Graham, Bradley. "It's Now OK with the Party to Acquire Riches in Hungary." *Washington Post*, March 29, 1985.

Gyertyán, Ervin. "Két Dokumentumfilm. Nyugodjak békében, Földi paradicsom." *Népszabadság* 251 (October 1984): 7.

Haney, Lynne A. *Inventing the Needy: Gender and the Politics of Welfare in Hungary.* Berkeley: University of California Press, 2002.

Hann, Chris M., ed. *Market Economy and Civil Society in Hungary.* London: Frank Cass, 1990.

Havel, Václav. *The Power of the Powerless,* trans. Paul R. Wilson. London: Vintage, 2018.

K. L.-H., J. Cs.-P. "Felemás az első maszek-strájk." In *Fejer Megyei Hírlap*, January 23, 1990, 1/3.

Kelley, Jonathan, and Krzysztof Zagorski, "Economic Change and the Legitimation of Inequality: The Transition from Socialism to the Free Market in Central-East Europe." *Research in Social Stratification and Mobility* 22 (2004): 319–64.

"Közért–Magamért, our company's advertising." *Ludas Matyi* 28, July 15, 1987.

"Living Conditions and Public Opinion." 15 February 1984, HU OSA 420-2-3, Records of the Hungarian Institute for Public Opinion Research TK/MKI: Open Publications, OSA at CEU, Budapest.

Lüdtke, Alf, and William Templer. *The History of Everyday Life: Reconstructing Historical Experiences and Ways of Life.* Princeton, NJ: Princeton University Press, 1995.

Mizsei, Kálmán. "Privatisation in Eastern Europe: A Comparative Study of Poland and Hungary." *Soviet Studies* 44, no. 2 (1992): 283–96.

Müller, Martin. "Goodbye, Postsocialism!" *Europe-Asia Studies* 71, no. 4 (April 21, 2019): 533–50.

Nadkarni, Maya. *Remains of Socialism: Memory and the Futures of the Past in Postsocialist Hungary.* Ithaca, NY: Cornell University Press, 2020.

Nyyssönen, Heino. "Salami Reconstructed: 'Goulash Communism' and Political Culture in Hungary." *Cahiers du Monde russe* 47, nos. 1–2 (2006): 153–72.

Phillips, Richard, Jeffrey Henderson, Laszlo Andor, and David Hulme. "Usurping Social Policy: Neoliberalism and Economic Governance in Hungary." *Journal of Social Policy* 35, no. 4 (2006): 588.

Pula, Besnik. *Globalization under and after Socialism: The Evolution of Transnational Capital in Central and Eastern Europe, Emerging Frontiers in the Global Economy.* Stanford: Stanford University Press, 2018.

Róna-Tas, Ákos. *The Great Surprise of the Small Transformation: The Demise of Communism and the Rise of the Private Sector in Hungary.* Ann Arbor: University of Michigan Press, 1997.

Scheiring, Gábor. *Retreat of Liberal Democracy: Authoritarian Capitalism and the Accumulative State in Hungary.* Basingstoke: Palgrave Macmillan, 2020.

Sík, Endre. "From Second Economy to Informal Economy." *Journal of Public Policy* 12, no. 2 (1992): 169.

"Súlycsoportmérkőzés." *Figyelő,* May 6, 1999, 35.

Tomka, Béla. *Austerities and Aspirations: A Comparative History of Growth, Consumption, and Quality of Life in East Central Europe since 1945.* New York: Central European University Press, 2020.

Valuch, Tibor. "Everyday Life." In *Social History of Hungary from the Reform Era to the End of the Twentieth Century,* edited by Gábor Gyáni, György Kövér and Tibor Valuch. New York: Social Science Monographs, 2004.

Valuch, Tibor. *Magyar hétköznapok: Fejezetek a mindennapi élet történetéből a második világháborútól az ezredfordulóig.* Budapest: Napvilág Kiadó, 2013.

Valuch, Tibor. *Magyarország társadalomtörténete a XX: század második felében.* Budapest: Osiris K, 2005.

Varga, Mária A. "Cipőt a Cipőboltból. Szaküzletek és hipermarketek versenye." *Népszabadság,* April 18, 2002, 32.

Varga, Mária A. "Igényesek a magyar vásárlók." *Népszabadság,* April 18, 2002, 32.

Varga, Mária A. "Jaj, de maszek." *Műszaki Élet,* September 15, 1983, 6.

Withers, Kay. "Hungarians Grow Increasingly Unhappy over State Plans for Personal Tax, VAT." *Toronto Globe and Mail,* October 22, 1987.

PART II

THE POLITICS OF EXCLUSION

4

"THERE'S A LOT OF TALK ABOUT TOLERANCE, BUT THAT'S JUST WORDS"

Being Gay in Postsocialist Poland[1]

AGNIESZKA KOŚCIAŃSKA

UNTIL RELATIVELY RECENTLY, THE PREVAILING NARRATIVE OF SEXUAL emancipation in Central and Eastern Europe operated on the assumption that this freedom was a belated outcome of progressive liberalization in the West. According to this narrative, it was not until the 1990s that LGBTQ communities in formerly socialist countries started to fight for their rights and self-organize.[2] However, recent research demonstrates that the situation across the region varied from country to country. While some countries, such as the USSR and Romania, openly persecuted homosexuals, queer communities enjoyed relative freedom in others, such as Poland and Czechoslovakia.[3] Despite these findings, the old narrative persists today in countries like Poland, where activists and the wider public alike tend to view the threat to LGBTQ rights posed by right-wing governments as symptomatic of an opposition between a developed European West and a backward East that has to catch up. For instance, a media presentation of an LGBTQ rights survey in thirty-four countries stressed that Poland is "closer to Russia than to Sweden," and graffiti in a residential neighborhood in Warsaw consisted of a rainbow flag (a symbol of LGBTQ rights) and the following comment: "this is Poland, not Russia."[4] Against this backdrop, this chapter examines the multiple, often conflicting, narratives of gay and lesbian lives during the early transformation from socialism to postsocialism, analyzing them with respect to the socialist past and the contemporary period, which is notable for the attacks on "LGBT ideology" that became central to Polish politics during the 2020 presidential campaign.[5] I am particularly interested in ideas and practices concerning, on the one hand, gay and lesbian rights, self-organizing, and visibility, and, on the other, Catholic attempts to regulate sexuality. As much as these different perspectives and practices are connected to the concept of Europe and the West–East divide, they are also strongly rooted in the everyday experiences and longings of Polish gays and lesbians. Consequently, I argue that we should not only view LGBTQ rights in Poland as following a Western path, but also as being rooted within the local political context and actual lives of LGBTQ people in Poland.

The narratives of early postsocialism that inform my analysis derive from two sources: letters sent to Wiesław Sokoluk, a sex educator, therapist, and the main author of the most progressive Polish school sex education handbook, *Przysposobienie do życia w rodzinie* (*Preparation for Family Life*), as well as a columnist for *Na Przełaj* (*Cross-Country*), a popular youth weekly published between 1957 and 1991, and interviews with older gay and lesbian individuals conducted in the late 2010s about their experiences of socialism and postsocialism.[6] While personal narratives offer an "incomplete and fragmentary" picture of the past, by putting them together and contextualizing them I hope to offer a fuller history of (homo)sexuality in Poland.[7]

HOMOSEXUALITY IN SOCIALIST AND POSTSOCIALIST POLAND

The Polish state's approach to homosexuality differed significantly from the majority of Western and Eastern European states.[8] From the late eighteenth century until the end of World War I, Poland was partitioned between the German, Russian, and Austrian Empires, each of which enforced its own system for the penalization of same-sex acts. Yet, the first modern criminal code, which was implemented in 1932 in independent Poland, did not penalize homosexuality. At the time, only homosexual prostitution was criminalized, though only until 1969, when it was decriminalized. Additionally, the 1932 penal code adopted a broad definition of sexual violence, stipulating that same-sex rapes could be subject to punishment, legislation that was retained in subsequent penal codes (1969, 1997).[9] Moreover, Polish legal codes never enforced discriminatory regulations, namely different ages of consent for homosexual and heterosexual intercourse; since 1932, the age of consent in Poland has been fifteen.[10]

Yet such progressive legislation did not reflect the general situation of homosexuals during state socialism, as they were often discriminated against in everyday life. Some of the interviewees reported violence in the proximity of cruising spaces in major Polish cities and hostile comments from kin or coworkers. As in other Eastern Bloc countries, official self-organizing was impossible and queers were under constant police and/

or secret service surveillance, which intensified in the mid-1980s.[11] Although there was no official socialist policy on homosexuality, such practices were motivated by the perception that homosexuality was antisocialist and antifamily. As in the USSR, homosexuality was often associated with criminality and prison culture.[12] As Lukasz Szulc writes about official discourses in Poland, "until 1980, male homosexuality was usually represented in stereotypical ways, either in a criminal context, especially in newspapers, or in a comical context, especially in films."[13] The only spaces where homosexual life was presented in a less pathologizing or comical fashion was in sex education publications, niche fine art, poetry, and literature.[14] Finally, in the 1980s, the first semi-legal gay and lesbian magazines appeared.[15] Nonetheless, queer life was mostly centered around cruising spaces and private parties.[16] Today, older gay people often emphasize that because homosexuality was shrouded in silence during socialism, its invisibility provided a sense of freedom, allowing them to live their lives unseen.[17] At the same time, many homosexuals, especially women, recall that queer communities were so deeply hidden that they rarely knew about one another's existence. As one of my interviewees, Maria, recalled: "In the 1970s I was so lonely, I didn't know any other lesbians, except for one, who also only knew me."[18] Everything changed for Maria in the early 1990s, when Lambda, the first Polish LGBTQ organization, was established.

Overall, Poland's history of homosexuality in the twentieth century is highly complex and multilayered. It encompasses progressive laws and local rights activism, combined with an invisibility that often allowed for open and free expression of non-normative sexuality. At the same time, little was done to prevent violence and everyday discrimination against homosexuals.

GAY AND LESBIAN EXPERIENCES OF THE EARLY 1990S

While working as a sex columnist for the scouting magazine *Cross-Country*, Sokoluk received many letters from nonheteronormative youth who were encouraged by his liberal approach to homosexuality (in which he referred to homosexual relationships as "analogues" to heterosexual ones). This approach was also presented in his sex education handbook that appeared in Polish schools in 1987, as the editors never tired of reminding their readers. In fact, the sex column was advertised as being written by the author of "the controversial sex education handbook." In their letters, readers expressed concern about sexual orientation, same-sex desire, and love. For instance, Anka wrote in 1991:

I think that in the past I didn't realize that I'm a lesbian. Now that I know it and feel it with every part of my body and soul—I'm scared. Why me? . . . I'm afraid now that

I've come to know this feeling, even though I am able to stand in front of the mirror and say, "I'm a lesbian." I try to be proud of it, but really, I can't come to believe it.... This year I'll be finishing high school.... It's getting harder for me to believe that I'll meet the woman of my dreams. I've lost hope. I know, however, what she should be like. I dream of a blonde, of medium height, and with blue eyes. Her long hair falls on her shoulders. But external appearance isn't so important. What's important is her tenderness and unique personality.[19]

This letter, like many others sent by lesbians to the Polish press, was not selected for publication.[20] However, letters expressing similar narratives were published in the *Cross-Country* sex column in the 1990s. Importantly, whereas homosexual men's voices could be found in the socialist press, women's homosexuality had largely been invisible under socialism.[21] Consequently, the letters written by lesbians that were later published by *Cross-Country* constitute some of the very first instances in post–World War II Poland of lesbians being granted a voice in mainstream publishing. The women expressed their desires and sexual anxieties by placing them within the context of their hopes, fears, and uncertainties about the new political and economic order.[22] For instance, Monika, like Anka, starts her letter to *Cross-Country* by talking about her experience of being a lesbian and describing her family situation:

From when I was very young, life taught me to hate men. My father is an alcoholic, who often times puts up his fist as an argument in relation to the rest of the family. My only brother, who is already grown, has up until now only showed indifference towards me.... I always differed from my friends who were girls. I could spend entire days surrounded by a band of boys, with whom I would fight, play ball and ride motorcycles. Yet romantic evenings lost their charm in the company of boys. In those moments I needed a friend who was a girl.[23]

Anka only sees one solution to her problem: self-organizing, which she mentions in the second part of her letter. Monika hopes to use the sex column in *Cross-Country* to network:

Everything would be O.K. if I could find myself in my own world. I've never talked with anybody about this, the reason of course, being fear. Of what? For fear of being banished, of losing my friends and for fear of my family's reaction. I've had enough of mute conversation, illusions, and loneliness. Ladies, if you feel that destiny has hurt you by making you love women, write! Together, let's try to find our common "I."[24]

Another letter published in the same issue, signed "Beata-lesbian," deals with the trauma caused by lack of equal rights:

> If I have enough courage to end my life, in a few months, I will pass away. I think it will happen under the influence of the moment, the mood and my hopelessness.... I wanted to live, just to live normally, and not have to constantly wander between emptiness and loneliness, between grief and hate. Only in scanning with our eyes over the writing on gravestones do we realize that life does not give us equal chances, chances for love, joy, hate, breaking up, and for forgiveness.[25]

The letters reveal the difficulties these young women experienced, which are not necessarily related to their sexuality. However, the fact that they are lesbians makes it more difficult for them to deal with such problems. Not only do they have to contend with discrimination based on sexual orientation, but they have no access to the kind of networks where they could find friends to join them in their fight for equal rights. Therefore, homosexual self-organizing appears to be a crucial element of these narratives.

In reply to these letters and another from Milena (who asked the magazine not to publish a testimony in which she confessed: "I know that I belong to a group of people who should be destroyed, and it is very difficult for me to live with this thought among normal people"), Sokoluk emphasizes that the problems homosexuals face are caused by societal "contempt" that "derives from the fear of otherness, and all that which doesn't fit into the mold." To underscore his point, he mentions another group who have similarly experienced stigma: "Geniuses are also subject to this type of treatment." He stresses: "No one has the right to condemn another person to social death just because they are different."[26] Sokoluk tries to convince Milena that things will get better and points to the importance of self-organizing and rights claims. "But there are people, Milena, who fight so that their difference is accepted and so that they are given a normal place among humans. They organize in support groups and publish texts about their problems. And besides that, they just live!"[27]

This response resonated with young nonheteronormative people. After publishing this article, Sokoluk and the editors of *Cross-Country* received more letters in which similar issues were raised, namely the social stigmatization of homosexuals and self-organizing as a means of overcoming these problems. For instance, a group of men established an informal gay club in northern Poland and wanted Sokoluk to publicize it among *Cross-Country*'s readers. Meanwhile, a letter from a seventeen-year-old called Zuza tells the story of her love for Magda, which contains the following confession: "I would like to write to Lambda, maybe one of the girls would write back to me, and maybe together it would be easier to get over the challenges that life throws at us."[28]

However, Sokoluk's replies to Milena, Beata, and Monika's letters contain one further element—a strong focus on Catholicism:

What can be said about a religion that discriminates, and even curses people who love differently, due to no fault of their own? Can an idea, even the most beautiful in its suppositions, justify the inhuman treatment of another person? Some churches, for example the Dutch church, have answered NO to both questions and strive toward the acceptance of homosexual relationships. This, of course, does not concern the sacrament of marriage, but acceptance in front of God and the religious community. Such a deeply humanistic approach of the Church toward homosexuals could contribute to changing the perspective of many people. Well, for now this is only wishful thinking.[29]

Sokoluk received many questions about religion from young people.[30] For instance, a boy who signed off as "Faggot" wrote, "you are literally 'my last resort.' There is no one else that I can turn to for help. I'm a homosexual. An older friend made me get into it. It all started when I was seven years old. Now I am nineteen."[31] He "read a lot of books about this" and understands "that homosexuality is not wrong," but he identifies as "a Christian-Catholic" and the Bible clearly condemns homosexuality.[32] "Faggot" continued:

I talked about all of this with a certain priest during confession and he said that I should try to spend as much time as possible in the company of girls. I have tons of female friends, but I don't feel as good with them as I do in the company of boys. I got propositions from men a few times, but I declined. You could say that I should get married and that this state will pass once I start a normal sex life. I don't want to hurt any girls just because this "state" might not pass.[33]

"Faggot" ends his letter with a cry for help: "You see for yourself that there is no other way left except for suicide. Unless you know another solution. If yes, please let me know as soon as possible, because I can't go on like this any longer. Hoping for your rapid assistance."[34]

These narratives show two dimensions of gay and lesbian life during the postsocialist transformation. On the one hand, there are opportunities for self-organizing, which, ideally, will help gay people overcome the problems they are facing; on the other hand, there are new restrictions caused by the political situation in Poland and the increased influence of the Catholic Church—especially its conservative wing—which had previously been unable (at least officially) to wield any influence over socialist policy on sexuality.[35]

Interviews conducted in the late 2010s confirm the two-dimensional character of the transition from socialism to democracy. For instance, one of my interviewees, a gay man in his seventies, told me that it was in the early 1990s that he finally started to call himself "gay" and divorced his wife, although he had been having sex with men for many years before that. He decided to get involved in LGBTQ activism: "I wanted to do something for our milieu, I joined Lambda . . . I got a Lambda ID on a pink paper." The previously quoted Maria also confessed that the first Lambda meetings in the early 1990s changed her life: "It was back then that legal associations were established and we were able to meet each other openly and get to know a lot of people. And you wouldn't have to be friends with everybody, but we could finally say, 'look, there are so many of us. This one I like, and this one I don't like.' There were so many of us, it was so empowering." Maria became an activist for the Lambda-Krakow women's section and established a PO box to which gay women in Poland could send letters. Based on these contacts, she organized lesbian meetings in Krakow throughout the 1990s. These initiatives enabled lesbian women to meet other lesbian women. But there is a second dimension to these memories that resembled what can be seen in letters sent to *Cross-Country*. Maria remembered that, already in the early 1990s, some women expressed concern about the influence of the Catholic Church. For instance, the women's section of Lambda received letters from Ewa, who was worried that too much lesbian visibility might create problems: "She was saying what lesbians should and should not do and she was talking about the Church all the time, [saying] that we should reckon with the Church."

The concerns Ewa expressed in letters in the early 1990s are echoed in recent interviews with older gay people. Although some, like Maria, complained about the invisibility of gay people under socialism for limiting opportunities to make contact with others, many praised this very same invisibility as a source of freedom. In many interviews, older gay individuals stressed that thanks to the lack of recognition granted to gay identity, cruising spaces and queer parties went unseen by the larger public. It was only the emergence of gay self-organizing and visibility that eventually triggered expressions of homophobia, including by the Catholic Church. Therefore, some homosexuals believe that their invisibility under socialism gave them greater freedom than their visibility under postsocialism.

This was what Ewa was worried about and what "Faggot" had already experienced. Thus, in accounts of the early postsocialist period, the 1990s are presented ambivalently: as a time of new political and social opportunities for gay people, but also a time when the growing power of the Catholic Church led to increased restrictions.[36] As Zuza wrote in her letter to Sokoluk: "There's a lot of talk of tolerance, but that's just words."[37]

THE SOCIALIST ROOTS OF
POSTSOCIALIST EXPERIENCES

Accounts of the 1990s, both in *Cross-Country* and in my interviews, reflect approaches toward sexuality in Poland during socialism. The prevailing elements in these accounts, including the need for social contacts and some kind of collective action or self-organizing in order to overcome discrimination, can be found in such publications as the semi-legal *Etap*, "the first Polish gay (but not lesbian) magazine," which was published by Andrzej Selerowicz, a Polish activist living in Vienna.[38] On the front page of a 1986 issue, there is a story about the International Lesbian and Gay Association, its involvement in the fight for homosexual rights, and its opposition to religious organizations that discriminated against sexual minorities. Page two is devoted to a section called "I am looking for a friend" and combines personal romantic or sexual goals with political ones. For instance, a twenty-year-old male reader from Wrocław wrote: "If you were born under a sign compatible with Gemini, write to me. . . . I would like to create a genuine and stable relationship. . . . I am not interested in one-night stands with irresponsible people. I will reply to every nice letter." Another young man said he lived in a small town in the Lublin area and it was hard for him to find a partner. *Etap* also included personal ads that were political. For instance, a nineteen-year-old gay activist from Yugoslavia wanted to meet Poles with similar political interests and asked for letters in English.[39]

References to rights and activism in Poland in the 1980s are not surprising. Contrary to widespread assumptions about the lack of self-organizing and rights claims under socialism, the socialist period—and late socialism in particular—was actually a time of (often illegal) self-organizing that provided a space for intensive deliberations around human rights and homosexuality.[40] Thus, discussions about sexual rights cannot be separated from the broader historical and social context of late socialism. The late 1970s and 1980s were permeated by discourses on rights, both in the official state-censored press and in anticommunist circles, where they were particularly prominent. The development of gender and sexual rights can thus be linked to these discussions.[41] During this period, the anticommunist opposition organized around workers' rights, freedom of association, and, more broadly, human rights.[42]

Increased focus on human rights discourse by groups and individuals within the Eastern Bloc—what scholars have termed the "Helsinki effect"—was a direct outcome of the 1975 Helsinki Accords, whereby states vowed to protect the human rights of their citizens and to which Poland, along with most states in Europe, were signatories.[43] Although the democratic opposition in Poland did not discuss sexual rights and they were not mentioned in the Helsinki Accords, the general human rights climate contributed to the proliferation of discussions about them. This was evident not only in letters sent by Polish homosexuals in the early 1980s to the Homosexual Initiative Vienna, a gay and lesbian organization that monitored the situation of homosexuals in communist Eastern Europe in cooperation with the International Lesbian and Gay Association (ILGA), but also in the illegal gay press.[44] Moreover, these claims were expressed publicly in the Polish press and supported by activists such as Mikołaj Kozakiewicz, a sexologist, sex educator, and the president of the Polish Planned Parenthood Association.[45] In the wake of the appearance of HIV/AIDS, a general understanding among sexologists and sex educators emerged that homosexual men needed the right to associate in order to combat the epidemic.[46] Even earlier, in the late 1970s, sexologists had supported the idea of homosexual rights and included extensive quotes in their writings encouraging homosexual men to demand the right to organize and live in accordance with their desires.[47] In socialist Poland, sexology developed as a multidisciplinary and patient-oriented field, and sexology books sold millions of copies. Thus, sexological voices were widely heard and often reflected popular sentiments as sexologists quoted extensively from their patients' and readers' letters. In this sense, homosexuals' insistence—visible in letters from the early 1990s—on their right to associate freely and live in accordance with their sexual orientation were rooted in the local (Polish) prodemocratic activities of the 1970s and 1980s (an orientation toward rights claims) *and* in the transnational trends that supported them (e.g., the Helsinki Accords, transnational LGBTQ activism).

At the same time, discussions about homosexual rights were gendered, focused first and foremost on men. *Etap* dealt exclusively with male homosexuality, while other semi-legal magazines from the 1980s had "women's sections," though they generally devoted little attention to lesbians. The same was true for sex experts. When writing about homosexual rights, sexologists usually referred exclusively to men.[48] That did not mean they ignored women altogether, as women's (heterosexual and traditional-gender-role-based) sexual pleasure and self-realization were widely discussed in highly popular sexological publications that provided women (including those who were gay) with the discursive tools to demand the right to sexual pleasure, albeit within marriage.[49]

Yet there is another side to this picture of rights in the 1980s, namely the influence of religious rights. Freedom of religion was actually mentioned in the Helsinki Accords, and Poles' right to be Catholic was stressed by Polish opposition leaders such as Lech Wałęsa. Meanwhile, the Catholic Church supported the opposition and its claims for rights, and offered space for prodemocratic deliberations.[50] However, there was no space within this model for sexual rights, as the church aimed to restrict these.[51]

WHAT HAPPENED NEXT

Maria, quoted earlier in this chapter, was very critical of the letters sent by Ewa, who had warned the gay community about the Catholic Church's intentions and had cautioned lesbians not to be too visible. Tensions in the 1990s thus centered around visibility and the church, and religiously fueled homophobia was crucial to the development of LGBTQ identities and activism over the next decades. Although homosexuals' appeals for self-organization and greater visibility did in fact increase the visibility of LGBTQ communities, these communities were nonetheless riven by internal conflicts over whether or not visibility was a good strategy. In her analysis of gay activism in the early 2000s, Monika Baer analyzes the continuous struggle between two forms of activism: the first oriented toward the "full emancipation" enjoyed by the heterosexual majority ("the fight for all civil rights") and the second toward "limited emancipation" (freedom in the private sphere).[52] Gradually, these tensions became linked to a concept of Europe in which "full emancipation" meant "European sexual citizenship," which "envisions LGBT persons as model (neo)liberal citizens, 'perfectly integrated into the social and political fabric of each member state.'"[53] This model was contested by right-wing nationalists and conservative Catholics in Poland, both of whom became more vocal on this issue in the 1990s and especially in the twenty-first century. As a result, LGBTQ Catholics like "Faggot," who wrote to Sokoluk, were not able to resolve their sexual–religious dilemmas in private.[54] Their identities and internal struggles became part of the political struggle over Polish national identity as LGBTQ rights began to be perceived as a foreign import, imposed on Poland from the outside. Accordingly, local genealogies, namely the needs and longings that gay people had expressed in the 1990s and which were embedded in the prodemocratic rights activism of late socialism, were not only overlooked but also undermined and actively silenced.[55] In this way, gay rights were, ironically, restricted by the same prodemocratic processes that contributed to their development. Although Law and Justice, the party of governance between 2015 and 2023, is now seen as an authoritarian and antidemocratic force due to its eagerness to restrict LGBTQ rights, its roots can be traced to the anticommunist democratic opposition.

The relationship between the Catholic Church and the anticommunist opposition, established in the 1980s and strengthened in the 1990s, provided the church with political influence in postsocialist Poland, including influence in the area of gender and sexuality policies.[56] Initially, the church focused on restricting reproductive rights, achieving success in 1993 when abortion, which had been accessible on demand under socialism, was nearly banned in Poland.[57] The church expanded its focus in subsequent years to incorporate other sexuality-related issues. In the mid-1990s, the church successfully challenged the inclusion, in the Polish constitution, of a provision designed to protect citizens from discrimination based on sexual orientation.[58] In the following decade the church, following global conservative trends and supported by the nationalistic right wing, became increasingly active in anti-LGBTQ initiatives. As a result, after socialism gay life was not only enriched by opportunities brought by rights appeals and activism, but also embedded in restrictions imposed by religion. This process was already evident in the early 1990s, as per the letters from "Faggot" and Ewa, and even earlier in the late-communist magazine *Etap*, which had devoted a great deal of space to religious attempts to restrict sexuality. The period between the late 1980s and early 2000s was when the Catholic Church, contrary to earlier hopes of the gay community, took a clear stance against LGBTQ rights.[59]

CONCLUDING REMARKS

Today's LGBTQ life and self-organizing are greatly affected by the strong politicization of non-normative sexuality. Poland is witnessing a significant backlash against LGBTQ rights: in 2019, 68 percent of Polish LGBTQ persons surveyed by the Fundamental Rights Agency reported that intolerance and prejudice against them had increased over the previous five years. Meanwhile, in 2019 and 2020, around 100 municipalities, mostly those supporting the ruling Law and Justice Party, declared themselves "LGBT-free zones."[60] This anti-LGBTQ atmosphere was exploited and reinforced during the 2020 presidential campaign when the sitting president, Andrzej Duda, was supported by Catholic officials and right-wing activists. When seeking reelection, Duda built his campaign around slogans such as "Defend Children from LGBT Ideology," causing an unprecedented outbreak of hate speech and violence against LGBTQ communities.[61] Within this framework, LGBTQ rights are presented as "foreign" impositions from Europe, particularly the European Union.[62] Influenced by this perspective, many Poles, rather than associating LGBTQ persons with concrete individuals who have feelings and longings, tend to see them as an embodiment of foreign "ideology."

To what extent are these ongoing developments rooted in the past? This politicization cannot be fully understood within the context of the East–West divide, Poland's postsocialist orientation toward Europe, or activists' attempts to implement "European sexual citizenship." LGBTQ self-organizing, rights, and visibility are very much rooted in Poland's socialist past, and a clear need for these was already being expressed by the early 1990s. The story of LGBTQ rights in Poland constitutes a history of ruptures and continuities as well as progress and backlash. It shows that the invisibility of LGBTQ communities under socialism was, for some, a space of freedom and emancipation, while for others it was a climate of suffering and loneliness. It also demonstrates that visibility and self-organizing contribute to freedom and emancipation, although some LGBTQ persons see such practices for clarity as counterproductive. The history of LGBTQ rights in Poland has much in common with other human rights issues. It highlights how the development of human rights under socialism not only contributed to the extension of sexual rights, but also of religious rights, since it strengthened the position of the Catholic Church, which, in the long run, caused disruptions in the development of sexual rights.

Positioning self-organizing, rights, and visibility—be it the voices of teenagers writing to *Cross-Country* or gays and lesbians engaged in early postsocialist activism—within the long history of socialism and real existing postsocialism allows us to understand their genealogies. It is also a political act because once these long histories are unveiled, it becomes apparent how they grew out of experiences of silence and loneliness, as well as prodemocratic struggles. And these struggles were certainly not imported from Europe. In fact, they arose from the needs of Polish homosexual boys and girls who grew up in the era of the proliferation of human rights in Poland.

NOTES

1. This chapter was made possible thanks to a Leverhulme Visiting Professorship at the Oxford School of Global and Area Studies (OSGA), an OSGA research allowance, and an Arts and Humanities Research Council grant ("Gender Wars: East and South," Grant Ref: AH/W009315/1). I am grateful to Philip Palmer for polishing my English writing.

2. See, for instance, Robert Kulpa and Joanna Mizielińska, eds., *De-Centring Western Sexualities: Central and Eastern European Perspectives* (Aldershot: Ashgate Press, 2011); and Dennis Altman, *Global Sex* (Chicago: University of Chicago Press, 2001). Other examples of this approach are discussed in Jill Owczarzak, "Introduction: Postcolonial Studies and Postsocialism in Eastern Europe," *Focaal: European Journal of Anthropology*, no. 53 (2009): 3–19; Dagmar Herzog, "Syncopated Sex: Transforming European Sexual Cultures," *American Historical Review* 114, no. 5 (2009): 1287–308; and Monika Baer, "Europeanization on the Move: LGBT/Q Activist Projects in Contemporary Poland," *Intersections: EEJSP* 6, no. 3 (2020): 53–73.

3. See, for instance, Łukasz Szulc, *Transnational Homosexuals in Communist Poland: Cross-border Flows in Gay and Lesbian Magazines* (London: Palgrave Macmillan, 2018); Tomasz Basiuk, "Od niepisanej umowy milczenia do protopolityczności: dyskursywny I sieciowy charakter społeczności osób homoseksualnych w 'długich latach 70,'" *Interalia. Pismo Poświęcone Studiom Queer*, no. 14 (2019): 28–50, https://interalia.queerstudies.pl/issues/14_2019/basiuk.pdf; Agnieszka Kościańska, "'Treatment is possible and effective'? Polish Sexologists and Queers in Correspondence in Late State Socialism," in *Queers in State Socialism: Cruising 1970s Poland*, ed. Tomasz Basiuk and Jędrzej Burszta (London: Routledge, 2021), 74–85; Anita Kurimay and Judith Takács,

"Emergence of the Hungarian Homosexual Movement in Late Refrigerator Socialism," *Sexualities* 20, nos. 5–6 (2017): 585–603; Kateřina Lišková, *Sexual Liberation, Socialist Style: Communist Czechoslovakia and the Science of Desire, 1945–1989* (Cambridge: Cambridge University Press, 2018); Agata Fiedotow, "Początki ruchu gejowskiego w Polsce," in *Kłopoty z seksem w PRL: Rodzenie nie całkiem po ludzku, aborcja, choroby, odmienności*, ed. Marcin Kula (Warsaw: Wydawnictwa Uniwersytetu Warszawskiego, 2012), 241–358; Jędrzej Burszta, "'Do czego się było przyznawać, jak nie istniał homoseksualizm?' Różowy język w narracjach pamięci o męskiej homoseksualności w PRL," *Interalia: Pismo Poświęcone Studiom Queer*, no. 14 (2019): 2–27, https://interalia .queerstudies.pl/issues/14_2019/burszta.pdf; Maria Dębińska, "Diagnosing Transsexualism, Diagnosing Society: The Blurred Genres of Polish Sexology in the 1970s and 1980s," in *Queers in State Socialism,* 59–73. For the history of homophobia in the context of the West/East divide, see Hadley Z. Renkin, "Homophobia and Queer Belonging in Hungary," *Focaal—European Journal of Anthropology*, no. 53 (2009): 20–37; and Hadley Renkin, "Biopolitical Mythologies: Róheim, Freud, (Homo)phobia, and the Sexual Science of Eastern European Otherness," *Sexualities* 19, nos. 1–2 (2016): 168–89.

4. Danuta Pawłowska, Stanisław Dudzik, and Dominik Uhlig, "Sondaż w 34 krajach: w ocenie homoseksualizmu bliżej nam do Rosji niż do Szwecji," *Gazeta Wyborcza*, online edition, June 24, 2020, https://biqdata.wyborcza.pl/biqdata/7,159116,260689 49,sondaz-w-34-krajach-polacy-w-ocenie-homoseksualizmu-sa.html; Author's fieldnotes, October 2020.

5. Shaun Walker, "Polish President Issues Campaign Pledge to Fight 'LGBT Ideology,'" *Guardian*, June 12, 2020, https://www.theguardian.com/world/2020/jun/12 /polish-president-issues-campaign-pledge-to-fight-lgbt-ideology.

6. Wiesław Sokoluk, Dagmara Andziak and Maria Trawińska, *Przysposobienie do życia w rodzinie* (Warszawa: Wydawnictwa Szkolne i Pedagogiczne, 1987). For more on Sokoluk and his work in the field of sex education and youth counseling, see Agnieszka Kościańska, *To See a Moose: The History of Polish Sex Education*, trans. Philip Palmer (New York: Berghahn Books, 2021); Agnieszka Kościańska, "'The Handbook of Masturbation and Defloration': Tracing Sources of Recent Neo-Conservatism in Poland," in *Gender, Intimacy and Mobility in the Era of Hardening Borders: Gender, Reproduction, Regulation*, ed. Frances Pine and Haldis Haukanes (Manchester: Manchester University Press, 2021), 218–34. The interviews I quote in this chapter were conducted within the CRUSEV project ("Cruising the 1970s: Un-Earthing Pre-HIV/AIDS Queer Sexual Cultures"), supported by the third HERA Joint Research Programme "Uses of the Past," which is co-funded by AHRC, BMBF via DLR-PT, MINECO, NCN, and the European Commission through Horizon 2020.

7. Agata Ignaciuk and Natalia Jarska, "Unawareness and Expertise: Acquiring Knowledge about Sexuality in Postwar Poland," *Journal of the History of Sexuality* 32, no. 2

(2023): 124.

8. For Hungary see Kurimay and Takács, "Emergence of the Hungarian Homosexual Movement"; for Czechoslovakia see Lišková, *Sexual Liberation, Socialist Style*; for East Germany, see Jose McLellan, *Love in the Time of Communism: Intimacy and Sexuality in the GDR* (Cambridge: Cambridge University Press, 2011), 114–18; for Russia, see Dan Healey, *Homosexual Desire in Revolutionary Russia* (Chicago: University of Chicago Press, 2001); for Britain, see Matt Cook, "From Gay Reform to Gaydar, 1967–2006," in *A Gay History of Britain*, ed. Matt Cook (Santa Barbara: Greenwood World Publishing, 2007), 179–214.

9. Agnieszka Kościańska, *Gender, Pleasure, and Violence: The Construction of Expert Knowledge of Sexuality in Poland*, trans. Marta Rozmysłowicz (Bloomington: Indiana University Press, 2021), 147–50.

10. Monika Płatek, "Sytuacja osób homoseksualnych w prawie karnym," in *Orientacja seksualna i tożsamość płciowa*, ed. Roman Wieruszewski and Mirosław Wyrzykowski (Warsaw: Instytut Wydawniczy EuroPrawo, 2009), 49–81; Kościańska, *To See a Moose*.

11. Szulc, *Transnational Homosexuals in Communist Poland*, 106–10; and Kościańska, *To See a Moose*, 188–94. Fiedotow, "Początki ruchu gejowskiego w Polsce," 271–72; Karolina Morawska, "'No authorities are interested in us, no one interferes in our affairs': Policing Homosexual Men in the People's Republic of Poland," in *Queers in State Socialism*; and McLellan, *Love in the Time of Communism*.

12. Healey, *Homosexual Desire*; Dan Healey, *Russian Homophobia from Stalin to Sochi* (New York: Bloomsbury, 2018); and Szulc, *Transnational Homosexuals in Communist Poland*, 98.

13. Szulc, *Transnational Homosexuals in Communist Poland*, 99.

14. Kościańska, *To See a Moose*; Kościańska, "'Treatment is possible and effective'"; Karol Radziszewski and Wojciech Szymański, "Queer (In)visibility in the Art of the People's Republic of Poland," and Błażej Warkocki, "'Transgression has become a fact': A Gothic Genealogy of Queerness in the People's Republic of Poland" both in *Queers in State Socialism*.

15. Szulc, *Transnational Homosexuals in Communist Poland*.

16. Remigiusz Ryziński, *Foucault w Warszawie* (Warsaw: Dowody na Istnienie, 2017); Jędrzej Burszta, "Three Circles of Male Homosexual Life in State-Socialist Poland," in *Queers in State Socialism*, 11–22.

17. See Jędrzej Burszta, "'Do czego się było przyznawać.'"

18. The authors of unpublished letters and interview partners are all pseudonyms.

19. Wiesław Sokoluk's private archive translated by Marta Rozmyłowicz.

20. For the process of selecting letters under state socialism, see Kościańska, "'Treatment is possible and effective'?"; Agnieszka Kościańska, "'Le droit de cité': Sexologie, homosexualité et le discours des droits de l'homme en Pologne socialiste dans les années 70,"

Sextant 37 (2020): 135–48.

21. Kościańska, "'Treatment is possible and effective'?"; Magdalena Staroszczyk, "'No one talked about it': The paradoxes of lesbian identity in pre-1989 Poland," in *Queers in State Socialism*, 105–15.

22. Frances Pine, "Migration as Hope: Space, Time and Imagining the Future," *Current Anthropology* 55 (2014): 95–104.

23. Quoted in Wiesław Sokoluk, "Dla tych, którzy kochają inaczej," *Na przełaj* 9, December 1990, 8, translated by Marta Rozmysłowicz.

24. Ibid., partly quoted in Kościańska, *To See a Moose*, 198.

25. Quoted in Sokoluk, "Dla tych, którzy kochają inaczej."

26. Sokoluk, "Dla tych, którzy kochają inaczej."

27. Sokoluk, "Dla tych, którzy kochają inaczej."

28. Wiesław Sokoluk's private archive.

29. Sokoluk, "Dla tych, którzy kochają inaczej."

30. Kościańska, *To See a Moose*.

31. Wiesław Sokoluk's private archive.

32. Wiesław Sokoluk's private archive.

33. Wiesław Sokoluk's private archive.

34. Wiesław Sokoluk's private archive.

35. See, for instance, Dorota Hall, "Shifting Silences: Changes in Living Religion and Homosexuality in Poland between 1970s and 2010s," *Intersections: EEJSP* 6, no. 3 (2020): 33–52; Kościańska, "'Le droit de cité."

36. See also Joanna Mishtal, *The Politics of Morality: The Church, the State, and Reproductive Rights in Postsocialist Poland* (Athens: Ohio University Press, 2015).

37. Wiesław Sokoluk, private archive.

38. Szulc, *Transnational Homosexuals in Communist Poland*, 138.

39. *Etap*, 1986, no. 4, 1–2.

40. For socialist self-organizing, see Szulc, *Transnational Homosexuals in Communist Poland*.

41. Kościańska, "'Le droit de cité.'" For the development of feminism in the context of the anticommunist opposition, see Magdalena Grabowska, "Bringing the Second World In: Conservative Revolution(s), Socialist Legacies, and Transnational Silences in the Trajectories of Polish Feminism," *Signs* 37, no. 2 (2012): 385–411.

42. Gunter Dehnert, "The Polish Opposition, the Crisis of the Gierek Era, and the Helsinki Process," in *The Breakthrough: Human Rights in the 1970s*, ed. Jan Eckel and Samuel Moyn (Philadelphia: University of Pennsylvania Press, 2014), 166–85.

43. According to the dominant Cold War narrative, human rights are linked to the capitalist and democratic West. Current research, however, points to the connection between human rights and socialism. See, for instance, Ned Richardson-Little, "Dictatorship

and Dissent: Human Rights in East Germany in the 1970s" and Celia Donert, "Whose Utopia? Gender, Ideology, and Human Rights at the 1975 World Congress of Women in East Berlin," both in *The Breakthrough*; Kristen Ghodsee, *Second World, Second Sex: Socialist Women's Activism and Global Solidarity during the Cold War* (Durham, NC: Duke University Press, 2019); and Dehnert, "The Polish Opposition."

44. Basiuk, "Od niepisanej umowy milczenia do protopolityczności."

45. Szulc, *Transnational Homosexuals in Communist Poland*, 106.

46. Jill Owczarzak, "Defining HIV Risk and Determining Responsibility in Postsocialist Poland," *Medical Anthropology Quarterly* 23, no. 4 (2009): 417–35.

47. Kościańska, "'Treatment is possible and effective.'"

48. Kościańska, "'Treatment is possible and effective.'"

49. Kościańska, *Gender, Pleasure, and Violence*.

50. Jose Casanova, *Public Religions in the Modern World* (Chicago: University of Chicago Press, 1994).

51. Kościańska, "The Handbook of Masturbation and Defloration."

52. Monika Baer, "'Let them hear us!' The politics of same-sex transgression in contemporary Poland," in *Transgressive Sex: Subversion and Control in Erotic Encounters*, ed. Hastings Donnan and Fiona Magowan (New York: Berghahn Books, 2009), 130–50.

53. Baer, "Europeanization on the Move," 54; and Baer quoting Francesca Romana Ammaturo, *European Sexual Citizenship: Human Rights, Bodies and Identities* (London: Palgrave Macmillan, 2017).

54. Dorota Hall, "Shifting Silences," 45.

55. Agnieszka Graff and Elzbieta Korolczuk, "'Worse than communism and Nazism put together': War on Gender in Poland," in *Anti-Gender Campaigns in Europe: Mobilizing against Equality*, ed. Roman Kuhar and David Patenotte (London: Rowman & Littlefield, 2017), 175–94.

56. Mishtal, *The Politics of Morality*.

57. Mishtal, *The Politics of Morality*.

58. Solongo Wandan, "Making New Rights: Constitutional Agenda-Setting in the Transitions of Poland (1989–1997) and South Africa (1990–1994)" (PhD diss., New School for Social Research, 2014).

59. Dorota Hall, "Shifting Silences," 37.

60. Anna Mazurczak and Mikołaj Winiewski, *Długa droga do równości osób LGBTQI: Komentarz badawczy i prawny do wyników badania Agencji Praw Podstawowych Unii Europejskiej dotyczących Polski* (Warszawa: Komisja Europejska Przedstawicielstwo w Polsce, 2020), https://poland.representation.ec.europa.eu/system/files/2021-12/ptpa_raport_2020_dluga_droga_do_rownosci.pdf; Lucy Ash, "Inside Poland's 'LGBT-free zones," BBC, September 21, 2020, https://www.bbc.co.uk/news/stories-54191344.

61. Walker, "Polish President Issues Campaign Pledge to Fight 'LGBT Ideology,'"; Krzysztof

Sobczak, "Amnesty: Ataki na osoby LGBT to w Polsce codzienność," https://www
.prawo.pl/prawo/ataki-na-osoby-lgbt-wg-amnesty-international-to-w-polsce,501026
.html.

62. Agnieszka Graff and Elzbieta Korolczuk, "'Worse than communism and Nazism put
together.'"

BIBLIOGRAPHY

Altman, Dennis. *Global Sex*. Chicago: University of Chicago Press, 2001.

Ash, Lucy. "Inside Poland's 'LGBT-Free Zones.'" BBC, September 21, 2020. https://www.bbc
.co.uk/news/stories-54191344.

Baer, Monika. "Europeanization on the Move: LGBT/Q Activist Projects in Contemporary Poland." *Intersections. EEJSP* 6, no. 3 (2020): 53–73.

Baer, Monika. "'Let them hear us!' The Politics of Same-Sex Transgression in Contemporary Poland." In *Transgressive Sex: Subversion and Control in Erotic Encounters,* edited by Hastings
Donnan and Fiona Magowan, 130–50. New York: Berghahn Books, 2009.

Basiuk, Tomasz. "Od niepisanej umowy milczenia do protopolityczności: dyskursywny i sieciowy charakter społeczności osób homoseksualnych w 'długich latach 70.'" *Interalia.
Pismo Poświęcone Studiom Queer*, no. 14 (2019): 28–50. https://interalia.queerstudies.pl
/issues/14_2019/basiuk.pdf.

Burszta, Jędrzej. "'Do czego się było przyznawać, jak nie istniał homoseksualizm?' Różowy język w
narracjach pamięci o męskiej homoseksualności w PRL." *Interalia: Pismo Poświęcone Studiom
Queer*, no. 14 (2019): 2–27. https://interalia.queerstudies.pl/issues/14_2019/burszta.pdf.

Burszta, Jędrzej. "Three Circles of Male Homosexual Life in State-Socialist Poland." In *Queers
in State Socialism: Cruising 1970s Poland*, edited by Tomasz Basiuk and Jędrzej Burszta, 11–
22. London: Routledge, 2021.

Casanova, Jose. *Public Religions in the Modern World*. Chicago: University of Chicago Press, 1994.

Cook, Matt. "From Gay Reform to Gaydar, 1967–2006." In *A Gay History of Britain*, edited by
Matt Cook, 179–214. Santa Barbara: Greenwood World Publishing, 2007.

Dębińska, Maria. "Diagnosing Transsexualism, Diagnosing Society: The Blurred Genres of Polish Sexology in the 1970s and 1980s." In *Queers in State Socialism: Cruising 1970s Poland*, edited by Tomasz Basiuk and Jędrzej Burszta, 59–73. London: Routledge, 2021.

Dehnert, Gunter. "The Polish Opposition, the Crisis of the Gierek Era, and the Helsinki Process." In *The Breakthrough: Human Rights in the 1970s*, edited by Jan Eckel and Samuel Moyn,
166–85. Philadelphia: University of Pennsylvania Press, 2014.

Donert, Celia. "Whose Utopia? Gender, Ideology, and Human Rights at the 1975 World Congress of Women in East Berlin." In *The Breakthrough: Human Rights in the 1970s*, edited by
Jan Eckel and Samuel Moyn, 68–87. Philadelphia: University of Pennsylvania Press, 2014.

Fiedotow, Agata. "Początki ruchu gejowskiego w Polsce." In *Kłopoty z seksem w PRL. Rodzenie nie całkiem po ludzku, aborcja, choroby, odmienności*, edited by Marcin Kula, 241–358. Warsaw: Wydawnictwa Uniwersytetu Warszawskiego, 2012.

Ghodsee, Kristen. *Second World, Second Sex: Socialist Women's Activism and Global Solidarity during the Cold War*. Durham: Duke University Press, 2019.

Grabowska, Magdalena. "Bringing the Second World In: Conservative Revolution(s), Socialist Legacies, and Transnational Silences in the Trajectories of Polish Feminism." *Signs* 37, no. 2 (2012): 385–411.

Graff, Agnieszka, and Elzbieta Korolczuk. "'Worse than communism and Nazism put together': War on Gender in Poland." In *Anti-Gender Campaigns in Europe: Mobilizing against Equality*, edited by Roman Kuhar and David Patenotte, 175–94. London: Rowman & Littlefield, 2017.

Hall, Dorota. "Shifting Silences: Changes in Living Religion and Homosexuality in Poland between 1970s and 2010s." *Intersections: EEJSP* 6, no. 3 (2020): 37, 33–52.

Healey, Dan. *Homosexual Desire in Revolutionary Russia*. Chicago: University of Chicago Press, 2001.

Healey, Dan. *Russian Homophobia from Stalin to Sochi*. New York: Bloomsbury, 2018.

Herzog, Dagmar. "Syncopated Sex: Transforming European Sexual Cultures." *American Historical Review* 114, no. 5 (2009): 1287–308.

Ignaciuk, Agata, and Natalia Jarska. "Unawareness and Expertise: Acquiring Knowledge about Sexuality in Postwar Poland." *Journal of the History of Sexuality* 32, no. 2 (2023): 121–43.

Kościańska, Agnieszka. "'Le droit de cité': Sexologie, homosexualité et le discours des droits de l'homme en Pologne socialiste dans les années 70." *Sextant* 37 (2020): 135–48.

Kościańska, Agnieszka. *Gender, Pleasure, and Violence: The Construction of Expert Knowledge of Sexuality in Poland*. Translated by Marta Rozmysłowicz. Bloomington: Indiana University Press, 2021.

Kościańska, Agnieszka. "'The Handbook of Masturbation and Defloration': Tracing Sources of Recent Neo-Conservatism in Poland." In *Gender, Intimacy and Mobility in the Era of Hardening Borders: Gender, Reproduction, Regulation*, edited by Frances Pine and Haldis Haukanes, 218–34. Manchester: Manchester University Press, 2021.

Kościańska, Agnieszka. *To See a Moose: The History of Polish Sex Education*. Translated by Philip Palmer. New York: Berghahn Books, 2021.

Kościańska, Agnieszka. "'Treatment is possible and effective'? Polish Sexologists and Queers in Correspondence in Late State Socialism." In *Queers in State Socialism: Cruising 1970s Poland*, edited by Tomasz Basiuk and Jędrzej Burszta, 74–85. London: Routledge, 2021.

Kulpa, Robert, and Joanna Mizielińska, eds. *De-Centring Western Sexualities: Central and Eastern European Perspectives*. Aldershot: Ashgate Press, 2011.

Kurimay, Anita, and Judith Takács. "Emergence of the Hungarian Homosexual Movement in Late Refrigerator Socialism." *Sexualities* 20, no. 5–6 (2017): 585–603.

Lišková, Kateřina. *Sexual Liberation, Socialist Style: Communist Czechoslovakia and the Science of Desire, 1945–1989*. Cambridge: Cambridge University Press, 2018.

Mazurczak, Anna, and Mikołaj Winiewski. *Długa droga do równości osób LGBTQI: Komentarz badawczy i prawny do wyników badania Agencji Praw Podstawowych Unii Europejskiej dotyczących Polski*. Warszawa: Komisja Europejska Przedstawicielstwo w Polsce, 2020. https://poland.representation.ec.europa.eu/system/files/2021-12/ptpa_raport_2020_dluga_droga_do_rownosci.pdf

McLellan, Jose. *Love in the Time of Communism: Intimacy and Sexuality in the GDR*. Cambridge: Cambridge University Press, 2011.

Mishtal, Joanna. *The Politics of Morality: The Church, the State, and Reproductive Rights in Postsocialist Poland*. Athens: Ohio University Press, 2015.

Morawska, Karolina. "'No authorities are interested in us, no one interferes in our affairs': Policing Homosexual Men in the People's Republic of Poland." In *Queers in State Socialism: Cruising 1970s Poland*, edited by Tomasz Basiuk and Jędrzej Burszta, 88–101. London: Routledge, 2021.

Owczarzak, Jill. "Defining HIV Risk and Determining Responsibility in Postsocialist Poland." *Medical Anthropology Quarterly* 23, no. 4 (2009): 417–35.

Owczarzak, Jill. "Introduction: Postcolonial Studies and Postsocialism in Eastern Europe." *Focaal*, no. 53 (2009): 3–19.

Pawłowska, Danuta, Stanisław Dudzik, and Dominik Uhlig. "Sondaż w 34 krajach: w ocenie homoseksualizmu bliżej nam do Rosji niż do Szwecji." *Gazeta Wyborcza*, June 24, 2020. https://biqdata.wyborcza.pl/biqdata/7,159116,26068949,sondaz-w-34-krajach-polacy-w-ocenie-homoseksualizmu-sa.html.

Pine, Frances. "Migration as Hope: Space, Time and Imagining the Future." *Current Anthropology* 55 (2014): 95–104.

Płatek, Monika. "Sytuacja osób homoseksualnych w prawie karnym." In *Orientacja seksualna i tożsamość płciowa*, edited by Roman Wieruszewski and Mirosław Wyrzykowski, 49–81. Warsaw: Instytut Wydawniczy EuroPrawo, 2009.

Radziszewski, Karol, and Wojciech Szymański. "Queer (In)visibility in the Art of the People's Republic of Poland." In *Queers in State Socialism: Cruising 1970s Poland*, edited by Tomasz Basiuk and Jędrzej Burszta, 116–44. London: Routledge, 2021.

Renkin, Hadley Z. "Biopolitical Mythologies: Róheim, Freud, (Homo)phobia, and the Sexual Science of Eastern European Otherness." *Sexualities* 19, no. 1–2 (2016): 168–89.

Renkin, Hadley Z. "Homophobia and Queer Belonging in Hungary." *Focaal—European Journal of Anthropology*, no. 53 (2009): 20–37.

Richardson-Little, Ned. "Dictatorship and Dissent: Human Rights in East Germany in the 1970s." In *The Breakthrough: Human Rights in the 1970s*, edited by Jan Eckel and Samuel Moyn, 49–87. Philadelphia: University of Pennsylvania Press, 2014.

Ryziński, Remigiusz. *Foucault w Warszawie*. Warsaw: Dowody na Istnienie, 2017.

Sobczak, Krzysztof. "Amnesty: Ataki na osoby LGBT to w Polsce codzienność." *prawo.pl*, June 14, 2020. https://www.prawo.pl/prawo/ataki-na-osoby-lgbt-wg-amnesty-international-to-w-polsce,501026.html.

Sokoluk, Wiesław. "Dla tych, którzy kochają inaczej." *Na przełaj*, December 9, 1990.

Staroszczyk, Magdalena. "'No one talked about it': The Paradoxes of Lesbian Identity in Pre-1989 Poland." In *Queers in State Socialism: Cruising 1970s Poland*, edited by Tomasz Basiuk and Jędrzej Burszta, 105–15. London: Routledge, 2021.

Szulc, Łukasz. *Transnational Homosexuals in Communist Poland: Cross-Border Flows in Gay and Lesbian Magazines*. London: Palgrave Macmillan, 2018.

Walker, Shaun. "Polish President Issues Campaign Pledge to Fight 'LGBT Ideology.'" *Guardian*, June 12, 2020. https://www.theguardian.com/world/2020/jun/12/polish-president-issues-campaign-pledge-to-fight-lgbt-ideology.

Wandan, Solongo. "Making New Rights: Constitutional Agenda-Setting in the Transitions of Poland (1989–1997) and South Africa (1990–1994)." PhD diss., New School for Social Research, 2014.

Warkocki, Błażej. "'Transgression has become a fact': A Gothic Genealogy of Queerness in the People's Republic of Poland." In *Queers in State Socialism: Cruising 1970s Poland*, edited by Tomasz Basiuk and Jędrzej Burszta, 33–73. London: Routledge, 2021.

5

REINVENTING POSTSOCIALISM AS HETERONATIONALISM

(Dis)continuities and Frictive Biopolitics in Orbán's Hungary

HADLEY Z. RENKIN

We must decide whether there will still be nations or if we want a united Europe? Do we want families and children, or can we not even determine who is a man and who is a woman?

—Viktor Orbán, Annual *Fidesz* Party Civil Picnic, Kötcse, Hungary, 2016

IN THE LAST SEVERAL YEARS, THE AUTHORITARIAN NATIONALISM OF PRIME Minister Viktor Orbán's Hungary has become an increasingly visible topic of discussion globally and locally, written about most typically as an icon of right-wing, "nativist" or "populist," reaction to the growing sway of transnational cultural, political, and economic forces. The very iconicity of that reaction has also positioned Hungary as a site emblematic of a related phenomenon: the derailing of postsocialism's democratic, inclusionary promise. In both these senses, Hungary's current cultural and political trajectory has become a powerful marker of postsocialism's increasingly troubling (dis)orientation, at once proof of a "transition" gone, despite initially triumphalist pronouncements, profoundly awry, and renewed evidence of Hungary's (and Eastern Europe's more generally) persistently precarious "modern," "European" belonging.[1]

Dominant debates about these concerns, both popular and scholarly, West and East, have overwhelmingly centered analysis of "what's gone wrong with (Hungarian) post-socialism?" on questions of resurgent authoritarian, nationalist ideologies, the promulgation of "illiberal" legal principles and mechanisms, and the deconstruction of recently formed democratic institutions. These discussions have focused largely on the formal pathways and dynamics of overtly authoritarian politics, such as Orbán and his *Fidesz* party government's open embracing of "illiberalism," its seizure of national media and public space and silencing of political opposition, its consolidation of economic resources, and the parallel rise of organized right-wing movements.[2] They have also typically seen such phenomena as indicators of postsocialism's fundamental temporality: whether its total escape from the socialist past (either through the resurrection of past national tradition, or by becoming the hypercapitalist future's laboratory), or its hopeless haunting by socialist "legacies" (inevitably corrupt, inefficient economies, habitually repressive societies and politics). Unquestionably illuminating crucial aspects of these trends, these emphases have unfortunately also meant that dominant narratives of postsocialist politics have frequently neglected people's concrete lives and practices in favor of formal, structural-level understandings. They have thus often obscured the intimate, embodied meanings through which ordinary people experience and negotiate such transformations, and the complex connections and disconnections between past, present, and future through which they construct actually existing postsocialisms that blur and transverse these very borders.

In Hungary one particularly potent site of such everyday consequential practice has been the intimate minutiae of gender and sexual identifications, interactions, and meanings. Indeed, while popular discourse under Hungarian socialism generally maintained a certain silence around the subject (making it very difficult to interpret general attitudes about non-normative sexualities), despite oft-repeated claims that "there was no homosexuality under socialism," sexuality was in fact a surprisingly visible and highly charged social and political site. Accusations of Western, bourgeois sexual decadence and deviance were key mechanisms for repressing political opposition, both through everyday police intimidation and in highly visible events such as show trials.[3] Hungary's decriminalization of homosexuality in 1961 was a potent tool in socialist maneuvering vis-à-vis the West for both closer social and economic connection and scientific-moral superiority.[4] Alternative forms of gender and sexual identity and community could often be seen, well before 1989, in the not-so-hidden queer scenes of Budapest's bars and restaurants, thermal baths, and cruising zones.[5] And during and after the collapse of socialism in 1989, gender and sexuality were critical sites of emerging civil society, as well as both global, liberal identification and heteronationalist backlash.[6] Gender and sexuality have also been salient elements of *Fidesz* and Orbán's intensifying national project. The Orbán government's 2012 rewriting of the Hungarian constitution explicitly defined marriage and family as heterosexual institutions, *Fidesz*'s openly heteronormative late-1990s "Family Policy" has since 2010 blossomed into a system of pronatalist state policies symbolically and financially rewarding heterosexual reproduction, and Orbán has denounced European civil society funding for feminist, queer, and human rights organizations as undermining the Hungarian nation. In May 2020, the government further modified the constitution to clarify that "marriage" meant "the mother is a woman, the father is a man"; made it illegal for trans and intersex people to change their assigned birth gender; and officially repudiated the Istanbul Convention.[7]

Beyond the domains of feminist, gender, and queer studies, however, the significance of these gender- and heteronormative moves has remained largely unrecognized; indeed, gender and sexual politics are typically seen as indexes of other meanings and tensions rather than sites of power and struggle in their own right. Yet, important threads of modern social theory have recognized gender and sexuality as critical elements of the disciplinary and subjectifying grip of modern nationalism, pinpointing figures like homosexuals and mothers as key "constitutive Others" of the proper national citizen.[8] Postsocialist scholarship, building upon such work, has viewed the politics of gender and reproduction as foundational to postsocialist nationalist resurgences.[9] More recently, a growing body of research, including my own work on Hungary, has argued that the exclusion of queer sexualities has been crucial to not only postsocialist national identity and community, but queer struggles to create alternative forms of belonging.[10] These analyses underscore a fundamental lesson of Foucauldian biopower: the profound intimacy of power, and the significance of gendered and sexualized bodily meanings and practices for its production and naturalization.[11] The persistent presence of gendered and sexualized Others in the entangled histories of biopolitical modernity and nationalism suggests that these constitute specifically heteronational forms of power.[12] Postcolonial scholars of sexuality have pointed out, however, that they also emerged in relation to imperial and colonial modernity's geotemporal, civilizational hierarchies,[13] and are not merely phenomena of the past, but continue to structure present relations of domination and resistance.[14] Recent scholarship has shown that this is as true of "Europe's (internal) East" as it is of non-European spaces: presocialist discourses defined Eastern Europeanness through reference to boundaries between "primitive" sexual passion and "modern" sexual control, and proper scientific knowledge of these;[15] practices such as homosexuality and oral sex served under socialism as indexes of the West's decadence and the East's moral (and scientific) superiority;[16] and, as we shall see, current Western representations of postsocialist Eastern Europe's problematic sexual intolerance are countered by the latter's assertions of greater sexual-moral authenticity.[17] These complex and comparative critical perspectives reveal crucial continuities, as well as significant shifts, across both space and time. They urge us to think in more nuanced ways about the relationships between sexualities and their politics, and processes of rupture and continuity both temporal and spatial, and how connected and disconnected, and divergent and convergent histories, and their personal and political meanings for different sexual subjects and communities, shape and are shaped by multiply located bodies and intimacies.[18]

Anthropologist Anna Tsing has noted that such complex, border-crossing negotiations cannot be approached in the abstract: they necessarily involve particular, practical "frictions": concrete and specific tensions at once productive and destructive of people, movements, communities, parties, and governments.[19] In this chapter, I explore some of these intimate, biopolitical frictions: two recent, interrelated controversies over gender and sexuality in postsocialist Hungary and their implications for Hungarian queer people and politics, Hungary's intensifying heteronationalism, and how we understand both. In their very concrete particularities, such frictions reveal the intimate, everyday ways in which not only postsocialism's original promise of greater social and political equality and inclusion, but postsocialism itself has fractured and fragmented. They can thus shatter our expectations of history's possible directions and ends as well.

BODIES AND BORDERS

Hungary's first queer rights march took place in Budapest in 1997. Comprising fewer than 200 people, it was nonetheless widely hailed as a crucial sign of postsocialist success: queer participants spoke of their joy at "finally feeling like normal people in a normal country"; analysts wrote of a "litmus test" for Hungary's progress on the path of democratic transition. Yet if the march, with rainbow flags and pink triangles, asserted global queerness and affiliation with a sexual-political history at odds with socialism's supposed erasures, its practical association with nationally symbolic sites like Heroes' Square (*Hösök tere*) claimed national belonging as well,[20] and thus connection with different postsocialist trajectories. These publicly signaled bonds to multiple pasts, presents, and futures, both national and global, inspired new everyday practices: new possibilities for postsocialist Hungarian queer people to live and build community more openly.

After ten years of peaceful marching with only scattered and peaceful opposition, however, in 2007 and again in 2008 the Budapest Pride March was violently attacked by massed nationalists and neo-Nazis. Stones, bottles, smoke bombs, and urine-filled eggs were thrown at marchers; numerous people were injured, some beaten so badly they were hospitalized.[21] As I have written elsewhere, for many Hungarian queer people, and others, the attacks occasioned a profound spatio-temporal shock, undermining assumptions of the country's, and their own, postsocialist location and directionality. In postattack discussions, queer people spoke of the "primitive" nature of their attackers, of how what had happened was "purely Balkan" in character, of wondering what country they were in. Such attacks, as one editorial on the queer website Pride.hu lamented, disrupted the nature of postsocialist history: "[The attacks go] against the precisely sketched progress of history . . . looking from this perspective it is also possible that the country is not sliding back in time, but rather in space." Hungary, the author observed, could now be counted as part of a "retrograde union" with Russia, Lithuania, Serbia, and Kazakhstan.[22]

The attacks also produced profound practical changes in the march. In the name of social minority "protection," police presence increased dramatically, and a double cordon of barricades was established along its entire route. These moves provoked intense debate in the queer community. While some marchers were grateful that the barricades prevented further attacks, others drew fraught comparisons with socialist-era repression, noting that the cordons had "hermetically sealed" the march off from what made Pride meaningful: its visibility in Budapest's everyday spaces and symbolic sites. These effects were both political and personal. One marcher next to me in 2009 muttered, "These damn fences make me feel like I'm some kind of strange animal inside a zoo." Another woman lamented, as we threaded lines of barricades and riot police at the 2012 march, "I feel like we're vanishing." The attacks also ushered in a new politics of queer respectability, creating other borders internal and external. In response to the first attacks, the 2008 Budapest Pride March was renamed the Gay Dignity Procession (*Meleg Méltóság Menet*). Mandatory premarch checks were introduced: volunteers searched people entering the cordon for potentially dangerous objects or signs of antiqueer intent. March organizers published safety guidelines advising against open display of queer symbols or behavior outside the march. Longstanding queer community debates about proper gender and sexual behavior intensified: some denounced trans presence and sexualized behavior at marches as "provocative"; others defended trans people and open sexuality as vital to queer life and politics. In concert with the now openly violent stance of the right wing, these debates shifted everyday queer behaviors far beyond the march. On one hand, several queer people confessed to me that the situation had led them to try to look less "queer" or to curtail public demonstrations of same-sex affection; on the other, tensions between those seeking "respectable" queerness and those whose saw queerness's essence precisely in challenging respectability tightened. Ultimately, these frictions led the march organizers, Rainbow Mission Foundation (*Szivárvány Misszió Alapítvány*), to reconsider the risks of too much safety and dignity. In 2012 they changed the name of the march back to Budapest Pride. In 2017, declaring it "outrageous that in Hungary today, police can cage a peaceful crowd instead of concentrating on violent protesters" and that the cordons violated marchers' constitutional rights, organizers implicitly invoked postsocialism's early democratic promise against both past socialist and present nationalist repressions and renounced the cordons, calling for "open, inclusive visibility."[23]

Yet the attacks on Pride, and its cordoning, reshaped the Hungarian right wing's bordering of belonging as well. Since 1997, opposition to the march had been situated in the spatialized and temporalized language of the heteronation, declaring queers and queerness "alien," "foreign," an un-Hungarian invasion from the West. Antimarch protesters bore posters with slogans like "Take your difference elsewhere!" and right-wing voices fulminated against queer presence amid the sacred sites of national history.[24] Both attacks and struggle over the cordon materialized this rhetoric as embodied practice. Although some right-wing voices decried the police barricades, for preventing them from reaching marchers, the intimate violence of the attackers' bodily brutality and resounding chants of "Filthy faggots!" (*Mocskos buzik!*") in fact mirrored those same cordons through which the Hungarian state "protected" queer people by rendering them separate and invisible. This profound postsocialist irony was underscored by the surreal juxtaposition of police and government insistence on maintaining the cordons despite both queer activists' rejection of such "protection" and the open avowal of the rabidly nationalist 64 Counties Youth Movement (*Hatvannégy Vármegye Ifjúsági Mozgalom*), some of Pride's most vicious attackers, that they wanted the cordon: by "caging the gays," they admitted, the state was actually fulfilling their antiqueer goals for them. The critical biopolitical slippage here, in which protecting sexual minorities from heteronationalist attack becomes protecting the heteronation from sexual minorities, in which the formal politics of the heteronational state blurs with the everyday practices of right-wing homophobic violence, and in which postsocialism functions simultaneously as imagined departure from both (antinational) socialist past and (perverse) Western present—and in which certain possibilities for postsocialist embodiment are foreclosed by others—was made still more intimately evident when, in response to Budapest Pride's 2017 rejection of the cordon's protective erasure, nationalists blockaded Budapest's Chain Bridge with a wall of black-clad bodies, bearing a banner announcing simply "We Are the Cordon."[25]

"IDEOLOGY, NOT SCIENCE": RE-PLACING GENDER STUDIES

In October 2018, almost immediately after being elected to a third term (with another overwhelming parliamentary majority), Viktor Orbán's government removed gender studies from the national Ministry of Resources list of state-accredited (and thus funded) academic disciplines in Hungary. While the move was not a surprise (the previous August the government had floated plans for a ban), the issue seemed a small one: there were only two such programs in Hungary in the first place, one at the elite state university *Eötvös Loránd Tudományegyetem*, the other at the international Central

European University.[26] As had been the case with the Pride March, however, gender and sexuality—and thus gender studies—were in fact at the heart of Orbán and *Fidesz*'s hopes and fears for the Hungarian nation and the intimate, everyday lives of its citizens.

Part of the problem with such programs, Deputy Prime Minister Zsolt Semjén argued, was what he claimed were consistently low levels of interest and enrollment. More tellingly, however, Semjén also claimed that their work was "ideology" rather than "science." Such a claim invoked powerful postsocialist tropes of the socialist past, and especially socialism's espoused goal of "gender equality," as unnatural social engineering. Through such tropes politicians, parties, and governments in Hungary and elsewhere had legitimized often contrasting visions of post-1989 postsocialist transformation as returns to not merely democratic capitalism or the presocialist nation, but to the natural gendered order imagined to undergird both.[27] This invocation allowed *Fidesz* to frame its attack on gender studies as a defense of natural, universal, and essentially Hungarian "truths" in several critical ways. First, its stance against gender studies allowed *Fidesz* to position itself as the guardian of not just science, but human nature itself. Dismissing as "absurd" the idea that gender was a social construct, Deputy Prime Minister Semjén argued: "There are things that are quite simply biologically determined, such as the issue of gender; whether someone is a woman or a man is a biological fact." Similarly, Orbán's chief of staff, Gergely Gulyás, declared: "The Hungarian government is of the clear view that people are born either men or women."[28] Second, their (anti)gender politics positioned Orbán and *Fidesz* as the defenders of Hungary and its future from the harmful ideologies of the past socialist and liberal postsocialist periods, creating a powerful relationship between gender borders and those linking Hungary's past, present, and future. Implicitly fusing the (imagined) psychic-spiritual damage of leftist socialism to the (also imagined) effects of liberal postsocialism, sociologist Balint Botond wrote in the progovernment newspaper Hungarian Times (*Magyar Idők*) that gender studies had to be eliminated because "gender-faithful liberals have already caused irreparable harm in the souls of generations growing up in the past decades [a period tellingly left undefined]. We need to fight them without compromise and achieve a complete victory, otherwise they will end up destroying us."[29] Critically, this threat to the simultaneously biological and spiritual nation was one of space as well as time: these "liberals" and their faith in "gender" were fundamentally alien to the nation. More than a year before the "ban," Lörinc Nacsa, head of the Association of Young Christian Democrats (*IKSZ; Ifjúsági Kereszténydemokrata Szövetséget*), declared gender studies' presence in Hungary the result of the "pressure" of a global "gender and gay lobby" (*gender- és meleglobbi*—a common bugbear of the Hungarian right). That cabal's proponents, Nacsa warned, "do not help the rise of our nation, they even destroy the value-centered thinking that is still present in Central European countries": the discipline not only "deal[s] with a subject that has no benefit to Hungarian society," but "by studying sexual minorities and deepening feminist philosophy" actively puts at risk "the future of Hungary" it-self.[30] *Fidesz* and Orbán thus blended rhetorics of rupture—positioning themselves as the saviors of a postsocialism that would at last restore the gender and sexual traditions of the presocialist Hungarian nation despite the damage of intervening socialist and postsocialist pasts—and continuity: resurrecting socialist sexual-political discourses to also suggest that only *Fidesz* could resist the decadent West's perverse existential threat. The existence of gender studies was thus far more than an academic question: it was a threat—both past and present, internal and external—to not only the Hungarian na-tion's survival, but its proper relationship to past, present, and future.

Rooted as far back as its late 1990s "Family Policy," *Fidesz*'s attack on gender stud-ies was also the inevitable consequence of the party's profound reorientation from its original vision of pro-Western, pro-democratic opposition to socialism to explicitly na-tionalist goals. Central to this stance was a vision of "traditional" gender and sexuality as key markers of national resistance to both the gender and sexual politics of Hungar-ian socialism, and what founding *Fidesz* member and then-president of the Hungarian Parliament László Kövér, at *Fidesz*'s party congress in 2015, called the West's "gender madness." These frictions between internal and external enemies, past and present, wove together symbolic and material structures, everyday gender and sexual behaviors, roles, and relationships; biopolitically, they also entwined individual self-realization with col-lective, national realization. They drove a marked proliferation of political speech fol-lowing Orbán's election in 2010 in which *Fidesz* more and more openly declared women biologically destined to be primarily mothers, childbearers, carers, and homemakers. In 2015, Kövér also commented, "When our girls give birth to our grandchildren, we want them to regard it as the defining moment of their self-realization"; in 2017 *Fidesz* vice president Szilard Nemeth exhorted women to "give birth for the country" to in-crease its population. The same frictions inspired *Fidesz*'s 2011 rewriting of the Hun-garian constitution to not only redefine marriage as a strictly heterosexual institution, "the conjugal union of a man and a woman," but the family as both based on the mar-riage of a man and a woman and "the basis for survival of the nation." That *Fidesz*'s vi-sion of Hungarian national survival was explicitly reproductive was made clear by the immediately following declaration that "Hungary shall promote the commitment to have and raise children"; that it was explicitly heteronormative was made clear by their further modification, in 2020, that marriage meant a situation "where the husband is a man and the wife is a woman." While the pronatalist tone of these rhetorics and policies was in important ways reminiscent of Hungarian socialism's moments of pronatalism, crucial disjunctures illuminate postsocialism's complexly cross-cutting and intersect-ing (dis)continuities: Orbán and *Fidesz* have positioned themselves with and against a range of competing pasts and presents: the shifting reproductive politics of the social-ist state, at times pronatalist, at others antinatalist; the briefly resurgent liberal gender and reproductive politics of early postsocialism; and an imagined West of declining (heterosexual) marriage and birth rates.

These symbolically potent pronatalist discourses were accompanied by concrete social and economic policies. A state regime financially encouraging reproductive marriage and family life, including cash rewards for families with multiple children, substantial tax reductions, and subsidized government loans for the purchase of cars or houses for parents of three or more children constructed a new biopolitical infrastructure for Orban's new Hungarian heteronation; revealingly, by 2021 the government had nationalized the country's entire fertility center network.[31] This reproductive heteronationalism implicated an extensive web of roles, relationships, and everyday practices, reshaping people's everyday lives, from reproductive choices to a wide range of other personal, social, and economic behaviors. As had socialist policies and practices in their own day, it articulated people's everyday gendered and sexual desires and practices with the structures of postsocialist national order. People had negotiated their everyday gendered and sexual lives around shifting pro- and antinatalist policies of Hungarian socialism, altering the balance of time and energy dedicated to domestic and state labor, and the rhythms and visibilities of their sexual lives.[32] *Fidesz*'s heteronational regime similarly encouraged couples to have previously unplanned third children, purchase new homes and cars, or, more painfully, bear and raise unwanted children—or in the case of same-sex couples, abandon dreams of legal partnership and parenthood. More indirectly, such discourses and policies have compelled nonmarried and nonreproductive individuals and couples to compete upon social fields at a material and symbolic disadvantage. The *Fidesz* gender regime has thus materialized a countermodel to both past socialism's and present Western "gender madness." It was precisely such madness and challenge to the everyday, intimate practices of national gender and sexuality, reproduction and kinship, that Orbán and *Fidesz* saw the field of gender studies to promote. As Kövér's 2015 speech also declared, further blurring dangers gendered and sexual, past and present, "We don't want to turn Hungary into a futureless society of man-hating women and woman-fearing, feminine men who only see children and families as an obstacle to self-fulfillment."

Most of the outrage that met Orbán's move against gender studies represented it as an effort to ban the discipline. What actually occurred, however, was more ingenious, and more revealing. Rather than a ban—the creation of mere absence where gender studies had been—the government officially established a new discipline in its place called Economics of Family Policy and Public Policies for Human Development (*Családpolitika és az emberi fejlődésre vonatkozó közpolitikák közgazdaságtanában*), with defined fields of expertise such as "family decisions," "population matters," "family assistance," and "child protection and children's rights." A fraudulent "ideology" undermining not merely gender distinctions but the national health and continuity that depended on them was thus replaced by a "scientific" field supporting both the natural facticity of the biological nation and the *Fidesz* government's heteronationalist claims about it. While, in the words on Facebook of a member of the Central European University (CEU) Gender Studies faculty, it seemed as if gender studies had "suddenly disappeared," in fact, in the place of both the discipline itself and the imagined gender regimes of socialism, liberal postsocialism, and the West a biopolitically reinforced Hungarian heteronation had emerged, its ideological character neatly naturalized by its contrast to all of these.

Critically, all these changes weave together material and symbolic practices, structures of practice and selfhood: the disappearance of not just an institutional discipline, but of ways of knowing and being. Everyday intimate practices, social networks, entire lives and communities traversing in imagination and action borders of gender, sexuality, and nation are replaced by others equally shaped by such borders, but in very different ways. Hungarian heteronationalism's "war on gender" has transformed the everyday lives of scholars and students engaging in these realms of inquiry. It has altered professional and life plans, and redirected or foreclosed real people's intellectual, emotional, and practical resources and capabilities. The flight to Vienna of CEU, with all its gender (and other) scholars and students, has erased from Hungarian life the everyday presence and visibility of countless words and actions opening alternative possibilities for gender and sexual life and thought, as has the lesser-known but very real silencing or self-exiling of numerous Hungarian queer and feminist activists. The case of Éva, a doctoral graduate of CEU Gender Studies who was simply unable to work or teach as a queer scholar in Hungary and who, although deeply attached to her life, queer activism, and family there, was forced to leave the country, is only one of many. The same is true of Márta, a long-time Hungarian lesbian activist, who told me, nearly a year after CEU's departure from Budapest, "Now there is nowhere in Hungary for me to go to learn these possibilities!" If they wish to explore scholarly perspectives on gender and sexuality, and the life options, personal and professional, these can open, Márta and others like her must turn westward, leaving behind other, once possible lives—and other, once possible Hungarys. Such changes profoundly shift the possibilities of intimate and everyday life—here, too, not a disappearance, but an *orienting away* from the nation of certain ways of knowing and being differently. For others, Hungary's increasing heteronationalism and both its politics of knowledge and biopolitical materialities may mean not merely the impossibility of ever learning about gender and sexual alternatives, and differing ways of looking, feeling, and acting, of living and loving, but vastly increased risks to exploring these, or mobilizing socially or politically on their behalf.[33] This has reshaped the everyday lives and practices of many queer Hungarians: those whose behaviors and experiences at Budapest Pride were constrained following the attacks described above, but also the young same-sex couple who angrily admitted to me that in the last several years they have stopped holding hands when they walk through Budapest's *Belváros* (City Center). Or the group of CEU Gender Studies students who, just a year or so before the university left Hungary, felt safe at a long-tolerant club to engage in a little gender and sexually transgressive dancing, only to be violently attacked by other, vocally antiqueer clubbers; and the attendees of a queer-friendly community center in Budapest in 2019 quietly watching a film about homophobic bullying in schools who, when violently invaded and threatened by thugs from the nationalist Our Homeland Movement (*Mi Hazánk Mozgalom*) carrying banners proclaiming "Stop LGBT Propaganda!" and "Zero Tolerance!" saw their relation to the heteronation brutally confirmed when the police, who finally arrived, simply stood there and watched.[34] Dramatically transforming the borders of gendered and sexual possibility, such changes crystallize the possible, and impossible, intimate, everyday practices of the heteronation, and locate other (im)possibilities elsewhere, beyond the temporal and spatial borders of Hungarian postsocialism.

CONCLUSION

There is a dividing line that starts from the Baltics and runs all the way along the western borders of Poland, the Czech Republic, Slovakia, Hungary and Slovenia. To the west of this line are those countries that have already abandoned the protection of the family; everywhere to the east of the line, on the other hand, family-friendly policies have prevailed; nowhere is same-sex marriage accepted.

—Viktor Orbán, in the progovernment newspaper
Hungarian Times (*Magyar Idők*), December 2015.[35]

As I write this conclusion, the *Fidesz*-dominated Hungarian Parliament has just passed, by 157 votes to 1, a new law, "On stricter action against pedophile offenders and amending certain laws to protect children."[36] Similar to (and likely modeled on) the notorious 2013 Russian "anti-gay propaganda" law, the Hungarian law bans the representation in advertising, educational materials, or any media content accessible to people under eighteen of any information considered by the government to promote "deviation from gender identity, gender reassignment and homosexuality." Justified as necessary for protecting the nation's children—as a Hungarian government spokesperson stated, "There are contents children under a certain age may misunderstand which may have a detrimental effect on their development (. . .) which could confuse their developing moral values or their image of themselves or the world"[37]—the ban is expected to profoundly curtail queer visibility, dramatically restrict queer and feminist activism, and perhaps even finally, after twenty-four years, ban the Budapest Pride march.

The shock occasioned for so many by this heteronationalist move seems to me a symptom of both our persisting expectations—despite all that has happened in the postsocialist world since 1989—of the apolitical nature of the intimate, and—despite all that has happened in the postsocialist world since 1989—of the necessarily (uni-)directional nature of history. Yet the stories I have related here challenge both these still all too dominant narratives of postsocialist (and other) transformation.

On the one hand, these stories reveal that, rather than merely marginal or indexical phenomena, gender and sexuality are in fact foundational elements of how postsocialist nations and nationalisms are secured and sustained, and everyday desires and practices articulated with their orders. Here gender and sexuality function as complex and crucial hinges: supporting Orbán's reinvention of Hungary as the necessary counterspace/time to both the socialist past's unnaturalness and the West's "deviant, failed Enlightenment"—a "real Europe" (in Orbán's words) of natural intimacies and stable gender, sexual, and national identities, roles, and relations.[38] Histories, then, are not merely (or even primarily) shaped by formal political structures, but in and through the frictions, fractures, and fragments, contingent structures and everyday practices, of knowledge, being, and power: worked out amid the frictions of past and present, national and transnational, state and society; fought out on the biopolitical terrain of bodies' everyday attractions and repulsions, tensions and confrontations, (in)visibilities and (im)possibilities.

On the other hand, these stories demonstrate clearly that history (always?) travels in more than one direction—and manner. Our imaginings of postsocialism have tended to present it in two mutually exclusive ways. One is as an upward trajectory of liberal reform and inclusive citizenship—a distinct rupture with socialism's unnatural, antidemocratic "deviation," a "return" to "Europeanness," "modernity," and "normal history" signaled by the "litmus tests" of Pride marches and gender studies. The other is as a history always already compromised—an inevitable continuity, in which both socialism and postsocialist nationalism's "return of the repressed" are merely differing expressions of essential Eastern difference, of a region again pursuing its natural path of deviance from modern morality and politics. Here, Hungarian heteronationalism's intolerance of queerness and critical approaches to "gender" ultimately serve as merely an Other litmus test: proving its inescapable geotemporality. Yet, as we have seen from these stories of gender and sexual politics, the postsocialist politics of heteronationalism do not in fact emerge from, or signify, either rupture or continuity, whether spatial or temporal: they are, rather, complex entanglements of both. In this sense, history itself can "shatter"—travel in multiple directions—precisely through the productive force of such intimate frictions. For it is ultimately through its complex, simultaneous targeting of the knowledges, discourses, and practices of the everyday intimacies of gender and sexuality that the multifarious, divergent, (dis)connecting enactment of the heteronation is most clearly revealed: happily heterosexist yet angrily heteronormative; profoundly structural yet deeply personal; creating both continuities and ruptures between different spaces—national and transnational; East and West—and different times—presocialist, socialist, and postsocialist; always at once past, present, and future.

NOTES

1. Stephen Holmes, "Introduction to 'From Postcommunism to Post-September 11,'" *East European Constitutional Review* 10 (Winter 2001): 78–81; Francis Fukuyama, *The End of History and the Last Man* (New York: Free Press, 1992); József Böröcz, "Goodness Is Elsewhere: The Rule of European Difference," *Comparative Studies in Society and History* 48, no. 1 (2006): 110–38; and Michał Buchowski, "The Specter of Orientalism in Europe: From Exotic Other to Stigmatized Brother," *Anthropological Quarterly* 79, no. 3 (2006): 463–82.

2. Timea Drinóczi and Agnieszka Bień-Kacała, eds., *Rule of Law, Common Values, and Illiberal Constitutionalism: Poland and Hungary within the European Union* (London: Routledge, 2020); Péter Krasztev and Jon Van Til, eds., *The Hungarian Patient: Social Opposition to an Illiberal Democracy* (Budapest: Central European University Press, 2015); Bálint Magyar, *A magyar maffiaállam anatómiája* [The Anatomy of the Hungarian Mafia-State] (Budapest: Noran Libor Kiado, 2015); András Pap, *Democratic Decline in Hungary: Law and Society in an Illiberal Democracy* (London: Routledge, 2018); and Gábor Scheiring, *The Retreat of Liberal Democracy: Authoritarian Capitalism and the Accumulative State in Hungary* (London: Palgrave Macmillan, 2020). I deliberately avoid the term "far right" to underscore the critical similarities between what are commonly seen as significantly different "far" and (unmarked) right-wing politics. In my view, both these similarities and their erasure through such distinctions are crucial to the power of parties like *Fidesz* and figures such as Orbán. I refer to Orbán's party, officially named *Fidesz*-Hungarian Civic Alliance [*Fidesz-Magyar Polgári Szövetség*] simply as Fidesz throughout the chapter.

3. István Rév, "In Mendacio Veritas (In Lies There Lies the Truth)," *Representations* 35 (Summer 1991): 1–20.

4. Judit Takács, "Liberating Pathologization? The Historical Background of the 1961 Decriminalization of Homosexuality in Hungary," *Hungarian Historical Review* 10, no. 2 (2021): 267–300.

5. Anna Borgos, ed., *Eltitkolt évek: Tizenhat leszbikus életút* (Budapest: Labrisz Leszbikus Egyesület, 2011); Péter Hanzli, ed., *Meleg férfiak, hideg diktatúrák: Életútinterjúk* (Budapest: Civil Művek, 2015); Anita Kurimay, *Queer Budapest, 1873–1961* (Chicago: University of Chicago Press, 2020); András Murai and Eszter Zsófia Toth, *Szex és szocializmus* (Budapest: Libri, 2014); Hadley Renkin, "Ambiguous Identities, Ambiguous Transitions: Lesbians, Gays, and the Sexual Politics of Citizenship in Postsocialist Hungary" (PhD diss., University of Michigan, Ann Arbor, 2007); Hadley Renkin, "Grief, Time, and a Postsocialist Queer Activist's Tears," *Lambda Nordica* (2024); and Judith Takács, "Disciplining Gender and (Homo)Sexuality in State Socialist Hungary in the 1970s," *European Review of History* 22, no. 1 (2015): 161–75.

6. Renkin, "Ambiguous Identities, Ambiguous Transitions"; Hadley Renkin, "Homophobia and Queer Belonging in Hungary," *Focaal—European Journal of Anthropology* 53, no. 1 (2009): 20–37; Hadley Renkin, "Perverse Frictions: Pride, Dignity, and the Budapest LGBT March," *Ethnos—Journal of Anthropology* 80, no. 3 (2015): 409–32; Renkin, "Grief, Time"; Anita Kurimay and Judit Takács, "Emergence of the Hungarian Homosexual Movement in Late Refrigerator Socialism," *Sexualities* 20, no. 5–6 (2017): 585–603. Interestingly, unlike in many other postsocialist countries, in Hungary religion does not seem to have been a critical vector in antiqueer politics until the late 1990s, and even into the 2000s.

7. The Istanbul Convention is officially known as the Council of Europe Convention on Preventing and Combating Violence against Women and Domestic Violence.

8. Lauren Berlant, *The Queen of America Goes to Washington City: Essays on Sex and Citizenship* (Durham, NC: Duke University Press, 1997); Kevin Moss, "Split Pride/Split Identities," *QED: A Journal in GLBTQ Worldmaking* 3, no. 2 (2016): 56–75; Andrew Parker, Mary Russo, Doris Sommer, and Patricia Yaeger, eds., *Nationalisms and Sexualities* (New York: Routledge, 1992); Nira Yuval-Davis, *Gender and Nation* (London: Sage, 1997); Nira Yuval-Davis, "Women and the Biological Reproduction of the Nation," *Women's Studies International Forum* 19, nos. 1–2 (1996): 17–24.

9. Susan Gal, "Gender in the Post-Socialist Transition: The Abortion Debate in Hungary," *East European Politics and Societies* 8, no. 2 (1994): 256–86; Susan Gal and Gail Kligman, *The Politics of Gender after Socialism* (Princeton, NJ: Princeton University Press, 2000); and Katherine Verdery, *What Was Socialism and What Comes Next?* (Princeton, NJ: Princeton University Press, 1996).

10. Renkin, "Homophobia and Queer Belonging"; Renkin, "Perverse Frictions"; Robert Kulpa and Joanna Mizielinska, eds., *De-Centering Western Sexualities: Central and Eastern European Perspectives* (London: Ashgate Press, 2011); Francesca Stella, *Lesbian Lives in Soviet and Post-Soviet Russia: Post/Socialism and Gendered Sexualities* (London: Palgrave Macmillan, 2015); Katja Kahlina, "Sexual Politics of Belonging: Sexual Identities, Nationalism, and Citizenship in Post-Yugoslav Croatia" (PhD diss., Central

European University, 2013); Gordon Waitt, "Sexual Citizenship in Latvia: Geographies of the Latvian Closet," *Social & Cultural Geography* 6, no. 2 (2005): 161–81; and Moss, "Split Pride/Split Identities."

11. Michel Foucault, *The History of Sexuality: Vol. 1, An Introduction* (New York: Pantheon, 1978).

12. George Mosse, *Nationalism and Sexuality: Middle Class Morality and Sexual Norms in Modern Europe* (Madison: University of Wisconsin Press, 1985). I use the term "heteronationalism" to draw attention to the foundational importance of heteronormative structures and practices for most modern nationalisms (see Mosse, *Nationalism and Sexuality*).

13. Ann Laura Stoler, *Race and the Education of Desire* (Durham, NC: Duke University Press, 1995).

14. Judith Butler, "Sexual Politics, Torture, and Secular Time," *British Journal of Sociology* 59 (2008): 1–23; Jasper Puar, *Terrorist Assemblages: Homonationalism in Queer Times* (Durham, NC: Duke University Press, 2007).

15. Renkin, "Perverse Frictions"; Kurimay, *Queer Budapest, 1873–196*; Larry Wolff, *Inventing Eastern Europe: The Map of Civilization on the Mind of the Enlightenment* (Stanford: Stanford University Press, 1994).

16. Dan Healey, "Homosexual Existence and Existing Socialism: New Light on the Repression of Male Homosexuality in Stalinist Russia," *GLQ: A Journal of Gay and Lesbian Studies* 8, no. 3 (2002): 349–78; Dan Healey, *Bolshevik Sexual Forensics: Diagnosing Disorder in the Clinic and Courtroom, 1917–1939* (Ithaca, NY: Cornell University Press, 2009); Kateřina Lišková, *Sexual Liberation, Socialist Style: Communist Czechoslovakia and the Science of Desire, 1945–1989* (Cambridge: Cambridge University Press, 2018); Agnieszka Kościańska, *Gender, Pleasure, and Violence: The Construction of Expert Knowledge of Sexuality in Poland* (Bloomington: Indiana University Press, 2020); Rév, "In Mendacio Veritas."

17. Eric Fassin, "National Identities and Transnational Intimacies: Sexual Democracy and the Politics of Immigration in Europe," *Public Culture* 22, no. 3 (2010): 507–29; Eric Fassin and Judith Surkis, "Introduction: Transgressing Boundaries," *Public Culture* 22, no. 3 (2010): 487–505; and Hadley Renkin, "'Far from the Space of Tolerance': The Biopolitical Geography of Postsocialist Homophobia," *Sexuality & Culture* 27 (2023): 2084–104.

18. Allan Berubé, *My Desire for History: Essays in Gay, Community, and Labor History* (Chapel Hill: University of North Carolina Press, 2011); Lee Edelman, *No Future: Queer Theory and the Death Drive* (Durham, NC: Duke University Press); Heather Love, *Feeling Backward: Loss and the Politics of Queer History* (Cambridge, MA: Harvard University Press, 2009); and Jose Muñoz, *Cruising Utopia: The Then and There of Queer Futurity* (New York: New York University Press, 2009).

19. Anna Tsing, *Friction: An Ethnography of Global Connection* (Princeton, NJ: Princeton University Press, 2005).

20. Renkin, "Homophobia and Queer Belonging in Hungary."

21. Renkin, "Homophobia and Queer Belonging in Hungary."

22. Renkin, "'Far from the Space of Tolerance.'"

23. *Budapest Pride Parade—We Stand for Our Freedom!* Wednesday, July 5, 2017, https://budapestpride.hu/hirek/buadpest-pride-felvonulas-kiallunk-a-szabadsagunkert. Despite police insistence that the barricades remain, the march that year occurred without them—and without renewed violence. See also Renkin, "Caging and Uncaging Pride: Di(s)visibility and the Borders of Budapest Pride," *Ethnos—Journal of Anthropology* (2024).

24. Renkin, "Homophobia and Queer Belonging in Hungary."

25. See also Renkin, "Caging and Uncaging Pride: Di(s)visibility and the Borders of Budapest Pride."

26. There was also a gender studies certificate program at the University of Szeged in southern Hungary. The legislation, however, only applied to actual MA or PhD program accreditation. In the interest of full disclosure, I should note that I am a member of the CEU Gender Studies department.

27. Daina Stukuls Eglitis, *Imagining the Nation: History, Modernity, and Revolution in Latvia* (University Park: Pennsylvania State University Press, 2002); Gal, "Gender in the Post-Socialist Transition"; Nancy Fraser, *Justice Interruptus: Critical Reflections on the "Postsocialist" Condition* (New York: Routledge, 1997).

28. http://www.atv.hu/belfold/20180813-Semjén-senki-nem-akar-genderologust-foglalkoztatni-igy-kepezni-sem-kell.

29. "Hungary to Stop Financing Gender Studies Courses: PM Aide," *Reuters,* August 14, 2018, https://www.reuters.com/article/us-hungary-government-education/hungary-to-stop-financing-gender-studies-courses-pm-aide-idUSKBN1KZ1M0.

30. https://444.hu/2017/02/17/hozza-tud-melto-modon-jarulni-a-jovohoz-az-elte-vagy-kiszolgalja-a-gender-es-meleglobbi-nyomulasat.

31. Éva Fodor, *The Gender Regime of Anti-Liberal Hungary* (London: Palgrave Macmillan, 2022). Here, too, while some of these policies and institutional structures resembled those of Hungarian socialism, their more explicitly national-reproductive ends reveal postsocialist heteronationalism's complex mixture of continuity and discontinuity.

32. Joanna Goven, "The Gendered Foundations of Hungarian Socialism: State, Society, and the Anti-Politics of Anti-Feminism, 1948–1990" (PhD diss., University of California, Berkeley, 1993); and Lynn Haney, *Inventing the Needy: Gender and the Politics of Welfare in Hungary* (Berkeley: University of California Press, 2002).

33. I certainly do not mean to imply that gender studies programs represent the only source of information for Hungarians (or anyone, anywhere) regarding alternative or

non-normative gender and sexual identities—or potential mobilization on their bases. There are, of course, other important sources such as the internet and social media—as well as the queer activists who continue to work in Hungary despite the weight of the heteronational atmosphere, and the knowledge transmitted by more private forms of everyday queer life and community. In this sense, there is no question that queer Hungarians continue to demonstrate resistance and agency despite the current conditions—as the recent publication of (and right-wing panic over) the 2020 publication of *Wonderland Is for Everyone* (*Meseország Mindenkié*), a book of gender, sexual, race, and disability-inclusive fairytales for children, so clearly shows (see Renkin, "Grief, Time"). Nonetheless, the public availability of knowledge about diversity of gender and sexuality, non-normative gender and sexual politics, and the possibility of their public visibility matters greatly as well for people's ability to find and pursue these kinds of questions—particularly in an environment where such representations and even the possibility of critical discourses has been, and continues to be, so authoritatively and intensively limited (see the conclusion to this chapter).

34. https://merce.hu/2019/09/26/budahazy-gyorgyek-megzavartak-egy-rendezvenyt -es-megszalltak-az-aurora-nevu-hely-egy-reszet/.

35. *Magyar Idők*, December 24, 2015.

36. See, https://www.parlament.hu/documents/129291/40734520/T16365_1.pdf/a244 e10a-33a1-df89-24c2-70edbe9f7622?t=1623263262629.

37. Jennifer Rankin, "Hungary Passes Laws Banning LGBT Content in Schools or Kids' TV," *Guardian,* June 15, 2021, https://www.theguardian.com/world/2021 /jun/15/hungary-passes-law-banning-lbgt-content-in-schools.

38. In another postsocialist irony, of course, the visibility of Orbán's and *Fidesz's* heteronational stance has ultimately made gender and sexuality more central, parts of the nation (and so of postsocialism and history itself)—thereby also making space for the intimate desires, practices, and relations of queer resistance: the embattled yet continuing struggles of Budapest Pride; the more hidden, yet persistent, work of Hungarian gender scholars.

BIBLIOGRAPHY

Berlant, Lauren. *The Queen of America Goes to Washington City: Essays on Sex and Citizenship.* Durham, NC: Duke University Press, 1997.

Berubé, Allan. *My Desire for History: Essays in Gay, Community, and Labor History.* Chapel Hill: University of North Carolina Press, 2011.

Borgos, Anna, ed. *Eltitkolt évek: Tizenhat leszbikus életút* [Secret years. Sixteen lesbian life stories]. Budapest: Labrisz Leszbikus Egyesület, 2011.

Böröcz, József. "Goodness Is Elsewhere: The Rule of European Difference." *Comparative Studies in Society and History* 48, no. 1 (2006): 110–38.

Buchowski, Michał. "The Specter of Orientalism in Europe: From Exotic Other to Stigmatized Brother." *Anthropological Quarterly* 79, no. 3 (2006): 463–82.

Butler, Judith. "Sexual Politics, Torture, and Secular Time." *British Journal of Sociology* 59 (2008): 1–23.

Drinóczi, Timea, and Agnieszka Bień-Kacała, eds. *Rule of Law, Common Values, and Illiberal Constitutionalism: Poland and Hungary within the European Union.* London: Routledge, 2021.

Edelman, Lee. *No Future: Queer Theory and the Death Drive.* Durham, NC: Duke University Press, 2004.

Eglitis, Daina Stukuls. *Imagining the Nation: History, Modernity, and Revolution in Latvia.* University Park: Pennsylvania State University Press, 2002.

Fassin, Eric. "National Identities and Transnational Intimacies: Sexual Democracy and the Politics of Immigration in Europe." *Public Culture* 22, no. 3 (2010): 507–29.

Fassin, Éric, and Judith Surkis. "Introduction: Transgressing Boundaries." *Public Culture* 22, no. 3 (2010): 487–505.

Fodor, Éva. *The Gender Regime of Anti-Liberal Hungary.* London: Palgrave, 2022.

Foucault, Michel. *The History of Sexuality: Vol. 1, An Introduction.* New York: Pantheon, 1978.

Fraser, Nancy. *Justice Interruptus: Critical Reflections on the "Postsocialist" Condition.* New York: Routledge, 1997.

Fukuyama, Francis. *The End of History and the Last Man.* New York: Free Press, 1992.

Gal, Susan. "Gender in the Post-Socialist Transition: The Abortion Debate in Hungary." *East European Politics and Societies* 8, no. 2 (1994): 256–86.

Gal, Susan, and Gail Kligman. *The Politics of Gender after Socialism.* Princeton, NJ: Princeton University Press, 2000.

Goven, Joanna. "The Gendered Foundations of Hungarian Socialism: State, Society, and the Anti-Politics of Anti-Feminism, 1948–1990." Unpublished PhD diss., University of California, Berkeley, 1993.

Haney, Lynn. *Inventing the Needy: Gender and the Politics of Welfare in Hungary.* Berkeley: University of California Press, 2002.

Hanzli, Péter, ed. *Meleg férfiak, hideg diktatúrák: Életútinterjúk* [Hot men, straight dictatorships. Life history interviews]. Budapest: Civil Művek, 2015.

Healey, Dan. *Bolshevik Sexual Forensics: Diagnosing Disorder in the Clinic and Courtroom, 1917–1939.* Ithaca, NY: Cornell University Press, 2009.

Healey, Dan. "Homosexual Existence and Existing Socialism: New Light on the Repression of Male Homosexuality in Stalinist Russia." *GLQ* 8, no. 3 (2002): 349–78.

Holmes, Stephen. "From Postcommunism to Post-September 11: Introduction." *East European Constitutional Review* 10, no. 4 (2001): 78–81.

Kahlina, Katja. "Sexual Politics of Belonging: Sexual Identities, Nationalism, and Citizenship in Post-Yugoslav Croatia." PhD diss., Central European University, Budapest, 2013.

Kościańska, Agnieszka. *Gender, Pleasure, and Violence: The Construction of Expert Knowledge of Sexuality in Poland.* Bloomington: Indiana University Press, 2020.

Krasztev, Péter, and Jon Van Til, eds. *The Hungarian Patient: Social Opposition to an Illiberal Democracy.* Budapest: Central European University Press, 2015.

Kulpa, Robert. "Nations and Sexualities—'West' and 'East.'" In *De-Centring Western Sexualities: Central and Eastern European Perspectives*, edited by Robert Kulpa and Joanna Mizielinska, 43–62. London: Ashgate Press, 2011.

Kurimay, Anita. *Queer Budapest, 1873–1961.* Chicago: University of Chicago Press, 2020.

Kurimay, Anita, and Judit Takács. "Emergence of the Hungarian Homosexual Movement in Late Refrigerator Socialism." *Sexualities* 20, nos. 5–6 (2017) 585–603.

Lišková, Kateřina. *Sexual Liberation, Socialist Style: Communist Czechoslovakia and the Science of Desire, 1945–1989.* Cambridge: Cambridge University Press, 2018.

Love, Heather. *Feeling Backward: Loss and the Politics of Queer History.* Cambridge, MA: Harvard University Press, 2009.

Magyar, Bálint. *A magyar maffiaállam anatómiája* [The Anatomy of the Hungarian Mafia-State]. Budapest: Noran Libor Kiado, 2015.

Moss, Kevin. "Split Pride/Split Identities." *QED: A Journal in GLBTQ Worldmaking* 3, no. 2 (2016): 56–75.

Muñoz, Jose. *Cruising Utopia: The Then and There of Queer Futurity.* New York: New York University Press, 2009.

Murai, András, and Eszter Zsófia Toth. *Szex és szocializmus* [Sex and socialism]. Budapest: Libri, 2014.

Pap, András. *Democratic Decline in Hungary: Law and Society in an Illiberal Democracy.* London: Routledge, 2018.

Parker, Andrew, Mary Russo, Doris Sommer, and Patricia Yaeger, eds. *Nationalisms and Sexualities.* New York: Routledge, 1992.

Puar, Jasper. *Terrorist Assemblages: Homonationalism in Queer Times.* Durham, NC: Duke University Press, 2007.

Renkin, Hadley. "Ambiguous Identities, Ambiguous Transitions: Lesbians, Gays, and the Sexual Politics of Citizenship in Postsocialist Hungary." PhD diss., University of Michigan, 2007.

Renkin, Hadley. "Caging and Uncaging Pride: Di(s)visibility and the Borders of Budapest Pride." *Ethnos—Journal of Anthropology* (2024). https://doi.org/10.1080/00141844.2024.2349656.

Renkin, Hadley. "'Far from the Space of Tolerance': The Biopolitical Geography of Postsocialist Homophobia." *Sexuality & Culture* 27 (2023): 2084–104. https://doi.org/10.1007/s12119-023-10155-2.

Renkin, Hadley. "Grief, Time, and a Postsocialist Queer Activist's Tears." *Lambda Nordica* (2024).

Renkin, Hadley. "Homophobia and Queer Belonging in Hungary." *Focaal—European Journal of Anthropology* 53, no. 1 (2009): 20–37.

Renkin, Hadley. "Perverse Frictions: Pride, Dignity, and the Budapest LGBT March." *Ethnos—Journal of Anthropology* 80, no. 3 (2015): 409–32.

Rév, István. "In Mendacio Veritas (In Lies There Lies the Truth)." *Representations* 35 (Summer 1991): 1–20.

Scheiring, Gábor. *The Retreat of Liberal Democracy: Authoritarian Capitalism and the Accumulative State in Hungary*. London: Palgrave Macmillan, 2020.

Stella, Francesca. *Lesbian Lives in Soviet and Post-Soviet Russia: Post/Socialism and Gendered Sexualities*. London: Palgrave Macmillan, 2015.

Stoler, Ann Laura. *Race and the Education of Desire*. Durham, NC: Duke University Press, 1995.

Takács, Judit. "Disciplining Gender and (Homo)Sexuality in State Socialist Hungary in the 1970s." *European Review of History* 22, no. 1 (2015): 161–75.

Takács, Judit. "Liberating Pathologization? The Historical Background of the 1961 Decriminalization of Homosexuality in Hungary." *Hungarian Historical Review* 10, no. 2 (2021): 267–300.

Tsing, Anna. *Friction: An Ethnography of Global Connection*. Princeton, NJ: Princeton University Press, 2005.

Verdery, Katherine. *What Was Socialism and What Comes Next?* Princeton, NJ: Princeton University Press, 1996.

Wolff, Larry. *Inventing Eastern Europe: The Map of Civilization on the Mind of the Enlightenment*. Stanford: Stanford University Press, 1994.

Yuval-Davis, Nira. *Gender and Nation*. London: Sage, 1997.

Yuval-Davis, Nira. "Women and the Biological Reproduction of the Nation." *Women's Studies International Forum* 19, nos. 1–2 (1996): 17–24.

6

ERADICATING SOCIALIST INTERNATIONALISM

The Expulsion of Foreign Students in Postsocialist Bulgaria

RAIA APOSTOLOVA

NEARLY A DECADE AGO, CHRISTINA SCHWENKEL ARGUED THAT INTER-national mobility was deeply woven into socialist societies—a point clearly demonstrated by the thousands of students and workers who took part in exchange programs between Asia, Africa, Latin America, and the Socialist Bloc.[1] In this respect, the People's Republic of Bulgaria (PRB) was no exception. Until the late 1980s, educating Third World students was encouraged as a form of solidarity that would ful-fill Bulgaria's "internationalist duties" in the training of future socialist cadres.[2] The end of socialism in 1989 signified a radical rupture from these practices and political rationales, as Bulgaria sought to take its place within the European order. Mass depor-tations, sacking of laborers, and changes in foreigners' legal rights were among the out-comes of this process in Bulgaria—and other parts of the Eastern Bloc—constituting a wave of expulsions in the 1990s.[3]

This chapter engages with the question of why and how previously held interna-tionalist values were eradicated from educational, institutional, and political struc-tures in Bulgaria after 1989. This question is not exclusively my own. Former exchange students who graduated in Bulgaria between the late 1980s and early 1990s posed sim-ilar questions, namely: Why isn't Bulgaria continuing its relationship with us? Why are educational programs between African countries and Bulgaria no longer in existence? These questions were posed by the twenty-seven individuals who were interviewed for the JustEdu project.[4] If the relation to the "Other" mirrors national aspirations, then exploring the conjunctural reconfigurations in the field of international mobilities il-luminates the racial dimensions of nation building during postsocialism. As such, it sheds light on the "whitening" of Eastern Europe more generally during this period. In the case of Bulgarian universities, such "whitening" involved rendering certain popu-lations invisible. As sociologist Svetla Koleva recently claimed in an interview for Bul-garian National Radio: the "institutional invisibility of [African students] is actually the most visible trace of Bulgaria's educational system prior to 1989."[5]

This chapter analyzes how students from Africa, Latin America, and Asia were con-stituted as "foreign friends" and part of socialist Bulgaria's internationalist project. As a corollary, it considers how this "friendship" produced aspirations within such students for continued enhancement of their material conditions. It then examines how politi-cal and economic measures implemented after 1989 were used to essentially coerce for-eign students to leave the country. These included administrative initiatives that turned foreigners' education into a free market enterprise—a necessary step in discontinuing previously established patterns of social inclusion deemed "communist." Efforts to ad-ministratively force foreigners out of the country, a political strategy designed to bring Bulgaria closer to a communist-free and democratic future, occurred simultaneously with increased everyday racial violence against African and Asian students and work-ers, revealing deep-seated postsocialist nationalist and anticommunist sentiments. In addition to administrative practices, this included discursive practices. Thus, the se-mantic cross-pollination of "foreigners" and "communists" in the 1990s transformed foreign nationals into unwanted residues of the communist past, culminating in the mass (and forced) exodus of foreign students from Bulgaria after 1989. This was part of larger transformations taking place throughout the former Eastern Bloc in the 1990s: as Eastern European countries sought to "return to Europe," they broke from earlier dis-courses and practices of inclusion, in particular socialist internationalism and engage-ments with countries in the Global South.

My analysis draws on archival documents from the Council of Ministers (CM), the Institute for Foreign Students (IFS), the Central Committee of the Bulgarian Commu-nist Party (CCBCP), the Ministry of Internal Affairs (MIA), and twenty-seven inter-views conducted with former students from Tanzania, Benin, Nigeria, Ghana, Zambia, and Congo who resided in Bulgaria between the early 1980s and the 1990s. Arriving in Bulgaria—a country many had never heard of—in their early twenties, these students were eager to receive an advanced education. Stemming from different socioeconomic backgrounds, the students viewed the exchanges as opportunities for upward mobility and for receiving an advanced education, which was unavailable to them in their home countries, though some also came to Bulgaria out of curiosity. While some were drawn to Bulgaria because of its socialist ideology, most students were apolitical and gener-ally ignored the ideological aspects of their education in Bulgaria.

FROM INCLUSION TO EXPULSION

In a 2005 study, Anna Krasteva claimed that Bulgaria's "ethnocultural diversity" creates epistemic conditions for the exclusion of immigrants as carriers of diversity—a result of communist societies' closed character.[6] Articles published in the same volume, however, revealed a starkly different reality, demonstrating how socialism, through student and worker exchanges in the 1960s and 1970s, created conditions for the formation of immigrant communities in Bulgaria. Given that socialist Bulgaria was not an inert or closed society, how might we explain the about-face of postsocialist governments after 1989? How, as a result of political conjuncture, did Bulgaria move from promoting socialist internationalism to promoting antiforeignism (in particular against Third World nationals), which it considered necessary for successfully transitioning to liberal democracy?

While research on the relationship between socialist and postcolonial spaces and peoples is prodigious, there has been no sustained analysis of the exclusion processes that occurred in the former Eastern Bloc during the 1990s. Saskia Sassen's notion of expulsion as "people, enterprises, and places expelled from the core social and economic orders of our time" is helpful in this regard, as it incorporates the social and political aspects of economic processes, enabling an examination of its workings in various contexts.[7] Although Sassen focuses on expulsions in economies that transitioned from Keynesian logics of social inclusion to neoliberal logics of exclusion, here I analyze them with reference to the transition from a planned to a free market economy. To understand the rationale behind postsocialist expulsions in Bulgaria, Sassen's "logics of social inclusion," which eventually became an expensive economic and symbolic burden for the restoration of "democracy," needs to be explored.

THE POLITICS OF FRIENDSHIP

In Bulgaria, students from postcolonial countries could enroll in undergraduate and graduate education via three types of stipends provided by states (either Bulgaria or the student's country of origin), international organizations (e.g., UNESCO), or Bulgarian-based mass organizations (e.g., the Committee for Solidarity with the Peoples of Africa and Asia; the Bulgarian Trade Union). Alternatively, they could be self-sponsored.[8] Foreign students were implicitly separated into two categories by the Bulgarian state: those who didn't have a particular affiliation with communist and progressive movements and those who associated with "communist, revolutionary-democratic, national-liberation, and progressive" parties.[9] Both types of students, however, had equal access to education and public services.[10] The training of cadres from postcolonial countries was considered necessary for socialist modernization, thus exchange programs aimed to provide students with knowledge for the "building of socialism" in their home countries.[11] To this end, the Bulgarian Communist Party's 1969 July Plenum called for comprehensive educational reform, including increasing the number of Third World nationals in the country at the expense of students from socialist countries, strengthening the class dimension in recruitment, and increasing the number of state sponsorships at the expense of self-sponsored arrivals.[12] This "Third World" turn in education was rationalized as an "important internationalist task" in accordance with COMECON's decision to widen member states' reception and training of foreign students to "respond to the needs of developing countries."[13] The relationship between socialist countries and revolutionary states took the form of "establishing friendships." While these friendships assumed different forms of cooperation, student exchanges between socialist and postcolonial countries enhanced the strategic importance of the concept.[14] Now, educators had to work with students who were not necessarily convinced communists as their countries often oscillated between capitalist and socialist modernity.

This semantic representation placed a distinctive figure at the center of educational politics: the "friends." Friends were constituted as subjects *of* politics from a part of the world that was organizing itself against a common enemy (i.e., capitalist imperialists). They were also a subject *in* politics as the PRB encouraged them to take part in federations that organized international symposiums, to distribute political pamphlets, and to participate in political demonstrations to raise awareness about the atrocities committed against the peoples of Africa, Asia, and the Arab world. Foreign students were also a subject of *future* politics, as they were expected to use their newly acquired knowledge to foster socialist relations at home. As a 1967 document written by the Commission for the Work with Foreign Students indicates, foreign students in the PRB were considered "capital" that "cannot be wasted."[15] Mass organizations and educational institutions were thus expected to continue their relationships with students after their return home. This included sending them scientific literature, encouraging them to actively participate in events organized by Bulgarian embassies, and continuously distributing socialist propaganda from Bulgaria.[16]

"Friendship" presupposed equal access to social reproduction infrastructures such as educational, leisure, transportation, and health care services. In some cases, these services did not live up to students' expectations, as Kafil, a Tanzanian who arrived in Sofia in 1984 when he was in his twenties, remembered:

> [In Tanzania] we lived in poverty, so we were expecting to see modern things [in Bulgaria]. But later, we discovered that life in Bulgaria is very equal. There was equality. Professors and students, we all rode the bus, the ticket was 0,06 BGN. With the stipend of 110 BGN, we could live quite securely.[17]

Integrationist strategies, which were part of the PRB's "friendly" policies, supported students' adjustment to everyday life in Bulgaria. As such, students were enrolled in Bulgarian language courses and had access to canteens, dormitories, subsidized holidays, and vocational training. Our interlocutors had fond memories of their teachers and professors, whose names they still remembered. Amadi, who is from Benin, recalled that IFS teachers walked around town with them and took them shopping in an effort to help them learn the language and experience everyday life in Bulgaria. In addition to enjoying state-sponsored vacations in Black Sea and mountain resorts, attending concerts, and traveling around Bulgaria, the students met people from all over the world. They also recalled interactions with "ordinary" Bulgarians, namely outside the educational sphere, including the warm welcome they received from Bulgarians who were genuinely curious about their lives back home. Such exchanges often led to long-lasting friendships.

Yet, foreign students' experiences were not always pleasant. Kafil recalled encountering everyday racism more than once, noting that African students had problems with the militia, who at times exhibited racist behavior. Additionally, other interviewees recalled hearing racist remarks in shops and on buses. This was especially the case when the foreign students were in the company of Bulgarian women. Indeed, stories of "whispering behind their backs" and fights due to their relationships with Bulgarian women were common. Racism was evident at official levels as well. In 1964 the Ministry of People's Education called attention to the "behavior of some Bulgarian female students" studying abroad. In a previously "top-secret" document, the Bulgarian ambassador in Hungary expressed concern about Bulgarian women who had entered into intimate relations with men from Africa and other "non-European countries." The alarmist tone of the letter reflected racialized undertones: "We [the country] either have to endure the situation . . . or undertake measures towards the ending of such relationships . . . which of course, if not done carefully, could have adverse consequences for us." The "adverse consequences" that concerned the ambassador were the internal contradictions related to antiracist policies and everyday practices exhibited toward the PBR's "friends."[18] As racism was antithetical to socialist ideology, such sentiments risked undermining the positive relations with "developing countries" that Bulgaria sought to cultivate. Members of the CCBCP sought to distance themselves from this inconvenient reality by ascribing expressions of racism to uneducated or psychopathic "elements" in Bulgaria, thereby avoiding the problem altogether.

The consequence of such avoidance would rear its head after the collapse of socialism, as racial violence became a vehicle for displaying anticommunism by skinhead groups.[19] This "friendship" between the PRB and anticolonial movements thus clashed with the approach taken by postsocialist governments, namely "the friends of my enemies are my enemies." Visible bearers of socialist internationalism, foreign students, after 1989, were constituted as residues of the communist past that needed to be rapidly extricated from the social fabric. As one of my interlocuters—a translator of Arabic who worked for the international department of the CCBCP and was later lecturer to Third World unionists—noted, "the conceptual apparatus [in the early 1990s] became completely confused." He concluded that intellectuals and opponents of communism started to identify as democrats, which, in the lexicon of that time, simply meant anti-communists. Thus, he could not help but notice that attitudes toward foreigners had changed because it was assumed they were communists. African, Asian, and Arab students were guilty by association.

FROM FRIENDSHIP TO ENMITY

At the beginning of 1989, nothing indicated that Bulgaria would soon suspend relations with "fraternal" states in the Third World. When, in 1985, Czechoslovakia dramatically decreased the number of Vietnamese workers allowed into the country and East Germany threatened to halt exchange programs altogether, the Bulgarian leadership invited Vietnamese laborers to Bulgaria.[20] The situation in the area of education was similar, with Bulgarian universities receiving students from abroad and the IFS continuing its training programs. Indeed, in 1989, the Academy of Social Sciences and Social Management (ASSSM) even called for an increase in foreign students' stipends and an improvement of their material circumstances.[21]

Within months, however, politically affiliated students (PAFS; foreign students who were associated with communist, trade unionist, and revolutionary movements or holders of scholarships sponsored by the Communist Party and affiliated organizations) went from being friends to enemies.[22] On November 3, 1989, Bulgaria witnessed its first demonstration against the BCP, organized by the environmental group *Ecoglasnost*. A week later, Communist Party leader Todor Zhivkov was forced by members of the Politburo to resign as first chairman of the State Council and general secretary of the CCBCP. Political crisis within the BCP, developments in the Eastern Bloc, and growing protests by dissident groups thus facilitated regime change in Bulgaria. Democratic elections were held in June 1990, with the Bulgarian Socialist Party (BSP) competing against the Union of the Democratic Forces (UDF).[23] Unlike other Eastern European countries, where the first democratic elections were won by opponents of communism, in Bulgaria the BSP earned a majority (52.75 percent). Nonetheless, the campaigns of both political parties were organized in view of the "recent past," with the BSP "demarcating itself from Zhivkov and his entourage" and the UDF issuing a slander campaign against the communist past.[24] The "recent past"—including Bulgaria's financial support for anticolonial movements and postcolonial states—would fuel political passions in the coming years.

As in other former socialist states, in Bulgaria internationalism and developmental aid to postcolonial states fell victim to micro- and macroeconomic restructuring and a nationalism cloaked in financial anxieties over excessive spending on "developing" countries.[25] Anthropologist Maxim Matusevich describes the departure of foreign students in the 1990s as a "logical end" to the encounter between Africa and the USSR; the result of a *perestroika* that blamed domestic shortcomings on expenses in the Third World and of disgruntled Bulgarians who construed foreigners as "privileged" because of their access to certain goods.[26] While the types of nationalisms in Bulgaria at the time were as varied as the political parties, a common trope used by all was the "intersection between anti-internationalism . . . and anti-communism."[27] Rossen Djagalov, in his analysis of the post-Soviet Russian liberal intelligentsia, concludes that their anticommunist and anti-internationalist hegemonic struggles transformed them into racializing actors in the 1990s.[28] While these conclusions apply to postsocialist Bulgaria as well, my concern is with how racism was institutionalized via the rationales and practices used to administer expulsions. In Bulgaria, intensification of racist violence and political commitment to anticommunism were mutually reinforcing practices that created a climate in which the removal of foreigners—both from Bulgarian territory and the social fabric constitutive of their inclusion—became a primary strategy in the disintegration of socialist structures.

The BSP did not quite know how to respond to the conflation of anticommunism and antiforeignism. As the "recent past" became a weapon for the "discrediting and elimination of political opponents," the party was forced to develop an ambiguous political identity vis-à-vis the socialist era.[29] On the one hand, it had to distance itself from the past and represent itself as its democratic alternative. On the other hand, it could not completely renounce the past as that would have meant total depersonalization.[30] Yet, as Iskra Baeva points out, the integration of the BSP into Western socialist internationalist structures required renouncing "totalitarian communists in the East." Thus, the BSP was compelled to end previously "friendly" internationalist relations with Third World revolutionary and communist movements to conform to its newly generated image of a social democratic party of a Western type. Essentially, foreign students could no longer rely on their local "communist friends."

ACCELERATION OF RACIST VIOLENCE

A common thread in our interviews was that although racist acts took place before 1989, their intensity was not comparable to that in the years that followed. Cipaye, a former student from Benin, recalled "there was a lot of effort put into ensuring foreigners lived securely . . . [but] towards the end of the socialist period things started to deteriorate."[31]

While Cipaye spoke of the decline in public services, he also mentioned openly racist behavior toward Africans. He noted that although he was on track to become a Bulgarian citizen in the 1990s, he chose to leave the country out of concern with growing material insecurity and racism.

The term "skinheads" appears in many former foreign students' memories, which is not surprising given that such subcultures developed in Eastern European countries in the 1980s.[32] However, such groups were not as prominent in Bulgaria as in the German Democratic Republic (GDR) or Hungary.[33] While some interlocutors mentioned skinheads' presence prior to 1989, they noted that they became more visible after the changes. Abeo, a Nigerian who studied at the ASSSM, claimed that starting in 1990, "nationalists became stern." He remembered how, at a bus station in 1991, someone waved a Philip Morris cigarette in front of him, malevolently shouting: "Look! Your time is over! I can now buy whatever I want!" This comment by a random citizen illustrates the conflation of "foreigner" with "communist," reflecting a common perception during the socialist period that foreign nationals were akin to the communist *nomenklatura* in their privileged consumption of Western goods, exemplified by the signifier "Philip Morris." The collapse of communism thus emboldened public displays of racism, which, while in existence before 1989, had been subdued.

Malike, a Ghanian who graduated with a PhD in philosophy in 1991, recalled that after *perestroika,* intense anticommunist agitation took place and foreign students became objects of "ruder behavior." He attributed this change to citizens' impression that "somehow foreigners were part of the problem inherited in communism." According to Malike, this created a sense among his compatriots that walking down the streets was not as safe as it had been. When asked whether such violence was provoked by the changes and if such sentiments existed prior to the collapse of socialism, Malike asserted: "Both. I think it is a bit mixed. Some wanted to do such stuff before that, but they could not. I believe there is a fine line."[34] Malike's "fine line" captures the extent of racist violence after 1989. As noted, under socialism "non-European" foreigners were constituted in racialized terms, exemplified in the letter of the Bulgarian ambassador. His conscious efforts to mask racism, CCBCP's uncomfortable murmur when faced with racist expressions and behaviors, and the party's requirements for more internationalism-in-action within the ranks of mass organizations reveal prior awareness of the contradictions faced by an officially antiracist state. Public sentiments that construed foreigners as privileged, along with racist manifestations, were viewed by CCBCP members as acts of nationalism inherited from interwar capitalism and as evidence of poor training in internationalism within the ranks of mass organizations. These rationalizations produced a political strategy according to which ideological education acquired a privileged position vis-à-vis internal struggles against racism. Intellectuals and the CCBCP often called for intensified education in the "spirit of internationalism" and for a "determined struggle to overpower the residues of bourgeois nationalism and chauvinism."[35]

In July 1990, Andrey Lukanov's (BSP) Council of Ministers created "conditions for the accelerated return of Vietnamese citizens," followed by the creation of an antiforeigner commission on August 5, 1991.[36] By mid-1990, racial violence had become intolerable. In a letter to President Zhelyu Zhelev (UDF) from October 1990, the Union of Vietnamese Students warned of intensified violence against foreign students.[37] They described the situation as "unacceptable" and feared it would grow out of control. At the same time, a symbolic war between different media outlets—those of the opposition and those of BSP—rapidly sought to define the place of Third World foreigners in the emerging postsocialist climate. Anticommunist newspapers such as *Demokratsia* and *Podkrepa* employed terms such as "Vietnamese syndrome" and "Vietnamada," construing Vietnamese nationals as imports of communism who accumulated wealth without working. In this manner, heretofore "foreign friends" were rapidly marked as "foreign enemies" whose presence threatened Bulgaria's efforts to "return" to a communist-free and democratic Europe.

The conflation of communist with foreigner and the transformation of foreign student as the subject *par excellence* of socialist internationalism to a carrier of a communist disease was politically expedient. Antiforeignism became a rhetorical device that signaled belonging to the democratic opposition and served as a basis for reinventing the national body, divorced from its postcolonial encounters. Accordingly, foreign workers were represented as an "impurity" (i.e., agents of social dumping), akin to the communist elite, impeding Bulgaria's immanent path toward a free market economy. As such, both needed to be eradicated from the body politic or country.

ADMINISTERING THE EXPULSIONS

By the 1989–1990 academic year, 2,300 foreign students had officially completed their education in Bulgaria as part of exchanges between Bulgarian communist organizations and foreign political organizations.[38] After Andrey Lukanov, prime minister of Bulgaria between September and December 1990, resigned, a coalition government supported by the BSP, the UDF, and the Bulgarian Agrarian National Union (BANU) was formed, led by the independent Dimitar Popov.[39] During Popov's time in office, the social expulsion and eventual departure of PAFS was raised repeatedly. In a letter to Popov from January 1991, the minister of science and higher education, Georgy Fotev (Independent), listed the number of PAFS, their distribution according to political organizations, and the budget allocated to them.[40] Fotev claimed that Lukanov had previously assured him that the government would work toward suspending PAFS applicants and stop subsidizing their travel, while allowing those already enrolled to finish their degrees. While Fotev was satisfied with the first two propositions, he demanded that the third one be reconsidered. Fotev was concerned that the financial support—4.2 billion leva for the 1990–1991 academic year for the remaining 940 PAFS (out of a total of 1,225 foreign students)—was beyond Bulgaria's budget.[41] Instead, Fotev suggested that the state suspend PAFS' stipends and that students continue their studies at the expense of the successor political organizations that brought them to Bulgaria in the first place—even though these had been or were in the process of being dissolved.[42]

In August, the CM approved Decision #255, suspending support for foreign high school pupils, higher education students, PhDs, and trainees admitted to communist organizations.[43] This soon led to a heated situation, including protests by foreign students and embassies. Addae, who was from Tanzania, recalls that prior to 1990, teachers "behaved with us like parents behave with children." Having established good relations with his colleagues, Addae "felt quite at home" and assured us that while there were "elements for whom it was not easy to interact, those people were there, we could see them … but that was not the norm; that was not what Bulgarians stood for." Addae graduated in fall 1991, and while he hoped to continue with his graduate studies, he was stuck in Bulgaria "without sponsorship, unable to continue [studying] as [he] couldn't pay the enrollment fees."[44]

In October 1991, new elections ousted Popov's cabinet and the UDF took power with Philip Dimitrov as prime minister. Decision #255 was annulled, creating a diplomatic scandal. Furthermore, it led to a chaotic situation as foreign students continued to attend lectures, ate in the canteens, slept in the dormitories, and were even "getting ready to take part in final exams" without paying their student fees.[45] "Practically, these students still have full student rights," wrote the deputy minister of education, Vassilev. In another report written by Vassilev and Ganev (minister of foreign affairs), we learn that "the previous MC has not sufficiently taken into account the complexity and complication [stemming from the suspension of PAFS], the consequences for the students, and the problems before higher education institutions and respectively before our country."[46] At the same time, many Bulgarian universities barred from campus foreign students who had not paid tuition for the 1992–1993 academic year. Foreign students in turn protested Decision #255 for "unexpectedly and unjustly" taking away their sponsorship and requested full restoration of student rights and an improvement of their material conditions.[47]

Dimitrov's government lost a no-confidence vote at the end of 1992, and the final decision regarding PAFS was left in the hands of Lyuben Berov's (an Independent, supported by the party of the Turkish minority, the Movement for Rights and Freedoms) cabinet.[48] Shortly after assuming power, Berov's cabinet took a retroactive decision that transferred the responsibility for foreign students from the state to higher education institutions, obliging universities to cover students' stipends from their own budgets.[49] While Fotev's initial questioning of continued support for foreign students concerned the PAFS, its effects would resonate throughout the entire foreign student body. As Professor Papazchev remarked, "How did it turn out?! Somebody invites them and now somebody else has to foot the bill."[50] As a result of neoliberal reforms, then, foreign students went from being "friends" to a profit-making enterprise. Today, foreign students pay eleven times more in student fees than Bulgarians and EU citizens.

CONCLUSION: FINE LINES

When speaking to Abeo about his experiences under socialism and postsocialism he became emotional:

> [Although there were attacks before 1989], the Changes empowered the nationalists. Imagine that! I came back to Bulgaria in 2014. I could not go out of the hotel. It was so scary. I could not walk in downtown Sofia. This is not the Bulgaria that I knew![51]

Despite official reports that portrayed socialist Bulgaria as a racism-free society, archival documents point to an uncomfortable awareness, among high-ranking officials, of the opposite. A struggle was unfolding within state structures between representatives of embassies and economic and educational units. Continuous calls on the part of the CCBCP for more decisive internationalism-in-action and intellectuals' appeals for a determined struggle against the remnants of bourgeois nationalism were not without situated meaning. They speak to a recognition that antiracist struggles were far from over. African students also struggled to make sense of how racism could exist in a socialist country. While posing as proud antiracists for the outside world, the socialist state and its mass organizations were ripped apart on the inside because of that painful awareness, a reality that affected the experiences of the foreign students. As Zhivka Valiavicharska asserts, to be able to critically examine socialism's legacies, including that of its promise to internationalism, we need to first acknowledge it as "a front of resistance."[52] From here, we can approach it as a continuous struggle against outside determinants, but also against internal conjunctures.

It would perhaps be easier to point to continuities between the abovementioned contradictions and the outbreak of racist violence in the postsocialist period. This, however, would undermine the micro and macro destructions of all that was, and still is, deemed "communist."[53] Indeed, Abeo's recollection from the beginning of this section necessitates a different approach. Malike's "fine line" continues to ring in my head and makes it difficult to speak of continuities between the socialist and postsocialist periods.

To point to continuities is to disregard the intentionality of the administrative procedures that secured the students' exodus. Otherwise, we risk dehistoricizing and flattening racializing grammars and thereby missing substantial nuances in the experiences of the objects of racism and the structural changes in racializing practices. It is precisely Malike's "fine line" that researchers need to interrogate and examine.

Something broke beyond recognition in the 1990s. Internationalism, as a political strategy, was made to disappear from the postsocialist horizon. These early forms of anticommunism and anti-internationalism continue to reproduce conditions for a "real existing" postsocialism, where, as the introduction to this volume argues, representations of socialism as a deviation from a "normal" path justify social exclusions. As demonstrated here, the postsocialist state perpetuated violent expulsions—both through severe social exclusion and forced exoduses—in the name of anticommunism. The expulsion of nonwhite foreigners was objectively inscribed in institutional settings and procedures. These processes entrenched deep structures of meaning that conditioned postsocialist xenophobic nationalisms, constituting a rupture with socialist practices and logics.

Racializing grammars found in "actual postsocialism" run on an imposed memory loss of the practice of "friendship" Bulgaria had once established with countries outside the Euro-Atlantic axis. "Real postsocialism" thrives on constant reinstitutionalization of whiteness—in education, in international migration practices, and in international relations—that allows for further implementation of budget cuts and desocialization of public services. The early 1990s continued to display *longue durée* effects on the local experiences of African, Asian, and Arab communities in postsocialist Bulgaria. The historical force with which anticommunism and anti-internationalism promised to end bad governance, in fact, reinforced a real existing postsocialism inhibited by violent makings of whiter streets, educational institutions, grammars, and political spaces. As a person of color, navigating the streets of real existing postsocialism in Bulgaria requires mapping them for the purpose of avoiding potentially violent spaces.[54] Indeed, African communities in Sofia have established a system of "alarm messaging," warning of racist packs, which Briga (a dual citizen of Bulgaria and Congo Brazzaville) angrily described when speaking about current racist violence in the city. Former prime minister Kiril Petkov's words, bluntly uttered in March 2022 to calm the public before the imminent Ukrainian refugee crisis, are telling. He assured Bulgarian citizens that Ukrainians are "Europeans, intelligent, educated, part of them, IT specialists. . . . This is not the usual refugee wave of people with unclear pasts."[55]

The restoration of capitalism occurred alongside a radical eradication of the forms of knowledge that governed socialist operations and socialist internationalism. These eradications were not exclusive to Bulgaria but occurred in other former socialist states such as the former GDR and the USSR as well. Previously established solidarities between Bulgaria and anti(neo)colonial struggles were narrated as a financial debt generator. Anti-internationalist sentiments grew so strong that Todor Zhivkov was accused of economic sabotage because of the PRB's international aid, in effect turning the operationalization of socialist internationalism into treason. Bulgaria's refusal to reestablish meaningful relations with its former students from Africa is subordinated precisely to this postsocialist deep structure.

NOTES

1. Christina Schwenkel, "Rethinking Asian Mobilities: Socialist Migration and Post-Socialist Repatriation of Vietnamese Contract Workers in East Germany," *Critical Asian Studies*, no. 2 (April 2014): 235–58. See also, James Mark, Artemy M. Kalinovsky, and Steffi Marung, eds, *Alternative Globalizations: Eastern Europe and the Postcolonial World* (Bloomington: Indiana University Press, 2020); Alena K. Alamgir, "Labor and Labor Migration in State Socialism," *Labor History* no. 3 (February 2018): 271–76; Mariya Ivancheva, "Paternalistic Internationalism and (De)Colonial Practices of Cold War Higher Education Exchange: Bulgaria's Connections with Cuba and Angola," *Journal of Labor and Society* 22, no. 4 (December 2019): 733–48.

2. Eduard Malhasyan, "Neokolonializmat i Osnovnite Protivorechia v Razvivashtite se Strani," *Mezhdunardoni Otnoshenia*, no. 3 (1974): 38–56.

3. Marcia C. Schenck, *Remembering African Labor Migration to the Second World: Socialist Mobilities between Angola, Mozambique, and East Germany* (Cham: Palgrave Macmillan, 2023).

4. The author gratefully acknowledges the support of the project "Dynamics of Inequalities in Participation in Higher and Adult Education: A Comparative Social Justice Perspective," JustEdu (2020–2024), funded by the Bulgarian National Science Fund within National Science Program VIHREN, contract number КП-06-ДВ-2/16.12.2019: https://justedu2020.eu/. Interviews were conducted between October 2021 and February 2022 by Svetla Koleva, Vesselina Kachakova, and Raia Apostolova.

5. Svetla Koleva, interviewed by Irina Nedeva, "Skasana e Vrazkata s Afrikanskite Specialisti, Zavarshili u Nas," *BNR*, November 1, 2019 [Скъсана е връзката с африканските специалисти, завършили у нас—Посоки—БНР Новини (bnr.bg)]. See also, Svetla Koleva, "The 'Useless' Other: African Specialists Trained in Bulgaria in the 1960–1990s," *Sociological Problems* 52, no. 1 (2020): 68–87.

6. Anna Krasteva, "Balgarskiat Imigratsionen Fenomen," in *Imigratsiata v Balgaria*, ed. Anna Krasteva (Sofia: IMIR, 2005), 7–18.

7. Saskia Sassen, *Expulsions: Brutality and Complexity in the Global Economy* (Cambridge, MA: Harvard University Press, 2014).

8. For a detailed analysis of the programs, see Vesselina Kachakova and Svetla Koleva, "Social Justice at Stake: Education of African Students in Bulgaria 1960–1990," *Sociological Problems* 54, no. 1 (2022): 49–70; and Gabriela Boneva, "Role and Functions of the Institute of Foreign Students in Sofia in the 1960s and the First Half of the 1970s," *Historical Review* 4 (2021): 120–39.

9. Most of the interviewees fall within the first group. For a similar composition in Czechoslovakia, see Barbora Buzássyová, "Repositioning of Czechoslovak Educational Strategies to the 'Least Developed Countries': The Rise and Decline of University of 17th November," in *Socialist Educational Cooperation and the Global South,* ed. Ingrid Miethe and Jane Weiss (Berlin: Peter Lang, 2020), 183–204.

10. The Academy of Social Sciences and Social Management was a CCBCP structure whose purpose was to create a vanguard of governmental cadres. At the end of 1987, none of the academy students were of Western origin. State Central Archive Fund 1Б-Inventory 83-Archival unit 433, 7-9 (hereafter, archival data will be cited as: SCA). Students enrolled in the Academy of Social Sciences and Social Management were given larger stipends than at "regular" universities.

11. Constantin Katsakioris, "Students from Portuguese Africa in the Soviet Union, 1960–74: Anti-Colonialism, Education, and the Socialist Alliance," *Journal of Contemporary History* 56, no. 1 (2021): 142–65; and Barbora Buzássyová, "Socialist Internationalism in Practice: Shifting Patterns of the Czechoslovak Educational Aid Programs to Sub-Saharan Africa, 1961–1989" (PhD diss., Slovak Academy of Sciences, 2021).

12. SCA 763-2-2, 20-24.

13. SCA 763-2-2, 20.

14. Rachel Applebaum, "The Friendship Project: Socialist Internationalism in the Soviet Union and Czechoslovakia in the 1950s and 1960s," *Slavic Review* 74, no. 3 (Fall 2015): 484–507.

15. SCA 858-1-15, 8.

16. SCA 858-1-15, 8-9.

17. All interviewees' names have been changed.

18. This clue comes from documents on which CCBCP members would correct racist grammars. See, for example, SCA 174Б-2-994, 5-6.

19. For further discussion of these contradictions, see Hilary Lynd and Thom Lloyd, "Histories of Color: Blackness and Africanness in the Soviet Union," *Slavic Review* 81, no. 2 (Summer 2022): 394–417; and Peter Wright, "'Are There Racists in Yugoslavia?' Debating Racism and Anti-Blackness in Socialist Yugoslavia," *Slavic Review* 81, no. 2 (Summer 2022): 418–41.

20. SCA 607-6c-10, 8.

21. SCA 1Б-54-186, 1-8.

22. These organizations included the Bulgarian Communist Party (BCP), the Bulgarian

Trade Unions, the Women's Committee, and the Committee for Solidarity with the Peoples of Africa and Asia, among others.

23. The BCP changed its name to Bulgarian Socialist Party in April 1990. The Union of Democratic Forces was an umbrella term for various ASSSM political groups such as *Ecoglasnost,* the trade union *Podkrepa,* and the Bulgarian Agricultural People's Union, among others.

24. Iskra Baeva, "BSP na Vlast i v Opositsia v Godinite na Prehoda," in *Izsledvania po Istoria na Sotsializma v Balgaria,* ed. Lilyana Kaneva, Maxim Mizov, and Evgenii Kandilarov (Sofia: Center for Historical and Political Research, 2011).

25. For the GDR, see Schenck, *Remembering African Labor,* 217–21.

26. Maxim Matusevich, "Probing the Limits of Internationalism," *Anthropology of East Europe Review* 27 no. 2 (Fall 2009): 19–39.

27. Kiril Kertikov, "Democratsia i Post-Totalitaren Natsionalisam," *Sociological Problems* 26, no. 3 (1994): 76–84.

28. Rossen Djagalov, "Racism, the Highest Stage of Anticommunism," *Slavic Review* 80, no. 2 (September 2021): 290–98.

29. Evgenii Kandilarov, "Otnoshenieto na BSP kam Sotsialisticheskoto Minalo," in *Izsledvania po Istoria na Sotsializma v Balgaria,* ed. Lilyana Kaneva, Maxim Mizov, and Evgenii Kandilarov (Sofia: Center for Historical and Political Research, 2011), 338–76.

30. Kandilarov, "Otnoshenieto na BSP," 348.

31. Cipaye, interview by Svetla Koleva, online, February 8, 2022.

32. Josef Smolík and Petr Novák, "Roots of the Czechoslovak Skinheads: Development, Trends and Politics," *Human Affairs* 29, no. 2 (May 2019): 157–73.

33. Gideon Botsch, "From Skinhead-Subculture to Radical Right Movement: The Development of a 'National Opposition' in East Germany," *Contemporary European History* 21, no. 4 (September 2019): 553–73. For Bulgaria, see Vihra Barova, "Genesis of the Subcultural Identity of the Football Fans," *Balgarska Etnologia,* no. 1 (2014): 7–22.

34. Malike, interview by author, online, October 27, 2021.

35. Todor Ganchev, "Edinstvoto na natsionalnoto i internatsionalnoto vav vanshnata politika na sotsialisticheskite strain," *Mezhdunarodni Otnoshenia* 3 (1975): 17–27.

36. SCA 136-85-347; SCA 136-85-387.

37. SCA 1224-2-821, 18-19.

38. SCA 136-87-565, p. 3, 1991. The author notes that this number is significantly underestimated.

39. His government was called "of national consent." Out of the nineteen ministers, seven were members of BSP, three of UDF, two of BANU, and seven were independent.

40. SCA 136-86-565, 6-9.

41. SCA 136-87-565, 4-5.

42. SCA 136-87-565, 5. Most of the organizations had already been dissolved.

43. SCA 136-87-565, 1.

44. Addae, interview by author, online, November 2, 2021.

45. SCA 136-88-1060, 29.

46. SCA 136-88-1120, 5.

47. SCA 136-88-1120, 9.

48. Lyuben Berov was a counselor to UDF President Zhelev. His cabinet (December 1992–October 1994) was a coalition government between the Alternative Social-Liberal Party, UDF, the Movement for Rights and Freedoms, and the Bulgarian Social-Democratic Party.

49. Meanwhile, those students who needed to repeat an academic year (except for cases of maternity and sick leave) were obliged to cover educational costs on their own. In the beginning of the 1992/1993 academic year, the PAFS in Bulgaria hosted 624 foreign students from 55 countries. SCA 136-88-1120, 12-14. Only two of the countries of origin (Greece and Portugal) were considered Western.

50. SCA 136-89-454, 9.

51. Abeo, interview by author, online, March 4, 2022.

52. Zhivka Valiavicharska, *Restless History: Political Imaginaries and Their Discontents in Post-Stalinist Bulgaria* (Montreal: McGill–Queen's University Press, 2021).

53. On the complexity of continuities and ruptures of nationalism in Bulgaria, see Neda Genova, "Recursive Lions and Strange Continuities of Bulgarian Nationalism," *European Review 30*, no. 4 (August 2022): 505–18.

54. Lea Vajsova, "Kakvo e da si Chernokoj Imigrant v Balgaria?" *Marginalia*, March 3, 2015.

55. Petkov, Kiril, "Kiril Petkov napravi rasistko izkazvane za bezhantsite [Kiril Petkov made a racist comment toward refugees]," *Glasove*, February 25, 2022. https://glasove.com/politika/kiril-petkov-napravi-rasistko-izkazvane-za-bezhantsite.

BIBLIOGRAPHY

Alamgir, Alena. "Labor and Labor Migration in State Socialism." *Labor History* 59, no. 3 (February 2018): 271–76.

Applebaum, Rachel. "The Friendship Project: Socialist Internationalism in the Soviet Union and Czechoslovakia in the 1950s and 1960s." *Slavic Review* 74, no. 3 (Fall 2015): 484–507.

Baeva, Iskra. "BSP na vlast i v opositsia v godinite na prehoda" [BSP in power and in opposition in the years of the transition]. In *Izsledvania po istoria na sotsializma v Balgaria* [Research in the history of socialism in Bulgaria], edited by Lilyana Kaneva, Maxim Mizov, and Evgenii Kandilarov, 248–87. Sofia: Center for Historical and Political Research, 2011.

Barova, Vihra. "Genesis of the Subcultural Identity of the Football Fans." *Balgarska Etnologia* no. 1 (2014): 7–22.

Boneva, Gabriela. "Rolia i funktsii na Instituta za chuzhdestranni studenti v Sofia prez 60-te iparvata polovina na 70-te godini na XX vek" [Role and functions of the Institute of Foreign Students in Sofia in the 1960s and the first half of the 1970s]. *Historical Review* 4 (2021): 120–39.

Botsch, Gideon. "From Skinhead-Subculture to Radical Right Movement: The Development of a National Opposition in East Germany." *Contemporary European History* 21, no. 4 (September 2019): 553–73.

Buzássyová, Barbora. "Repositioning of Czechoslovak Educational Strategies to the 'Least Developed Countries': The Rise and Decline of University of 17th November." In *Socialist Educational Cooperation and the Global South*, edited by Ingrid Miethe and Jane Weiss, 183–204. Berlin: Peter Lang, 2020.

Buzássyová, Barbora. "Socialist Internationalism in Practice: Shifting Patterns of the Czechoslovak Educational Aid Programs to Sub-Saharan Africa, 1961–1989." PhD diss., Slovak Academy of Sciences, 2021.

Djagalov, Rossen. "Racism, the Highest Stage of Anticommunism." *Slavic Review* 80, no. 2 (September 2021): 290–98.

Ganchev, Todor. "Edinstvoto na natsionalnoto i internatsionalnoto vav vanshnata politika na sotsialisticheskite strani" [The unity of the national and the international in the external politics of the socialist countries]. *Mezhdunarodni Otnoshenia* 3 (1975): 17–27.

Genova, Neda. "Recursive Lions and Strange Continuities of Bulgarian Nationalism." *European Review* 30, no. 4 (August 2022): 505–18.

Ivancheva, Mariya. "Paternalistic Internationalism and (De)Colonial Practices of Cold War Higher Education Exchange: Bulgaria's Connections with Cuba and Angola." *Journal of Labor and Society* 22, no. 4 (2019): 733–48.

Kachakova, Vesselina, and Svetla Koleva. "Social Justice at Stake: Education of African Students in Bulgaria 1960–1990." *Sociological Problems* 54, no. 1 (Spring, 2022): 49–70.

Kandilarov, Evgenii. "Otnoshenieto na BSP kam sotsialisticheskoto minalo." In *Izsledvania po istoria na sotsializma v Balgaria* [Research in the history of socialism in Bulgaria], edited by Lilyana Kaneva, Maxim Mizov, and Evgenii Kandilarov, 338–76. Sofia: Center for Historical and Political Research, 2011.

Katsakioris, Constantin. "Students from Portuguese Africa in the Soviet Union, 1960–74: Anti-Colonialism, Education, and the Socialist Alliance." *Journal of Contemporary History* 56, no. 1 (2021): 142–65.

Kertikov, Kiril. "Democratsia i post-totalitaren natsionalisam." *Sociological Problems* 26, no. 3 (Summer 1994): 76–84.

Krasteva, Anna. "The Bulgarian Immigration Phenomenon." In *Immigration in Bulgaria*, edited by Anna Krasteva, 7–18. Sofia: IMIR, 2005.

Koleva, Svetla. *Horizont do obed*. Interviewed by Irina Nedeva. Bulgarian National Radio, November 1, 2019.

Koleva, Svetla. "'Izlishniat drug': afrikanskite spetsialisti, formirani v Balgaria prez 1960–1990 ['The Useless Other': African Specialists Trained in Bulgaria in the 1960s–1990s]." *Sociological Problems* 52, no. 1 (Spring 2020): 68–87.

Lynd, Hilary, and Thom Lloyd. "Histories of Color: Blackness and Africanness in the Soviet Union." *Slavic Review* 81, no. 2 (Summer 2022): 394–417.

Malhasyan, Eduard. "Neokolonializmat i osnovnite protivorechia v razvivashtite se strani" [Neocolonialism and the main contradictions in the developing countries]. *Mezhdunardoni Otnoshenia*, no. 3 (Winter 1974): 38–56.

Mark, James, Artemy Kalinovsky, and Steffi Marung, eds. *Alternative Globalizations: Eastern Europe and the Postcolonial World*. Bloomington: Indiana University Press, 2020.

Matusevich, Maxim. "Probing the Limits of Internationalism." *Anthropology of East Europe Review* 27 no. 2 (Fall 2009): 19–39.

Sassen, Saskia. *Expulsions: Brutality and Complexity in the Global Economy*. Cambridge, MA: Harvard University Press, 2014.

Schenck, Marcia. *Remembering African Labor Migration to the Second World: Socialist Mobilities between Angola, Mozambique, and East Germany*. Cham: Palgrave Macmillan, 2023.

Schwenkel, Christina. "Rethinking Asian Mobilities: Socialist Migration and Post-Socialist Repatriation of Vietnamese Contract Workers in East Germany." *Critical Asian Studies* 46, no. 2 (April 2014): 235–58.

Smolík, Josef, and Petr Novák. "Roots of the Czechoslovak Skinheads: Development, Trends and Politics." *Human Affairs* 29, no. 2 (May 2019): 157–73.

Vajsova, Lea. "Kakvo e da si chernokoj imigrant v Balgaria?" [What it is to be a Black immigrant in Bulgaria]. *Marginalia*. March 3, 2015.

Valiavicharska, Zhivka. *Restless History: Political Imaginaries and Their Discontents in Post-Stalinist Bulgaria*. Montreal: McGill–Queen's University Press, 2021.

Wright, Peter. "'Are There Racists in Yugoslavia?' Debating Racism and Anti-Blackness in Socialist Yugoslavia." *Slavic Review* 81, no. 2 (Summer 2022): 418–41.

PART III

SOMETHING OLD,
SOMETHING NEW

7

THE SPECTER OF SEX

Continuities and Changes in Sex Education in Postsocialist Romania

BEATRICE SCUTARU AND LUCIANA JINGA

I would like to know more about my body, to know about STIs, about how one becomes pregnant. But I want it from specialists, not from the religion teacher who blushes when we mention "sex." I grew up in a traditional family, my mother was ashamed to talk about menstruation and sex. I don't think it's shameful. The more you know, the better. And then you learn how to avoid bad people, you learn to protect your body, to understand it. . . . When I got my period, I thought I was dying. My belly hurt a lot; I was bleeding a lot. I didn't know what was happening to me. Grandma came and laughed at me: "Ha, the dog bit you!" I was ashamed and I cried. It troubled me so much that I am still ashamed.[1]

—Isabela, aged 13

SINCE THE COLLAPSE OF SOCIALISM, YOUNG PEOPLE IN ROMANIA HAVE REPEAT-edly demanded the introduction of mandatory sex education in schools. Although the topic has produced intense debates among parents, politicians, and in society at large, young people's viewpoints are rarely heard, let alone taken into account, when policies are made. This is most regrettable, for while adults debate, youth suffer the dire consequences of lack of access to information, evident in numerous health indicators. For instance, within the European Union (EU) Romania ranks among the highest in terms of rates of teen pregnancy, sexually transmitted diseases (STIs), and gender-based violence.[2] Moreover, during the first half of 2022, every day a minor was raped or sexually assaulted in Romania.[3] Despite these alarming statistics, because many young people do not know what constitutes sexual abuse, they are not always able to recognize it when it occurs.[4] Romania not only has one of the highest teen pregnancy rates in Europe, but also has some of the highest rates of maternal and child mortality, school dropout, and child abandonment.[5] In addition, Romania and Albania have the highest rates of newly diagnosed HIV/AIDS cases in Eastern Europe, despite decreases in new HIV/AIDS cases globally.[6]

Such outcomes are avoidable. Since the early 1990s, organizations and reproductive health specialists have been recommending mandatory reproductive health and sex education courses in schools to educate youth about their bodies and their rights (e.g., consent), to encourage safe sex, and to prevent teen pregnancies.[7] Surveys from the 1990s and early 2000s demonstrate that Romanian women and men of reproductive age overwhelmingly support sex education in schools.[8] Moreover, organizations representing Romanian students have long requested "an educational system that meets the needs and interests of all Romanian students, and the implementation of sex education in schools as part of a larger concern for health education."[9] However, despite the troubling sex-related health outcomes, as well as the aforementioned recommendations and requests, there is no mandatory sex education in Romanian schools—be they public or private.

At the end of June 2022, Romanian deputies voted in favor of "systematic health education programs in schools . . . for the purpose of preventing sexually transmitted diseases and the pregnancy of minors."[10] While the adoption of this law is welcome, it has two major limitations: sex education classes can begin only in eighth grade (with students aged fourteen or older) and enrollment in these courses requires the written consent of a parent or legal guardian. Such stipulations undermine the potential effectiveness of the law by denying young people the right to learn about sexual health (if their parents are opposed to it) or by delaying instruction until the early teen years (after some youths have already become sexually active). This is ironic given that the aim of the law is to reduce teen pregnancy, which has been consistently high over the last decades, with around 700 girls under fifteen years of age giving birth each year.[11] Most teen mothers in Romania live in rural areas, give birth to their first child at age 15.8, and drop out of school.[12] According to the new law, then, those most in need of sex education would receive this information too late, if at all. That said, the Romanian Parliament's law 191 (of June 29, 2022), modifying law 272/2004 regarding the protection and promotion of the rights of the child, would increase young people's access to health and sex education and represents some progress.

This chapter explores sex education in Romania from late communism to the present from the perspective of policy and everyday life, with a particular focus on young people's perspectives. We examine debates surrounding mandatory sex education with respect to religion, ethnicity, and class, considering their relationship to broader disputes between anti-abortion, anti-LGBTQ individuals, antiliberal movements, and Euroskeptics on the one hand, and supporters of the EU on the other. As such, we examine the national particularities of conflicts over sex education, as well as their transnational inspirations and connections. We demonstrate that 1989 did not signify a decisive rupture with respect to sexual health and rights, the decriminalization of abortion notwithstanding. Instead, the postsocialist period represents a nonlinear transition zone where past and present, expectations and reality intermingle and overlap.

SEXUAL PLEASURE AND REPRODUCTION DURING SOCIALISM

While women in Romania did not necessarily have better sex under socialism, sex was not a taboo topic. Indeed, sexology emerged as an important field of study across Eastern Europe during the Cold War, designed to improve people's sexual lives and overall happiness, as well as increase the birth rate. The Romanian National Commission for Demography believed that educating citizens about sex would ensure a higher birth rate, while also reducing the number of illegal abortions. In this context, Romanian medical practitioners, primarily endocrinologists, published sex manuals for young adults and married couples. The texts included information on reproductive anatomy and physiology, STIs, and the family under socialism. Promoting the sanctity of (heterosexual) marriage, the manuals often reinforced prevailing cultural norms: young women were advised to abstain from sexual relations until marriage, when their husbands would educate them in sexual matters.[13] Meanwhile, young men were encouraged to be prudent in their sexual pursuits.[14] Other books went beyond reproductive anatomy and physiology, providing information on the female orgasm, the best sexual techniques, homosexuality, and masturbation. These publications sold on average 100,000 copies per edition, reflecting their popularity.[15]

The women's and youth presses echoed much of the information presented in official sex manuals and included articles by endocrinologists and gynecologists. During the 1970s, the state socialist women's magazine, *Femeia* (*The Woman*), featured surveys about couples' sex lives, which included questions about the female orgasm and the relationship between gender equality and sexual fulfillment.[16] The magazine also published articles warning about the dangers of fertility control, some of which peddled disinformation: natural methods such as coitus interruptus were correlated with frigidity, while oral contraceptives were correlated with cancer and infertility. Finally, socialist organizations such as *Uniunea Tineretului Comunist* (Union of Communist

Youth) and *Consiliul Național al Femeilor* (National Women's Council) organized seminars for high school students and young workers, during which medical practitioners gave talks on how to have a "responsible, happy, and fulfilled family life."[17] The communist approach to sexuality thus aimed to democratize knowledge and emphasized the importance of pleasure for both individuals, albeit within a heterosexual, ideally legal (married) partnership.

Although sex education was not part of the school curriculum during the communist period, biology teachers instructed middle and high school students on reproductive anatomy and physiology, and homeroom teachers could, if they chose, lead discussions on special topics, among them sexual health and hygiene, though most preferred to avoid the subject altogether. Short classes on venereal diseases were sometimes taught by visiting health professionals, though they were held separately for boys and girls.[18] Thus middle and high school students had minimal access to sex education, and, when they did, it was heavily medicalized, focused primarily on reproductive health and the risks of pregnancy and STIs. This approach was designed to inform—and also scare—youth and, thereby, encourage abstinence until marriage, especially for females. As C. recalled, both teachers and parents were prudish and alarmist:

> They [the teachers] didn't say a word about sexuality and relationships . . . they were condemned during that period. If you had a boyfriend in high school it wasn't very socially acceptable. . . . Girls who had boyfriends were categorized as promiscuous . . . and we [my sister and I] were not allowed. The prevailing belief was that you needed to be careful because "boys can ruin your future reputation."[19]

Thus, while sex was featured in some print media (sex manuals; articles and surveys in *Femeia*) and sexual health was covered by science teachers or medical health professionals at some schools, it was generally expected that sex would be discussed in the private sphere, between parent and child. Alongside curricular limitations, there were significant rural and urban disparities with respect to access of information. Moreover, the Orthodox Church perpetuated traditional notions about sexuality, presenting premarital and extramarital sex as sinful and limiting access to information about sex. Therefore, at the time of the Romanian Revolution in 1989, views toward sex education were diverse, ranging from genuine curiosity among (probably) large segments of the population to prudish and highly conservative perspectives, which often forestalled any discussion of sex.

During the communist period many parents refused to discuss sexual health and hygiene with their children; meanwhile, schools also failed to educate young people about the topic. Indeed, even youth attending school in large cities had no knowledge about the basics of female physiology, such as menstruation. As a result, when young people did learn about sex, it was often too little, too late. Lack of knowledge about reproduction meant that abortion continued to be a primary form of birth control, both after it was decriminalized in 1957 and after it was recriminalized in 1966, especially since modern forms of fertility control were either unavailable or illegal.[20] For instance, IUDs (intrauterine devices) and hormonal methods (i.e., the Pill) were only permitted for women diagnosed with serious health conditions such as infectious and neuropsychiatric diseases and genetically transmitted maladies.[21] The toll of these restrictions on female youth and women was dramatic, and, after abortion was criminalized, tragic. Between 1979 and 1989 Romania had the highest maternal mortality rate in Europe—ten times higher than any other European country—largely abortion-related. Moreover, abortion-related complications contributed to female infertility. Finally, the rise in unwanted pregnancies, coupled with the deteriorating economic situation (characterized by the rationing of food, heat, and electricity), resulted in increases in child abandonment. Many of these abandoned children ended up in institutions, where their physical and mental health was gravely neglected.[22]

THE 1990S: UNFULFILLED PROMISES

The fall of the communist regime in December 1989 brought the promise of sexual revolution. The decriminalization of abortion was among the first laws passed by the new democratic government, the National Salvation Front (NSF), causing a surge in the abortion rate. This was accompanied by the end of state censorship, and Romanians now had access to explicit sexual content on television and in magazines. Despite these dramatic ruptures, continuities remained: sexual education was still not mandatory in schools, and middle and high schools continued to use pre-1989 materials, primarily biology texts that focused on anatomy and physiology.[23] Moreover, according to testimonials from youth who grew up in the 1990s, many parents were reluctant to speak about sex, just as their own parents had been.

Andra recalled that her parents would cover her eyes whenever a scene with nudity appeared on TV, while Ioana noted that none of the adults she grew up around dared mention the word "sex" in her presence. This left its mark. Unlike her parents, Ioana is willing to talk about sex; however, having internalized the shame attached to the word, she only feels comfortable using coded language:

> Nobody ever taught me anything about cars. They didn't think I needed to know about driving and thought I would learn about crossing the street from the kids around me . . . that I will know what I have to do when the time comes. They didn't tell me anything, because they were ashamed to talk about it.[24]

In addition, parents transmitted views about sex that they had grown up with: for girls it was the importance of abstinence (until marriage) and that boys were potentially dangerous since they were only interested in sex. In such a context, there was little or no discussion about contraception and STIs. As Kati recalled:

> A woman's virginity until marriage was put on a pedestal. My parents did not restrict me, but I started believing, during my high school years, that I could play as much as I wanted but stop at penetration. I was curious, I wanted to experiment, but at the same time, I was also afraid of sexual intercourse, of pain, of pregnancy, of people's opinion, of men's contempt.[25]

Despite having relatively liberal parents, Kati internalized broader cultural scripts, namely that motherhood was the primary objective of sex for women and premarital sex was a source of shame and should be avoided at all costs. Boys, by contrast, did not encounter such proscriptions in Romanian culture.

Adult reticence to discuss sexual matters in a mature and objective manner is a continuity with the socialist (and even presocialist) period, perpetuating a vicious cycle of ignorance. Numerous women who started their sex lives in the 1990s expressed regret over their lack of knowledge about their bodies and sex more generally. While Kati noted that she postponed penetrative sex for such a long time that she no longer remembers when and with whom she "lost her virginity," Irina did not know she was still a virgin, even though she had been in a long-term relationship:

> I realized that I had still been a virgin after the pain I felt when I got involved with another guy. That's how I found out that losing one's virginity is not really pleasant. . . . I can say that I really discovered sex only in my 30s. . . . I just didn't know how to control the situation. I let myself be dominated, it seemed to me that it did not depend on me.[26]

Another consequence of lack of sex education is continued reliance on abortion as a contraceptive method: in the 1990s, abortion was the primary means of fertility control among youths.[27] While these numbers slowly decreased over time, partly as a result of improved sex education, the abortion rate in Romania continues to be high for all age groups in comparison with other EU countries.[28]

After the fall of communism, sex education was initially under the direction of international nongovernmental organizations (NGOs) that had come to Romania to help "Ceaușescu's orphans" and reduce abortion and child abandonment rates. Along with national actors, these NGOs developed local programs that targeted mostly female youth and medical practitioners (e.g., doctors, nurses, psychologists).[29] For instance,

Doctors without Borders and Doctors of the World organized local seminars focused on reproductive health and contraception. In addition, with the support of several international agencies, local NGOs such as *Tineri pentru Tineri* (TpT; Youth for Youth), *Societatea de Educație Contraceptivă și Sexuală* (SECS; Society for Sexual and Contraceptive Education), and *Societatea Româna Anti-SIDA* (ASAS; Romanian Society Against AIDS) organized lectures in high schools about sexual health and fertility. However, as these were not nationally coordinated efforts, classes varied from locality to locality and were not available in remote, rural areas.[30]

While many parents and teachers were generally unsupportive of the Sex Education curriculum in schools, when the same content was renamed Health Education or Education for Life, they were more supportive. This was illustrated by the success of Procter and Gamble's School Program for boys and girls (grades five through seven), launched in the mid-1990s. This program organized teams of trained volunteers (primarily university students) who visited schools to speak with students about puberty, reproductive anatomy and physiology, sexual health, and the characteristics of healthy relationships.[31] During the visits, girls were provided with hygienic pads—a novelty as, prior to 1989, Romania did not produce or import feminine hygiene products. Unsurprisingly, the campaign was tremendously successful and today women still remember "the Always Girls" who visited their middle and high schools.[32] However, due to limited funds, the initiative did not reach most rural areas and children under twelve were not included.

Given that there was no state-mandated curriculum for sex education, Romanians continued to consult communist-era sex education manuals, which could often be found on the family bookshelf. In addition, teen publications such as *Bravo* magazine, which appeared in Romania in 1997, included a column dedicated to sex education.[33] As Andra recalled:

I learned about sex from the pages of Bravo magazine. . . . I learned that sex was a taboo, not to be talked about, not to be looked at. Because, every time my family bought the most recent *Bravo*, they made sure to glue the sex pages together before allowing me to see the magazine. With infinite care, I tried to cut through the glue with a razor blade. I failed to save the edges . . . but I saved enough that my heart started racing: two naked bodies, facing each other, a he and a she, Adam & Eve as for Beverly Hills 90210 fans. I read and reread the technical tips on nipples and the definition of arousal, looking disgustedly at the guy with a toned abdomen, under which hung the best hidden trunk in the world.[34]

Andra's reflections reveal young people's thirst for knowledge—and the ways they tried to circumvent limitations imposed by their parents. On the heels of *Bravo,* other publications such as *Popcorn* and *Salut* (Hi) began including pieces on sex education, becoming among the most common mediums for young people to learn about sex. According to the 1999 Romania Reproductive Health Survey, one in three (38 percent) of young females (aged fifteen to twenty-four) learned about contraception from friends or acquaintances, 25 percent from mass media or books, and 7 percent from a health care provider. Meanwhile, only 9 percent claimed their parents had taught them about contraception, and 4 percent learned about it in school.[35]

TOWARD A MORE HOLISTIC AND YOUTH-CENTERED APPROACH TO SEX EDUCATION

The 2000s brought new initiatives, as well as Romania's admission to the EU, finalized in 2007. EU admission requires alignment with a host of laws and conditions per the Copenhagen criteria, among them safeguarding children's rights and improving their living conditions. To prepare for such alignment, in 1999 the Romanian government created the National Agency for the Protection of the Rights of the Child.[36] In 2001, the Ministries for Education and Research (MEC) and Health and Family (MSF) launched a national pilot program entitled Education for Health in Romanian Schools, which, in 2004, became an optional subject for first through twelfth grades.[37]

The curriculum, which was created by primary and secondary school teachers and national and international organizations, was designed "to ensure pupils learn what a healthy lifestyle is, to facilitate access to accurate information (in both urban and rural areas), to promote adult education about sex [through their children] and to reduce illness and risky behaviors."[38] Reflecting a more holistic approach to sex education that goes beyond basic information about personal hygiene, reproductive health, and STIs, the curriculum included topics such as sexual relations, mental health, substance abuse, and violence, among other topics.[39] As such, the curriculum aimed to tackle pervasive social problems and involve parents and guardians in this process.

Education for Health, an optional class, has a number of shortcomings. First, its effectiveness has not been consistently evaluated.[40] Second, few students have access to the subject due to parental opposition and limited adoption of the curriculum.[41] Third, as sex education is not mandatory for teacher certification, only teachers willing to follow a special training program can teach Education for Health.[42] Finally, teachers can decide how—including how many hours—they want to teach the subject. As a result, many Romanian youths do not have access—or at least consistent access—to sex education classes and thus rely on their peers, NGOs, mass media, and parents to learn about sexual health and hygiene. The situation is different in private schools, which are not limited by national rules. Most private schools in Romania were established after 2010 as Romanian branches—or adaptations—of foreign secular schools (e.g., the French School, the British School, the Cambridge School). Therefore, in terms of access to education, the discrepancy is not only between rural and urban, but also between private and public schools.

After EU accession, Romania no longer received international development funds (i.e., USAID), which had subsidized sex education training programs and contraceptives for a range of groups. Without engagement and resources from international agencies, many of these efforts were not sustained. Two Romanian organizations have worked to fill this void: SECS and TpT.[43] With the help of volunteers (mainly medical students) these organizations developed sexual awareness campaigns and organized classes in rural areas, which have the highest teen pregnancy and school dropout rates. Topics covered in these classes include reproductive anatomy and physiology, STIs, contraception, pregnancy, and gender roles. Since the 2010s, sexual minorities have also been included in the classes.[44] However, due to lack of funding these initiatives have been less extensive than anticipated.

In 2013 Adriana Radu launched Sexul vs Barza (Sex vs. Stork), an online platform dedicated exclusively to sex education in Romania. Information about legislation, relationships, LGBTQ individuals, pornography, and sexual violence is shared in videos and via a YouTube channel.[45] This is the first interactive platform that features youths' questions, opinions, and concerns (the information provided is based on questions received on the platform). In addition, Radu visits schools, where she offers discussions about sex, sometimes at the pupils' request. As Monica recalled about the project:

> While I was a pupil at the George Coşbuc High School, I was the social media editor, and I did my best to help Adriana reach young people who follow us on Facebook. Why Sexul vs Barza? Because we don't know. We don't know what we want, we don't know who we are and what path we are taking. What we're doing here is teaching young people to better understand what's happening: starting with themselves.[46]

For Lorena (b. 1998), Radu's visit was transformative:

> In less than two hours, Adriana presented to us, in the simplest way possible, what sex education is and how it is presented in schools in economically developed countries. . . . Many students were thrilled with the initiative and appalled at its absence from schools. We talked about rape and when one can say no, a discussion that led to disagreements between students. The discussion continued so naturally that one wouldn't think there could be someone who couldn't understand why we need sex education in schools, leaving aside the grim statistics on the number of teenage pregnancies in Romania. . . . What is even more surprising is that, before this meeting, no

one around me had brought up the subject in any way! Of course, three years ago, there was a failed attempt to explain human anatomy to us in biology class, where it seemed normal to divide us into two groups, "boys with boys and girls with girls," for no logical reason other than to avoid jokes. Jokes. Because yes, it seemed normal for the boys to laugh when they heard words like menstruation.[47]

While these reflections point to continuities in cultural attitudes toward sex, evident in the lack of a comprehensive sex education curriculum in schools and parents' general silence around the topic, they also underscore discontinuities, namely the existence of a more open and liberal climate in which youths can speak freely about sex and sexuality.

Young people now have access to pornography, but also high-quality information, even if this is not provided by the state, but rather private initiatives. The individuals who launched these private initiatives are usually medical practitioners and/or activists for human rights, gender equality, and so on. The success of different online campaigns shows that the retrograde, prudish attitude is more a political and religious construct and does not reflect the prevailing public opinion. While Sexul vs Barza has been instrumental in transmitting information about sexuality to young people, given that not everyone has internet access, its reach is difficult to gauge.

THE BATTLE FOR CHILDHOOD: DEBATES ON MANDATORY SEX EDUCATION

Efforts to make Education for Health (and sex education more generally) mandatory in public schools began in the early 2000s. By the 2010s, mandatory sex education had become a topic of heated debate in the Romanian Parliament, Senate, and society at large, receiving widespread media coverage. Three arguments were put forward in support of mandatory sex education in schools.[48] First, by not having implemented mandatory Sex Education and Education for Health classes in its school curriculum, Romania lags behind other European countries. Second, Romania has some of the highest rates of teen pregnancy, abortion, maternal and infant mortality, school abandonment, and STI rates within the EU.[49] Third, educating the population about sex, hygiene, and nutrition will improve public health outcomes in the country more generally.[50] Proponents of mandatory sex education also juxtaposed a "modern Europe" against a "backward Romania."[51] Accordingly, the only way to close the gap and fully enter the modern era is by following Western countries' examples.

Meanwhile, those opposed to mandatory sex education in schools ("the oppositionists"), including conservative civil society organizations and religious groups, tap into parents' fears, citing threats to children's innocence. As the Romanian media thrive on controversy and panic, the oppositionists receive far more coverage than the supporters. The oppositionists began mobilizing in 2013, after the Minister of Health declared the government's intention to make health education a mandatory subject in schools.[52] They argue for the *status quo*, namely that sex education should remain an optional subject as per the Education for Health curriculum, and that abstinence until marriage should be promoted in schools. The first two arguments are based on the belief that parents should decide when and what their children should learn because, as teacher Tiberiu Paul argued, "School should not be involved in students' intimate life. These things are discussed and settled in the family."[53] MP Alin Colesa, member of AUR (Alliance for the Union of Romanians), a right-wing, nationalist party founded in 2019, went even further, noting: "We need freedom, not ideology, we need the freedom to choose how to raise our children. In a word, we don't need child masturbation, gender ideology, teenage abortion, sexualizing children."[54]

As previously noted, sex education is often presented as a threat to children's innocence and a pathway to masturbation and homosexuality. The unsuccessful Childhood Innocence Law, proposed in 2016, epitomizes these arguments: sex education will introduce young people to "pornography, LGBT proselytism, and incite various forms of deviant sexuality."[55] Efforts to curtail youths' access to sex education and depictions of sexual minorities as deviant and a threat to children's innocence fit squarely within the broader antigender movement embraced by right-wing policymakers in Poland, Hungary, and Russia. In these countries, "gender ideology" serves as the justification for a host of regressive initiatives, including anti-gender equality, anti-same-sex marriage, and anti-LGBTQ rights. These same individuals also oppose teaching about gender and sex education in schools. Antigenderism is also mobilized to condemn the European project, which critics present as a medium for the cultural and economic colonization of Eastern Europe.[56] Adherents of antigenderism argue that their countries embody authentic European values, which they are trying to safeguard from foreign forces (i.e., liberal elites) seeking to impose a cosmopolitan ideology on their country.[57] As UDSCR (Democratic Union of Slovaks and Czechs from Romania) MEP Adrian-Miroslav Merka argued in June 2022, "Do you think that Europe represents all that is good? I think you are looking too much at a Europe that is changing. We are a democratic country, but also a Christian country."[58] According to this logic, Romania and other East European countries are bastions of traditional European civilization, and, as such, best poised to protect the interests of the nation and its children.

Finally, those against sex education curricula believe youth should be taught self-control in the form of abstinence: "Children need to know how to prevent sexual intercourse," emphasized MEP Robert Sighiartău (PNL); meanwhile, Colesa asserted: "They should be encouraged to decrease the need for physical attraction by promoting sports."[59] Currently, a number of programs promote a "non-sexual alternative [to sex education] with a religious touch." These programs, which openly promote abstinence, present themselves as neutral and claim to act in children's best interests, while concealing their religious impetus and intent. Moreover, they are opposed to abortion, even in the case of rape. With support from international NGOs such as the US Institute in Basic Life Principles, the Italian Pro Life, and the Latin American ALAFA (Latin American Alliance for the Family), they are also part of a broader, transnational movement designed to limit children's access to education and undermine reproductive freedom.[60]

WHAT ABOUT CHILDREN'S RIGHTS?

In all these debates one actor is usually voiceless: young people. Indeed, even though youths' opinions are solicited, they are not considered in policymaking. In July 2021, the Romanian NGO Semper Musica invited young people to participate in a national survey about access to human rights education, reproductive health (including sex education), and access to family planning services. In response, 1,200 teenagers expressed concern about the lack of sex education in the national school curriculum.[61] As two young people emphasized:

> Don't decide for us, please! We also have a voice, we know what we need, what we lack. It's not your battle, it's our right to information. Many children have nowhere to go, only to school [to have information about sex education . . .] Maybe they are raised by illiterate parents, maybe they experience physical and emotional abuse. Where to learn about contraception, bodily changes, sexually transmitted diseases? We need to learn all that, and we need it now![62]

> Yes, we need sex education like we need air. My father is a priest, and even he agrees with learning about it [sex education] at school. Many parents are embarrassed, many teachers are embarrassed, and now I see politicians are embarrassed too. Adults should think about us, not about their fears and prudishness. I have schoolmates who have already had an abortion and they are 14–15 years old. And that's because there is no sex education in schools.[63]

Because young people's voices are absent in discussions about sex education, they have started organizing with the aim of making themselves heard. In July 2022, one thousand teens protested in front of the Bucharest District School Department against sexual abuse in Romanian schools. Moreover, on August 16, 2022, the Students National Council publicly asked the minister of education to resign, criticizing the forthcoming "Law of Education" and the introduction of a new subject, Education for Life.

CONCLUSIONS

While in certain respects postsocialism represented a decisive rupture with the pre-1989 era, with regard to sex education this has been less pronounced. Marriage continues to be seen as a heterosexual union, and women are urged to postpone sex until marriage. For men, premarital sex is condoned and, in some cases, encouraged, though they are urged to protect against STIs and to avoid deviant practices (i.e., homosexuality). Moreover, as during earlier periods, adults (parents, teachers, and politicians) are generally unwilling or ashamed to speak about sex, including sexual health, with their children. Finally, public schools still lack a mandatory sex education curriculum.

The transition to liberal democracy and the codification of new rights and civil liberties, such as freedom of speech and association, facilitated several ruptures that positively impacted youths' access to sex education. With the lifting of censorship after 1989, individuals had access to a range of information, including explicit sexual content via television, print media, and the internet. While this was not followed by a comprehensive sex education curriculum, by the early 2000s, international NGOs and national programs (e.g., Sexul vs Barza) began to fill this educational void by providing youths with information about sex. Although initially focused on fertility control and STIs, reflecting a preventive approach, by the 2010s this broadened to include sexual relations, mental health, substance abuse, and sexual violence, among other topics. Romanians increasingly considered sex education important for youths' physical and emotional well-being. Yet, it was also around this time that debates emerged about when, how, and by whom sex education should be taught. In contrast to the communist period, when state propagandists controlled the narrative about sex education, now a host of actors—politicians, international and national organizations, and ordinary citizens—weigh in on the issue.

Nonetheless, among these voices an essential one was—and still is—missing: young people's. Lack of interest in youths' needs and perspectives represents another unfortunate continuity. Throughout the twentieth and early twenty-first centuries, numerous actors have debated what is best for children and teens, with little or no input from young people themselves. Young people are thus the subject of these debates but never actors within them. Indeed, even when youths' views are solicited, they are rarely mentioned during debates, let alone taken into account. Yet, as demonstrated here, many young people do have access to information about sex, largely from the internet and their peers. At the same time, access to information about reproductive and sexual health is not universally available as a result of demographic disparities. The absence of a coordinated, comprehensive, and mandatory sex education curriculum in schools is evident in the aforementioned health indicators for young people. Clearly, the current form of adult "protection" is not working. More than ever, youths need to be equipped with information that will help them not only navigate potential dangers but also fully understand their bodies and their rights as human beings. This requires soliciting young people's opinions *and* taking them into consideration when policies and programs are being devised.

NOTES

1. Simona Chirciu, "Ce cred elevii despre educația sexuală: Da sau ba pentru SexEd în curricula școlară?" *Mediafax*, June 23, 2021, https://www.mediafax.ro/social/interviuri -ce-cred-elevii-despre-educatia-sexuala-da-sau-ba-pentru-sexed-in-curricula-scolara -20152973.

2. For the situation before 1989, see Luciana Jinga, "Comrade First, Baba Second: State Violence against Women in Communist Romania," *History of Communism in Europe*: *The Other Half of Communism: Women's Outlook*, 8 (2017): 61–84.

3. Ramona Ciobanu, "Gabriela Firea: 'E strigator la cer, dar aproape in fiecare zi, un minor este violat sau agresat sexual,'" *Libertatea,* July 25, 2022.

4. *SONDAJ World Vision România cu privire la abuzul sexual asupra copiilor*, January 2020, 5, https://worldvision.ro/wp-content/uploads/2021/07/Sondaj-cu-privire -la-violenta-sexuala-asupra-copiilor.pdf.

5. Smaranda Diaconescu, et al., "Teenage Mothers, an Increasing Social Phenomenon in Romania: Causes, Consequences and Solutions," *Revista de cercetare si interventie sociala*, 51 (2015): 162–75; and Cristian Iftimoaiei, "O perspectiva statistica asupra maternitatii mamelor minore," *Ziarul de Iasi*, August 3, 2021. The record for the youngest grandmother in the world was set by a twenty-five-year-old Romanian girl, who had had her first child at age twelve. Kathy Bradeanu, "Youngest Grandmother: World Record Set by Rifca Stefanescu," *World Record Academy*, April 7, 2021, https://www.huffpost.com /entry/rifca-stanescu-became-wor_n_833108.

6. Deniz Gökengin et al., "The Growing HIV Epidemic in Central Europe: A Neglected Issue?" *Journal of Virus Eradication* 2, no. 3 (2016): 156–61.

7. IOMC and CDC, *Reproductive Health Survey Romania (RSHR) 1993*, 1995; Florina Șerbănescu, Leo Morris, and Mona Marin, *RHSR 1999* (September 2001); UNICEF and Asociatia SAMAS, *Sarcina la adolescente in Romania: Raport* (January 2021).

8. Șerbănescu, Morris, and Marin, *Reproductive Health Survey Romania (RSHR) 1999*, 276–82.

9. Consiliul Național al Elevilor, Alianța Națională a Organizațiilor Studențești din România, Consiliul Tineretului din România, *Press Release Concerning the Introduction of Sex Education in the Romanian School System*, https://anosr.ro/slide/tinerii-sustin -implementarea-educatiei-sexuale-in-scoli/30921.

10. Law no. 191 of 29 June 2022 to modify law 272/2004 regarding the protection and promotion of the rights of the child, *Monitorul Oficial* no. 652, June 30, 2022.

11. Institutul National de Statistics (INSEE), *Nascuti vii pe grupe de varsta ale tatalui si grupe de varsta ale mamei, macroregiuni, regiuni de dezvoltare si judete* (POP201B), http://statistici.insse.ro/shop/index.jsp?page=tempo2&lang=ro&context=11.

12. Mihail Peticila, "Introducerea educației sexuale în școli ca disciplină obligatorie sub denumirea de Educație sexuală, susținută de ministrul Educației," https://www.edupedu.ro/introducerea-educatiei-sexuale-in-scoli-ca-disciplina-obligatorie-sub-denumirea-de-educatie-sexuala-sustintuta-de-ministrul-educatiei-care-spune-ca-este-nevoie-si-de-educatie-parentala/.

13. Radu Dumitriu, *De vorbă cu tinerii: Probleme de educație a sexelor* (București: Editura Tineretului, 1972), 146.

14. Maria Camelia Zavarache, "Educația moral-sanitară și pentru căsătorie a tinerilor din România (1918–1939)" (PhD diss., Academia Română, Institutul de Istorie, Nicolae Iorga, 2016).

15. Luciana M. Jinga, "Tinerii și sexualitatea în România Comunistă: Manualele de educație sexuală," in *Tineri și Tineret în Romania Socialistă: Identitate, ideologie și dinamici socio-culturale*, ed. Mioara Anton, Bogdan Cristian Iacob, and Cristian Vasile (Târgoviște: Cetatea de Scaun, 2022), 135–58.

16. Jinga, "Tinerii și sexualitatea în România Comunistă."

17. Luciana M. Jinga, *Gen și reprezentare în România Comunistă: 1944–1989* (Iași: Polirom, 2015), 140–43.

18. Elena Zamfir and Cătălin Zamfir, *Politici sociale: Romania în context European* (Bucharest: Editura Alternative, 1995), 461.

19. Cited in Jill Massino, *Ambiguous Transitions: Gender, the State, and Everyday Life in Socialist and Postsocialist Romania* (New York: Berghahn Books, 2019), 122, 201.

20. Luciana Jinga, "Science et politique pendant la guerre froide: La sexologie dans la Roumanie communiste," in *Le rideau déchiré: La sexologie à l'heure de la guerre froide*, ed. Sylvie Chaperon, Carla Nagels, and Cécile Vanderpelen-Diagre (Bruxelles: Sextant, 2021), 85.

21. Luciana M. Jinga and Florin S. Soare, *Politica Pronatalistă a Regimului Ceaușescu*, vol. II (Iași: Polirom, 2011), 169.

22. IOMC and CDC, *Reproductive Health Survey Romania 1993. Final Report*, 1995, 11.

23. Florina Șerbănescu and Leo Morris, eds., *Young Adult Reproductive Health Survey Romania 1996* (February 1998), 24–27.

24. Testimonial of Ioana Pelehatăi, published in "Anchetă: Ne-educația noastă non-sexuală," *Scena9*, June 2, 2016, https://www.scena9.ro/article/ne-educatia-noastra-non-sexuala.

25. Testimonial of Kati, published in Teo Dumitriu, "Poveștile româncelor despre pierderea virginității îți arata cat de pudica era lumea in anii '90,'" *Vice*, February 29, 2016,

https://www.vice.com/ro/article/9ayakd/povestile-romancelor-despre-pierderea
-virginitatii-iti-arata-cat-de-pudic-era-lumea-in-anii-90-535.

26. Testimonial of Irina in Teo Dumitriu, "Poveștile româncelor despre pierderea virginității îți arata cat de pudica era lumea in anii '90.'"

27. In 1990, 992,265 abortions were registered in Romania.

28. Jiřina Kocourková, "East-West Divide in Abortion Behaviour in the EU Countries
since 1990: Ongoing or Vanished Differentiation?" in *Induced Abortion and Spontaneous Early Pregnancy Loss: Focus on Management*, ed. Igor Lakhno (London: IntechOpen, 2019).

29. *Istoria SECS*, https://secs.ro/istoric/.

30. Center for Reproductive Law and Policy, *Women of the World: Laws and Policies Affecting Their Reproductive Lives in East Central Europe* (2003), 144, https://
reproductiverights.org/wp-content/uploads/2020/12/Romania.pdf.

31. "The Talk," https://www.always.com/en-us/tips-and-advice/the-talk.

32. "Always" is the name of the maxi pads. "Voi de unde ati invatat/ invatati care ii treaba
cu sexul? (serios, dacă se poate)," https://www.reddit.com/r/Romania/comments
/3ggdoq/voi_de_unde_ati_invatat_invatati_care_ii_treaba/.

33. Carmen Maria Andronache, "Bravo Magazine Closes Its Print Edition: Super
Bravo Girl Remains on the Market," *Paginile de media*, April 28, 2014, https://www
.paginademedia.ro/2014/04/bravo-magazine-closes-its-print-edition-super-bravo
-girl-remains-on-the-market/.

34. Testimonial of Andra Matzal, published in "Anchetă: Ne-educația noastă non-sexuală,"
Scena9, June 2, 2016, https://www.scena9.ro/article/ne-educatia-noastra-non-sexuala.

35. Șerbănescu, Morris, and Marin, *RHSR 1999*.

36. Yves Denéchère and Beatrice Scutaru, "International Adoption of Romanian Children
and Romania's Admission to the European Union (1990–2007)," *Eastern Journal of
European Studies* 1, no. 1 (2010): 142–43.

37. OMECS (Ordinul Ministrului Educatiei si Cercetarii Stiintifice), 4496/2004.

38. Administratia Prezidentiala, *Educatie pentru sanitate*, ed. Departamentul de Educatie
si Cercetare, Departamentul Sanatate Publica (2015), 3.

39. Ministerul Educatiei si Cercetarii, Consiliul National pentru Curriculum, eds., *Programme scolare revizuite pentru disciplina optionala Educatie pentru Sanatate. Clasele
Ia-XIIa* (Bucharest, 2004).

40. Anamaria Suciu and Cabriel Brumariu, *Raport de analiza a disciplinei optionale Educatie pentru sanatate componenta educatie sexuala* (2015).

41. For example, 6 and 7 percent of all pupils took Education for Health in 2014–2015 and
2014–2015 respectively. Administratia Prezidentiala, *Educatie,* 3; Ministerul Educatiei Nationale, eds., *Scrisoare de la Ecaterina Andronescu pentru Cristina-Ionela Iurisniti* (December 4, 2018); "Anchetă: Ne-educația noastă non-sexuală." Since the subject

is part of the School Decision Curriculum, schools can choose to teach the subject one year and not the next. Moreover, subjects that are not part of the school curriculum cannot be taught. Finally, parents can choose whether their child can take this subject.

42. Administratia Prezidentiala, *Educatie*, 3.

43. Cosmin Dinu, "Cum s-a născut proiectul 'Redevenim,'" https://redevenim.ro/. Societatea de Educatie Contraceptiva si Sexuala, homepage, https://secs.ro/.

44. "De ce este atât de controversată educația sexuală în România. BOR: Poate deveni educație de tip homosexual," *Digi24*, March 18, 2018. https://www.digi24.ro/stiri /actualitate/educatie/de-ce-este-atat-de-controversata-educatia-sexuala-in-romani a-897395.

45. At: http://www.sexulvsbarza.ro and https://www.youtube.com/c/SEXULvsBARZA.

46. "Despre noi," *Sexul vs Barza*, https://www.sexulvsbarza.ro/despre-noi/.

47. Testimonial of Lorena Iacob, published in "Anchetă: Ne-educația noastă non-sexuală."

48. These ideas are taken from the laws' explanatory memorandums, as well as the discussions that took place in the Chamber of Deputies, available at http://www.cdep.ro/pls /proiecte/upl_pck2015.proiect?idp=16756; "Dezbaterea Propunerii legislative pentru modificarea si completarea Legii 272/2004 privind protectia si promovarea drepturilor copilului" (PI-x 119/2019), (*ramasa pentru votul final*), March 10, 2020.

49. Alexandru Rotaru, "Cum se face educația sexuală în Europa: Diferența între Vest și Est," *Digi24,* June 2021, https://www.digi24.ro/stiri/actualitate/politica/cum-se-face -educatia-sexuala-in-europa-diferenta-intre-vest-si-est-1568067.

50. See Law 272/2004 from July 21, 2004 regarding the protection and promotion of the rights of the child, *Monitorul Oficial* no. 557, July 23, 2004.

51. Ruxandra Gubernat and Henry P. Rammelt, "'Vrem o țară ca afară!': How Contention in Romania Redefines State-Building through a Pro-European Discourse," *East European Politics and Societies* 35, no. 1 (2021): 247–68.

52. Claudia Spiridon, "Educatia Sanitara ar putea deveni disciplina obligatorie in scoli, Ministrul Sanatatii vrea sa majoreze orele de sport din invatamantul gimnazial si superior," *Adevarul*, October 18, 2013.

53. Mirela Ionela Achim, "Discuții aprinse, între profesori, despre disciplina Educație sexuală," *B1tv,* December 15, 2020, https://www.b1tv.ro/eveniment/discutii-aprinse-intre -profesori-despre-disiplina-educatie-sexuala-o-singura-vorba-a-vreunui-profesor -catre-copilul-meu-si-ii-scot-ochii-nu-va-mai-certat-tampitilor-bateti-va -354350.html.ai-certat-tampitilor-bateti-va-354350.html.

54. "Camera: In scoli se vor derula, incepand cu clasa a VIII-a, programe de educatie pentru sanitate, cu acordul parintilor," *Agerpres*, June 21, 2022, https://www .agerpres.ro/viata-parlamentara/2022/06/21/camera-in-scoli-se-vor-derula-incepand -cu-clasa-a-viii-a-programe-de-educatie-pentru-sanatate-cu-acordul-parintilor --937836.

55. "Explanatory memorandum Lege pentru 'Inocenta Copilariei,' privind interzicerea cursurilor de educatie sexuala in invatamantul prescolar, primar si gimnazial fara acordul scris al parintilor sau tutorelui," L515/2016, https://www.senat.ro/legis/PDF/2016/16L515EM.PDF.

56. Ov Cristian Norocel and Ionela Băluță, "Retrogressive Mobilization in the 2018 'Referendum for Family' in Romania," *Problems of Post-Communism* (2021), 1–10; and Elżbieta Korolczuk and Agnieska Graff, "Gender as 'Ebola from Brussels': The Anticolonial Frame and the Rise of Illiberal Populism," *Signs: Journal of Women of Culture and Society* 43, no. 4 (2018): 797–821.

57. Elżbieta Korolczuk, "'Worse than communism and Nazism put together': War on Gender in Poland," in *Anti-Gender Campaigns in Europe: Mobilizing against Equality,* ed. Roman Kuhar and David Paternotte (New York: Rowman & Littlefield International, 2017), 175–94.

58. Sabina Fati, "Educatie sexuala, ipocrizia si anti-occidentalismul," *Deutsche Welle,* June 22, 2022, https://www.dw.com/ro/educația-sexuală-ipocrizia-și-anti-occidentalismul/a-62214180.

59. Florin Puscas, "Lovitură pentru Iohannis: cererea de reexaminare a legii referitoare la educația sexuală, respinsă de Comisia de muncă din Camera Deputaților," *stiripesurse.ro,* March 22, 2022, at https://www.stiripesurse.ro/lovitura-pentru-iohannis-cererea-de-reexaminare-a-legii-referitoare-la-educatia-sexuala-respinsa-de-comisia-de-munca-din-camera-deputatilor_2303220.html.

60. Diana Meseșan and Roma Gavrila, "Batalia pe adolescenta," *Scena 9,* May 13, 2019, https://www.scena9.ro/article/batalia-pe-adolescenta.

61. Silvia Trașcă, "Am întrebat liceeni din România de ce educația sexuală trebuie făcută în școli, nu pe TikTok," *Vice,* July 13, 2021, https://www.vice.com/ro/article/n7bqnx/liceeni-din-romania-educatie-sexuala.

62. Trașcă, "Am întrebat liceeni din România de ce educația sexuală trebuie făcută în școli."

63. Trașcă, "Am întrebat liceeni din România de ce educația sexuală trebuie făcută în școli."

BIBLIOGRAPHY

Achim, Mirela Ionela. "Discuții aprinse, între profesori, despre disciplina Educație sexuală." *B1tv,* December 15, 2020. https://www.b1tv.ro/eveniment/discutii-aprinse-intre-profesori-despre-disiplina-educatie-sexuala-o-singura-vorba-a-vreunui-profesor-catre-copilul-meu-si-ii-scot-ochii-nu-va-mai-certat-tampitilor-bateti-va-354350.html.

Administratia Prezidentiala. *Educatie pentru sanitate,* ed. Departamentul de Educatie si Cercetare, Departamentul Sanatate Publica (2015).

Andronache, Carmen Maria. "Bravo Magazine Closes Its Print Edition: Super Bravo Girl Remains on the Market." *Paginile de media*, April 28, 2014. https://www.paginademedia.ro/2014/04/bravo-magazine-closes-its-print-edition-super-bravo-girl-remains-on-the-market/.

Center for Reproductive Law and Policy. *Women of the World: Laws and Policies Affecting Their Reproductive Lives: East Central Europe* (2003). https://reproductiverights.org/wp-content/uploads/2020/12/Romania.pdf.

Chirciu, Simona. "Ce cred elevii despre educația sexuală. Da sau ba pentru SexEd în curricula școlară?" *Mediafax*, June 23, 2021. https://www.mediafax.ro/social/interviuri-ce-cred-elevii-despre-educatia-sexuala-da-sau-ba-pentru-sexed-in-curricula-scolara-20152973. https://www.reddit.com/r/Romania/comments/3ggdoq/voi_de_unde_ati_invatat_invatati_care_ii_treaba/.

Ciobanu, Ramona. "Gabriela Firea: 'E strigator la cer, dar aproape in fiecare zi, un minor este violat sau agresat sexual.'" *Libertatea*, July 25, 2022.

Denéchère, Yves, and Beatrice Scutaru. "International Adoption of Romanian Children and Romania's Admission to the European Union (1990–2007)." *Eastern Journal of European Studies* 1, no. 1 (2010): 142–43.

Diaconescu, Smaranda, et al. "Teenage Mothers, an Increasing Social Phenomenon in Romania: Causes, Consequences and Solutions." *Revista de cercetare si interventie sociala*, 51 (2015): 162–75.

Dinu, Cosmin. "Cum s-a născut proiectul 'Redevenim.'" https://redevenim.ro/. Societatea de Educatie Contraceptiva si Sexuala. https://secs.ro/.

Dumitriu, Radu. *De vorbă cu tinerii: Probleme de educație a sexelor*. București: Editura Tineretului, 1972.

Dumitriu, Teo. "Poveștile româncelor despre pierderea virginității îți arata cat de pudica era lumea in anii '90.'" *Vice*, February 29, 2016. https://www.vice.com/ro/article/9ayakd/povestile-romancelor-despre-pierderea-virginitatii-iti-arata-cat-de-pudic-era-lumea-in-anii-90-535.

Fati, Sabina. "Educatie sexuala, ipocrizia si anti-occidentalismul." *Deutsche Welle*, June 22, 2022.

Gökengin, Deniz Cristiana Oprea, Serhat Uysal, and Josip Begovac. "The Growing HIV epidemic in Central Europe: A Neglected Issue?" *Journal of Virus Eradication* 2, no. 3 (2016): 156–61.

Gubernat, Ruxandra, and Henry P. Rammelt. "'Vrem o țară ca afară!': How Contention in Romania Redefines State-Building through a Pro-European Discourse." *East European Politics and Societies* 35, no. 1 (2021): 247–68.

Iftimoaiei, Cristian. "O perspectiva statistica asupra maternitatii mamelor minore." *Ziarul de Iasi*, August 3, 2021.

Institutul National de Statistics (INSEE). *Nascuti vii pe grupe de varsta ale tatalui si grupe de varsta ale mamei, macroregiuni, regiuni de dezvoltare si judete* (POP201B). http://statistici.insse.ro/shop/index.jsp?page=tempo2&lang=ro&context=11.

Jinga, Luciana M. "Comrade First, Baba Second: State Violence against Women in Communist Romania." *History of Communism in Europe: The Other Half of Communism: Women's Outlook*, 8 (2017): 61–84.

Jinga, Luciana M. *Gen și reprezentare în România Comunistă: 1944–1989*. Iași: Polirom, 2015.

Jinga, Luciana M. "Science et politique pendant la guerre froide: La sexologie dans la Roumanie Communiste." In *Le rideau déchiré: La sexologie à l'heure de la guerre froide*, edited by Sylvie Chaperon, Carla Nagels, and Cécile Vanderpelen-Diagre. Bruxelles: Sextant, 2021.

Jinga, Luciana M. "Tinerii și sexualitatea în România Comunistă. Manualele de educație sexuală." In *Tineri și Tineret în Romania Socialistă: Identitate, ideologie și dinamici socio-culturale*, edited by Mioara Anton, Bogdan Cristian Iacob, and Cristian Vasile, 135–58. Târgoviște: Cetatea de Scaun, 2022.

Jinga, Luciana M., and Florin S. Soare. *Politica Pronatalistă a Regimului Ceaușescu*, vol. II. Iași: Polirom, 2011.

Kocourková, Jiřina. "East-West Divide in Abortion Behaviour in the EU Countries Since 1990: Ongoing or Vanished Differentiation?" In *Induced Abortion and Spontaneous Early Pregnancy Loss: Focus on Management*, edited by Igor Lakhno. London: IntechOpen, 2019.

Korolczuk, Elżbieta. "'Worse than communism and Nazism put together': War on Gender in Poland." In *Anti-Gender Campaigns in Europe: Mobilizing against Equality*, edited by Roman Kuhar and David Paternotte, 175–94. New York: Rowman & Littlefield International, 2017.

Korolczuk, Elżbieta, and Agnieska Graff. "Gender as 'Ebola from Brussels': The Anticolonial Frame and the Rise of Illiberal Populism." *Signs: Journal of Women of Culture and Society* 43, no. 4 (2018): 797–821.

Massino, Jill. *Ambiguous Transitions: Gender, the State, and Everyday Life in Socialist and Postsocialist Romania*. New York: Berghahn Books, 2019.

Meseșan, Diana, and Roma Gavrila. "Batalia pe adolescenta." *Scena 9*, May 13, 2019. https://www.scena9.ro/article/batalia-pe-adolescenta.

Ministerul Educatiei si Cercetarii, Consiliul National pentru Curriculum, eds. *Programme scolare revizuite pentru disciplina optionala Educatie pentru Sanatate. Clasele Ia-XIIa* (Bucharest, 2004).

Ministerul Educatiei Nationale, eds. *Scrisoare de la Ecaterina Andronescu pentru Cristina-Ionela Iurisniti* (December 4, 2018).

Norocel, Ov Cristian, and Ionela Băluță. "Retrogressive Mobilization in the 2018 'Referendum for Family' in Romania." *Problems of Post-Communism* (2021): 1–10.

OMECS (Ordinul Ministrului Educatiei si Cercetarii Stiintifice), 4496/2004.

Peticila, Mihail. "Introducerea educației sexuale în școli ca disciplină obligatorie sub denumirea de Educație sexuală, susținută de ministrul Educației, care spune că este nevoie și de educație parentală." *Edupedu*, June 18, 2021. https://www.edupedu.ro/introducerea-educatiei-sexuale-in-scoli-ca-disciplina-obligatorie-sub-denumirea-de-educatie-sexuala-sustintuta-de-ministrul-educatiei-care-spune-ca-este-nevoie-si-de-educatie-parentala/.

Puscas, Florin. "Lovitură pentru Iohannis: cererea de reexaminare a legii referitoare la educaţia sexuală, respinsă de Comisia de muncă din Camera Deputaţilor." *stiripesurse. ro*, March 22, 2022. https://www.stiripesurse.ro/lovitura-pentru-iohannis-cererea-de -reexaminare-a-legii-referitoare-la-educatia-sexuala-respinsa-de-comisia-de-munca -din-camera-deputatilor_2303220.html.

Rotaru, Alexandru. "Cum se face educaţia sexuală în Europa: Diferenţa între Vest şi Est." *Digi24*, June 2021. https://www.digi24.ro/stiri/actualitate/politica/cum-se-face-educatia -sexuala-in-europa-diferenta-intre-vest-si-est-1568067.

Şerbănescu, Florina, and Leo Morris, eds. *Young Adult Reproductive Health Survey Romania 1996* (February 1998).

SONDAJ World Vision România cu privire la abuzul sexual asupra copiilor, January 2020.

Spiridon, Claudia. "Educatia Sanitara ar putea deveni disciplina obligatorie in scoli, Ministrul Sanatatii vrea sa majoreze orele de sport din invatamantul gimnazial si superior." *Adevarul*, October 18, 2013.

Suciu, Anamaria, and Cabriel Brumariu. *Raport de analiza a disciplinei optionale Educatie pentru sanatate componenta educatie sexuala* (2015).

Traşcă, Silvia. "Am întrebat liceeni din România de ce educaţia sexuală trebuie făcută în şcoli, nu pe TikTok." *Vice*, July 13, 2021. https://www.vice.com/ro/article/n7bqnx/liceeni -din-romania-educatie-sexuala.

Zamfir, Elena, and Cătălin Zamfir. *Politici sociale: Romania în context European* (Bucharest: Editura Alternative, 1995).

Zavarache, Maria Camelia. "Educaţia moral-sanitară şi pentru căsătorie a tinerilor din România (1918–1939)." PhD diss., Academia Română, Institutul de Istorie, Nicolae Iorga, 2016.

8

NO COUNTRY FOR (POOR) WOMEN

Reproductive Rights, Conservatism, and Neoliberalism in Postsocialist Romania[1]

CORINA DOBOȘ

IN AUGUST 2017, ALEXANDRA, A YOUNG WOMAN FROM BRĂNEȘTI (A VILLAGE near Bucharest), killed herself and her three children by jumping in front of a train. At the time of her suicide, Alexandra was pregnant and did not want to have another child. Because she could not afford an abortion, she had previously attempted to provoke a miscarriage by repeatedly punching her stomach, a method she had successfully used in the past. Alexandra was married, but she often quarreled with her husband, who was also the primary breadwinner, and the family experienced dire poverty. Alexandra also suffered from severe depression, having been admitted to mental institutions several times in the past. A suicide note was found on her, in which she apologized for taking her and her children's lives, but emphasized she simply could not take it anymore.[2]

This chapter examines family planning and elective abortion services in Romania. My research reveals women's—particularly poor women's—limited agency with respect to fertility control and reproductive rights in Romania, a country traumatized by the harsh pronatalist policies of socialist leader Nicolae Ceaușescu between 1966 and 1989.[3] After the expansion of family planning services and subsidized contraception during the first two decades of postsocialism, in the 2010s, access to modern contraception and elective abortion services decreased considerably, especially for poor, vulnerable, and uneducated women. I demonstrate how elements of Ceaușescu's infamous pronatalist policies reemerged in an ideological, political, and socioeconomic context significantly different from the one in which they originated. Thus, the late socialist pronatalist ethos has recently experienced a revival, primarily as a result of rising social conservatism, neoliberal policies, and concerns about demographic decline. This renewed pronatalism, while not legislatively imposed, is manifest in lack of access to subsidized contraceptives, disinformation about Romania's abortion laws, and reduced access to abortion services (in public hospitals). The result is an increase in unwanted pregnancies and a growing reliance on doctors in private clinics for abortion services, most of which are beyond the means of low-income women. Women thus resort to self-inducing an abortion or to cheap doctors—some poorly trained and using unhygienic methods—to control their fertility, practices that echo the era of Ceauşescu's draconian pronatalism. In the most desperate circumstances, they resort to suicide.

REPRODUCTIVE POLICIES IN CEAUŞESCU'S ROMANIA

As elsewhere in socialist Eastern Europe, in Romania pronatalist policies were rooted in concerns about declining birth rates and their negative impact on the labor force and economic productivity.[4] Yet, rather than provide positive incentives (i.e., economic support for children), as most states in the Eastern Bloc did, Ceauşescu's pronatalism was characterized by meager social entitlements and widescale repression.[5] In 1966, after nearly a decade of being legal upon demand, abortion was criminalized under the infamous Decree 770. The law permitted abortion only in a few circumstances: at the recommendation of a socio-medical commission for women older than forty-five or for those who already had four children in their care. In addition, the law mandated that such abortions be performed in a state medical facility during the first twelve weeks of pregnancy. Women who sought illegal abortions or who tried to self-induce were punished, as were abortion providers, the latter receiving two or more years imprisonment. In addition to criminal sanctions, medical practitioners charged with illegally providing an abortion were sanctioned professionally, in some cases losing their medical licenses altogether. The sudden change in the abortion law in 1966 decisively affected reproductive behavior and everyday life in Romania. In the absence of modern contraception, abortion continued to be the most common method of pregnancy termination, in spite of the drastic limitations introduced by Decree 770. After an initial explosion of the birth rate, which doubled between 1967 and 1969, women began adapting to the new realities and found alternative, illicit, and often dangerous ways to terminate unwanted pregnancies.

Inducing abortions through abortifacients and other techniques often had dramatic effects on women's health. The escalation of illicit abortive practices, coupled with medical neglect in hospital units and emergency rooms, led to the death of more than 12,000 women between 1967 and 1989. Possibilities of medical intervention to save a woman's life in urgent situations were dependent on the patient revealing details about the abortion (who performed it, where, etc.). Attending doctors could only access necessary medical instruments (which were locked up) if the woman, usually in agonizing pain, provided such details. Accordingly, the emergency room became an inquisitorial space where the patient's admission of guilt—real or not—was often her only chance to receive specialized treatment and, ultimately, to survive.[6]

In addition to women, children were victims of Ceaușescu's pronatalism. Thousands of children were orphaned or abandoned by their parents—usually due to desperate poverty—and subsequently placed in state institutions, where they experienced neglect, malnutrition, and abuse.[7] Thus, Ceaușescu's inhumane pronatalist policies traumatized many generations in Romania. These *decreței* (as children born after 1967 were colloquially called), who had been abandoned and institutionalized before 1989, were not integrated into society after the collapse of communism. As a result, in the 1990s, many ended up on the streets, left to fend for themselves. During the era of loosely regulated international adoptions of the early 1990s and 2000s, some even became victims of human trafficking.[8]

REPRODUCTIVE POLICIES AFTER 1989

The repeal of Decree 770 was among the first legislative measures taken by the new government after the collapse of communism in December 1989. Elective abortion was legalized, and women's access to modern contraception was facilitated by support from US donors and the Romanian Ministry of Health (MoH). An overview of the evolution of abortion practices and family planning services in postsocialist Romania demonstrates how, under a complicated web of neoliberal economic policies, growing social inequalities, and the increasing influence of neoconservatism, access to elective abortion and modern contraceptives is no longer subsidized for low-income women.

Family planning services were introduced in 1992, when 240 offices for family planning were established by the MoH across the country. These services were organized with the support of a World Bank grant and implemented by the Society for Contraceptive and Sexual Education (SECS), a national NGO created in the early 1990s by leading Romanian gynecologists and supported by the International Planned Parenthood Federation (IPPF). The program included a series of trainings in family planning for doctors (GPs), who began working in the newly established family planning offices. In an interview in 2020, Dr. Iuliana Balteș, one of the pioneers of the family planning system in Romania, remembered how helpful these trainings were at the beginning of her career as a family planning physician.[9] Determined to educate women about contraception and reproductive health, she began by building trust among them:

> In the first three years I did a lot of talking [explaining to women how important contraception was]. Afterwards, there was no need for me to explain anymore, as women, especially from rural areas, came by themselves. There were a lot of women from rural areas who came down to my office. Many of them learned how to correctly take contraceptive pills and came regularly to see me. They quickly understood the benefits of modern contraception. They were coming from rural areas, where they were working hard but were not financially independent, and were facing a lot of pressure from their abusive husbands. They were coming regularly to take their contraceptive pills or to have their contraceptive shot.[10]

Balteş also recalled:

> At first, the contraceptive pills that were distributed by family planning offices were cheaper than what you could find on the market . . . soon we realized that many women, especially from rural areas, could not afford to buy contraception, even at a subsidized price. Thus, the Ministry of Health began—at the insistence of SECS— to provide free contraception (pills), through family planning offices, for vulnerable individuals: students, the unemployed, or women who came to have an abortion in a state hospital; women who could not afford contraception; all women from rural areas.[11]

During the 1990s and early 2000s, these family planning initiatives proved successful: the percentage of women using any form (traditional or modern) of contraception grew steadily from 41 percent in 1993 to 58 percent in 2004, while the percentage of those who used modern contraception tripled between 1993 (when modern contraceptive methods were used only by 10 percent of women of fertility age) and 2004 (when the percentage of women using modern contraception grew to 34 percent).[12] However, family planning initiatives that relied on support from US donors (USAID) and the expertise of SECS began decreasing with Romania's accession to the European Union (EU) in 2007.[13] Since then, sexual and reproductive health and rights (SRHR) have suffered from the termination of international development funding, as well as political instability and lack of political will. Dr. Balteş recounted the unfortunate ramifications of this outcome on women's fertility control:

> The Ministry of Health did not distribute free contraception anymore. The injectable contraception—which used to be widely used—slowly disappeared, and . . .

everything finished. We were told that papers are done, that soon free contraception would be again available—but nothing happened.... The few of us who remained in this specialization, we tried our best to get the Ministry's support, to help us rebuild the family planning system in Romania. There are still good specialists in family planning, but no one seems to care.... The ministers [of Health] are coming and going, but reproductive health does not represent a priority for any of them.[14]

Data gathered by several Romanian NGOs confirm Dr. Bălteş's remarks. A 2020 study conducted by the Association Sexul vs. Barza found that between 2014 and 2020, thirty-six offices for family planning were shut down in Romania, and two counties were left without any family planning services.[15] Out of the 117 family planning centers functioning across the country in 2020, only two still provided modern contraceptives (pills and condoms) free of cost.[16] Although overall use of modern contraception in Romania increased between 2004 and 2016, its use by poor women decreased due to suspension of subsidies for targeted groups, underscoring distinct socioeconomic differences in women's ability to control their fertility.[17] Borbala Koo, president of SECS, emphasized that in spite of existing laws, which were designed to provide low-income and impoverished women with free contraception, subsidies are dependent upon the budget allocated by the MoH. In January 2015, for example, the MoH did not allocate any funds for contraceptives to low-income women and made no plans in the budget to subsidize them the following year.[18] In addition, contraceptives are no longer covered by health insurance companies.

In an analysis of reimbursement schemes across sixteen EU countries between 2013 and 2016, Romania scored the lowest for reimbursement of contraception and was ranked among the last with respect to social and economic inequalities that negatively affect access to contraceptives.[19] The report stated that, in the 2010s, "the government has not renewed, in recent years, a reimbursement provision that used to allow free access to certain contraceptives for certain vulnerable groups, including students and low-income or unemployed people."[20] The report concluded that the austerity measures implemented by the Romanian government during the 2009–2012 financial crisis negatively affected contraception reimbursement schemes, and recommended that reimbursement schemes should target young women and vulnerable groups to overcome inequalities in accessing reproductive health services.[21] The 2020 Contraception Atlas, released in October 2020 by the European Parliamentary Forum for Sexual and Reproductive Rights (EPF), also registered a decrease in access to subsidized contraception in Romania, noting that the provision of free contraception "ended unexpectedly in 2013 when the last public procurement of supplies took place."[22] Challenges in accessing contraception are often correlated with an increase in unwanted pregnancies, abortions, and child abandonment, and in this regard Romania is no exception.[23]

ONE STEP FORWARD, TWO STEPS BACK: DECLINING ACCESS TO ABORTION

Alongside family planning services, access to elective abortion services has declined over the last decade. As noted, elective abortion was (re)legalized in Romania in December 1989, and is permitted on demand during the first fourteen weeks of pregnancy. However, abortion is not covered by public health insurance, and the fees for an abortion in public hospitals, while still lower than in private health clinics, are considerable for low-income individuals. For instance, in Bucharest in 2019, the cost for an abortion in a public hospital ranged from 350 to 500 lei (70–100 euros). Meanwhile, the cost in a private facility was double and even triple that: from 700 to 1,200 lei (170–250 euros) depending upon the type of anesthesia provided. In the rest of the country, costs are lower, though still significantly less in public facilities, as the woman's magazine *Unica* documented.[24] In 2021, this disparity was even more pronounced, as the results of a daring project of investigative journalism, published in the daily news journal *Libertatea*, showed.[25]

Doctors' refusal to provide abortion on demand in public facilities and the cost-prohibitive nature of an abortion in private facilities affects, first and foremost, economically and socially vulnerable women—the very same women who no longer have access to subsidized contraception and other family planning services.[26] A study published in 2019, found that, in 2016, elective abortion was more common in rural than urban areas and was most in demand among poor and uneducated women.[27] With the onset of COVID-19 in March 2020, women's access to elective abortion was further curtailed as public medical facilities restricted interventions to medical emergencies. The MoH reported that out of 134 public and 16 private hospitals, more than half (57.7 percent) did not provide abortion services. As a result, the number of elective abortions performed in the first six months of 2020 declined by nearly one-half when compared with the same period in 2019. Meanwhile, the number of abortions provided on medical grounds (during the same period in 2020) decreased by nearly one-fifth when compared to 2019.[28] National Institute of Public Health (NIPH) data showed that while in 2017 only one-third of elective abortions were performed in private facilities, in 2020 this figure had increased to almost half, while in 2021 the majority of elective abortions (62 percent) were performed in private hospitals. This means that in more than one-fourth of Romania's counties, no abortions were performed in the public health system in 2021.[29]

Studies conducted by several NGOs over the past ten years concluded that for combined reasons—religious, professional, financial—fewer public facilities have provided elective abortion services. While in 2011, six public hospitals refused to provide elective abortions, that figure increased to thirteen in 2013 and to fifty-one in 2019.[30] Between 2011 and 2014, substantial changes in the ethical norms of medical professionals have seemingly occurred.[31] For example, in March 2012, the basis upon which physicians could refuse to perform an abortion expanded to include situations that could be harmful to a physician's "professional independence," "image," and "moral values," or that "did not respect the fundamental principles of the medical profession, its main goals and social role."[32] Indeed, medical professionals have increasingly cited respect of "ethical norms" in justifying their refusal to perform elective abortions, including in public medical facilities. This is despite the fact that elective abortion is still legal in Romania and should, like "any other lawful medical service," be available upon demand in public hospitals and clinics.

From a legal point of view these "ethical norms" are recommendations and, as such, not legally binding.[33] Indeed, they actually contravene legal provisions and thus do not constitute valid legal grounds for refusing to perform an elective abortion in a public hospital.[34] However, they do de facto; as a result, the number of public hospitals that no longer provide abortion upon demand has increased over the last decade.[35] For instance, in 2019, only forty public health facilities in the country (all outside of Bucharest) provided abortion services year round, a quarter of which did not offer these services around major Orthodox holidays such as Christmas or Easter.[36] Refusal to provide elective abortions in public health facilities has been accompanied by a change in medical personnel's attitude toward abortion more generally as "women who ask for details about the procedure are often stigmatized by doctors who increasingly invoke their 'right' to refuse this procedure for ethical or religious reasons."[37]

FOLLOW THE MONEY!

Yet these changes in service provisions, both on institutional and interpersonal levels, appear not only to be a matter of conscience, but also material gain. An exposé revealed that (cheaper) elective abortions are denied by physicians at a growing number of public facilities on the basis of their "moral sensibilities," and abortion-seekers are directed to private clinics, where abortion services are often provided by the very same physicians who had previously refused to perform the procedure in public facilities.[38] Indeed, in some instances abortion seekers are told that elective abortion is no longer legal in public hospitals in Romania. For instance, Dr. Usruf Wajdy, when asked by the independent newspaper, *The Decree Chronicles*, why he performs (elective) abortions at a private practice after refusing the same service at the state hospital where he works, cynically replied: "I cannot give you this information, and you cannot ask for it, if you don't have a special document. It is my personal life, it is not your business, and I am not obligated to give you this information. Private medical practices are different, but here, in state hospitals, we simply do not provide this service."[39] Abortion seekers are thus caught in a web of secrecy, misinformation, and greed.

The tragic death of Magdalena Clisaru, a forty-five-year-old mother of three who died in September 2020 at a gynecologist's (private) clinic in Ploiești after intense hemorrhaging following a surgical abortion, illustrates well the difficulties women in Romania currently face in trying to control their fertility. Clisaru's abortion was performed by Dr. Virgil Mircea Burciu at his clinic; however, there was no medical staff on hand to attend to her after she began hemorrhaging. Although her eldest daughter, who was with her at the clinic, called an ambulance, by the time it arrived it was too late to save Clisaru. As a form of compensation, the doctor offered to refund the cost for the surgical procedure (around 100 euros) to the deceased's family, though he insisted that he had performed the procedure correctly and was thus not responsible for Clisaru's death. An autopsy determined that the cause of death was massive hemorrhaging and Dr. Burciu was charged with manslaughter. A subsequent police investigation revealed that Dr. Burciu's office did not meet hygienic standards and that he lacked appropriate medical instruments for performing abortions. When asked by the press to comment upon Clisaru's death, the MoH's spokeswoman asserted:

We do not encourage terminations of pregnancy. The Ministry does not assume responsibility for someone's own personal decision. . . . A physician has no obligation to perform an abortion on demand. A doctor's obligation is to save the life of a fetus or the mother when a pregnancy cannot be brought to term. And the Ministry, as I've already told you and I repeat, as maybe you don't understand what I'm saying in Romanian, the Ministry encourages giving birth. . . . These are Ministry of Health policies. It's up to the doctor to agree or not to perform an abortion procedure. It's not an obligation. In 2020, if you don't want to have any children, there is contraception.[40]

The spokeswoman's declaration sparked protests, and several NGOs demanded her resignation, claiming she had peddled erroneous information about access to contraception and elective abortion.[41] At the same time, the declaration reflected the attitude of a considerable segment of the population toward fertility control (e.g., that it's a woman's responsibility; that abortion should be a final resort; or that it should not be permitted at all). After 2007, when US donors and agencies discontinued support for family planning services and contraception in Romania, the MoH failed to assume this responsibility—or find alternative means of subsidizing fertility control. Nor did the MoH officially underscore that abortion in Romania continued to be legal (up to fourteen weeks) and available in public hospitals on demand.

REPRODUCTIVE RESTRICTIONS AND CUTS IN SOCIAL EXPENDITURES

Restrictions in accessing elective abortion and modern contraception cannot be understood without reference to social, economic, and demographic realities in Romania. According to various studies, declining birth rates in Romania since the 1990s, combined with massive outmigration, has caused "the worst demographic crisis in Romania's contemporary history," producing concern about future population size and age structure.[42] It is women, however, who are blamed for this worrying situation, not the economic uncertainty and social dislocation produced by Romania's transition to a market economy.

As Dorothee Bohle and Béla Greskovits have demonstrated, the postsocialist reconfiguration of the political sphere, macroeconomic structures, and social relations in East-Central Europe contributed to the emergence of different types of market societies.[43] After an initial state characterized by "economic and political disorder," the transition to market capitalism in Romania combined neoliberal economic features and weak state institutions, leading to social disintegration.[44] Thus, macroeconomic coordination was characterized by minimal taxation and a meager welfare state.[45] Welfare entitlements and labor conditions were further eroded by austerity measures (including cuts to health care facilities, maternal and child support, and public salaries) in response to the financial crisis at the end of the 2000s.[46] For many Romanians, this translated into declining standards of living and financial difficulties. Some responded by leaving Romania, for which then-president Traian Băsescu thanked them, as they "relieved the burden that the crisis had put on Romania's safety net."[47] Yet, in 2010, Băsescu also declared that "Romania has no [working] women and children anymore. Romania has become a country of mothers and babies [*mămicuțe* and *bebeluși*]," implying that Romanian women, in order to avoid working, have children and live on state subsidies—an absurd claim given the meager maternal and child benefits women received at the time.[48]

Census data from 2011 revealed a significant decrease in Romania's population in general and a fall in the birth rate in particular, placing the government party (PDL) in an uncomfortable position.[49] It was difficult for them to openly acknowledge that the austerity measures of 2010–2011, especially major cuts in social expenditures such as for mother and child welfare, had contributed to declining birth rates. Thus, they blame women's reproductive choices (i.e., having an abortion rather than bringing their pregnancy to term) for this demographic decline, rather than acknowledge that the austerity measures implemented after 2008 had contributed to increased emigration.[50]

In April 2012, the PDL introduced a law that would have required women to undergo counseling before being approved for an elective abortion. Its initiators argued that the high number of abortions registered in Romania was due to lack of information about the medical aspects and consequences of the procedure. In reality this "counseling" involved showing the pregnant woman a graphic video of an abortion being performed, with the aim of inducing fear and guilt in her. After the "counseling" session, if the woman still opted for an abortion, she had to sign a declaration that read: "I was informed that abortion involves ending a life, as the fetus is a living being from the very beginning of its conception."[51] The MoH officially supported such mandatory "counseling" for abortion seekers, declaring in April 2012 that "it would be useful if physicians could give advice to the woman before she has an abortion, to explain the procedure to her and the risks involved in it. To give her some time to think it over, to discuss it with her husband or with her family, with her friends."[52] The MoH's reasoning shares much with late socialist medical discourse, which emphasized the supposed psychological and physical perils of abortion—and also presented the fetus as a human being.[53]

While the MoH openly supported the initiative, civil society groups stressed the potential trauma this supposed "counseling" might produce within abortion seekers.[54] After the fall of the PDL government (in May 2012) the proposal was tabled; however, such legislative initiatives exemplify typical attitudes toward elective abortion, evident in local efforts to dissuade women from having an abortion. For instance, *A Study on Reproductive Health*, issued in February 2020 by the Vaslui County Public Health Services, reinforced the message outlined in the 2012 "pre-abortion counseling proposal," referring to abortion as a "traumatic experience, with long-lasting effects."[55] The report continued:

> Given the serious effects upon woman's mental and physical well-being, the woman seeking an abortion should be informed about the consequences before making her decision. Moreover, the woman who has suffered an interruption of pregnancy should be given psychological support afterwards, especially if one takes into consideration that the "uncured trauma [of abortion]" could be projected on her next offspring(s). In order to get over this painful experience, in order for her to have a healthy relationship with her future child, a woman has to be given support.[56]

The document not only peddles misinformation, but also displays a paternalistic attitude toward women, reflective of medical officials' prejudices toward women and their reproductive choices in Romania.[57]

By blaming ordinary women for demographic decline, the government evades its own responsibility for this outcome, while at the same time employing discourses that evoke Ceaușescu's pronatalism. These conservative or, more aptly, neoconservative discourses have been increasingly mobilized by various political parties in Romania over the last decade, reflecting similar tendencies in another postsocialist country—Poland. Yet, whereas in Poland generous subsidies are provided to mothers and families to encourage childbearing, in Romania these incentives, along with public services and social safety nets, have been systematically dismantled by neoliberal policies. The alliance of ideological conservatism and neoliberal economics has resulted in a "disembedded neoliberalism, a hybrid extensively stripped of arguments defending the role of the state in buffering society against market dislocations."[58] According to historian Cristian Cercel, this type of neoliberal society is characterized by,

> on the one hand, "privatization," "market" withdrawal of the State from many areas in which it should normally be involved, and, on the other hand, a fatal embrace of conservatism, based on an ideological alliance with the Romanian Orthodox Church and all sorts of foundations and organizations that promote undemocratic ideas. Neoliberalism and Orthodoxy are joining in their efforts [in the form of] indoctrination in schools from the earliest ages, and as little sex education as possible: Under our eyes, Romania is transforming itself into the Neoliberal Orthodox Republic of Romania.[59]

Since 2017 conservatism has increasingly shaped the agenda of political elites and NGOs in Romania. The Coalition for the Family (Coaliția pentru familie; CpF), an alliance of pro-life and religious organizations, has attacked "gender ideology" and the rights of sexual minorities, their efforts culminating, in autumn 2018, in a national referendum to amend the constitutional definition of the "family" (from a "union of two persons" to a "union of two persons of the opposite sex"). The aim was to prevent same-sex marriage from ever being legalized in Romania; however, the referendum failed due to the lack of a quorum.

FINAL REMARKS

The evolution of women's reproductive rights in postsocialist Romania is puzzling and troubling at the same time: since Romania's accession to the EU, women's—especially low-income and impoverished women's—access to elective abortion and modern contraception has declined. After over a decade and a half of support by US donors and local NGOs, through which the Romanian MoH provided family planning services and free contraception to designated groups of women across the country, the situation changed abruptly and dramatically. Contraceptive pills and injectables ceased to be subsidized by the state, and doctors in public hospitals increasingly refused to provide elective abortions, claiming it was against their ethical norms. Meanwhile, doctors in private hospitals (some using unhygienic and unsafe methods) increasingly provided abortions, albeit at fees that are cost-prohibitive for many low-income women. The consequences of these developments evoke the latter part of socialist rule, when accessibility to safe abortion was dependent on money, bribery, and connections. Like their socialist foremothers, vulnerable women in postsocialist Romania who do not wish to carry their pregnancy to term are left with few choices, unsafe abortion through empirical means being one of them.

The legacy of Ceaușescu's pronatalism is also evident in the approach of the current MoH, which employs tropes similar to those used under socialism (i.e., "the perils of abortion to woman's health"). This paternalistic attitude, which represents childbearing as one of women's civic roles, reflects a clear continuity with the pre-1989 period. This pronatalist ethos is, in turn, supported by medical professionals who deceive or misinform women about the reproductive choices available to them and the health risks associated with abortion and contraception. It is also supported by their refusal to provide abortions in public hospitals on "ethical grounds" and their willingness to do so in private hospitals for exorbitant sums. While legal restrictions on elective abortion in the 1970s and 1980s created a profitable black market for abortion providers—of which medical and nonmedical professionals took advantage—since 2010, some medical professionals have invoked their "freedom of conscience" to refuse performing (cheaper) elective abortions in the public system, only to redirect abortion seekers to their private and more lucrative practice. Like their socialist forebears, some of these medical professionals have thus transformed elective abortion into a lucrative business.

Finally, as in late socialist Romania, women are blamed for the country's demographic decline, even though entitlements for families and children remain meager, as they had been under Ceaușescu. Similarly, they suffer from the combined effects of austerity measures and restrictions, albeit de facto, of their reproductive rights. However, there are also discontinuities such as the increased influence of the Orthodox Church and religious and conservative groups (some supported by neoconservative groups in the United States) on Romanian politics. Appealing to women on moral and religious grounds, they aim to guilt them into not having an abortion. In the complex equation of neoliberal economics infused with neoconservatism and pronatalism, expressed through limited access to abortion services in public hospitals and lack of subsidized contraception, it is low-income women who suffer the most. In light of such realities, it is perhaps no surprise that the mother of the first child born in Romania in 2021 was a girl of fifteen.[60]

NOTES

1. This work was supported by a grant from the Romanian Ministry of Research, Innovation and Digitization, CNCS-UEFISCDI, project number PN-III -P1-1.1-BSH-3-2021-0009 within PNCDI III.

2. Ionel Stoica, "Sinucidere macabră: o mamă şi 3 copii, călcaţi de tren: Poliţiştii au găsit un bilet de adio. Mărturiile conductorului locomotivei şi ale rudelor femeii," *Adevărul*, August 17, 2017, https://adevarul.ro/news/eveniment/o-femeie-trei-copii-deceda t-fost-loviti-tren-halta-branesti-1_59954d805ab6550cb81125f6/index.html.

3. Gail Kligman, *The Politics of Duplicity: Controlling Reproduction in Ceausescu's Romania* (Berkeley: University of California Press, 1998).

4. Corina Doboş, "Disciplining Births: Population Research and Politics in Communist Romania," *The History of the Family. Special Issue: Sex Education and Reproductive Politics in Cold War Europe* 25, no. 4 (September 2020): 599–626.

5. Corina Doboş, "Măsurile socioeconomice de stimulare a natalităţii şi susţinere a familiei din România ceauşistă (1966–1989)," in *Politica pronatalistă a regimului Ceauşescu: O perspectivă comparativă*, ed. Corina Doboş (Iaşi: Polirom, 2010), 223–63.

6. Corina Doboş, "Decesul s-a produs din vina femeii: fragmente din universul medico-juridic al pronatalismului ceauşist," in *Statutul femeii în România comunistă: Politici publice şi viaţă privată*, ed. Alina Hurubean (Iaşi: Editura Institutul European, 2015), 171–200.

7. Luciana Jinga, "Copilărie şi abandon familial în România anilor '80," in *Copilăria românească între familie şi sociatate (secolele XVII–XX)*, ed. Nicoleta Roman (Bucureşti: Nemira, 2015), 310–36; Jean-Philippe Légaut, "Les enfants de l'État: Histoire d'un orphelinat roumain sous Ceausescu," *Bulletin de l'Institut Pierre Renouvin* 29, no. 1 (Spring 2009): 79–88.

8. Ingi Iusmen, "The EU and International Adoption from Romania," *International Journal of Law, Policy and the Family* 27, no. 1 (April 2013): 1–27, 7–8.

9. Adelina Miron, "Sistemul naţional de planificare familială, încă o poveste despre indolenţa statului român: Medicii sunt bine pregatiţi, dar nimeni nu ne bagă în seama," *Ziare.com*, October 18, 2020, https://ziare.com/stiri/eveniment/sistemul -national-de-planificare-familiala-inca-o-poveste-despre-indolenta-statului-roman -medicii-sunt-bine-pregatiti-dar-nimeni-nu-ne-baga-in-seama-1637882.

10. Miron, "Sistemul naţional de planificare familială."

11. Miron, "Sistemul naţional de planificare familială."

12. Ministerul Sănătăţii, *Studiul sănătăţii reproducerii: România 2004* (Bucharest: Ministerul Sănătăţii, 2005).

13. Andrada Fişcutean, "Romania's Communist-Era Abortion Ban Harmed Hundreds of Thousands of Children: Is History Repeating Itself?" *Grid*, August 8,

2022, https://web.archive.org/web/20230525031114/https://themessenger.com
/grid/romanias-communist-era-abortion-ban-harmed-hundreds-of-thousands-of
-children-is-history-repeating-itself.

14. Miron, "Sistemul național de planificare familială"; Iolanda Mihalache, ed., *Plan de
măsuri pentru creșterea accesului la servicii de planificare familială: Propuneri alternative la politici publice formulate de ONG-uri* (Asociația pentru Dezvoltare Durabilă, December 2019), 38, https://programsamas.ro/materiale/propunere-alternativa
-in-domeniul-sanatatii-reproducerii.pdf.

15. Sexul vs. Barza, "Numărul cabinetelor de planificare familială în 2020 raportat la 2014,"
Facebook, October 12, 2020, https://www.facebook.com/sexulvsbarza/photos/a.4489
83561806357/3456990274338989/.

16. Sexul vs. Barza, "Distribuția gratuita de contraceptive și prezervative în cabinetele
de planificare familială în anul 2020," Facebook, October 14, 2020, https://www
.facebook.com/sexulvsbarza/photos/a.448983561806357/3462910917080258.

17. The percentage of women who used modern contraception increased from 23 percent
in 1999 to 38.7 percent in 2016. The percentage of women who procured contraception
on the market (i.e., from pharmacies) also increased during this period, from 51 percent
in 1993 to 54 percent in 2004, reaching 82 percent in in 2016. See Nicolae Suciu et al.,
Studiul sănătății reproducerii: România 2016 (Bucharest: Ministerul Sănătății, 2019).

18. International Planned Parenthood Federation and SECS, *Barometru: Accesul femeilor
la opțiuni de contracepție modernă în 16 țări UE. Principalele constatări și recomandări
privind politicile. România 2015*, 7. https://europe.ippf.org/sites/europe/files/2016-12
/Barometer%20of%20Women%27s%*

19. International Planned Parenthood Federation, *Barometer of Women's Access to Modern
Contraceptive Choice in 16 EU Countries. Extended 2015*, 24. https://europe.ippf.org
/resource/womens-access-modern-contraceptive-choice-barometer-2015

20. IPPF, *Barometer 2015*, 23.

21. IPPF & SECS, *Barometru 2015*, 10, 14–15.

22. European Parliamentary Forum for Sexual and Reproductive Rights (EPF), *European
Contraception Policy Atlas—Romania*, https://www.epfweb.org/node/747.

23. Suciu et al., *Studiul sănătății 2016*, 48.

24. "Cât costă un avort în România în 2019," *Unica*, January 8, 2019, https://www.unica
.ro/sanatate/cat-costa-un-avort-romania-2019-263787.

25. As of 2021, the most expensive surgical abortion in public facilities cost 1,000 lei (200
euros), while in private facilities the cost ranged from 1,200 lei (250 euros) to 4,500 lei
(1,000 euros). See Diana Meseșan, "În 11 județe din România nu s-a făcut niciun avort
la cerere în 2021, în spitalele publice," *Libertatea*, June 30, 2022, https://www.libertatea
.ro/stiri/in-11-judete-din-romania-nu-s-a-facut-niciun-avort-la-cerere-in-2021-in
-spitalele-publice-exista-femei-care-sunt-nevoite-sa-mearga-in-alt-judet-4195786.

26. Meseşan, "În 11 judeţe din România."

27. Suciu et al., *Studiul sănătăţii 2016*, 45, table 4.2.1.

28. FILIA, *Cum a modificat COVID19 accesul româncelor la avortul la cerere?* 2020, https://coronavirus.centrulfilia.ro/avortul-si-covid19/.

29. Meseşan, "În 11 judeţe din România."

30. ECPI, *Refuzul pe motive de religie sau conştiinţă la efectuarea avortului lacerere în România* (2014), 4, http://www.ecpi.ro/wpcontent/uploads/2015/03/Raport_Refuzul_la_efectuarea_avortului_la_cerere_in_Romania.pdf; ECPI & FILIA, *Refuzul pe motive de religie sau conştiinţă la efectuarea avortului lacerere în România* (2019), 10, https://cdn.edupedu.ro/wp-content/uploads/2019/06/Raport_Avorturi_2019-1.pdf.

31. ECPI, *Refuzul pe motive de religie* (2014), 2.

32. ECPI, *Refuzul pe motive de religie* (2014), 8.

33. ECPI, *Refuzul pe motive de religie* (2014), 8.

34. ECPI, *Refuzul pe motive de religie* (2014), 7.

35. ECPI, *Refuzul pe motive de religie* (2014), 2.

36. ECPI & Filia, *Refuzul pe motive de religie* (2019), 8.

37. ECPI, *Refuzul pe motive de religie* (2014), 2.

38. Diana Meseşan, "Ce treabă aveţi dumneavoastră cu privatul meu?" *DelaO.ro*, November 7, 2021, https://beta.dela0.ro/ce-treaba-aveti-dumneavoastra-cu-privatul-meu/.

39. Diana Meseşan, "None of Your Business: How Private Clinics Have Become the Leading Providers of Abortion Services in Romania, *The Decree Chronicles*, November 7, 2021, https://decreechronicles.com/none-of-your-business-how-private-clinics-have-become-the-leading-providers-of-abortion-services-in-romania/.

40. "Romania: Campaign Blog—After the Death of the Woman, He Offers Them the Money Back," *International Campaign for Women's Right to Safe Abortion*, September 3, 2020, https://www.safeabortionwomensright.org/news/romania-campaign-blog-after-the-death-of-the-woman-he-offers-them-the-money-back/?fbclid=IwAR0I1vgDPkRD7mbHf5K3WHKJk73W_MLQ5JI7wzR-OJ8u6a_k98Wyhla4g-g.

41. Cristian Andrei Leonte, "Centrul FILIA cere demiterea purtătorului de cuvânt al Ministerului Sănătăţii, după declaraţiile controversate despre avort," *G4Media.ro*, September 3, 2020, https://www.g4media.ro/centrul-filia-cere-demiterea-purtatorului-de-cuvant-al-ministerului-sanatatii-dupa-declaratiile-controversate-despre-avort.html?fbclid=IwAR0tDumIyLV9s8M_ckbQLVB1Wmx_FpX66M0mnPlgkR1VBRmdIr8lygrbjAw.

42. Romania's population decreased from 22.8 million in 1992 to 19,603,879 in 2014. Meanwhile, the total fertility rate (TFR) decreased from 2.22 in 1989 to 1.76 in 2020. Vasile Surd, Bogdan-Nicolae Pacurar, and Camelia Kantor, "Major Demographic Changes in the Dynamics and Structure of the Romanian Population after the Fall of

Communism," *Zbornik Matice srpske za drustvene nauke* 148 (201): 803–11, 809.

43. Dorothee Bohle and Béla Greskovits, *Capitalist Diversity on Europe's Periphery* (Ithaca, NY: Cornell University Press, 2012).

44. Bohle and Greskovits, *Capitalist Diversity*, 22.

45. Bohle and Greskovits, *Capitalist Diversity*, 183.

46. Sabina Stan and Roland Erne, "Explaining Romanian Labor Migration: From Development Gaps to Development Trajectories," *Labor History* 55, no. 1 (2014): 21–46.

47. Stan and Erne, "Explaining Romanian Labor Migration," 36. See also "Băsescu: Să nu mai facem o dramă din faptul că românii pleacă să muncească în afara țării," *Adevărul*, August 5, 2010, adevarul.ro/news/societate/basescu-nu-mai-facem-drama -faptul-romanii-pleaca-munceasca-afara-tarii-1_50ae30367c42d5a6639a83de/index.html.

48. "Băsescu: Romania a devenit o țară de mamicuțe și bebeluși," *Știrile ProTV*, July 22, 2017, https://stirileprotv.ro/stiri/politic/basescu-solutia-privind-indemnizatia-si -concediul-pentru-mame-este-buna.html.

49. Iulia Popovici, "Știu femeile ce fac atunci cînd avortează?," *Observatorul Cultural*, April 6, 2012, https://www.observatorcultural.ro/articol/stiu-femeile-ce-fac-atunci-cind -avorteaza-2/; Cristian Cercel, "Întreruperea de sarcină în Republica Neoliberală Ortodoxă România," *Observatorul Cultural*, April 12, 2012, https://www.observatorcultural .ro/articol/intreruperea-de-sarcina-in-republica-neoliberala-ortodoxa-romania-2/.

50. Popovici, "Știu femeile"; Cercel, "Întreruperea de sarcină; and Stan and Erne, "Explaining Romanian Labor Migration."

51. Cercel, "Întreruperea de sarcină."

52. "Ministerul Sănătății: Ar fi util ca medicii să consilieze femeia care dorește să facă avort," *Mediafax*, April 9, 2021, https://www.mediafax.ro/social/ministerul-sanatatii -ar-fi-util-ca-medicii-sa-consilieze-femeia-care-doreste-sa-faca-avort-9500741.

53. Dobos, "Disciplining Births."

54. Popovici, "Știu femeile"; "Ministerul Sănătății: Ar fi util ca medicii să consilieze."

55. DSP Vaslui, *Campania Sănătatea reproducerii 2020*, 21, http://www.dspvs.ro/dsp2 /images/Campania%20Sanatatea%20reproducerii.pdf.

56. DSP Vaslui, *Campania Sănătatea reproducerii 2020*, 21.

57. M. Antonia Biggs, et al., "Women's Mental Health and Well-Being 5 Years after Receiving or Being Denied an Abortion: A Prospective, Longitudinal Cohort Study," *JAMA Psychiatry* 74, no. 2 (Feb. 2017): 169–78.

58. Cornel Ban, *Ruling Ideas: How Global Neoliberalism Goes Local* (Oxford: Oxford University Press, 2016), 5.

59. Cercel, "Întreruperea de sarcină."

60. "România, pe locul doi în UE la rata de naștere în rândul mamelor adolescente," *Europa Liberă. România*, January 8, 2021, https://romania.europalibera.org/a/romania-pe -locul-doi-in-ue-la-rata-de-nastere-in-randul-mamelor-adolescente-/31038834.html.

BIBLIOGRAPHY

Ban, Cornel. *Ruling Ideas: How Global Neoliberalism Goes Local*. Oxford: Oxford University Press, 2016.

"Băsescu: Romania a devenit o țară de mamicuțe și bebeluși." *Știrile ProTV*, July 22, 2017. https://stirileprotv.ro/stiri/politic/basescu-solutia-privind-indemnizatia-si-concediul -pentru-mame-este-buna.html.

Biggs, M. Antonia, et al. "Women's Mental Health and Well-Being 5 Years after Receiving or Be- ing Denied an Abortion: A Prospective, Longitudinal Cohort Study." *JAMA Psychiatry* 74, no. 2 (Feb. 2017): 169–78.

Bohle, Dorothee, and Béla Greskovits. *Capitalist Diversity on Europe's Periphery*. Ithaca, NY: Cornell University Press, 2012.

"Cât costă un avort în România în 2019." *Unica*, January 8, 2019. https://www.unica.ro/sanatate /cat-costa-un-avort-romania-2019-263787.

Cercel, Cristian. "Întreruperea de sarcină în Republica Neoliberală Ortodoxă România." *Ob- servatorul Cultural*, April 12, 2012. https://www.observatorcultural.ro/articol/intreruperea -de-sarcina-in-republica-neoliberala-ortodoxa-romania-2/.

Doboș, Corina. "Decesul s-a produs din vina femeii: fragmente din universul medico-juridic al pronatalismului ceaușist." In *Statutul femeii în România comunistă: Politici publice și viață pri- vată*, edited by Alina Hurubean, 171–200. Iași: Editura Institutul European, 2015.

Doboș, Corina. "Disciplining Births: Population Research and Politics in Communist Roma- nia." *The History of the Family. Special Issue: Sex Education and Reproductive Politics in Cold War Europe* 25, no. 4 (September 2020): 599–626.

Doboș, Corina. "Măsurile socioeconomice de stimulare a natalității și susținere a familiei din România ceaușistă (1966–1989)." In *Politica pronatalistă a regimului Ceaușescu: O perspec- tivă comparativă*, edited by Corina Doboș, 223–63. Iași: Polirom, 2010.

ECPI. *Refuzul pe motive de religie sau conștiință la efectuarea avortului lacerere în România* (2014), 4, http://www.ecpi.ro/wpcontent/uploads/2015/03/Raport_Refuzul_la_efectuarea _avortului_la_cerere_in_Romania.pdf.

European Parliamentary Forum for Sexual and Reproductive Rights (EPF). *European Contra- ception Policy Atlas—Romania*. https://www.epfweb.org/node/747.

FILIA. *Cum a modificat COVID19 accesul româncelor la avortul la cerere?* 2020. https:// coronavirus.centrulfilia.ro/avortul-si-covid19/.

Fișcutean, Andrada. "Romania's Communist-Era Abortion Ban Harmed Hundreds of Thou- sands of Children: Is History Repeating Itself?" *Grid*, August 8, 2022. https://web.archive .org/web/20230525031114/https://themessenger.com/grid/romanias-communist -era-abortion-ban-harmed-hundreds-of-thousands-of-children-is-history-repeating-itself.

International Planned Parenthood Federation. *Barometer of Women's Access to Modern Contraceptive Choice in 16 EU Countries Extended, January 2015*. https://europe.ippf.org/resource/womens-access-modern-contraceptive-choice-barometer-2015.

International Planned Parenthood Federation & SECS. *Barometru: Accesul femeilor la opțiuni de contracepție modernă în 16 țări UE. Principalele constatări și recomandări privind politicile. România 2015.* https://europe.ippf.org/sites/europe/files/2016-12/Barometer%20of%20Women%27s%20Access%20to%20Modern%20contraceptive%20Choice%20in%20Romania.pdf.

Iusmen, Ingi. "The EU and International Adoption from Romania." *International Journal of Law, Policy and the Family* 27, no. 1 (April 2013): 1–27.

Jinga, Luciana. "Copilărie și abandon familial în România anilor '80." In *Copilăria românească între familie și sociatate (secolele XVII–XX)*, edited by Nicoleta Roman, 310–36. București: Nemira, 2015.

Kligman, Gail. *The Politics of Duplicity: Controlling Reproduction in Ceausescu's Romania*. Berkeley: University of California Press, 1998.

Légaut, Jean-Philippe. "Les enfants de l'État. Histoire d'un orphelinat roumain sous Ceausescu." *Bulletin de l'Institut Pierre Renouvin* 29, no. 1 (Spring 2009): 79–88.

Leonte, Cristian Andrei. "Centrul FILIA cere demiterea purtătorului de cuvânt al Ministerului Sănătății, după declarațiile controversate despre avort." *G4Media.ro*, September 3, 2020. ntrul-filia-cere-demiterea-purtatorului-de-cuvant-al-ministerului-sanatatii-dupa-declaratiile-controversate-despre-avort.html?fbclid=IwAR0tDumIyLV9s8M_ckbQLVB1Wmx_FpX66M0mnPlgkR1VBRmdIr8lygrbjAw.

Meseșan, Diana. "Ce treabă aveți dumneavoastră cu privatul meu?" *DelaO.ro*, November 7, 2021. https://beta.dela0.ro/ce-treaba-aveti-dumneavoastra-cu-privatul-meu/.

Meseșan, Diana. "În 11 județe din România nu s-a făcut niciun avort la cerere în 2021, în spitalele publice." *Libertatea*, June 30, 2022. https://www.libertatea.ro/stiri/in-11-judete-din-romania-nu-s-a-facut-niciun-avort-la-cerere-in-2021-in-spitalele-publice-exista-femei-care-sunt-nevoite-sa-mearga-in-alt-judet-4195786.

Meseșan, Diana. "None of Your Business: How Private Clinics Have Become the Leading Providers of Abortion Services in Romania." *The Decree Chronicles*, November 7, 2021.

Mihalache, Iolanda, ed. *Plan de măsuri pentru creșterea accesului la servicii de planificare familială: Propuneri alternative la politici publice formulate de ONG-uri*. Asociația pentru Dezvoltare Durabilă, December 2019.

"Ministerul Sănătății: Ar fi util ca medicii să consilieze femeia care dorește să facă avort." *Mediafax*, April 9, 2021. https://www.mediafax.ro/social/ministerul-sanatatii-ar-fi-util-ca-medicii-sa-consilieze-femeia-care-doreste-sa-faca-avort-9500741.

Ministerul Sănătății. *Studiul sănătății reproducerii: România 2004* (Bucharest: Ministerul Sănătății, 2005).

Miron, Adelina. "Sistemul national de planificare familiala, inca o poveste despre indolenta statului roman: Medicii sunt bine pregatiti, dar nimeni nu ne baga in seama." *Ziare.com*, October 18, 2020. https://ziare.com/stiri/eveniment/sistemul-national-de-planificare-familiala-inca-o-poveste-despre-indolenta-statului-roman-medicii-sunt-bine-pregatiti-dar-nimeni-nu-ne-baga-in-seama-1637882.

Popovici, Iulia. "Știu femeile ce fac atunci cînd avortează?" *Observatorul Cultural*, April 6, 2012. https://www.observatorcultural.ro/articol/stiu-femeile-ce-fac-atunci-cind-avorteaza-2/.

"Romania: Campaign Blog—After the Death of the Woman, He Offers Them the Money Back." International Campaign for Women's Right to Safe Abortion, September 3, 2020. https://www.safeabortionwomensright.org/news/romania-campaign-blog-after-the-death-of-the-woman-he-offers-them-the-money-back/?fbclid=IwAR0I1vgDPkRD7mbHf5K3WHKJk73W_MLQ5JI7wzR-OJ8u6a_k98Wyhla4g-g.

"România, pe locul doi în UE la rata de naştere în rândul mamelor adolescente." *Europa Liberă. România*, January 8, 2021. https://romania.europalibera.org/a/romania-pe-locul-doi-in-ue-la-rata-de-nastere-in-randul-mamelor-adolescente-/31038834.html.

Sexul vs. Barza. "Distributia gratuita de contraceptive si preservative in cabinetele de planificare familiala in anul 2020." Facebook, October 14, 2020. https://www.facebook.com/sexulvsbarza/photos/a.448983561806357/3462910917080258

Sexul vs. Barza. "Numarul cabinetelor de planificare familiala in 2020 raportat la 2014." Facebook, 12 October 2020. https://www.facebook.com/sexulvsbarza/photos/a.448983561806357/3456990274338989/.

Stan, Sabina, and Roland Erne. "Explaining Romanian Labor Migration: From Development Gaps to Development Trajectories." *Labor History* 55, no. 1 (2014): 21–46.

Stoica, Ionel. "Sinucidere macabră: o mamă şi 3 copii, călcaţi de tren: Poliţiştii au găsit un bilet de adio. Mărturiile conductorului locomotivei şi ale rudelor femeii." *Adevărul*, August 17, 2017. https://adevarul.ro/news/eveniment/o-femeie-trei-copii-deceda t-fost-loviti-tren-halta-branesti-1_59954d805ab6550cb81125f6/index.html.

Suciu, Nicolae, et al. *Studiul sănătății: Reproducerii Romania 2016*. Bucharest: Ministerul Sanatatii, 2019.

Surd, Vasile, Bogdan-Nicolae Pacurar, and Camelia Kantor. "Major Demographic Changes in the Dynamics and Structure of the Romanian Population after the Fall of Communism." *Zbornik Matice srpske za drustvene nauke* 148 (2014): 803–11.

PART IV

ORIGIN STORIES

9

THE "TURNCOAT" AS A SOCIAL FORM

Tracing Everyday Moral Grammars of Justice in Post-1989 East Germany and Czechia

TILL HILMAR

WHO IS THE "TURNCOAT"? THOUGH SEMANTICALLY OPEN, IT IS A NOtion rich in dramatic associations. The turncoat is a person whose true identity has been disclosed. Their insincere, fraudulent commitment to the values of a group has come to light: they have betrayed others. Their behavior has deeply troubling implications not just for interpersonal relations, but for the larger community. Their decision to break the bonds of loyalty and abandon their commitments signals that those older beliefs, and the very people who hold them dear, do not count any longer—and perhaps never did.[1]

The turncoat may be an instance of what Georg Simmel called a "social form": an elementary category of personhood that provides a framework to think about society, that structures people's everyday understanding of the relationship between individual and community. In this sense, the turncoat symbolizes disconcerting aspects of societal change.[2]

The turncoat is everywhere to be found where regimes collapse, states are in transition, and political fortunes are reshuffled.[3] The history of twentieth-century Eastern Europe is rich in such episodes. The breakdown of communist rule is merely the most recent instance: Nazi occupation, genocidal mass violence, and the crushing of national elites by the Soviets before and after World War II shook the social fabric of societies in this part of the world. In territories occupied by both the Nazis and the Soviets, "collaborators" were ubiquitous; to define whose actions counted as such was as much an exercise of military supremacy as it was an act of political and ideo-logical power. During and long after the war, the Jewish population of Eastern Europe was most consequently deemed "disloyal" to the nation, as acting in the service of "foreign" political forces. Today, the image of the turncoat is thus necessarily intertwined with the murderous legacies of the ostracization, persecution, and annihilation of Jewish citizens.[4]

The memory of this violent past also impacts the texture of social relationships in the present. To be Jewish and Polish in post-1989 Poland, for instance, means to be cognizant of particular historical experiences, which may generate a sense of deep attachment and affect how one relates to one's friends and confidants in the present.[5] Yet, in turn, knowledge about the twentieth century is never innocent. There is always the possibility of abandoning shared memories. Shifting and conflicting interpretations of the past may burden and fracture social bonds when they are seen as problems of loyalty. In recent times, with the rise of authoritarian populism across the globe, value conflicts in proximate social relations are often understood as instances of political polarization. However, these contestations arguably run deeper when they are rooted in the dynamics of socially segmented historical memories.

In this chapter, I explore the significance of the turncoat in relation to popular experiences of the 1989 revolutions and the subsequent changes in East Germany and Czechoslovakia, drawing on excerpts from interviews with individuals who experienced the breakdown of communism as young adults. I ask: What value antagonisms and conflicting loyalties does the notion of the turncoat invoke from the perspective of those who lived through the post-1989 changes? By focusing on the transformation period, I narrow the time frame and the depth of this exploration. However, there is a particular benefit to such a perspective: foregrounding interpretations of the relatively recent events of 1989 grants important insights into popular ideas about political and economic justice as they are nourished by the social experience of change after the collapse of communism.

APPROACHING VALUE CHANGE POST-1989

Jan Kubik suggests that the study of postsocialism calls for a "contextual holism" approach, a perspective that takes the meaning of life-worlds in transition as its point of departure and, at the same time, links biographical trajectories and their interpretation to the institutions of state and society.[6] Modernization theory, with its unidirectional assumption about how Easterners would gradually morph into Westerners (and learn to be better citizens along the way), has justifiably lost its dominant position in this respect. Yet, the mere description of a given set of individual and community experiences after 1989—culture as the way we do things around here—is not a satisfactory epistemological alternative. Instead, following Kubik, we need to look for shifting patterns of social relationships and their normative interpretation; for how societal institutions such as work, gender, welfare, and the state, all of which transitioned after the collapse of communism, shaped individual trajectories, as well as the horizons of meaning by which everyday experiences of the transformation were enacted, narrated, and justified. Social and oral history approaches that regard biographies as embedded in institutional change provide rich examples for such a view.[7] I situate my contribution in this perspective, albeit with an important limitation: I do not reconstruct biographical horizons in detail. Instead, I aim to trace a recurring pattern of meaning-making in the way people apprehend value change after 1989. By tracing the meaning of the turncoat from an everyday perspective, I focus on what people deem to be a particularly negative, disconcerting instance of value change. Examining the ways in which this category is imbued with meaning by individuals who experienced the rupture of 1989 firsthand promises to offer revealing, if necessarily fragmentary, insights into this larger set of problems.

In postsocialist societies, the issue of value change is inseparable from the reality of elite continuity after 1989. In many instances, former elites and their families managed to hold onto power—if not political, then economic power. Mechanisms of transitional justice, if any were in place, often failed.[8] States were generally weak in enforcing the rule of law and in overseeing privatization, deregulation, and the liberalization of the economy after 1989.[9] To be sure, there was great variation across countries in terms of the nature and extent of malfeasance. Still, today, elite kleptocracy is widely seen as a defining outcome of this period, and wide swaths of the population across the postsocialist world associate the transformation period with corruption.[10] In this respect, the meaning of the transformation period is precisely the opposite of value change: it signifies the continuation of practices of theft and non-meritocratic privilege that are associated with the late socialist *nomenklatura* (administrative elite). Elite continuity thus symbolizes a barely subtle transformation of undeserved advantage pre-1989 into newer variants of illegitimate wealth accumulation in post-1989 market society.

EAST GERMAN AND CZECH EXPERIENCES COMPARED

In the following, I discuss excerpts from semi-structured interviews with sixty-seven respondents who experienced the 1989 revolutions as young adults. Interviewed in 2016 and 2017, the respondents were invited to participate in conversations on biographical experiences of economic change after the collapse of communism: I asked them to recount their work biography in the first part of the conversation, followed by questions on the topics of social relations and justice orientations after 1989.[11] The focus on work experiences guides the conversations; the salience of economic issues in the interviews is thus also determined by the framework for this study. There are two ways in which the turncoat appears in them. First, the notion was invoked by respondents directly. Second, respondents were asked to define it in a later part of the conversation.[12] In this way, it is possible to compare the cultural classifications employed by respondents across interviews systematically. An advantage of asking this particular question is that it does not come with any assumptions about the content of the normative framework by which to evaluate other people's actions after 1989: respondents were invited to reveal the specific moral concerns (and justifications) through which they evaluate the matter. From a methodological point of view, the notion works well as a prompt as it encourages an invitation to reflect on one's everyday experience with more general reflections about the nature of social change.

The conversations were held in (former East) Germany and the Czech Republic, two very different transformation contexts. Politically, the dissolution of East Germany and its incorporation into the West German Federal Republic in 1990 resulted in the East Germans losing their former polity. For Czechs, in contrast, the divorce from Slovakia facilitated the independence of a new Czech nation-state at the beginning of 1993. Economically, East Germans experienced a radical break with the German Democratic Republic (GDR) model of a socialist "welfare dictatorship," with the dissolution of industry and skyrocketing unemployment during the 1990s.[13] West Germans soon became the new proprietors and bosses of the East German workforce, while East Germans experienced diminished opportunity for upward mobility after the fall of the Wall. In this case, former East German political elites were effectively kept from retaining positions of power or making use of pre-1989 political networks. Czechs, by comparison, experienced relative continuity thanks to a social policy priority of keeping unemployment low.[14] There was also elite continuity, as many former technocrats and firm insiders (in what Czech sociologists have labeled a "revolution of the deputies") were able to capitalize on privatization and weak regulation of the financial sector.[15] Against this background, it could reasonably be assumed that the turncoat meant different things in each case—perhaps because of varying salient concerns about political and economic justice after 1989.

JUDGING THE TURNCOAT: FROM POLITICAL ALLEGIANCE TO ECONOMIC INCOMPETENCE

Václav is a middle-aged Czech structural engineer who left his job at a large state-owned company and became a successful entrepreneur in the early 1990s. Overall, his view of the 1990s is very positive as it was a time of freedom (in political and economic terms), self-realization, and growth. When it comes to the turncoat, however, his mood sours. In his view, the turncoat is someone who was attached to the Communist Party before the revolution and managed to profit from these prior connections after the 1989 revolutions:

> I was not friendly with those people because I didn't have many communist friends before the revolution . . . but it was clear that there were post-1989 politicians and people who were riding the privatization wave and so on who were linked with the regime before the revolution, and after the revolution they were . . . grand privatizers. In the '80s, there weren't many people in the party for ideological reasons, who actually believed, who wanted to build communism. So [after 1989], they remained silent for a moment, waiting, and after it was clear that no one would go after them, nothing happened—well they started knocking on doors after one or two years. They had opportunities, they had contacts. They would enter management positions; they had the means from pre-revolutionary times unlike 90 percent of the rest of the nation. [16]

According to Václav, the turncoat combines two instances of undeserved advantage: he enjoyed a position of relative power under communist rule and continues to rely on nepotism after 1989. [17] Crucially, Václav links this kind of post-1989 profiteering directly to the privatization process.

Privatization in the Czech Republic was accompanied by major corruption scandals, with banks handing out foul loans to scheming business insiders and misinformed citizens losing their share of the former "people's property" in the process. [18] For Václav, the turncoat is a person who profited from what has been a disappointment to many Czechs. In his view, privatization is not a market mechanism, but a politically coordinated scheme, something that only the well-connected were able to profit from, but never those who were genuinely committed to meritocratic principles. Václav took pride in having never "privatized anything." What is problematic about the turncoat, then, is not so much the act of transitioning from a socialist into a capitalist, but the means by which the person remained attached to politics in one way or another. It deserves mentioning that this antipolitical reading of the 1990s is itself grounded in a somewhat mythical narrative that tends to ignore the role of the state in the economy. There was hardly a branch of the emerging Czech private economy that was not affected or enabled by the transfer of public resources to private hands.[19]

The turncoat, according to Václav, is a careerist and an opportunist, a person who acts out of purely instrumental motives with no ideological allegiance. Thus, the turncoat was not a socialist and is not necessarily a capitalist. Yet, there is a tension inherent in this interpretation, for how can we truly know a person's beliefs about state and society in late socialist Czechoslovakia? Václav, understandably, argues that communist ideals were already long dead in the 1980s. But this also suggests that the definition of the turncoat depends on an interpretation (and, in this case, a certain simplification) of the relationship between state and society in late socialist society, both in terms of the dominant values at the time and in terms of who was equipped with relative power in this system.[20]

According to respondents, a person's economic success after 1989 appears to be an important indicator of being a turncoat. For them, it is particularly hurtful—and unfair—to see someone who was involved with the secret police, who might have spied on friends and family and was complicit in the network of state-socialist terror, be materially rewarded in the post-1989 system. Yet the turncoat is not necessarily linked to a nouveau-riche type of wealth made possible by privatization. When describing the turncoat, some respondents have much less glamorous careers in mind. Jan, a Czech railway engineer in his early fifties, recounted the story of someone who he is convinced was affiliated with the Communist Party before the revolution.[21] After 1989, because this person wanted to "avoid having to work," he made a career as a union functionary. Later, according to Jan, he managed to secure a high position in the labor office, "distributing jobs" among his network and exercising a kind of arbitrary power in this way: "They say that around four people had to leave their jobs just so that he could keep his position."[22] What really defines the turncoat, according to Jan, is a reckless drive for and abuse of power. This, again, is a story of continuity rather than change, and respondents often linked the turncoat to elite change and continuity.

In the German context, the historical parameters of this problem are very different. In this case, there was minimal elite reproduction after the fall of the Wall. Thanks to an extensive lustration program and West German institutional and personnel transfer, the German transformation effectively blocked former communist elites from maintaining or regaining power.[23] As a result, West German elites soon occupied dominant roles in politics, administration, economics, journalism, and the cultural sphere. Against this backdrop, it is surprising that East German respondents put forward themes similar to their Czech counterparts. Many former East Germans characterize the turncoat as a person who enjoyed a privileged position before 1989 as a result of being proximate to the center of communist power and who became a full-fledged capitalist after 1989. Lukas, a sixty-seven-year-old German ultrasound technician, experienced bouts of unemployment after the fall of the Wall. His narrative of the 1990s is strongly marked by the themes of resilience and individual responsibility. Asked about the turncoat, he explains that he himself was not able to advance his career before 1989 because he refused to become part of the social infrastructure of the Communist Party:

> I was not part of the combat group, not part of the civil organization, things that one had to do to rise further. And the people who did . . . they disgusted me, I have to say, because you knew exactly what they were like. They were preaching water and drinking wine. . . . And precisely these people turned into pure market ideologues afterwards. They put themselves at the top of the firms and the spin-offs. In this way they secured for themselves the privileges. Because they still had the connections and things like that. Just like that, from party secretary to business consultant![24]

According to Lukas, the turncoat enjoyed undeserved advantages within a firm's hierarchy before 1989. Meanwhile, after 1989, he profited from business spin-offs and the splitting up of the firms into more and less valuable parts. This is exceptional because, on the whole, successful East German entrepreneurship after the fall of the Wall was a rather rare phenomenon.[25] Lukas also mentions a particular profession that former party functionaries assumed after 1989: the "business consultant." By doing so, he designates a somewhat generalized role more than describing the actions of a particular person—in Simmel's terms, he defines a more general social principle by delineating individual qualities.[26] In a similar vein, other respondents referenced "insurance brokers" or "sales people" whom they contrasted with productive and useful workers. In this way, they demarcate the turncoat's distance from the values of the (East German) community.

East German respondents are no less concerned with the problem of elite continuity after 1989 than Czechs. Still, in this context, the relevant interpretations are often associated with various aspects of the relationship to West Germans. Some respondents associate the turncoat with the German federal privatization agency, the *Treuhand* (Trust). This is again counterintuitive: the *Treuhand* was a West German project through and through. In fact, it was arguably the paradigmatic example of the absence of an East German voice and agency in the transformation of the GDR economy. Others argue that the turncoat had no second thoughts about aligning himself with West Germans after regime change.[27] Before the collapse of the communist regime, Laura, fifty-two, was trained as a cartographer and worked for a company that produced maps for the East German army. She remembered how the downsizing of her firm in the 1990s prompted some of her former colleagues—notably, those who used to be affiliated with the party—to take up work for a West German employer. This she interpreted as a form of defection:

It was at the point where the issue was, who can stay and who has to go, who has to go only at a later point, that the ones who were Party members suddenly turned and said, "well that West German publishing house, I'll go there right away!" Now how could they—if they had ever been real comrades—how could they go and suddenly work for the "class enemy"! I was shocked, I'd say because that meant it was all a charade, or a show, or a lot of it at least.[28]

Laura draws an analogy between being affiliated with the communist elite and associating oneself with West Germans, or, even worse, turning into a West German. Clearly, this is a rejection of the official German narrative of reunification, which emphasizes East Germans' desire and struggle to become more like their Western counterparts.

What might be made of such classifications? The turncoat references a range of vague perceptions, a set of issues that are associated with regime change and the ways in which elites, or people in privileged positions more generally, assert power in one way or another. Is it therefore also an arbitrary category, a kind of one-size-fits-all terminology, detached from people's social experience of the transformation period? I would argue against such a view. People in fact reveal serious normative commitments when invoking this category. A certain pattern emerges here: in most of the respondents' descriptions the turncoat is understood to be bad at doing things that actually matter. Specifically, he is notoriously incapable or unwilling to perform useful work or fulfill tasks that are beneficial and valuable to the community. Thus, respondents attach value to particular types of economic knowledge and skills, values that the turncoat lacks. He is often poorly trained, lacks professional ambition, and has questionable priorities. He cares about power, not about competence. This is why he affiliates himself with "politics" before and after 1989. He tries to avoid getting his hands dirty at all costs.

To Werner, a fifty-seven-year-old East German business professor, the distinction between a shallow and a profound work ethic is key. The fact that he always put his technical competence first enabled him to deal with the problem of his political involvement before 1989, and, subsequently, with the need to make sense of his past in the course of the turbulent 1990s:

I solved this in the following way: I said, alright, I was politically active to some degree during GDR times, but I have always put my technical competence first.... That was also because of my parents, my dad was a party hardliner, my mother was not. I was baptized, too. My parents were married, too, and so that affected me, that is why I have always put the technical aspects first. I made sure that I kept my personal integrity, that I stayed morally clean.[29]

For Werner, work ethic and competence animate his biographical trajectory. This was a frequent theme among German and Czech respondents alike: to attain knowledge and expertise in order to advance in a field of work was for him a sign of ideological neutrality as well as integrity. The turncoat violates such principles, as they seek to profit by way of superficial knowledge and through the "the art" of selling, advertising, or siphoning off money. They might be good at "rhetoric," as another respondent conceded, but the turncoat does not possess genuine skill or qualification for the job. By virtue of their unwillingness—or inability—to be a productive member of society, the turncoat has lost moral credibility.

In the course of these discussions, the meaning of the turncoat seemingly shifted from the political domain to the economic realm. Perhaps this does not come as a surprise: after all, popular accounts of the 1990s are deeply interlinked with problems of distributive justice and whether society was meritocratic, rewarding skills and effort, or cronyistic, based on connections and favoritism. In addition to broader questions about post-1989, such questions were deeply personal, related to identity and self-worth. Individuals had to negotiate them biographically, as the value of their skills was shifting in post-1989 labor markets.[30]

REJECTING THE CLASSIFICATION

Some respondents, meanwhile, rejected classifications altogether. They posited that discussions about the turncoat were merely a superficial diagnosis (and perhaps an artificial concern) that distracted from a larger, underlying truth, namely the fact that people change as circumstances change. To be sure, there is a range of gradations in meanings and interpretations possibly associated with such a position. It can be advanced as a fatalistic attitude, in which human nature is defined as ever-changing and opportunistic; or as a universal binary classification of people with "good" or "bad" character. Eva, a Czech nurse in her early fifties, interpreted the turncoat as a fundamental problem of human nature, independent of regime change.[31] Others, specifically those who did relatively well after 1989, reject the category because they associate it with social resentment and material envy after the revolutions.

Finally, some problematize this desire to expose the turncoat, viewing it as a larger problem haunting the social experience of the transformation period—the need to judge others for their choices and convictions at the time. This troubles Irene, a sixty-year-old East German who was trained as a technician in the GDR, shifted to social work after the fall of the Wall, and currently works in an elder care organization:

I had my qualms, my questions about [the turncoat]. It was like that, maybe I was naïve, but it was at a time when the transition of 1989 wasn't even a thing yet, some of my colleagues always knew, "this person works for the secret police, that person does," and so on, and I always asked: "How do you know?" I might have thought of the person as a dumb dumb, but I wouldn't have dared to make these kinds of claims. . . . And [after 1989] suddenly, people thought they knew, this or that person has to go, be dismissed from their job, as if they knew exactly what they were doing. I'd say they had no way of knowing. It's like I cannot know for sure whether a tool-maker is qualified for his job or not because I don't know what it is that he is doing. But now this and that person suddenly felt entitled to say, "this person has to go, he's just idling time away!"[32]

Irene criticizes the fact that, after 1989, people were ready to judge each other even if they lacked information about their choices and the context that informed them. Whatever it was that motivated them—perhaps revenge—it was nasty and undermined the possibility of coming to terms with the complexity of change around 1989. For Irene it is too late to solve this problem. The social scars run deep, and people are still living with the consequences of devaluing each other's work and life choices after the collapse of communism.

THE UNBOUNDEDNESS OF CHANGE AND THE NEED FOR PURITY AFTER 1989

Change in post-1989 societies is generally understood as a complex mix of political, economic, and cultural processes. Beyond unidirectional assumptions of where this journey is going, we must embrace the possibilities that varying trajectories interact and study the ways in which people interpret, and thereby also shape, these processes from the standpoint of their everyday experience. Understanding the realms of meaning and the cultural classifications that the category of the turncoat invokes proves to be a useful point of departure for such a perspective.

As demonstrated, the turncoat is often associated with an instrumental, cold-blooded, value-free striving for power. To claim that the turncoat never really believed in socialism, of course, is to suggest that one, personally, was not naïve about the precariousness of values in late socialist society. Accordingly, if there were no normative ideas to be shared, if there was no moral texture to be maintained in community bonds, then the turncoat cannot be accused of betraying anything of substance. Yet, as the widespread concern with this phenomenon demonstrates, this view is only part of the story. This is one of the complexities that this analysis has revealed: to engage with definitions of the turncoat after the collapse of communism is to engage the question of guilt and the problem of collaboration, complicity, and complacency during late socialism. The very resources that individuals could draw on after 1989—their education, contacts, and knowledge about the world—were also part of their socialization in late socialist society.

"The question remains," writes Marci Shore in an essay that eloquently links problems of transitional justice to larger issues of social and intellectual history, "when the vast majority was complicitous, how can anyone be held responsible?" And, she adds, "in some ways the legacy of dissidents has become nostalgia for moral purity—the moral purity of speaking truth against power—and suffering from it."[33] This desire for innocence and biographical purity is evident not only in the memories of dissidents and in the political realm, but also in the way people comprehend economic change, in how they make sense of the many and rapid shifts that have affected their work biography after the collapse of communism. In this domain, too, people's experiences shape how they think about justice in society today.

When invoking the turncoat, Czech and German respondents alike were concerned with what they deem as undeserved success after 1989—even if many do not define success as lavish wealth, but as successfully muddling through, something made possible by the lack of an adequate (economic) punishment for the actions and dispositions that these individuals are considered guilty of. These small stories from the 1990s may also transcend this context and take on a larger meaning as a criticism of persistent, systemic problems, such as in the denunciation of a political system that is understood to reward the wrong kinds of individuals, those who are flawed both in terms of their actions and in terms of their moral character. It is not hard to imagine how right-wing interpretations of the 1990s may resonate with such views. At the same time, the salience of the turncoat also serves as a reminder that justice has, in fact, not been done in postsocialist societies. To this day, the humiliating social and political experiences of late socialist authoritarianism have not been fully reckoned with.

However, it may also be the case that the turncoat is not just specific to this context. The phenomenon doubtless also plays a role in many other contexts of rapid social change. It makes sense, then, to link the problem back to sociological theory, and specifically to Georg Simmel's writings about sociation and the social form.[34] Simmel's famous example was "the stranger": the stranger represents a danger to the cohesion of the community because he stands, at the same time, "inside" and "outside" of it, and thus represents the formal possibility of this way of being. Analogously, the turncoat might simultaneously index the "old" and the "new" regime; they represent the danger of inner change—the possibility of a change to heart and soul—and thus of an undermining of community bonds from the inside.[35]

At the same time, the turncoat has a much longer, protracted history in the Eastern European context so there is a need to reveal these historical legacies and emphasize their current salience. Whether the problem is approached from the perspective of social theory or history, it is clear that, when thinking about the meanings and ramifications of the post-1989 transformations in Eastern Europe today, the turncoat cannot be avoided.

NOTES

1. Avishai Margalit, *On Betrayal* (Cambridge, MA: Harvard University Press, 2017).

2. Georg Simmel, *Georg Simmel on Individuality and Social Forms,* ed. Donald N. Levine (Chicago: University of Chicago Press, 1971).

3. The German word for turncoat is *"Wendehals"* (which carries a physical association, as it refers to a person's neck); the Czech expression is a phrase, *"převléct kabát"* (literally, turning one's coat).

4. See Timothy Snyder, *Bloodlands: Europe between Hitler and Stalin* (New York: Basic Books, 2012); Jeffrey Burds, "'Turncoats, Traitors, and Provocateurs:' Communist Collaborators, the German Occupation, and Stalin's NKVD, 1941–1943," *East European Politics and Societies* 32, no. 3 (2018): 606–38; Kateřina Šimová, "Turncoats, Traitors, Murderers in White Coats: The Image of the 'Jew' as the 'Enemy' in Late Stalinist Propaganda," *Czech Journal of Contemporary History* 3 (2015): 25–56; and Paul A. Hanebrink, *A Specter Haunting Europe: The Myth of Judeo-Bolshevism* (Cambridge, MA: Harvard University Press, 2018).

5. Marci Shore, *The Taste of Ashes: The Afterlife of Totalitarianism in Eastern Europe* (New York: Random House, 2013).

6. Jan Kubik, "From Transitology to Contextual Holism: A Theoretical Trajectory of Postcommunist Studies," in *Postcommunism from Within: Social Justice, Mobilization, and Hegemony,* ed. Jan Kubik and Amy Lynch (New York: New York University Press 2013), 27–94.

7. See Jill Massino, *Ambiguous Transitions: Gender, the State, and Everyday Life in Socialist and Postsocialist Romania* (New York: Berghahn Books, 2019); Adam Mrozowicki, *Coping with Social Change: Life Strategies of Workers in Poland's New Capitalism* (Leuven: Leuven University Press, 2011); Miroslav Vaněk and Pavel Mücke, *Velvet Revolutions: An Oral History of Czech Society* (Oxford: Oxford University Press, 2016). Subjective interpretations of change are constituted by varying patterns of life changes (such as labor market changes), so they are not independent of social structure and the salient experiences that people make within the relevant institutions. At the same time, moral evaluations are not determined by individual economic outcomes after 1989. They are

generated by human agency and the capacity to reflect on experiences.

8. Lavinia Stan and Nadya Nedelsky, *Post-Communist Transitional Justice: Lessons from Twenty-Five Years of Experience* (Cambridge: Cambridge University Press, 2015).

9. Hilary Appel and Mitchell A. Orenstein, *From Triumph to Crisis: Neoliberal Economic Reform in Postcommunist Countries* (Cambridge: Cambridge University Press, 2018).

10. In this context, it is interesting to note that the relative size of the dominant class (the group at the top of the wealth and income distribution) in Eastern Europe is much smaller than in Western Europe. See, for instance, Cedric Hugrée, Etienne Penissat, and Alexis Spire, *Social Class in Europe: New Inequalities in the Old World* (London: Verso Books, 2020), 134–37. What is more, key industries in Eastern European economies are predominantly foreign owned. See Nina Bandelj, *From Communists to Foreign Capitalist: The Social Foundations of Foreign Direct Investment in Postsocialist Europe* (Princeton, NJ: Princeton University Press, 2011). The transformation experience seems to have left many people with the impression that excessive wealth accumulation after 1989 was much more widespread than it actually was.

11. Herbert J. Rubin and Irene S. Rubin, *Qualitative Interviewing: The Art of Hearing Data* (Thousand Oaks: Sage, 2012).

12. After a few initial interviews, I noticed that the turncoat was an important term with respect to the social experience of the transformation period so I included it in the questionnaire.

13. See Konrad H. Jarausch, "Care and Coercion: The GDR as Welfare Dictatorship," in *Dictatorship as Experience: Towards a Socio-cultural History of the GDR*, ed. Konrad Jarausch (New York: Berghahn Books, 1999), 47–69.

14. Mitchell A. Orenstein, *Out of the Red: Building Capitalism and Democracy in Postcommunist Europe* (Ann Arbor: University of Michigan Press, 2001), 71.

15. For this concept see Jiří Večerník and Petr Matějů, *Ten Years of Rebuilding Capitalism: Czech Society after 1989* (Prague: Academia, 1999), 165.

16. Interview conducted by Till Hilmar and Petr Kubala, April 13, 2017, Brno, Czech Republic (CZ_ENG7).

17. In Czech discourse, these individuals are also sometimes referred to as "dinosaurs," a term that has a specific generational meaning. Another associated pair of words is "careerist" and "opportunist." Unlike the turncoat, both of these terms lack the explicit reference to a historical event.

18. See Orenstein, *Out of the Red*, 100–11.

19. Appel and Orenstein, *From Triumph to Crisis*.

20. Often, characterizations like this depict the late socialist firm as an environment made up of a majority of *ordinary* people who kept their distance from politics and some individuals—whom one generally knew to avoid—affiliated with the party. For late socialist Czechoslovakia, historian Michal Pullman has problematized this clear-cut,

sanitized image of social order that still dominates the social memory of the period today. See Michal Pullman, *Konec Experimentu* (Prague: Scriptorium, 2011).

21. Interview conducted by Till Hilmar and Petr Kubala, April 7, 2017, Brno, Czech Republic (CZ_ENG4).

22. There are, however, some exceptions. One person observed that after the revolution Czechs suddenly made a habit of attending church and questioned the sincerity of their beliefs. In this example, the connection to a lust for power is not given, or perhaps not made explicit.

23. Hilary Appel, "Anti-Communist Justice and Founding the Post-Communist Order: Lustration and Restitution in Central Europe," *East European Politics & Societies* 19, no. 3 (2005): 379–405; Heike Solga, "The Rise of Meritocracy? Class Mobility in East Germany before and after 1989," in *After the Fall of the Wall: Life Courses in the Transformation of East Germany,* ed. Martin Diewald, Anne Goedicke, and Karl Ulrich Mayer (Stanford: Stanford University Press, 2006): 140–69. The "petrification" of social mobility chances was true for the East German population more broadly. See Steffen Mau, *Lütten Klein: Leben in der Ostdeutschen Transformationsgesellschaft* (Berlin: Suhrkamp, 2019), 171–72.

24. Interview conducted by Till Hilmar near Leipzig, Germany, November 11, 2016 (GER_ENG11).

25. Early retirement—something that tens of thousands of East Germans took advantage of in this situation—seems like a more ethical alternative to pursuing one's career here, as it can be read as a kind of voluntary economic passivity. But it was also often seen, especially by those who were slightly too young to be eligible for it, as a kind of unfair advantage enjoyed by a specific (older) generation.

26. Simmel, *Georg Simmel on Individuality and Social Forms.*

27. A related category in this context is the term "*Einheitsbrüller,*" which roughly translates as someone who would embrace German unity overenthusiastically. It is similarly associated with the problem of betraying East German communal obligations by switching sides and aligning oneself with West German interests all too eagerly.

28. Interview conducted by Till Hilmar in Halle/Saale, Germany, October 27, 2016 (GER_ENG08).

29. Interview conducted by Till Hilmar in Saxony, Germany, November 29, 2016 (GER_ENG13).

30. In this respect, it also matters whether someone believes that the turncoat is a thing of the past or not: for some, this was a problem of the early 1990s. For others, it is still the same issue today, which implies that the sense of injustice persists.

31. Interview conducted by Till Hilmar and Petr Kubala in Brno, Czech Republic, April 25, 2017 (GER_ENG17).

32. Interview conducted by Till Hilmar near Jena, Germany, December 7, 2016

(GER_ENG17).

33. Marci Shore, "'A Spectre Is Haunting Europe . . .' Dissidents, Intellectuals and a New Generation," in *The End and the Beginning: The Revolutions of 1989 and the Resurgence of History*, ed. Vladimir Tismaneanu and Bogdan Iacob (Budapest: Central European University Press 2012), 491.

34. Simmel, *Georg Simmel on Individuality and Social Forms*.

35. Margalit, *Betrayal*.

BIBLIOGRAPHY

Appel, Hilary. "Anti-Communist Justice and Founding the Post-Communist Order: Lustration and Restitution in Central Europe." *East European Politics & Societies* 19, no. 3 (2005): 379–405.

Appel, Hilary, and Mitchell A. Orenstein. *From Triumph to Crisis: Neoliberal Economic Reform in Postcommunist Countries*. Cambridge: Cambridge University Press, 2018.

Bandelj, Nina. *From Communists to Foreign Capitalist: The Social Foundations of Foreign Direct Investment in Postsocialist Europe*. Princeton, NJ: Princeton University Press, 2011.

Burds, Jeffrey. "'Turncoats, Traitors, and Provocateurs:' Communist Collaborators, the German Occupation, and Stalin's NKVD, 1941–1943." *East European Politics and Societies* 32, no. 3 (2018): 606–38.

Hanebrink, Paul A. *A Specter Haunting Europe: The Myth of Judeo-Bolshevism*. Cambridge, MA: Harvard University Press, 2018.

Hugrée, Cedric, Etienne Penissat, and Alexis Spire. *Social Class in Europe: New Inequalities in the Old World*. London: Verso Books, 2020.

Jarausch, Konrad H. "Care and Coercion: The GDR as Welfare Dictatorship." In *Dictatorship as Experience: Towards a Socio-Cultural History of the GDR*, edited by Konrad Jarausch, 47–69. New York: Berghahn Books, 1999.

Kubik, Jan. "From Transitology to Contextual Holism: A Theoretical Trajectory of Postcommunist Studies." In *Postcommunism from Within: Social Justice, Mobilization, and Hegemony*, edited by Jan Kubik and Amy Lynch, 27–94. New York: New York University Press, 2013.

Margalit, Avishai. *On Betrayal*. Cambridge, MA: Harvard University Press, 2017.

Massino, Jill. *Ambiguous Transitions: Gender, the State, and Everyday Life in Socialist and Postsocialist Romania*. New York: Berghahn Books, 2019.

Mau, Steffen. *Lütten Klein: Leben in der Ostdeutschen Transformationsgesellschaft*, 171–72. Berlin: Suhrkamp, 2019.

Mrozowicki, Adam. *Coping with Social Change: Life Strategies of Workers in Poland's New Capitalism*. Leuven: Leuven University Press, 2011.

Orenstein, Mitchell A. *Out of the Red: Building Capitalism and Democracy in Postcommunist Europe*. Ann Arbor: University of Michigan Press, 2001.

Pullman, Michal. *Konec Experimentu*. Prague: Scriptorium, 2011.

Rubin, Herbert J., and Irene S. Rubin. *Qualitative Interviewing: The Art of Hearing Data*. Thousand Oaks: Sage, 2012.

Shore, Marci. "'A Spectre Is Haunting Europe…' Dissidents, Intellectuals and a New Generation." *In the End and the Beginning: The Revolutions of 1989 and the Resurgence of History*, edited by Vladimir Tismaneanu and Bogdan Iacob. Budapest: Central European University Press 2012.

Shore, Marci. *The Taste of Ashes: The Afterlife of Totalitarianism in Eastern Europe*. New York: Random House, 2013.

Simmel, Georg. *Georg Simmel on Individuality and Social Forms*, edited by Donald N. Levine. Chicago: University of Chicago Press, 1971.

Šimová, Kateřina. "Turncoats, Traitors, Murderers in White Coats: The Image of the 'Jew' as the 'Enemy' in Late Stalinist Propaganda." *Czech Journal of Contemporary History* 3 (2015): 25–56.

Snyder, Timothy. *Bloodlands: Europe between Hitler and Stalin*. New York: Basic Books, 2012.

Solga, Heike. "The Rise of Meritocracy? Class Mobility in East Germany before and after 1989." In *After the Fall of the Wall: Life Courses in the Transformation of East Germany*, edited by Martin Diewald, Anne Goedicke, and Karl Ulrich Mayer, 140–69. Stanford: Stanford University Press, 2006.

Stan, Lavinia, and Nadya Nedelsky. *Post-Communist Transitional Justice: Lessons from Twenty-Five Years of Experience*. Cambridge: Cambridge University Press, 2015.

Vaněk, Miroslav, and Pavel Mücke. *Velvet Revolutions: An Oral History of Czech Society*. Oxford: Oxford University Press, 2016.

Večerník, Jiří, and Petr Matějů. *Ten Years of Rebuilding Capitalism: Czech Society after 1989*. Prague: Academia, 1999.

IO

FROM STEPPE TO STATE

Alternative Histories, Amateur Knowledge, and the Search for Origin in Post-1989 Bulgaria

VICTOR PETROV

IN THE MID-2000S, I STOOD BEFORE A BULGARIAN ARMY MAJOR WHO RAN Varna's national service commission, asking me if I was ready for the draft. I answered "no" as I was planning to go to university. Learning that I would study history, his eyes lit up and he launched into a twenty-minute quasi-monologue, during which he expounded on the hidden origins of the Bulgarians, who, according to him, originated in Iran and carried a civilizing mission to the world. Apart from eliciting exasperated glances from the other boys waiting by the open door—the procedure usually took a minute at most—his "revelations" reminded me of "theories" I had encountered in certain popular history books that sold well on the Bulgarian market at the time.[1]

The major's interest in Bulgaria's ancient origins was not unique, but part of a burgeoning popular engagement with renewed historical narratives that abounded in the country after 1989. Freed from the constraints of official historiography per the Bulgarian Communist Party (BCP; Българска Комунистическа Партия), yet often parroting the same narratives it had advanced, professional and amateur historians felt compelled to reveal knowledge that "had been previously hidden," assuming the role of sleuth on the cusp of discovering a new truth about Bulgaria's past.

Many aspects of Bulgarian history were up for reimagination after 1989: the "national revival" period of the nineteenth century, medieval history, and, of course, the communist period. Yet, the genesis of the Bulgarian nation and the origin of the Bulgarians (and others who lived on Bulgarian soil in ancient times) proved to be particularly gripping subjects for both historians and the public. This chapter focuses on the "origin stories" that emerged in Bulgaria in the 1990s and 2000s, many of which either reframed older narratives from before—and after—1944 or advanced new, in some cases outlandish, ideas about the ancient roots of modern Bulgaria. I first examine the production of such histories by professional historians or those who claimed historical knowledge and published works on the topic: Bozhidar Dimitrov, Petŭr Dobrev, the Madzharov family, and Stefan Tsanev.[2] I then examine, through the prism of social media, popular responses to their work. What emerges is a symbiotic relationship between audience and authorship, with the audience often assuming an authorial tone and advancing novel ideas. Rather than a niche topic appealing to a few people in ivory towers, the search for Bulgaria's origins became a burgeoning industry, attracting people from various walks of life. Looking back to a glorious past that showcased a powerful, independent Bulgaria was alluring for a society uncertain about its future. Unable to control the direction of the democratic transition and frustrated with Bulgaria's political climate (evidenced by declining voter turnout, which reached historic lows in 2021), the past offered Bulgarians a means for asserting agency and drawing out the civilizational, almost cosmic, mission of their nation. Thus, two main themes emerge in the texts and discussions under review here: the supposed state-building capacity of the ancient Bulgarians and their contribution to world, and especially European, civilization. The appeal of these works is evident in publication figures, some garnering over 100,000 copies (in Tsanev's case). Meanwhile, posts on social media are authored by a wide variety of individuals, from history teachers to those wholly unaffiliated with history.

According to cultural theorist Boris Buden, post-1989 societies like Bulgaria were "guided" by the democratizing hand of Western experts—often in the guise of international economic organizations—which employed a language that infantilized local choices and experiences.[3] This patronizing approach dictated that Bulgaria's present and future would be determined by already established (Western) democratic and free market ideas. For a small state like Bulgaria, there was truly no alternative; it could not hew to its own political road as it relied on Western investments and expertise to get to the "right side of history." An obsession with chronological primacy and the states that the nomadic Bulgars established throughout Eurasia is thus closely connected to the geopolitical and historical uncertainty of the postsocialist transition.[4]

Yet, debates on Bulgaria's origins reveal not only anxieties about democracy but also antidemocratic sentiments, as the "plenty" promised by both Western experts and Bulgarian politicians has not come to fruition. Thus, certain intellectuals and a significant portion of the reading and TV-watching public found refuge in a mystical Bulgarian past. As if to answer Kant's question "What is enlightenment?" Bulgarians turned to their "origins" as a guide and source of inspiration for navigating the challenges of postsocialism. Other Bulgarians chose a different road, namely the road out of town, and emigrated.

Bulgaria's "origin stories" have become a field where political games can be played—including by those who lack the public influence of the intellectuals who wrote many of these post-1989 texts—and social media platforms have become increasingly important channels for disseminating them. To quote Todor Hristov, "Such a tactic allows even those with unequal access to 'truth-telling' channels—such as books published by respected presses or national TV channels—to participate in the creation of 'truth.'"[5] Indeed, the internet has provided not only a medium for popularizing these theories, but also tools and sources for crafting them. As a result, older studies or fragments of information that have been debunked can be endlessly reconfigured by amateurs in their quest for the "truth." As these amateur authors are not associated with socialist institutions, they are considered untainted and more "authentic," and thus capable of uncovering truths that were not ideologically driven or the product of a discredited regime. Their engagement with Bulgaria's origin stories can therefore be read as a revolt against the mass professionalization of late socialist culture, when history was the purview of those accredited by the state and holding positions in academic or cultural institutes. Accordingly, after 1989, the dilettantes were back in fashion, paradoxically repackaging the late socialist narratives that had emerged during the "nationalist mysticism" period, while at the same time distancing themselves from communism.

The 1990s and early 2000s were a time of immense social and economic dislocation, as Bulgaria was subject to international monetary oversight, or under the "tutelage of capitalism and democracy," seeking "entry to Europe" as a panacea for both economic and political woes.[6] By the mid-1990s, entire sectors of the economy had disappeared as a result of deindustrialization, and unemployment and inflation continued rising. In 1996–97, high energy prices and political corruption sparked protests, which continued on and off throughout the 2000s and 2010s. Accession to the European Union (in 2007) did little to minimize Bulgaria's sense of marginality, as Europe's leading powers treated Bulgaria as an unequal partner. Moreover, the gap between haves and have-nots increased, and in 2016 Bulgaria ranked highest within the EU in terms of income inequality.[7] There was not much exogenous proof that the transition had ended—or would end anytime soon—as the Bulgarian elites seemed incapable of delivering on their promises.[8] For those who had not benefited from the transition, alternative visions of Bulgarian statehood, in particular narratives about Bulgaria's propensity to build strong states civilizing other societies, served as a foundation for instilling confidence within a significant portion of the population. It is these alternatives I now turn to, first investigating the trendsetting texts and intellectuals that shaped this discourse after 1989.

THE UNIQUENESS OF BULGARIA AND
THE CONSPIRACIES AGAINST ITS PAST

While many pundits in the West present 1989 as a clean break, very few in the East—as this volume shows—do so. Striking continuities with socialism are evident in the realm of politics, the economy, and culture. This holds true for historical narratives as well. From the 1960s onward the socialist regime promoted nationalist narratives, with Bulgarian Communist Party (BCP) leader Todor Zhivkov publicly challenging, in March 1963, the existence of a Macedonian national identity and mobilizing medieval history to proclaim Bulgaria the region's cradle of civilization.[9] This signified a volte-face from the late 1940s and 1950s, when the BCP followed a policy of "Macedonization" in the southwest of the country as part of its internationalist policy. This extended to history as well, with Marxist scholars replacing the "Grand National" narrative with the "Slavicization" narrative. These "counternarratives" accentuated the contribution of the Slavs in the nation's genesis and culture and downplayed that of the Bulgars.[10] This interpretation, which dated back to the nineteenth century, was prominent during the Stalinist period, serving as a vehicle for underscoring the historical similarity and "natural affinity" of Bulgaria and the Soviet Union and, thereby, promoting Soviet-Bulgarian friendship.

In 1964, the Second National Conference of Historians was held, a key moment in the "thawing" of Bulgarian historiography. Previously banned "bourgeois" historians were rehabilitated, and the role of the Bulgars and Thracians in the ethnogenesis of the nation was reappraised. The works of noted medievalist Ivan Dujcev were published, as were other nationalist histories.[11] Beginning in the late 1970s, this grand narrative received full backing by the state under Lyudmila Zhivkova, daughter of Communist Party leader Todor Zhivkov and head of the Bulgarian Ministry of Culture. Under Zhivkova's direction new areas of study such as Thracology (the study of ancient Thrace) flourished, as did narratives about the Bulgarian nation in film, art, and monuments, culminating in the celebration of the 1,300th anniversary of the Bulgarian state in 1981. Zhivkova's fascination with esoteric Eastern ideas such as theosophy also engendered an officially sanctioned entry of new narratives into national thinking, encouraging the search for links between Bulgaria and Eurasian cultures.[12] The political dimension of these cultural and historiographical narratives was elaborated in the regime's anti-Muslim campaigns, culminating in the Revival Processes of the 1970s and 1980s. This state-led project of forced assimilation of the Pomaks (Bulgarian-speaking Muslims) and Bulgarian Turks was legitimated by regime historians. After forced assimilation failed, the regime adopted more inhumane methods, expelling over 360,000 Turks from Bulgaria in the summer of 1989. In response, dissidents organized in solidarity with the Bulgarian Turks and in resistance to state policy, laying the foundations for the end of communist rule.[13]

A CERTAIN PAST FOR AN
UNCERTAIN PRESENT

When communism collapsed in 1989, Bulgarian society had already been subjected to a sustained campaign of nationalism, sometimes virulent in character. However, while the communist regime was dead, nationalist discourses survived and eventually flourished, repackaged by entrepreneurial historians and others who took advantage of the end of censorship to position themselves as "truth tellers." While some, like Bozhidar Dimitrov and Petŭr Dobrev, were established scholars who moved from academic to popular history, others, such as Hristo Madzharov, Galya Madzharova, and Stefan Tsanev, were amateur newcomers to the scene who, over the course of the 1990s, increasingly captured more and more of the reading market.

Dimitrov was a prolific writer of popular histories as well as the host of popular history television shows, most famously *Pamet Bŭlgarska* (*Bulgarian Memory*), which aired on Channel 1 (the national channel) from 2002 to 2012. Educated under socialism, Dimitrov was a State Security agent (DS; Държавна Сигурност) for over two decades, during which he succeeded in acquiring materials about Bulgaria housed in the Vatican archives, among them Peter Bogdan's 1667 *History of Bulgaria*.[14] Thus, Dimitrov's access to "hidden truths" was already solidified in the public mind prior to the collapse of communism. His credibility was further enhanced by media appearances and in his role as director of the country's National Museum of History.

Dimitrov often emphasizes Bulgarian contributions to Slavic civilization. In his 1993 *Bulgarians: Civilizers of the Slavic World*, a glossy book with pictures aimed at a general audience, Dimitrov asserts: "Few, however, know that the Bulgarians are the ones who created the foundation for European medieval Christian civilization (the base upon which contemporary Europe is built, too)."[15] Moreover, contrary to previous claims that the Slavs assumed a leading role in establishing the Bulgarian nation, in his narrative Slavs are presented as incapable of establishing states, even as they pushed the Byzantines into their cities. Accordingly, they needed others, such as the Bulgars, to create states for them.[16] Tolerant of others, the Bulgars, Dimitrov argues, incorporated Slavic aristocrats into their new state, emphasizing that the Bulgar state existed far earlier than 681 CE, the year historians typically date its establishment.[17]

As proof of the country's unique contributions to civilization, the book lists some of the Bulgars' "greatest hits": its defense of Europe at the walls of Constantinople in 717–718; the Christianization of the population; and the development of the Cyrillic alphabet. Dimitrov's most unique claim, however, is that Bulgaria saved Europe by forestalling its domination by the "universal empire" (a reference to the Eastern Roman Empire and the newly formed Holy Roman Empire, which sought to resurrect the Roman Empire).[18]

Bulgaria's role as "the savior" of national identity can and should be read against the background of a newly emerging postsocialist state. So too should Dimitrov's other claims, which challenge the pro-Russian line—popular in socialist-era histories—by emphasizing Bulgaria's cultural "mission" in the Slavic lands. Dimitrov argues that Serbia, Croatia, and Romania, but especially Russia, have the Bulgarians to thank for their language and Christian culture. In this rendition, Bulgaria almost providentially plants the seed for its eventual rescue from the hands of the Turks by sending its culture to a country that would eventually save it—Russia.[19] By claiming that Slavic culture originated in Bulgaria, Dimitrov reverses the imperial-satellite relationship of the Cold War, where the USSR's primacy was often propagated in official publications. This polemic reached epic proportions in Dimitrov's 2005 book, *12 Myths in Bulgarian History*, in which he advanced the thesis of Bulgarians' "genetic predisposition to state-building."[20]

But what was the reach of Dimitrov's work? While sales figures are unavailable, the popularity of his books can be gauged by the fact that many went through second and third editions—a rarity in the Bulgarian publishing market. Moreover, English and French translations of the book were sponsored by the Bulgarian government, which viewed Dimitrov as the ideal public relations persona for popularizing this aggrandizing narrative.[21] Interviews with Dimitrov and back episodes of his show *Pamet Bŭlgarska* (*Bulgarian Memory*) can be found on YouTube and the Bulgarian video site VBox7, with view counts ranging from a few thousand to well over 100,000, an impressive figure for the Bulgarian streaming sphere. Additionally, Dimitrov's announcement during the 2015 dig at the Pliska Grand Basilica (the first medieval capital and its first Christian temple) that "holy water" had gushed forth from the ground was met with widespread media and political coverage. Then–prime minister Boyko Borisov even participated in the spectacle, going so far as to "wash" government ministers' hands with the supposed holy water. This episode marked the culmination of Dimitrov's influence as narrator of Bulgaria's heritage, illustrated in the growth of his viewership and readership after the event. As ethnologist Ana Luleva writes about it: "Cultural heritage is not so much about the artefacts or the past itself, but the meanings they carry and communities they are associated with. Dimitrov's success as an author, TV persona, and at the 'holy water' event, thus served to reconstruct Bulgaria's past."[22]

Petŭr Dobrev, a historian Dimitrov often cites, also highlighted the Bulgars' state making. His 1994 book, *The World of the Proto-Bulgarians: Realities and Misunderstandings*, is a typical example. Claiming to draw on Indian, Arab, Armenian, and Caucasian chronicles (which he inconsistently quotes), Dobrev locates the ancestral land of the Bulgars in the Pamir region. A cornerstone of his thesis, which he uses to prove the Bulgar provenance of many ancient states—or at least their close relation to "proto-Bulgarians"—is linguistic affinity. Accordingly, the Bulgars' language is akin to Sumerian rather than Turkish or Magyar, "proving" the Bulgars are older than anyone suspected. Dobrev argues that Bulgarians' ignorance of this history has had profound sociopolitical reverberations, asserting: "Until we are armed with a clear idea on this last question [the specificities of the Bulgars' origin] we will always be in danger of someone selfishly taking advantage of our lack of knowledge." He contends that Bulgarians would listen like a "child listens to fate" and believe they are Mongols or Turks.[23] Moreover, he claims that Slavs and Thracians were sponsored by the "Moscow and Zhivkova lobbies," which pushed Bulgars unfairly to the background. An "objective rehabilitation of the Bulgars'" ancient mission thus "uncovers the invisible roots that connects Bulgaria with many ancient peoples."[24]

Dobrev's primary aims are to discount previous interpretations of Bulgarian history and, through the rehabilitation of ancient and medieval history, provide a blueprint for post-1989 state making. For Dobrev, the apogee of Bulgarian statehood was the medieval "just state," governed by a political class that ruled in the interest of the people.[25] Thus, in his 2003 book, *On the State and Power*, he claimed that the transition's ills, such as poverty and demographic decline, which he attributes to rapid privatization, can only be remedied with a dose of medieval politics.[26] For Dobrev, this entails the creation of a centralized and autarkic state, in which Bulgaria relies on its own resources and distributes wealth among the people (though not like under communism, when a small elite monopolized wealth just as they do today). Ignoring the differences between medieval and modern economies and between medieval subjecthood and modern citizenship, Dobrev anachronistically combines populist economics with medieval state building.

ENTER THE AMATEURS

Alternative histories were not only the purview of classically educated historians. Fringe amateur historians also engaged in "history making," often infusing their narratives with the mysticism inherited from Zhivkova or spiritual movements such as the White Brotherhood.[27] Among the more prolific amateur historians are Hristo Madzharov and Galya Madzharova, who authored historical and spiritualist books in the 1990s and 2000s. Lacking formal historical training and steeped in esoteric teachings and experiences, the authors bring ideas advanced by academic historians, such as Dobrev, to their logical ends. Madzharov's *The Great Conspiracy Against Bulgarians* (2001) is described in a fawning review by a martial artist-turned-amateur historian as akin to "a stone thrown in the swamp of our 'official' historical science."[28] In his own mission statement, Madzharov is unrestrained:

A visa for the entrance of peoples into the Third millennium is a developed national self-consciousness. That is why it is imperative to shake off this tendentiously implanted national nihilism; to stop bending the back before East and West, and to search for our dignity where we lost it—in our own historical roots.[29]

He celebrates the fact that truth can now flourish: "Democracy, elevated free thought, and widened opposition brought pluralism. Every idea has the right to be said, until it is proven bankrupt"—a paean to the new climate of open, postsocialist discourse.[30] While Madzharov draws on original sources, he also uses dubious translations to prove the Bulgarian origin of almost all ancient civilizations—or at least Bulgarian contributions to events such as the building of the Great Wall of China. Sumer, Egypt, India, and lost kingdoms in Siberia are also part of the march of the Bulgars through world civilization. In certain instances, Madzharov issues a call to arms in an attempt to raise people's spirits rather than engage with the "specialists" (i.e., professional historians and archaeologists). He rhetorically asks: "Does the historian or the literary writer persuade more? Which one reveals the Truth first? The mind or the heart? The most important [truth] is invisible to the eye."[31] Madzharova's work, meanwhile, expands this narrative from a gendered perspective, tracing the power of ancient Bulgarian women, particularly the influence of "amazon queens." According to her, rejuvenation lies in a rebirth of the spirit inherent in us, rather than in pure politics: "In every woman lives a queen, priestess, amazon, and in every man a prince, troubadour, a knight."[32] As with Madzharov, there is minimal reflection on the social stratification of ancient and medieval societies. Moreover, Madzharova fails to mention the lack of evidence for women's political power in Bulgarian history. One wasn't a queen or prince by virtue of a romantic "inner power," but by birth.

Such flights of fancy, together with the work of academic historians, informed the most widely sold history book in post-1989 Bulgaria: Stefan Tsanev's four-volume *Bulgarian Chronicles*, published between 2006 and 2009. A popular Bulgarian playwright whose plays from the 1960s onward focused on historical themes, Tsanev devoted himself to history writing in the 1990s, selling over 100,000 copies of *Bulgarian Chronicles* in its first run—a phenomenal achievement in the Bulgarian market.[33] Tsanev's first volume begins in 2137 BCE, near China, cementing his work among those that push Bulgarian origins to the earliest possible date.[34] The book's first chapter lays out the story's narrative arc, which borrows liberally from the historical and fringe works cited above. In the first sentence of the book he declares, "It is unlikely there is any other people in the world that knows its history so poorly," continuing: "or maybe the truth is even more discouraging: our old history exceeds our current pathetic self-confidence as a people, the comparison to the past depresses us and we don't want to remember it."[35] In a whirlwind tale, the Bulgars create twelve states throughout Eurasia, carrying cosmic knowledge, "because simple peoples can't make states."[36] In this respect, Tsanev's work is a synthesis of the narratives that abounded after 1989.

The aforementioned books are stocked by reputable bookshop chains in Bulgaria, such as Ciela and Helikon. Additionally, Dimitrov's and Tsanev's works are often found in museum bookshops or at tourist sites around the country. Although professional historians and cultural commentators have criticized these works for their inaccuracies and distortions, public reactions are typically positive.[37] Tsanev's work has a 4.5 rating on the Goodreads website with over 835 ratings, being one of the most-viewed Bulgarian works there. As one reviewer remarked: "This is the history that should be taught in schools!" Indeed, even the more critical reviews noted that this is a "fun read" that will hopefully prompt readers to delve deeper into Bulgarian history.[38] In addition, reviews in an online bookstore call it "gold" and a "must-read for every Bulgarian family."[39]

In terms of sales, TV audiences, and presence, Dimitrov and Tsanev (both of whom often quote Dobrev) are far more likely to be known to the average reader. Current television shows, particularly those on the Bulgarian national channel's Monday night *Istoria.bg*, feature professional historians who debate topics in Bulgarian history, typically emphasizing Bulgarian achievements and victories.[40] What they all have in common is a link to their audience, mostly through Facebook, where users are encouraged to submit questions—similar to Dimitrov's TV shows, where he fielded phone calls live.

FACEBOOK NATION

The aforementioned "theories" not only sell books, but shape popular perceptions of the past. According to historian Desislava Lilova, the internet has blown up the normative canon of Bulgarian identity, facilitating its renegotiation.[41] In his study of the "Thracian canon," Ivo Strahilov traces the blogs of self-proclaimed amateurs who create a new, in a sense "democratized," science. According to them, while old institutions act as gatekeepers and thus compromise historical inquiry, the internet, by housing sources from myriad repositories throughout the world, enables ordinary citizens to contribute to scientific knowledge and "put things right" again.[42]

This culture of "history writing" has taken strong root on social media platforms, where groups dedicated to Bulgarian history claim tens of thousands of members. Articles by academic and novice historians, as well as anonymous writers, are posted on designated sites, facilitating lively discussions. Typically members do not quote historians or particular sources, but rather reproduce themes from the alternative narratives discussed above, juxtaposing them against textbooks and "received knowledge" from school lessons that they deem politically suspect and false; evidence of a national nihilism born of outdated pro-Russian views or association with the EU and the West.

The largest group, with over 380,000 members, often links to a website where historians—usually graduate students—write about particular topics. The Facebook comments, however, are as insightful as the articles themselves. For example, an article on Paisiy of Hilendar's 1762 *History of the Slavo-Bulgarians* triggered vitriolic debates over the inclusion of the word "Slavo" in the title. Many claimed that "Slav" meant "glory" rather than "Slav" (the addition of a single letter changes the meaning in Bulgarian). One user opined: "If you knew Bulgarian history, you would never call your site that!" blaming, in a different post, current professors for falsifying Paisiy's title page.[43] Another user posted a video by Bozhidar Dimitrov, which claimed that the word Slav was not widely used in the eighteenth century, while another explicitly called such views "socialist myths" and asserted that there are few real scientists who defend the "Bulgarians."[44] The juxtaposition of an authentic Bulgarian source versus the Russian-backed "Slavicization" of history is even more explicit in other posts, where the former is seen as "objective" and the latter as communist propaganda aimed at destroying Bulgarian national identity.[45]

Bulgaria's historical achievements such as the alphabet or the Bulgars' primacy in ethnogenesis also dominate discussions. Users stretch the origin of the Bulgars back to 5500 BCE, or rail against historians who portray them as nomadic barbarians, presenting them instead as autochthonous to the Balkans—a theme popular with other post-1989 writers such as Madzharov.[46] In another discussion, the creation of Cyrillic is portrayed as an achievement financed by the Bulgarian state and Boris I himself, meaning it has always been a "Bulgarian alphabet"; it has just been hidden in textbooks that contain "stupidities."[47] Other posts borrow more liberally from Madzharov's fringe ideas, referring to Bulgarians as the most ancient people—not just in Europe but the world.[48]

Discussing the defeat of the Byzantines by Krum in 813 CE, one user bemoans the loss of "Bulgarian characteristics such as honor, fighting spirit, and purity of spirit" and asserts: "It is time to end the last years of the Mafia and stupidity, to offer education and decent work to all . . . to be real Europeans, as Levski wanted!"[49] Krum is often evoked in such depictions, with users hoping that current politicians might learn from him by applying his laws to rich and poor alike. "If he was in charge today," one poster asserted, "the national riches would not be embezzled and Bulgaria would in fact be the Switzerland of the Balkans."[50]

The endless sea of Facebook comments could be quoted ad infinitum, but one need only survey a selection to get a sense of their users' understanding of Bulgarian history. In a society that ranks lowest in the EU with respect to income, health outcomes, and media freedom, among other indicators, and suffering from political gridlock and widespread corruption, highlighting origin stories and historical achievements is designed to divert attention away from unfortunate realities and to assert

Bulgaria's prestige on the global stage. The message is clear: today's Bulgaria might be weak and confused, but it has a glorious past that can also point to a potentially equally glorious future.

CONCLUSION

Shortly before his death in 2018, Bozhidar Dimitrov founded a national movement named Kan Kubrat in honor of the ruler of Old Bulgaria. On media platforms Dimitrov called for a presidential republic with a strong leader and noted that in the 1930s professors—the true elite of the nation—were granted power and managed to make the country "flourish in eight years."[51] The road from bookish arguments about Bulgaria's state-building capacity logically ended in the authors' own political ambitions, evident in his political promiscuity: he switched from the Bulgarian Socialist Party to the center-right GERB party in 2009, assuming a ministerial position in the latter until 2011. Dimitrov's change in political affiliation and his close links to state institutions illustrate the appeal of the nationalist narrative among parties of all political stripes. For them, celebrations of a glorious past are a soothing balm used to shore up consensus much like they were under late socialism.

The nationalist narrative has demonstrated remarkable continuities over the last sixty years, used to showcase Bulgaria's contributions to world civilization and to foster national pride in times of ideological weakness. If, by the 1960s, the mobilizational power of Marxist-Leninism had waned, by the 2000s enthusiasm for democracy had similarly lost its pull. Bulgaria, as an ancient nation once of "world importance," thus reemerged as a useful trope. As we have seen, these tropes had their origins or boost in the late socialist period and were resurrected and reworked to suit post-1989 needs. Bulgaria's glorious past, its links to other world cultures, and its mystical aspirations were narratives that were bolstered by Zhivkova and endured well beyond 1989. Baked into the official narrative, they nonetheless contained other possibilities that were exploited in the post-1989 sphere of free speech and publishing. In the context of pervasive corruption and perceived government incompetence, a glorious past narrative, when the state was strong and society flourished, could be used by authors such as Dimitrov to present themselves as potential leaders of the nation, calling for unity and a Bulgarian resurrection—Dimitrov being the clearest example considering his political role. Others, such as the Madzharov family, could use them for religious-mystical purposes and for advancing their own private projects. Meanwhile, for nonprofessionals these origin stories, by highlighting episodes of national pride and glory, provided succor during uncertain times. They also enabled amateurs to participate in the creation of "knowledge" and to see that "knowledge" widely disseminated on the internet.

Despite the different uses of these popular narratives, their coherence lies in the ideological need they fulfill. The use of the past in countries undergoing political turbulence is well documented, as politicians in postcommunist countries are similarly masters of mobilizing the past. In this respect, the post-1989 period in Bulgaria was not decisively different from earlier periods, as the "search for origins" and the use of the national past in securing consensus for political projects is centuries old. The true rupture was the opening of the public sphere to alternative voices. It was also in the devaluation of institutions that had previously narrated the nation's history, which, after 1989, were presented as tainted by socialism and pro-Russian distortions. Technological change and the creation of an online reading public deepened this process. The increasing participation of ordinary people in these projects has created a new stage in the development of historical narratives, which are no longer the purview only of the state and, at the same time, are highly dependent on theories propagated by professional authors with disproportionate access to the markers of status such as publications or television programs. The internet has created the conditions for both challenging narratives and more widely disseminating them. It has also created a new archive that historians can use to better understand the postsocialist world. As elsewhere in the region, socialist narratives continued to be popular after 1989, but now they could be repackaged by new authors, often lacking academic credentials, which they wear with a badge of honor. The true rupture of postsocialism was thus in the widening of authorship and in the reductive belief that institutions under socialism, such as universities and academies, were tainted, even though many of the theories advanced by them are now unquestionably used by these new "truth tellers."

NOTES

1. In this essay, I use "theory" to describe the arguments and narratives advanced by the writers under consideration. Despite their self-confident tone, these authors often present their work as a "very likely" interpretation of the evidence they are presenting and are often at odds with the general histories produced by Bulgaria's institutional guardians of the national narrative, such as the Ministry of Education and the Academy of Sciences.

2. Bozhidar Dimitrov, probably the most well-known public historian in Bulgaria, was a politician and director of the National Museum of History. Petŭr Dobrev is a historian at the Bulgarian Academy of Sciences who has written extensively on economic history. Hristo and Galya Madzharov write both popular histories and esoteric texts on the ancient Bulgarians. Stefan Tsanev is a Bulgarian writer and playwright who authored the best-selling popular history book series in postsocialist Bulgaria.

3. Boris Buden, *Zona na Prehoda: Za Kraya na PostKomunizma* (Sofia: Kritika I Humanizum 2016), 37; first published as *Zone des Übergangs: Von Ende des Postkommunismus* in 2009.

4. Throughout this text I will use "Bulgars" to denote the groups and confederations that are sometimes referred to as proto-Bulgars (*prabulgari*) and that created Danubian Bulgaria in the seventh century.

5. Todor Hristov, "Istinata na Konspirativnite Teorii ili Prezidentut e Izvunzemen," *Seminar*, issue 7 (2012), April 22, 2022, https://www.seminar-bg.eu/spisanie-seminar-bg/broy7-kiberfolk.html.

6. Vesselin Dimitrov, *Bulgaria: The Uneven Transition* (Abingdon: Routledge, 2002).

7. Jean-Jacques Hallaert, *Inequality, Poverty, and Social Protection in Bulgaria*, IMF Working Paper WP/20/147, International Monetary Fund (2020), 6.

8. Venelin Ganev, *Preying on the State: The Transformation of Bulgaria after 1989* (Ithaca, NY: Cornell University Press, 2013).

9. Tchavdar Marinov, "Ot Internacionalizum kam nacionalizum, Komunisticheskiyat Rezhim, Makedonskiyat Vupros I Politikata kum Etnicheskite I Religioznite Obshtestva," in *Istoriya na Narodna Republika Bulgaria: Rezhimut I Obshtestvoto*, ed. Ivaylo Znepolski (Sofia: Institut za izsledvane na blizkoto minalo, "Siela," 2009), 492.

10. Rumen Daskalov, *Golemite Razkazi za Bulgarskoto Srednovekovie* (Sofia: Riva, 2018), 46–47.

11. Ivan Elenkov, *The Science of History in Bulgaria in the Age of Socialism: The Problematic Mapping of Its Institutional Boundaries*, CAS Working Paper Series Issue 1, Centre for Advanced Study Sofia (2007), 10.

12. For more on Zhivkova, see Veneta Ivanova, "Socialism with an Occult Face: Aesthetics, Spirituality, and Utopia in Late Socialist Bulgaria," *East European Politics and Societies* 36, no. 2 (2022), 558–81; and Theodora Dragostinova, *The Cold War from the Margins: A Small Socialist State on the Global Cultural Scene* (Ithaca, NY: Cornell University Press, 2021).

13. Mikhail Gruev, *Vuzroditelniyat Protzes: Myusulmanskite Obshnosti I Komunisticheskiya Rezhim* (Sofia: Ciela, 2008).

14. Decision 267/20.09.2011 by the Commission for Uncovering Documents and Declaring the Service of Bulgarian Citizens in State Security, Ministry of Culture.

15. Bozhidar Dimitrov, *Bulgarite: Tzivilizatori na Slavyanskiya Svyat* (Sofia: Borina, 1993), 9.

16. Dimitrov, *Bulgarite*, 11–16.

17. Dimitrov, *Bulgarite*, 31–32.

18. Dimitrov, *Bulgarite*, 43–49.

19. Dimitrov, *Bulgarite*, 80.

20. Bozhidar Dimitrov, *12 Mita v Bulgarskata Istoriya* (Sofia: Fondatziya KOM, 2005), 3–11.

21. Stefan Detchev, "Za Istoriyata na Bozhidar Dimitrov, bozhidimitrovskata istoriya I oshte neshto: Chast I," *Marginalia*, August 15, 2018, April 21, 2022, https://www.marginalia.bg/aktsent/stefan-dechev-za-istoriyata-na-bozhidar-dimitrov-bozhidar dimitriovskata-istoriya-i-oshte-neshto/#_ftn35.

22. Ana Luleva, "Introduction," in *Contested Heritage and Identities in Post-Socialist Bulgaria*, ed. Ana Luleva, Ivanka Petrova, and Slavia Barlieva (Sofia: Gutenberg Publishing House, 2015), 7–11.

23. Petŭr Dobrev, *Svetŭt Na Prabŭlgarite: Istina i Zabludi* (Sofia: IKK Slavika-REM, 1994), 5–6.

24. Dobrev, *Svetŭt Na Prabŭlgarite*.

25. Luleva, Petrova, and Barlieva, *Contested Heritage*, 106–8, 250–54.

26. Petŭr Dobrev, *Za Durzhavata I Vlasta* (Sofia: IK Galika, 2003), 5.

27. The movement, founded by Peter Deunov in the early twentieth century, combines Christian esoteric beliefs with practices such as physical musical exercises called pan-eurhythmy.

28. Hristo Madzharov, *Golemiyat Zagovor Sreshtu Bulgarite* (Varna: Alfiola, 2001), 3.

29. Madzharov, *Golemiyat Zagovor Sreshtu Bulgarite*, 6.

30. Madzharov, *Golemiyat Zagovor Sreshtu Bulgarite*, 15.

31. Madzharov, *Golemiyat Zagovor Sreshtu Bulgarite*, 19.

32. Galya K. Madzharova, *Bulgarski Tsaritsi-Amazonki: Misteriite na Devetnadesetiya Put* (Varna: Alfiola, 2010), 256.

33. Silviya Nedkova, "Knigite s Fenomanalen Tirazh v Bulgariya," *Ploshtad Slaveikov*, October 6, 2019, https://www.ploshtadslaveikov.com/knigite-s-fenomenalni-tirazhi-v-balgariya/.

34. Stefan Tsanev, *Bulgarski Hroniki–Tom I: Istoriya na Nashiya Narod ot 2137 pr. Hr. do 1453 sl. Hr* (Plovdiv: Zhanet 45, 2006), 5.

35. Tsanev, *Bulgarski Hroniki–Tom I*, 21.

36. Tsanev, *Bulgarski Hroniki–Tom I*, 33.

37. For a representative critique of Tsanev's work see Boris Popivanov's "Mahmurlukut na Edin Natsionalizum," *Kultura*, no. 31 (2690), September 15, 2006.

38. https://www.goodreads.com/book/show/7114536-1.

39. https://www.book.store.bg/p9345/bylgarski-hroniki-tom-i-stefan-canev.html.

40. Keta Marcheva, "Pet Godini Istoriya.BG—A Sega Nakude?" *Marginalia*, April 2, 2022, https://www.marginalia.bg/aktsent/pet-godini-istoriya-bg-a-sega-nakade/.

41. Desislava Lilova, "Istoriyata na Viktor Krum: Natsionalnata Identichnost v Internet," *Kritika i Humanizum* 25, no. 1 (2008): 115–38.

42. Ivo Strahilov, "Trakite Otvrushtat na Udara: Antichnoto Nasledstvo i Kulturata na Uchastieto," *Seminar*, no. 14 (2017), April 21, 2022, https://www.seminar-bg.eu/spisanie-seminar-bg/broy14/item/470-trakite-otvrashtat-na-udara.html.

43. Angel Kiyrakov, "Българска история ако знаехте" and "Georgi Dichev проверете го вие," *Facebook*, January 11, 2021, https://www.facebook.com/bulgarian.history1/photos /a.386150848075206/3953267568030165/.

44. Boyko Prumov, "URL of Dimitrov video" and Ivan Hristov, "Dimo 'Много е лошо да робуваш на соц. Митове,'" *Facebook*, January 11, 2021, https://www.facebook.com /bulgarian.history1/photos/a.386150848075206/3953267568030165/.

45. Ivan Hrisov, "Мартин Вачев То заради такива" and Georgki Nikolov Kocharkov, "История славно Българска—това трябва," *Facebook*, December 29, 2020, https:// www.facebook.com/bulgarian.history1/posts/3919270418096547.

46. Yordan Radenkov, "Българите са автохонното население" and Alexander Atanasov, "Българите са автохтонното (коренното)," *Facebook*, February 17, 2021, https://www .facebook.com/bg.istoriq/posts/2782970898582099.

47. Simeon Grudev, "Няма такова нещо като Кирилица" and Svetla Nikolova, "Интересно и поучително," *Facebook*, February 17, 2021, https://www.facebook.com /bg.istoriq/posts/278291095192142.

48. https://www.facebook.com/photo/?fbid=294733131982195&set=a.112771423511701.

49. Martina Dragomirova, "От тези времена насам наистина," *Facebook*, July 26, 2020, https://www.facebook.com/bulgarian.history1/posts/3459460584077535.

50. Ivan Ivanov, "Велик наш Владетел," *Facebook*, February 20, 2021, https://www.face book.com/istoriqtasd.gilev/posts/3720109088025464.

51. "Bozhidar Dimitrov Vliza v Politikata s Dvizhenia 'Khan Kubrat,'" *Vesti.bg*, March 5, 2018, https://www.vesti.bg/bulgaria/politika/bozhidar-dimitrov-vliza-v-politikata -s-dvizhenie-kan-kubrat-6079963.

BIBLIOGRAPHY

Buden, Boris. *Zona na Prehoda: Za Kraya na PostKomunizma*. Sofia: Kritika I Humanizum, 2016.

Daskalov, Rumen. *Golemite Razkazi za Bulgarskoto Srednovekovie*. Sofia: Riva, 2018.

Detchev, Stefan. "Za Istoriyata na Bozhidar Dimitrov, bozhidimitrovskata istoriya I oshte neshto: Chast I." *Marginalia*, August 15, 2018.

Dichev, Ivaylo. "Erata na Amatyora." *Seminar* 14 (2017).

Dimitrov, Bozhidar. *Bulgarite: Tzivilizatori na Slavyanskiya Svyat*. Sofia: Borina, 1993.

Dimitrov, Bozhidar. *12 Mita v Bulgarskata Istoriya*. Sofia: Fondatziya KOM, 2005.

Dimitrov, Vesselin. *Bulgaria: The Uneven Transition*. Abingdon: Routledge, 2002.

Dobrev, Petŭr. *Istoriya Razpunata na Krustopat—Chast Vtora: Manipulatsiite na 20ti Vek*. Sofia: IKK Slavica-Rim, 1998.

Dobrev, Petŭr. *Svetŭt Na Prabŭlgarite: Istina i Zabludi*. Sofia: IKK Slavika-REM, 1994).

Dobrev, Petŭr. *Za Durzhavata I Vlasta*. Sofia: IK Galika, 2003.

Dragostinova, Theodora. *The Cold War from the Margins: A Small Socialist State on the Global Cultural Scene*. Ithaca, NY: Cornell University Press, 2021.

Elenkov, Ivan. *Kulturniyat Front: Bulgarskata Kultura prez Epohata na Komunizma—Politichesko Upravlenie, Ideologicheski Osnovaniya, Institutsionalni Rezhimi*. Sofia: Ciela, 2008.

Elenkov, Ivan. *The Science of History in Bulgaria in the Age of Socialism: The Problematic Mapping of Its Institutional Boundaries*. CAS Working Paper Series Issue 1. Centre for Advanced Study Sofia, 2007.

Ganev, Venelin. *Preying on the State: The Transformation of Bulgaria after 1989*. Ithaca, NY: Cornell University Press, 2013.

Gruev, Mikhail. *Vuzroditelniyat Protzes: Myusulmanskite Obshnosti I Komunisticheskiya Rezhim*. Sofia: Ciela, 2008.

Hallaert, Jean-Jacques. *Inequality, Poverty, and Social Protection in Bulgaria*. IMF Working Paper WP/20/147. International Monetary Fund, 2020.

Hristov, Todor. "Istinata na Konspirativnite Teorii ili Prezidentut e Izvunzemen." *Seminar* 7 (2012).

Ivanova, Veneta T. "Socialism with an Occult Face: Aesthetics, Spirituality, and Utopia in Late Socialist Bulgaria." *East European Politics and Societies* 36, no. 2 (2002): 558–81.

Lilova, Desislava. "Istoriyata na Viktor Krum: Natsionalnata Identichnost v Internet." *Kritika i Humanizum* 25, no. 1 (2008): 115–38.

Luleva, Ana, Ivanka Petrova, and Slavia Barlieva, eds. *Contested Heritage and Identities in Post-Socialist Bulgaria*. Sofia: Gutenberg Publishing House, 2015.

Madzharov, Hristo. *Golemiyat Zagovor Sreshtu Bulgarite*. Varna: Alfiola, 2001.

Madzharova, Galya. *Bulgarski Tsaritsi-Amazonki: Misteriite na Devetnadesetiya Put*. Varna: Alfiola, 2010.

Marcheva, Keta. "Pet Godini Istoriya.BG—A Sega Nakude?" In *Marginalia, Sudut nad Istoritsite: Bulgarskata Istoricheska Nauka: Dokumenti I Diskusii 1944–1950*, vol. 1, edited by Vera Mutafchieva et al. Sofia: AI Prof Marin Drinov, 1995.

Nedkova, Silviya. "Knigite s Fenomanalen Tirazh v Bulgariya," *Ploshtad Slaveikov*, October 6, 2019.

Popivanov, Boris. "Mahmurlukut na Edin Natsionalizum" *Kultura*, 31, September 15, 2006.

Strahilov, Ivo. "Trakite Otvrushtat na Udara: Antichnoto Nasledstvo i Kulturata na Uchastieto." *Seminar* 14, 2017.

Strahilov, Ivo. "We Are the New Thracians: Modern Bulgarians and the Making of Ancient Heritage Living Again." *Seminar* 4, 2018.

Tsanev, Stefan. *Bulgarski Hroniki—Tom I: Istoriya na Nashiya Narod ot 2137 pr. Hr. do 1453 sl. Hr.* Plovdiv: Zhanet 45, 2006.

Znepolski, Ivailo, ed. *Istoriya na Narodna Republika Bulgaria: Rezhimut I Obshtestvoto*. Sofia: Institute for the Study of the Recent Past, Ciela, 2009.

I I

"I'M AN OUTSIDER, I'M AN INSIDER, AND OH, HOW HAPPY I AM"

Narratives of Former Communist Party Members in Hungary

SÁNDOR HORVÁTH

T HIS CHAPTER EXAMINES THE VARIOUS WAYS THAT FORMER MEMBERS OF the Hungarian communist party narrated their experiences of party membership after the fall of socialism.[1] Given that party membership was relatively high in Hungary (in 1987, one in every four households included a party member), such autobiographical refashioning was relatively common after 1989. Rather than nuanced recollections of past experiences, these narratives were intentionally crafted to address the exigencies of postsocialism—and former party members' places within it. As many party members belonged to wealthier, well-educated, and urban groups who advanced socially as a result of joining the communist party, membership provided a host of opportunities, which they in turn translated into economic and cultural capital after 1989. Accordingly, people's professional aspirations after 1989 typically informed how they represented both their work and political roles during socialism.

While some claimed that they joined the party for the purposes of securing work in their areas of expertise and career advancement, others emphasized commitment to social justice, highlighting concern for the common good and distancing themselves from the repressive aspects of the regime. This included those who joined the party during the early years of socialist consolidation in the late 1940s and early 1950s and those who joined during the renaissance of Marxism and subsequent emergence of the new left in the 1960s. By contrast, those who joined in the late 1970s and 1980s typically did not reference ideological conviction, namely leftist (e.g., "reform communist" or social democratic) sympathies.

While strategic mobilizations of the past, the arguments advanced by the individuals featured here run counter to hegemonic instrumentalizations by political elites. Rather than presenting themselves as victims of a coercive dictatorship or downplaying their agency, they emphasized the choices they made within the system, be it promotion of social equality or efforts to acquire the job of their choosing, be promoted, and expand their social networks. Stressing their "independence"—and in some cases representing themselves as extraordinary—former party members strategically connect past and present to provide a coherent narrative of their lives, values, and professional aspirations.[2] As such, their accounts illustrate the diverse ways that everyday practices from the socialist period remain salient today.

These narratives were designed to showcase the expertise and acumen they had developed under socialism, which they in turn emphasized to claim access to particular jobs after 1989. For instance, as a result of their educational level (undergraduate and postgraduate degrees), former party members were often able to retain senior positions in Hungarian institutions after 1989. Thus, they drew on the educational capital they had acquired under socialism to justify their previous party membership *and* to legitimate their continued employment in these positions in the 1990s.[3] Educational level and status under the old regime also enabled former party members to participate in the privatization process, either in their workplace or via the public housing they had been provided at reasonable prices before 1989 and which was eligible for purchase at below-market rates after 1989. As such, former party members were key actors in the privatization of public assets. Indeed, those who remained in the public (state) sector until 1989 were more likely to acquire a dominant place in the privatization process than those who had left the public sector earlier (or had been simultaneously active in the private sector and the socialist sector).[4] Thus, most of the new, large entrepreneurs were former party members. Although constituting a small segment of society, they had enormous influence and power, participating in one of the most spectacular property acquisition schemes of the 1990s, which, as will be examined, influenced how they narrated their career trajectory.

PARTY AND CAREER

Membership in the Hungarian communist party peaked in 1956 and then again in 1987. In the year leading up to the 1956 Revolution, party membership increased dramatically to roughly 870,000 (or more than one in ten adults).[5] After the period of retribution following 1956, the newly established Hungarian Socialist Workers' Party (MSZMP) increased its membership with similar rapidity. Despite the fact the MSZMP was the party of the "working class," white-collar workers constituted the largest percentage of members, while blue-collar workers constituted the smallest. By 1986, party membership had risen to 883,131, prompting a review of party members in 1987. During this process, which included the introduction of new party membership books, the party removed more than one thousand members. Scholars have portrayed this purge as an attempt by the leadership to consolidate power and, at the same time, "cleanse" the party. Moreover, they have identified it as the beginning of the end of "the disintegration of the party-state."[6] However, similar trends in party membership can be observed in other countries of the Eastern Bloc; thus, changes in party membership were not necessarily related to the stability of the system.[7] For instance, according to Anna Grzymala-Busse, "the Polish and Hungarian parties recruited from the outside, using skill, style, and pragmatism as criteria, while the Czechoslovak party advanced its elites from within, using ideological loyalty as the chief criterion."[8] How was this recruitment strategy reinterpreted and mobilized by former party members in the postsocialist period?

Former party members' reasons for joining are widely known: workplace promotion, enjoyment of certain benefits (improved working and housing conditions), a genuine belief in socialism, and a commitment to social reform. Yet, in examining former party members scholars have tended to focus on secret police files rather than people's actual recollections.[9] This is not because former party members are ashamed of their past or reluctant to discuss it. Indeed, despite the fact that the MSZMP, and communism more generally, is stigmatized in current Hungarian public and political discourse, former party members frequently share their stories, including positive recollections of their party membership. How is this possible in a climate dominated by anticommunist rhetoric, and what motivations lie behind such accounts?

WHY THEY JOINED

Under socialism party membership was a prerequisite for career advancement; thus, after 1989 many claimed they had joined the party for the purpose of workplace promotion. According to this narrative, party membership was a compromise required for thriving professionally. As a former party member, who became the owner of a large company after 1989, explained:

> That's what the secretary of the district party committee asked me to do [to join the party]. But I gave up in a minute because I wanted to train myself at all costs. I don't mind, but I've never been interested in helping myself as a member of the party. I'll

tell you honestly, at the time I was half afraid that if I didn't do it, it would have put pressure on the company and the business would not have moved forward. I said I'd rather sacrifice myself, do it. And I didn't regret it.[10]

For this former member, the party represented opportunities for education and training. The narrative of promotion through party membership may also explain why, conversely, blue-collar workers did not join the party in larger numbers, as they had considerably fewer prospects for promotion than did professionals, technocrats, and office workers.[11] As such, managers and other professionals constituted the bulk of communist party members.[12] This suggests that the expectation of party membership was almost automatically associated with high office.

Interviews with non–party members confirmed these rationales. Gábor Bojár, founder of the successful Graphisoft CAD software development company and the Aquincum Institute of Technology in Budapest, explained that he was unable to work as a physicist during the communist period because he was not a party member. Thus he went into programming:

> If I had been a party member, I might have gotten it [a position as a physicist], but of the five or six people who really worked as physicists, I'd say three or four got them [their positions] based on their merits, and they were better than me, but there were two or three who were able to achieve this through their membership in the party. [That was] in 1973. Well, I was not a member of the party, there was no job for a physicist, so I got a job as a programmer.[13]

Gábor draws a clear demarcation between "us" (non–party members) and "them" (party members), and claims that "they" sought to break "us" (i.e., pressure us into joining the communist party) but failed, and therefore "they" made it impossible for "us" to get promotions as non–party members.[14] This widespread and persistent narrative is based on the prevailing assumption that communist parties offered career opportunities as a reward for political loyalty.[15]

It is unsurprising that narratives emphasizing careerist motivations as the primary reason for party membership were common after 1989, enabling former members to excuse or justify their decisions (i.e., they argued they had joined the party not for ideological reasons but out of professional considerations). Another strategy among former party members was to make their stories acceptable from the vantage point of regime change, which they often linked to the decline of their workplace and the collapse of the party, as if everything was heading toward 1989.[16] By claiming they joined the party for practical reasons, rather than ideological ones, and by emphasizing that they joined when it was clear that socialism was disintegrating and the regime would

soon fall, these individuals could retain a modicum of moral authority, even presenting themselves as prophetic.[17]

Former party members also justified their choices on the basis of ingenuity and their
ability to outwit a rigged system.[18] In other words, party membership was based on cal-
culation and shrewdness; a means for career advancement or to avoid trouble, which
should not be confused with a belief in the communist party or its political stances.
In this narrative, former party members are clever individuals who worked the system; they never really wanted to be party members, but because they were intelligent
and hoped to progress professionally, as well as get in the good graces of the authorities, they did so. A school principal who had been imprisoned for his revolutionary activities in 1956, after which he became a party member, used this tack. While depict-
ing his entry into the party as a sign of his social responsibility, he also explained that
this was the only way he could avoid problems associated with his earlier, antistate activities. Furthermore, he claimed that other party members forced him to join; that he
himself had never wanted this:

> It was already raised at my previous school, [that] the requirement for promotion was
> that I needed to settle my relationship with the party. . . . They told me that I could
> join the party, they would accept me if I asked for admission. I said "alright, please
> let me in, but not so that I get anything for myself," but I thought it would enable me,
> looking back, to better justify the [1956] events.[19]

This could work the reverse way as well. A former member of a 1956 workers' council claimed that he refused to join after the revolution because it would mean collabo-
rating with—and thus legitimizing—the János Kádár regime, for which he had no respect. He noted, "After a visit to the Cotton [factory], the management of the MSZMP
in Csepel visited me and asked the whole workers' council to join the party. The answer
was clear: we will never join under any circumstances."[20]

GENERATIONS AND VALUES

Motivations for joining the party also varied with respect to generation. In the accounts
offered by former communist party members, different recollection strategies, often
based on when they joined the party, are evident. "Early" party members (those who
joined the party before the 1960s) emphasized social responsibility and their role in
consolidating socialism, while those who became party members in the 1960s (many
of whom were born during the 1940s and belonged to the younger generation) highlighted professional reasons and possibilities for effecting political change. Meanwhile,

"latecomers" (those who joined in the mid-1970s and especially the 1980s) stressed that since they joined an already disintegrating party, their membership in it had minimal impact on their careers and was thus not strategic.

Political motivations (i.e., faith in the movement) were mentioned primarily in the recollections of party members who joined in the 1960s. In the second half of the 1960s, it became customary among philosophy students at the Faculty of Arts at Eötvös Loránd University (ELTE) in Budapest (many of them from the late Lukács school) to join the party a year before graduation.[21] Some, however, withdrew their applications for party membership after the invasion of Czechoslovakia in 1968. Such was the case of Sándor Radnóti, a philosopher and one of the most influential intellectual figures of his generation.[22] Tibor Huszár, a member of the Faculty of Arts and also a prominent party member, wrote in 1990 about the appeal of the party for young intellectuals during the 1960s: "The chances of an international and domestic renaissance of Marxism and also the emergence of the new left played a significant role in attracting talented groups of young intellectuals and university students to the party."[23] Huszár, who belonged to the earlier generation, emphasized that party membership signified a declaration of loyalty to the regime, which meant better chances of getting a leading position in the communist bureaucracy (as opposed to nonmembers).[24] Therefore, some former party members who were part of the intelligentsia and joined the party in the 1960s do not regard membership as collaboration with the communist regime. Instead, they portray it as a sign of their earlier political commitment and as a form of activism. Miklós Almási, who became head of the aesthetics department at ELTE at the end of the 1970s, described his membership in the party as a tactic that involved "keeping distance," noting, "'I'm an outsider, I'm an insider, and oh how happy I am.' That became my slogan. Happily, outside, inside. In the party I joined, they kicked my ass I don't know how many times! I was able to get back to the university position only after twenty years had passed."[25] By assuming an insider-outsider position, Almási distanced himself from official expectations, while at the same time enjoying the benefits of party membership.

A university student who joined the party in 1969 and later became a literary historian recalled her decision as having been motivated by a kind of enthusiasm to do something meaningful: "Looking back from a distance of forty years, I can say that I was uninformed about daily political and public issues, and my views were immature and uncertain. As a consequence of my age, perhaps, and my attraction to the career I had chosen as a teacher, I longed to take part in meaningful acts."[26] In this woman's interpretation, joining the party is related to her belief that she could promote social justice and improve society, as well as her youthful naivete.

The question arises as to why people's relationships to the party changed over the course of a mere decade. Throughout the Eastern Bloc and, indeed, the globe, 1968 reshaped prevailing conceptualizations of political participation among the generation born after World War II. During the 1960s, politics expanded to include different forms of engagement for the postwar generation, especially university students.[27] After years of reprisals in the wake of the 1956 Revolution and the amnesties issued in 1960 and 1963, Hungary seemed to be more open, evident in changes in travel rules, visits by Western tourists, and increased access to consumer goods. In addition, Western news was partially available, and popular media, including new television shows and the tabloid press, expanded.[28] Hungarian media now featured pieces about Western youth who were critical of capitalist-imperialism, participated in occupations of universities, and withdrew from conventional society. In this climate, party membership might have appeared to young Hungarians as a vehicle for meaningfully participating in politics, including reforming socialism in Hungary and promoting it globally. As Iván Szelényi described this cohort of young party members:

> These Hungarian intellectuals who graduated in the 1960s were driven by ethical motives in their careers. They had a sense of mission or vocation. They wanted to lead society towards an enlightened, rational, humanist, and definitely socialist future.... Many joined the party because they wanted to bring about change, they wanted to seize power, and they wanted to change society with the help of a reformed party.[29]

In contrast to the prewar generation, which represented compromise, submission to power, intimidation, and "doublespeak," in this interpretation the generation that came of age in the 1960s was favorably portrayed as a generation embodying new standards of morality. Thus, 1968 symbolized a change in the prevailing understanding of the past, which was accompanied by a kind of lifestyle revolution.[30] Everyday activities and consumer habits such as travel, clothing, and even social research acquired a political meaning.[31] As a result, people who joined the party in the 1960s were later able to portray themselves as moral entrepreneurs of a sort, whether they were youth workers, rebellious sociologists, or rock musicians who imitated Western music.

This revolutionary narrative played an important role in creating a generational identity, which, in the 1990s, reflected a more empathetic recollection of former party membership, one that explains it as part of the "new leftist" and "neo-Marxist" movement. In the 1990s, an important feature of this memory politics was that the history of the 1960s was not simply a story of the "powerful" versus the "powerless," but rather a tale that involved "ordinary" party members as protagonists. According to this narrative, members of this "big generation" had taken initiative; they were not simply passive observers of their history but active agents who played an essential role in shaping it. As such, this narrative could be used to explain why they were active party members during the 1960s. At the same time, their activism within the party could be presented as altruistic, rooted in concern for the collective good rather than a selfish form of opportunism.

Meanwhile, some from the 1960s generation claimed that they joined the party as an act of rebellion against the older generation, including their parents. As Ferenc Kulin, a member of the conservative Hungarian Democratic Forum (Magyar Demokrata Fórum, MDF) and former parliamentary member who, during the communist era, was (between 1974 and 1983) deputy editor-in-chief and later editor-in-chief of the critical periodical *Mozgó Világ* (*World on the Move*), emphasized: "In order to be a member of the editorial staff of *Mozgó Világ* I had to be a party member. Of course I didn't join the party to be an editor. The truth is that from the age of eighteen to twenty-something, I rebelled against my family traditions and against my church, and I wanted to go in a very independent direction."[32]

TRANSFORMING NETWORKS AFTER 1989

Between 2009 and 2011, Mihály Csákó surveyed over four thousand university students about major events in twentieth-century Hungarian history and their family's (nuclear and extended) relationship to the communist regime.[33] According to the students, there were far more members of the "resistance" among their parents than communist party members, even though in the 1980s the number of dissidents came nowhere near the number of party members. Meanwhile, he found that topics that were taboo under communism (the expulsion of the so-called kulaks, the deportations in the early 1950s, and the 1956 Revolution and subsequent reprisals) were rarely discussed in families in which one parent was a former communist party member. Based on Csákó's findings, it appears that the past is not a major topic of family conversation if one parent was once a member of the communist party, leading him to conclude that former party membership "does not stifle memory, at most it just hampers its survival."[34]

In contrast, when former party members talked about their membership with people outside of their family, they tended to exaggerate its importance. James Mark argues that former party members were confronted with conservative nationalist voices after 1989, which demonized them as careerist collaborators. In response, former party members revived their antifascist stories. This was a means of distancing themselves from the negative aspects of the communist regime and underscoring their commitment to ethical principles, which "they hoped would make their lives morally acceptable to a postcommunist audience."[35]

CONCLUSION

Based on the discussion above, former party members presented their membership in numerous ways. For some it was an expression of educational achievement, moral commitment to the common good, and identification with a particular intellectual community, while for others it was necessary for securing a job in one's field and advancing professionally. Although it is impossible to know the degree to which these representations reflected genuine motivations at the time, because of the way they represented their party membership, none of the individuals featured here considered membership shameful. Instead, they claimed to have worked hard for their positions, which provided them with at least limited opportunities for genuine political participation. More generally, they characterized themselves as ordinary people who had some political power, which they used for "good" purposes. In this way, they reinterpreted the recruitment strategy of the party to legitimize their social positions.

Those who joined the party in the 1950s and especially in the 1960s, during the period of Marxist revisionism, emphasized commitment to the principles of socialist egalitarianism and upward mobility. By justifying their former party membership on collectivist and ethical grounds, they sought to defend themselves from charges of opportunism or having supported a dictatorial regime, which non–party members typically accused them of. Thus, individuals who joined the party in the 1960s could assume a moral high ground, distancing themselves from the older generation of party members of the Stalinist period. Finally, those who joined the "diluted" party in the 1970s and 1980s, when communism was waning, could also present their choice as morally uncompromising.

In addition to playing the morality card, former party members invoked educational credentials in explaining why they became members (since party membership was often necessary for securing work in one's field and advancing professionally). This explanation served dual purposes: it allowed them to present their decision to join the party as a rational act in a system that was based more on loyalty than merit, and it helped them preserve their pre-1989 privileged status after the collapse of the regime. By highlighting their educational merits, former party members legitimated their suitability for positions in politics, business, and public administration. Yet, in reality, securing such jobs after 1989 often had more to do with the connections they had built up prior to 1989, which they did not mention in their narratives. Their transition from socialism to postsocialism thus reflects continuities: just as they belonged to the educated elite during socialism, so too many continued to belong to the educated (and privileged) elite after 1989. They also continued to benefit from insider networks and connections.

Yet, the significance of such refashioning went well beyond job security and personal enrichment. It also had political implications as the Hungarian Socialist Party (Magyar Szocialista Párt; MSZP, the post-1989 successor to the Hungarian Socialist Workers' Party) could count on the support of former party members, enabling it to secure electoral victory in 1994. It did so again in 2002 and 2006, with about half of its votes coming from former communist party members.[36] This was a strategic rather than ideological move as former party members realized they would likely be rewarded for their support. As a result, to quote András Körösényi, "the strata that were the beneficiaries of the communist system, the nomenklatura of the communist regime and its wider social clientele, formed the base of the same political camp in the emerging multi-party plural democracy."[37]

By strategically crafting their autobiographies, former party members retained jobs in leading Hungarian institutions and used their networks and status to secure positions in politics and business. By presenting their previous choices in a positive light, they also challenged prevailing discourses that vilified communist party membership. Despite the fact that most Hungarians who had not been party members believed former party membership should disqualify individuals for political office, many former party members retained or secured political influence at local and national levels, largely by virtue of their status, education, and social capital. Thus, it is perhaps unsurprising that in 1994 more people claimed to be former communist party members (14 percent of those surveyed) than had actually been (around 10 percent of all adults). This reveals the utility of communist party membership in facilitating individuals' privileged status both before and after 1989, and that for this cohort, the collapse of communism did not signify a definitive rupture.[38]

NOTES

1. From 1948 to 1956: Magyar Dolgozók Pártja (MDP) and from 1956 to 1989: Magyar Szocialista Munkáspárt (MSZMP). This chapter was prepared with the support of the MTA-BTK Lendület "Momentum" Work Research Group.

2. For critical meanings of the term *extraordinary*, see Yanni Kotsonis, "Ordinary People in Russian and Soviet History," *Kritika: Explorations in Russian and Eurasian History* 12, no. 3 (2011): 739–54.

3. János Ladányi, *Rétegződés és szelekció a felsőoktatásban* (Budapest: Educatio, 1994).

4. Mihály Laki, "A nagyvállalkozók tulajdonszerzési esélyeiről a szocializmus után," *Közgazdasági Szemle* 69, no. 1 (2002): 55–56.

5. Roland Hell, "Adalékok a Kádár-rendszer politikai elitjének vizsgálatához: Az MSZMP tagságának és függetlenített apparátusának összetétele a számok tükrében," *Jog, állam,*

politika 2, no. 3 (2010): 117–37, 119–20. The total population at the time was 9.8 million.

6. Attila Réfi, "Az MSZMP bomlási folyamata a párt és tagjai viszonya tükrében (1985–1989)," *Múltunk* 54, no. 4 (2009): 64–91.

7. The proportion of communist party members in Hungary to the overall population was slightly higher than average in the 1980s, especially when compared to Czechoslovakia and Poland. The Romanian Communist Party (RCP) was proportionally the largest "Leninist party" in Eastern Europe with approximately 3.7 million members in 1988 (or an estimated 33 percent of Romania's employed population). Anna M. Grzymala-Busse, *The Regeneration of Communist Parties in East Central Europe* (Cambridge: Cambridge University Press, 2002), 32–65; Catalin Augustin Stoica, "Once upon a Time There Was a Big Party: The Social Origins of the Romanian Communist Party (Part I)," *East European Politics & Societies* 19, no. 4 (2005): 686–716, 687; Andreas Malycha and Peter Jochen Winters, *Die SED: Geschichte einer deutschen Partei* (Munich: C. H. Beck, 2009), 409–16.

8. Grzymala-Busse, *The Regeneration*, 29.

9. On the functions of secret police files in memory politics see Lavinia Stan, "The Vanishing Truth? Politics and Memory in Post-Communist Europe," *East European Quarterly* 40 (2006): 392–410.

10. Laki, "A nagyvállalkozók," 53.

11. See also Miroslav Vaněk and Pavel Mücke, *Velvet Revolutions: An Oral History of Czech Society* (New York: Oxford University Press, 2016), 175; and Grzymala-Busse, *The Regeneration*, 31.

12. Szonja Szelényi, "Social Inequalities and Party Membership: Patterns of Recruitment into the Hungarian Socialist Workers' Party," *American Sociological Review* 52 (1987): 559–73.

13. Interview with Gábor Bojár, *Óbuda*, November 9, 2014.

14. Vaněk and Mücke, *Velvet Revolutions*, 172–74.

15. Andrew G. Walder, "Career Mobility and the Communist Political Order," *American Sociological Review* 60 (1995): 310–11.

16. See Eszter Zsófia Tóth, *"Puszi Kádár Jánosnak": Munkásnők élete a Kádár-korszakban mikrotörténeti megközelítésben* (Budapest: Napvilág, 2007), 146–48.

17. Alexei Yurchak, *Everything Was Forever, Until It Was No More: The Last Soviet Generation* (Princeton, NJ: Princeton University Press, 2005).

18. György Majtényi, *A tudomány lajtorjája. "Társadalmi mobilitás" és "új értelmiség" Magyarországon a II. világháború után* (Budapest: Gondolat, 2005), 119.

19. Recollections of E. J. in 2000, in Adrienne Molnár, *A "hatvanas évek" emlékezete* (Budapest: 1956-os Intézet, 2004), 134–35.

20. Gyula Kozák and Adrienne Molnár, eds., *"Szuronyok hegyén nem lehet dolgozni!" válogatás 1956-os munkástanács-vezetők visszaemlékezéseiből* (Budapest: Századvég, 1993), 43.

21. For them, Marxism remained a reference point and theoretical basis for a democratic revival of real socialism. André Tosel, "The Late Lukács and the Budapest School," in *Critical Companion to Contemporary Marxism*, ed. Jacques Bidet and Stathis Kouvelakis (Leiden: Brill, 2008), 163–73.

22. András Lénárt, "Egy sorozatról: a Társadalomtudományi Könyvtár," in Gyula Kozák, ed., *Kádárizmus: Átereszek. Az 1956-os Intézet Évkönyve 2010* (Budapest: 1956-os Intézet, 2011), 154–84.

23. Tibor Huszár, *Mit ér a szellem, ha . . . Értelmiség, politika, értelmiségpolitika (1957–1987)* (Budapest: Szabad Tér, 1990), 42.

24. Recollections of Tibor Huszár, in Lénárt, "Egy sorozatról," 176.

25. Máté Pálos, "'Kint is, bent is, boldogan': Interjú Almási Miklós esztétával." Interview with aesthete Miklós Almási, *Magyar Narancs*, November 15, 2020, https://magyarnarancs.hu/konyv/kint-is-bent-is-boldogan-134005.

26. Éva Standeisky, "Az én hatvannyolcam," in *Kádárizmus atereszek: Évkönyv XVII*, ed., Gyula Koz.k (Budapest: 1956-os Intézet, 2010), 263–74.

27. Robert Gildea and James Mark, "Conclusion: Europe's 1968" in *Europe's 1968: Voices of Revolt*, ed. Robert Gildea, James Mark, and Anette Warring (Oxford: Oxford University Press, 2013), 326–38.

28. János M. Rainer, "A 'hatvanas évek' Magyarországon: (Politika)történeti közelítések," in *Hatvanas évek" Magyarországon,* ed., János M. Rainer (Budapest: 1956-os Intézet, 2004), 11–30.

29. Iván Szelényi, *Új osztály, állam, politika* (Budapest: Európa, 1990), 58.

30. Ágnes Heller, "1968," *Beszélő* 3, no. 11 (1997): 70–79.

31. "Olyan világról ábrándoztunk, amelyet a saját értékeink uralnak," *Mozgó Világ*, 34, no. 8 (2008): 3–17.

32. "Bukásunk lesz a vesztetek," *Szcenárium* 2, no. 8 (2014): 99–109.

33. Mihály Csákó, "Családi emlékezet és történelem," *Socio Hu* 1 (2014): 81–107, https://doi.org/10.18030/SOCIO.HU.2014.1.81;https://socio.hu/uploads/files/2014_1/4csako.pdf.

34. Csákó, "Családi," 106.

35. James Mark, "Antifascism, the 1956 Revolution and the Politics of Communist Autobiographies in Hungary 1944–2000," *Europe-Asia Studies* 58, no. 8 (2006): 1209–40.

36. Róbert Angelusz and Róbert Tardos, "A választói magatartás egy mögöttes pillére," *Politikatudományi Szemle* 4, no. 3 (1995): 5–18; András Körösényi, "Nómenklatúra és törésvonal," *Társadalmi Szemle* 52, no. 2 (1997): 63–75.

37. Körösényi, "Nómenklatúra," 73.

38. Angelusz and Tardos, "A választói," 8.

BIBLIOGRAPHY

Angelusz, Róbert, and Róbert Tardos. "A választói magatartás egy mögöttes pillére." *Politikatudományi Szemle* 4, no. 3 (1995): 5–18.

Csákó, Mihály. "Családi emlékezet és történelem." *Socio Hu* 1 (2014): 81–107. https://socio.hu/uploads/files/2014_1/4csako.pdf.

Gildea, Robert, and James Mark. "Conclusion: Europe's 1968." In *Europe's 1968. Voices of Revolt*, edited by Robert Gildea, James Mark, and Anette Warring, 326–38. Oxford: Oxford University Press, 2013.

Grzymala-Busse, Anna M. *The Regeneration of Communist Parties in East Central Europe*. Cambridge: Cambridge University Press, 2002.

Hell, Roland. "Adalékok a Kádár-rendszer politikai elitjének vizsgálatához: Az MSZMP tagságának és függetlenített apparátusának összetétele a számok tükrében." *Jog, állam, politika* 2, no. 3 (2010): 117–37.

Heller, Ágnes. "1968." *Beszélő* 3, no. 11 (1997): 70–79.

Huszár, Tibor. *Mit ér a szellem, ha . . . Értelmiség, politika, értelmiségpolitika (1957–1987)*. Budapest: Szabad Tér, 1990.

Körösényi, András. "Nómenklatúra és törésvonal." *Társadalmi Szemle* 52, no. 2 (1997): 63–75.

Kotsonis, Yanni. "Ordinary People in Russian and Soviet History." *Kritika: Explorations in Russian and Eurasian History* 12, no. 3 (2011): 739–54.

Kozák, Gyula, and Adrienne Molnár, eds. *"Szuronyok hegyén nem lehet dolgozni!" válogatás 1956-os munkástanács-vezetők visszaemlékezéseiből*. Budapest: Századvég, 1993.

Ladányi, János. *Rétegződés és szelekció a felsőoktatásban*. Budapest: Educatio, 1994.

Laki, Mihály. "A nagyvállalkozók tulajdonszerzési esélyeiről a szocializmus után." *Közgazdasági Szemle* 69, no 1 (2002): 55–56.

Lénárt, András. "Egy sorozatról: a Társadalomtudományi Könyvtár." In *Kádárizmus. Átereszek. Az 1956-os Intézet Évkönyve 2010*, edited by Gyula Kozák, 154–84. Budapest: 1956-os Intézet, 2011.

Majtényi, György. *A tudomány lajtorjája. "Társadalmi mobilitás" és "új értelmiség" Magyarországon a II. világháború után*. Budapest: Gondolat, 2005.

Malycha, Andreas, and Peter Jochen Winters. *Die SED: Geschichte einer deutschen Partei*. Munich: C. H. Beck, 2009.

Mark, James. "Antifascism, the 1956 Revolution and the Politics of Communist Autobiographies in Hungary 1944–2000." *Europe-Asia Studies* 58, no. 8 (2006): 1209–40.

Molnár, Adrienne. *A "hatvanas évek" emlékezete*. Budapest: 1956-os Intézet, 2004.

Rainer, János M. "A 'hatvanas évek' Magyarországon. (Politika)történeti közelítések." In *"Hatvanas évek" Magyarországon*, edited by János M. Rainer, 11–30. Budapest: 1956-os Intézet, 2004.

Réfi, Attila. "Az MSZMP bomlási folyamata a párt és tagjai viszonya tükrében (1985–1989)." *Múltunk*, 54, no. 4 (2009): 64–91.

Stan, Lavinia. "The Vanishing Truth? Politics and Memory in Post-Communist Europe." *East European Quarterly* 40 (2006): 392–410.

Standeisky, Éva. "Az én hatvannyolcam." In *Kádárizmus atereszek*, edited by Gyula Kozák, 263–74. Budapest: 1956-os Intézet, 2010.

Stoica, Catalin Augustin. "Once Upon a Time There Was a Big Party: The Social Origins of the Romanian Communist Party (Part I)." *East European Politics & Societies* 19, no. 4 (2005): 686–716.

Szelényi, Iván. *Új osztály, állam, politika.* Budapest: Európa, 1990.

Szelényi, Szonja. "Social Inequalities and Party Membership: Patterns of Recruitment into the Hungarian Socialist Workers' Party." *American Sociological Review* 52 (1987): 559–73.

Tosel, André. "The Late Lukács and the Budapest School." In *Critical Companion to Contemporary Marxism*, edited by Jacques Bidet and Stathis Kouvelakis, 163–73. Leiden: Brill, 2008.

Tóth, Eszter Zsófia. *"Puszi Kádár Jánosnak": Munkásnők élete a Kádár-korszakban mikrotörténeti megközelítésben.* Budapest: Napvilág, 2007.

Vaněk, Miroslav, and Pavel Mücke. *Velvet Revolutions: An Oral History of Czech Society.* New York: Oxford University Press, 2016.

Walder, Andrew G. "Career Mobility and the Communist Political Order." *American Sociological Review* 60 (1995): 309–28.

Yurchak, Alexei. *Everything Was Forever, Until It Was No More: The Last Soviet Generation.* Princeton, NJ: Princeton University Press, 2005.

PART V

HOME IS WHERE THE HEART IS

12

CHILDREN OF THE *WENDE*

Everyday Experiences of the Postsocialist Transformation in (East) Germany

FRIEDERIKE KIND-KOVÁCS

I N AN ARTICLE PUBLISHED IN THE EAST GERMAN DAILY *NEUE ZEIT* (*THE NEW Times*) on January 13, 1990, a woman expressed concern about the challenges that *die Wende* (regime change) posed for East Germans, singling out children in particular: "Overnight, parents, teachers, educators, and children were confronted with life circumstances they had not known until then," all of which caused "special risks for children."[1] As some of the most vulnerable members of society, children, she argued, should be of paramount importance, otherwise they could face major disadvantages during the transformation.[2] Meanwhile, contemporaries remarked on the mix of emotions they observed among children, who seemed "hopeful and irritated at the same time," as they were both "impressed by the range of consumer goods and greater freedom of choice" but also "depressed because of the crisis and losses caused by family problems, the dissolution of care facilities, and problems facing their teachers."[3] By October 1990, the Child Commissioner of the Bundestag (the German Parliament), Wilhelm Schmidt, feared East German children "will be the big losers of German reunification," as parents' loss of work would lead to divorces, separations, and the dissolution of friendships, which could, in turn, impair children's upbringing.[4]

Kathleen K., who was a second-grader during *die Wende*, recalled in 2020 that her understanding of the period was filtered through the experiences of the adults in her midst: "I think I mainly mirrored what the people around me reacted to. Everyone was like, didn't really know yet, was excited, [but] no one really knew what was coming."[5] This linguistically fragmented recollection illustrates how Kathleen attempted to make sense of what was happening by way of adults' responses to the transformation. In effect, she became their sounding board during this time of crisis. In light of such sentiments, exploring how young people experienced and emotionally processed the collapse of state socialism and the early transition merits sustained analysis.

Drawing on oral histories, autobiographical novels, letters, and print media, this chapter explores the everyday experiences of the *Wendekinder* (children born between 1975 and 1985) during the early postsocialist transformation.[6] While recent research has focused on "the long history of the transformation" (*die lange Geschichte der Wende*), as Kerstin Brückweh contends, the years 1989–1990 can serve as a magnifying glass, enhancing our understanding of how change affected people in the short term.[7] As children's routines, families, and social relationships were deeply embedded in the socialist system before 1989, they were particularly affected by the subsequent political and social transformation. Rather than examining "how 'large processes were passively experienced in the 'small worlds' of [young people's] everyday existence," I render visible the ways in which people positioned themselves and evaluated the early postsocialist transformation, both contemporaneously as children and retrospectively as adults.[8] Many of the individuals featured here entered puberty just as the world around them began crumbling. As such, they experienced multiple transformations, living simultaneously through a political, social, and personal transformation. While views of reunification tended to be celebratory during the 1990s, the *Wendekinder* featured here express a range of sentiments, revealing that the immediate post-*Wende* years were accompanied not only by happiness and hopefulness, but also loss, disappointment, and disillusionment. Centering on these critical recollections, this chapter seeks to complicate current tendencies in East Germany to— retrospectively—idealize everyday life in the German Democratic Republic (GDR) and demonize what came after. Understanding why some children experienced the postsocialist transformation and its immediate aftermath as a fundamental rupture might help us grasp the historical roots of the disillusionment with 1989 and its original promises.

By examining children's often ambiguous narratives of transition, this chapter goes beyond the heroic story of German reunification on the one hand and totalitarian-inflected depictions of the GDR on the other, providing a complex portrait of the socialist regime and the liberal democratic government that followed it. As such, it serves as a barometer for gauging state commitment to its citizens, offering insight into which groups it prioritized and which it subordinated or overlooked.[9] To quote a German policymaker: "Tell me how you deal with the children of your country, and I will tell you what kind of politics you conduct."[10]

AMBIGUOUS FEELINGS: YOUNG
PEOPLE'S EXPERIENCES OF 1989

When discussing the collapse of the Soviet Union, Alexei Yurchak claimed that "the system collapse had been profoundly unexpected and unimaginable . . . until it happened, and yet, it quickly appeared perfectly logical and exciting when it began."[11] In East Germany, children greeted socialism's collapse with a host of sentiments: excitement, anticipation, confusion, disorientation, relief. Andrea H., who was a pedagogy student in 1989, recalled the natural momentum and rapidity of change, noting: "If you have such strict rules and regulations, the moment the wall fell, it became an automatic process, which could not be stopped."[12] For Heike H., who was a teenager during the early 1990s, the transition was associated with relief. In an interview in September 2020, she recalled what it had meant to experience the transformation as a sixteen-year-old: "I was at that age when you start questioning everything actively," emphasizing that she was "so rebellious" that she would have had problems with the previous regime had it not collapsed.[13] Meanwhile, Sabine Rennefanz, author of the novel *Eisenkinder* (*Children of Iron*), recalled the period more ambivalently: "When I see old pictures on TV from the time after the fall of the Berlin Wall, people always seem so euphoric, relaxed, happy. Wasn't it the best time to be in puberty? In the middle of a new beginning? Were the younger ones not the winners of the transformation? My notes don't seem to go with it. I didn't feel any joy, any optimism."[14] Similarly, Jana Hensel, who was thirteen in November 1989, felt confused and uncertain, noting in her memoir *Zonenkinder* (*After the Wall*), "Something happened to this country, which had always been my home, something I did not understand, and that no adult could explain to me, what it was and would actually lead to."[15]

The unification of East and West Germany also elicited concern among many young people that their previous experiences and identities would no longer be important and would no longer matter. Pamela Hess emphasized that while "the GDR was indeed a dictatorship, it was also a place where people loved and lived."[16] Such realities were seemingly forgotten, however, as new values based on individualism replaced the old (i.e., East German) ones based on collectivism. Hensel poignantly captured the feeling of being unmoored after 1989: "These are the last days of our childhood, which of course I didn't know back then, just like doors to another time zone that has the smell of a fairy tale and for which we can no longer find the right words." Hensel thus looked nostalgically to her childhood before 1989 as a time "when the clocks had a different rhythm, the winter smelled different, and the bows in our hair were tied differently," adding that it is hard "to remember this fairytale time, because for a long time we wanted to forget it, we wished for nothing more than for it to disappear as quickly as possible. It was as if it should have never existed." Yet, years later she realized that it did hurt her to "part with the familiar," when "one day the doors did actually close. Suddenly they were gone, the old days."[17]

THE ROAD TO UNCERTAINTY: THE TRANSFORMATION OF LIFE AS WE HAVE KNOWN IT

As daily life was upended virtually overnight, many of the values, certainties, and convictions people had shared no longer seemed to matter or resonate. Hensel's feelings of loss about her "GDR childhood" and uncertainty about the future were echoed by others who experienced 1989 as a child or teen. The aforementioned teenager Heike H. expressed ambivalence about the system change, recounting her enthusiastic—and fearless—participation in demonstrations in 1989, while also mourning "those things from my childhood and my country [that] no longer exist." She further reflected: "Somehow, I lost my country, didn't I?" She compares this loss to refugees' loss of home: "[It was like] refugees who can't go back to their country, who miss it; that was hard for me too."[18] Admittedly, the comparison with refugees is misleading in that East German citizens neither had to flee nor relocate to another country. Nonetheless, they did harbor feelings of loss and disorientation as the country in which they had grown up—the GDR—ceased to exist.

Children's memories of the transition were also mediated through their parents' experiences, which at times affected them deeply. In a letter to *Neues Deutschland* (*New Germany*), the official newspaper of the GDR, on December 15, 1989, Anne Zimmermann, an eleven-year-old from Lübz, described how, when watching the news of the regime collapse, her "father had tears in his eyes and was very depressed," something she had never experienced before. Thus, she wished for "all the old men of the old government to be punished so that my parents can be happy again," because "Erich Honecker and our old government had not been honest with us, they had lied to the people of the GDR."[19]

In 1993, German writer Regina Rusch, hoping to give voice to those who had experienced the postsocialist transformation as children, published a collection of over three hundred letters from children aged seven to fourteen.[20] The letters capture the void the transformation had created in children's lives, be it in the realm of leisure, socialization, or daily routines. Walter Bärsch, a German psychologist, criticized in the afterword of the book "how little thought had been given to the situation of children during the transformation," noting that they had "generally identified" with the GDR and that in their youth clubs "they cheered Honecker and learned that 'socialism is good, capitalism is bad.'" Because many had "felt at home in their pioneer groups," they now seemed lost, since "all has been taken from them and nothing new has been put in its place."[21] To children, real existing postsocialism, in many respects, signified a rupture from their former lives, and this required finding new ways of coping. In response to social upheaval, private life and the family became increasingly important, underscoring continuities with the socialist period when the family served as a refuge, albeit from state interference. During the early transformation in particular, the family acquired a stabilizing function, serving as a "'protective wall' against imminent losses."[22]

POST-1989: RUPTURED LIVES AND UNFULFILLED DREAMS

The most fundamental challenge for families after 1989 was economic, as many parents lost their jobs. During socialism many people had been employed in large factories and enterprises; however, the privatization and closure of factories created mass layoffs in the former East. Already by 1992, almost one million people had lost their jobs, with women experiencing the greatest job loss: between 1990 and 1995, the unemployment rate for women reached 8.2 percent—almost twice as high as male unemployment (4.9 percent).[23] Moreover, women remained unemployed for a longer period, especially those with small children in their care. These new circumstances forced many (East) German women into the role of housewife, which they had generally rejected under socialism. Deindustrialization had psychological effects as well. The East German state had been a "workers' state," in which labor was fundamental and unemployment nonexistent—at least officially. As such, job loss after 1989 was experienced as a stigma, producing feelings of shame and frustration.[24]

While the family often served as a protective shield during the transition, not all parents could insulate loved ones from feelings of insecurity, disillusionment, and sadness. Indeed, with the adoption of capitalism in the East after German unification, parents faced a host of economic challenges, which at times compromised their ability to support their children in navigating change and new challenges. Parents' abrupt loss of work, in particular, had marked repercussions on their children. As Sabine Rennefanz recalled: "That was perhaps most challenging about growing up in the transformation period: to see how helpless and hurt our parents were. How shall one find a place in the world if those who are supposed to help you are lost themselves? Not all shared this destiny, but many fathers and mothers lost their jobs."[25]

Adapting to the new labor market often involved professional reorientation and retraining. Kathleen K., another child of the transformation who had grown up with the conviction that "work is important" and that "it is secure as long as you do your best," witnessed how her parents were forced to "completely reinvent themselves," which required participating in job requalification programs. While her parents successfully adapted to the changes, others did not fare so well and were ultimately unable to secure work. Witnessing the regime change as a fourteen-year-old, Dana R. recalled that her father had accepted the need to learn another skill; however, despite his best efforts, he failed to find work and was thus deeply disappointed by the post-1989 changes.[26] Having relied on their parents for guidance, support, and comfort, many children and adolescents found such realities jolting.

Families were also ambiguously affected by the consumer revolution that emerged after the collapse of the East German regime, when Western goods flooded into the East. Under the GDR's economy of shortage, East Germans often looked at West Germany's consumer culture with envy. For instance, Heike H. recalled how jealous she had been of West German children's access to certain sweets, which she had learned about from a comic book, *Die Biene Maja* (*Maya the Bee*), she received from her grandmother. Through these comics she became familiar with Müller chocolate rice pudding, something she had never seen or eaten. Thus, for her "the West was always paradise"; it "was colorful, light, while the GDR was always grey."[27]

Hopes of engaging fully in this consumer paradise were soon dashed, as prosperity was unevenly felt due to the social inequalities that emerged under capitalism. As Frank Budy, who was thirteen in 1990, recalled: "Before the transformation my mother regularly bought me something… now she often says that we need to cut down on expenses. Now, when I need something to wear, I do get something, but only what is absolutely necessary."[28] As Frank's recollection demonstrates, the increased choice and availability of consumer products meant little for those experiencing economic difficulties; instead, they produced disappointment, particularly among children.

Pierre Spiller, who was twelve years old in 1990, emphasized in a letter that people were "happy that the borders were finally open and that we, children, were also allowed into the West," adding that it felt "like a dream." Yet, he also realized that "the beautiful dream is no longer so beautiful because completely new worries also emerged, which we didn't expect before." While tempted by the many beautiful things from the West that he had learned about in advertisements before 1989, he soon realized that his family "cannot afford many of the things which we would like to have," which is why his parents "talk almost every day about money, complaining that it is not enough."[29] Pierre's letter underscores the ambiguous, even bittersweet, nature of the transformation: his initial happiness about the opening of the border and the possibility of buying things he had once only dreamed about on the one hand, and his family's inability to actually purchase those things due to lack of means on the other. Pierre was thus frustrated with the discrepancy between his initial expectations and the reality that shattered his dreams.

While this discrepancy was difficult for children, it was even more difficult for single mothers who struggled to support their children, let alone treat them to the new consumer goods on offer. In 1990, a single mother of two (aged nine and thirteen) recalled the challenges in affording basic goods for her children. As the rent had quadrupled, there was no money left for anything extra. She explained: "Already now, I need to say all the time, 'we cannot afford this.' I need to save for months to be able to buy clothes or shoes. A common vacation is an illusion. For birthdays and Christmas, I can only give practical gifts."[30] As the initial fascination with Western consumer goods faded among some East Germans, feelings of "*Ostalgie*" (a nostalgia for East German material objects) emerged. East German consumer goods thus became symbols of a romanticized East German past that had been wiped out.

PHYSICAL AND MENTAL MIGRATION

Due to unemployment, but also the long-cherished dreams to live a "better life," after 1989 many families seized the opportunity to leave for West Germany. However, mass migration had several unanticipated repercussions. As people fled due to unemployment, entire East German villages began to simply die out. Meanwhile, families who arrived in the West faced difficulties they had not foreseen. Even though they shared a common language and rapidly found well-paid work, many felt alienated or even like second-class Germans. The forty-year division between the two Germanys was evident in daily encounters. Johannes Nichelmann, a post-*Wende* child, recalled how he felt in his new school in Bavaria. While he was born after the regime change and moved to the West only in 2002, he nonetheless felt a psychological divide and the stigma of being East German. Prior to moving to the West, he almost "never thought about being (East) German," however, once he arrived in Bavaria, he realized that he was now an "Ossi," which made him feel excluded and marginalized, hindering his ability to "enter into wonderful friendships."[31] Feeling "pushed into the same corner" against his will, without exactly comprehending what was going on, he noted: "I defend East Germany and the GDR. Without knowing exactly what I am defending. It's a feeling of double powerlessness. The fight against discrimination and the feeling of not being able to explain one's origin."[32]

These westward departures did not always include the entire family, as thousands of parents left their children behind in the East, either temporarily or permanently. A mother from Hellersdorf, for instance, was reported to have left with a friend to West Berlin on the night of November 13, 1989, leaving her four-year old twins Sascha and Sebastian with another friend. After some time, it was clear that the mother did not intend on returning.[33] Meanwhile, an article in *Neue Zeit* on November 30, 1989, related the story of three children in Berlin-Friedrichshain (Christoph, 3, Katharina, 2, and Steffen, 9 months) whose mother, now in Werneck, West Germany, had stated she was not planning on returning to the East and that "the concerned father should take care of them."[34]

This type and level of parental neglect triggered heated discussions in the media. On December 6, 1989, the Schubert family wrote to the East German *Neue Zeit*, expressing indignation about child abandonment: "Parents quietly leave our country without their children. What kind of mothers are they, what kind of fathers? Don't they have any conscience? It's pre-Christmas time, so slowly we are getting into the mood for the celebration of the year, and what can these children expect? A pile of broken pieces, no more home with child love, lots of tears and certainly mental disorders."[35] Youth councils in the East tried to locate parents via newspaper ads, and orphanages took in many children who had been left behind; however, they were unable to take them all in. Only recently have the stories of these forgotten children attracted scholarly attention, bringing to light the more heartrending effects of the transition.

CHILDCARE AND LEISURE

The transition to a market economy also affected East Germany's childcare system. As a "welfare dictatorship" the GDR provided a range of social entitlements, including subsidized childcare.[36] In 1989, 98 percent of all children aged three to six attended kindergarten, and 80 percent of children aged two months to three years were cared for in a state nursery. With German reunification, state expenditures on welfare provisions in the East were scaled back, resulting in the closing or privatization of childcare facilities. In addition, as factories closed, so too did the childcare centers that were housed within them. The loss of affordable childcare created particular challenges for blue-collar families. In a letter published in *Neues Deutschland* in early 1990, parents complained about the shuttering of a children's nursery, demanding that it should be reopened, as their children had been "optimally cared for" at this institution.[37]

The closing of daycares and kindergartens was also jolting for care workers, many of whom lost their jobs. As Kerstin S. lamented, "there were no more children in the nursery," adding that her kindergarten was so fundamentally restructured that "we, the young, had to leave." Meanwhile, some private childcare facilities refused to hire East German care workers, believing they had been "tainted by socialist ideology." Rosemarie K., a former care worker, emphasized that her proximity to the former regime, rather than her competence, was what seemed to matter after 1989.[38] This produced bitterness within care workers, who felt that their expertise and experience no longer mattered.

Some care workers resisted efforts to displace them from the workforce. For instance, workers at a nursery in Berlin Treptow invited parents from West Berlin to observe the quality of care they provided, demonstrating that "the pedagogical work and the everyday life of children had been improved to such a degree that it could be compared with the quality of a West German nursery."[39] Such acts were influenced by both economic need and a desire to challenge stereotypes about East German childcare institutions and their staff.

In the immediate aftermath of the fall of the Berlin Wall, East German pedagogues and childcare institutions were under constant pressure to prove their pedagogical quality and financial sustainability. This critical evaluation process, while creating common childcare standards, also produced inequalities between the East and West German labor markets. For instance, Stefanie H., an East German mother and care worker at the time, felt that her West German colleagues had looked down on her. While she acknowledged that East Germany could not "catch up overnight with what the West had achieved in forty years," she nevertheless recalled feeling "personally hurt" when she heard some West Germans on television say that "we East Germans should first learn how to work," as she had always been a diligent and conscientious worker.[40]

Insults aside, many East German pedagogues were keen on learning new approaches to teaching and caregiving. Veronika K., a former East German daycare manager, recalled a pedagogical training trip during which East German kindergarten teachers learned about West German approaches to childcare: how important the individual child was, what methods they employed "to support and encourage children," and "how to turn their weaknesses into strengths."[41] For East German care workers, this transformation entailed a shift from a collective to a more individualized understanding of childhood and childcare. It also involved reducing the caretaker–child ratio and the formulation of new pedagogical agendas. The newly established "program for care in nurseries" (*Programm für die Erziehungsarbeit in den Kinderkrippen*) resulted in the awareness of the need "to respond sensitively to the needs of each individual child, establish positive social contacts, and foster [children's] innovative and creative abilities." At the same time, it acknowledged that nurseries "could not replace the warmth, security, and love of families."[42]

Childcare was also diversified and schedules were made more flexible. New types of care such as "*kinderläden*" and "nanny projects" emerged as an alternative to nurseries, enabling parents to freely choose their preferred care facilities.[43] In addition, parents of children with disabilities were given the choice of having their children attend a facility for children with special needs or a "normal school."[44] This signified a decidedly positive rupture, ending the state-mandated institutionalization by school and health authorities that had resulted in the isolation and discrimination of children with special needs.[45] Parents were also allowed and expected to be more involved in childcare decisions, including how quickly their child should be acclimated to a care facility. In 2020, Veronika K. recalled that before 1989 "the children were handed over and good-bye," but now they had to consider the process of attachment and their acclimatization to caretakers. Moreover, she noted that emphasis was placed on play, rather than just learning. Overall, then, childcare witnessed an ambiguous transformation: on the one hand, a reduction in childcare facilities, which resulted in job loss for many care workers; on the other hand, improvements in the quality of care at existing childcare centers.

Heike M., a childcare worker, felt that attitudes and relationships changed most after 1989, which she welcomed and found liberating. In 2020 she recalled how "suddenly there were topics that were really interesting. And they talked about it and parents asked questions: 'How do you want to do that?' And we honestly admitted: 'We don't know yet. We can't tell you yet. You can see what's going on here and we're changing a lot right now. We'll have to decide it at some point.'"[46] This exchange reveals how the democratization of the political regime also resulted in the democratization of childcare. It hints at the slow negotiation process that accompanied the pedagogical transformation. As little instruction was given to care workers about the new pedagogical agenda, they had to shape their institutions' future by themselves. Heike emphasized greater openness between caregivers and parents, as well as children's increased input in determining the nature of their leisure activities.

Children's leisure also witnessed fundamental reconfiguration. State organizations for youth leisure, such as the pioneers and the *Freie Deutsche Jugend* (FDJ; Free German Youth), were either disbanded or lost so many members that they were forced to shut down. As a result, the sense of community and belonging that had been forced through and fostered by these organizations waned as well. Verena, who was eleven in 1990, lamented the loss of such social relations, noting, "I dislike it that they got rid of the pioneers. . . . I liked the feeling of belonging." Verena preferred to say that she had once belonged (to the young pioneers) than to say that she now belonged nowhere. She concluded: "We were all part of something, it was this feeling of belonging together, that's very important to me, that you are not a loner. With the *Wende* everyone is now for themselves."[47] Meanwhile, in an article in *Neues Deutschland* from January 1990, a woman wrote, "The kids in the neighborhood lack places to play and meet," adding that schools were increasingly leaving children to their own devices.[48] As Veronika K., whose own children were young at the time, recalled, "I felt that all of a sudden my own children didn't know what to do with their free time."[49] In addition to youth organizations, children's holiday camps were closed, leaving many East German families without childcare during the summer months.[50] Many teenagers were, however, also relieved from the pressure they had experienced through their membership in the children's and youth mass organizations of the GDR. New social and economic inequalities also affected children's access to leisure opportunities. Only those children whose parents were among the "winners" of the transformation could enjoy the wide range of fee-based leisure and travel opportunities on offer—and their parents were free of worry as well.

Although new youth groups were established after 1989, children increasingly spent more time alone, including at home watching television. Kathleen K. described this change in her own life once she became a latchkey child: "So then I started to be outside less. And then I sat in front of the TV more. And just like that, a bit of the framework that surrounded us was suddenly gone."[51] Like Kathleen, many other children of the *Wende* lost a substantial part of their common institutional coherence and had trouble coping with this social void. The transformation thus undermined the sense of community and belonging that many young people had experienced in socialist organizations, producing isolation and loneliness.

CONCLUSION

As explored in this chapter, (East) German children often experienced—and remembered as adults—1989 and the early transition in similar ways.[52] More generally, what many young people had considered to be eternal before 1989 simply vanished into thin air or abruptly lost its meaning. For them, 1989 represented the end of everyday routines and relationships, triggering feelings of disorientation and sadness. Alongside losing outlets for socializing with their peers, young people witnessed the complete dissolution of their country and its integration into a different one. Herein we can detect a fundamental difference from other postsocialist societies. While German unification was expected to be easier, smoother, and more natural due to the formerly shared past and identity of the once unitary German state, this expectation did not turn out to be true. The disappearance of the GDR as a country caused widespread feelings of loss and disappointment among East German children. Even in 2023, thirty-four years after 1989, heated debates revolve around the supposedly failed mental reunification of both states and the ongoing division of Germany into "Ossis" (East Germans) and "Wessis" (West Germans).[53]

In the past decade the former children and adolescents of the *Wende* have played a key role in the current debate over the reevaluation of the GDR and the transformation. Back then, during the process of the *Wende*, those entering their teens not only faced social transformation, but they also experienced the developmental changes of adolescence. Understandably, then, young people recall feeling overwhelmed by these rapid and simultaneous changes and by the disappearance of life as they had known it. An eleven-year-old girl from Berlin expressed shock and anger that everything she had believed in seemingly ceased to matter overnight: "I am afraid. I cannot understand that everything I had learned in eight years of school will be useless and wrong."[54] Other children similarly felt that the rug had been pulled out from under them, as the structures that had given their lives meaning ceased to exist. For Kathleen K., these changes had long-term effects on her personality. She noted: "I was used to being guided and then that was gone. And I believe that this haunts me until today. . . . If there are too many paths, too many possibilities, then I'm a bit overwhelmed."[55] Herein we can also see how deeply the East German dictatorship had intervened in the private lives of its youngest generations. Due to the overtly defined daily routines—starting from nursery school—that left little freedom of choice to children in the GDR, the newly gained freedom after 1989 overwhelmed many children. Others, however, felt an amazing relief from the fading influence of the state in their individual lives and were happy to spend this newly gained time with old and new friends.

Some also felt that their youth simply disappeared after 1989. Christiane M., who was twenty when the wall came down, describes how political rupture went hand in hand with personal rupture. She explained that "the time back then was very exciting and nerve-wracking," which expressed itself in "this break between childhood, youth, and growing up." Until then, she noted, "life was just babbling along, which suited me quite well. But "then came the regime change, and since then everything has been racing." Despite acknowledging all the opportunities available to her now, she longs for the time before 1989, even if life during real existing socialism had also meant more restrictions: "I didn't lack anything, but there are certainly others who felt restricted. But nowadays you are also restricted. That's my impression." Christiane feels not only the pressures of fast-paced life under everyday postsocialism, but also its disappointments, as her financial situation never enabled her to make use of the many new opportunities. She expressed the greatest pain, however, when describing her parents' sense of helplessness after 1989, as they did "not understand the world anymore."

Thus, young people were confronted with new worries, specifically the financial challenges their parents faced as a result of unemployment and rising costs for housing and basic goods. As children typically relied on their parents for emotional support, these new realities were jolting. In some cases, parents' responses to the transition had lingering effects, influencing how young people responded to change in adulthood. Christiane noted that her parents' responses to rapid change were "handed down" to the next generation, which is why she felt as if "you never really get rid of it. . . . I think I've never really gotten rid of it."[56] This retrospective reflection on the intergenerational transmission of loss and disorientation underscores the possible long-term repercussions of the transformation. While children who succeeded in "getting rid" of such inherited emotional responses were able to fill the void created by the collapse with something meaningful, their memories of the time before 1989 nonetheless still constitute a central part of their memory—and their identity—today.

NOTES

1. Gudrun Skulski, "Gefahren für Kinder?" *Neue Zeit*, January 13, 1990, 46.

2. Skulski, "Gefahren für Kinder?" 8.

3. Gudrun Leidecker, Dieter Kirchhöfer, and Peter Güttler, *Ich weiss nicht, ob ich froh sein soll: Kinder erleben die Wende* (Stuttgart: JB Metzler, 1991), 6. See also Else Blankenburgh, "Jugendliche Erfahrungen der Wendezeit," *Neue Zeit*, April 18, 1991, 47.

4. "Einheit Kann Für Kinder Negative Folgen Haben," *Berliner Zeitung*, October 15, 1990, 46.

5. Kathleen K., narrative interview, September 7, 2020, Digital Archive of the Hannah Arendt Institute for Totalitarianism Studies, (hereafter HAIT), Dresden, Germany.

6. The interviews were conducted between 2020 and 2022 by students of TU Dresden for the research and teaching project "Die 'Wende' der Kinder: Kindheit in der ostdeutschen Transformation" at the HAIT at TU Dresden, https://hait.tu-dresden.de/ext/forschung/forschungsprojekt-5143/?lang=en; Sara Jones, "(Extra)Ordinary Life: The Rhetoric of Representing the Socialist Everyday after Unification," *German Politics & Society* 33, no. 1/2 (2015): 119–34, 125.

7. Kerstin Brückweh and Clemens Villinger, *Die lange Geschichte der "Wende": Geschichtswissenschaft im Dialog* (Berlin: Ch. Links Verlag, 2020).

8. David F. Crew, "Alltagsgeschichte: A New Social History 'From Below'?" *Central European History* 22, no. 3/4 (1989): 394–407, 396.

9. Joachim Maaz and Lydia Heller, "'Wir Sollten Reden!'—Mutter, Vater, Staat, Kind," in *Wie War Das für Euch? Die Dritte Generation Ost Im Gespräch mit Ihren Eltern*, ed. Judith Enders, Mandy Schulze, and Bianca Ely (Berlin: Ch. Links Verlag, 2016), 11–27, 17.

10. Rosi Blaschke, "Kinder Können Nicht Wählen," *Neues Deutschland*, March 14, 1990, 45.

11. Alexei Yurchak, *Everything Was Forever, until It Was No More: The Last Soviet Generation* (Princeton, NJ: Princeton University Press, 2013), 4.

12. Andrea H., narrative interview, July 22, 2020, Digital Archive of the HAIT.

13. Heike H., narrative interview, September 24, 2020, Digital Archive of the HAIT.

14. Sabine Rennefanz, *Eisenkinder: Die Stille Wut Der Wendegeneration* (München: Luchterhand, 2013), 66.

15. Jana Hensel, *Zonenkinder* (Reinbek: Rowohlt, 2004), 13–14.

16. Pamela Hess, "Was Bleibt von Der DDR? Erinnerungen Verbinden Wendekinder," in *Die Generation Der Wendekinder: Elaboration Eines Forschungsfeldes*, ed. Adriana Lettrari, Christian Nestler, and Nadja Troi-Boeck (Wiesbaden: Springer, 2016), 71–86, 77.

17. Hensel, *Zonenkinder,* 14.

18. Heike H., narrative interview, September 24, 2020, Digital Archive of the HAIT.

19. Anne Zimmermann, "'Kinder brauchen eine Zukunft' (Leserbrief 11-jährige Schülerin)," *Neues Deutschland*, December 15, 1989, 44 (295), 4.

20. Regina Rusch, *Plötzlich ist alles ganz anders. Kinder schreiben über unser Land* (Frankfurt am Main: Eichborn Verlag, 1992).

21. Walter Bärsch, "Die Kinder ernster nehmen," in *Plötzlich ist alles ganz anders*, ed. Regina Rusch (Frankfurt am Main: Eichborn Verlag, 1992), 123–26, 124.

22. Hanna Haag, "Nachwendekinder zwischen Familiengedächtnis und öffentlichem DDR-Diskurs," in *Ostdeutsche Erinnerungsdiskurse nach 1989: Narrative Kultureller Identität*, ed. Elisa Goudin-Steinmann and Carola Hähnel-Mesnard, vol. 1 (Berlin: Fank & Timme, 2013), 59–78, 63.

23. *Die Generation der Wendezeit: Erfolgreich, nüchtern und enttäuscht*, Working Paper 49 of the SFB 186 at Bremen University 1998, http://www.sfb186.uni-bremen.de /download/paper49.pdf.

24. Christoph Klessmann, *Arbeiter im "Arbeiterstaat" DDR: Deutsche Traditionen, sowjetisches Modell, westdeutsches Magnetfeld (1945 bis 1971)* (Bonn: Dietz, 2007).

25. Rennefanz, *Eisenkinder*, 71.

26. Dana R., narrative interview, September 26, 2020, Digital Archive of the HAIT.

27. Heike H., narrative interview, September 24, 2020, Digital Archive of the HAIT.

28. Rusch, *Plötzlich ist alles ganz anders*, 60.

29. Bärsch, "Die Kinder ernster nehmen," 123–24.

30. "Nur noch 'Praktisches' für meine Kinder," *Berliner Zeitung*, March 2, 1990, 11.

31. Johannes Nichelmann, *Nachwendekinder: Die DDR, unsere Eltern und das große Schweigen*, Sonderausgabe für die Zentrale für politische Bildung (Berlin: Zentrale für politische Bildung, 2019), 94.

32. Nichelmann, *Nachwendekinder*, 99.

33. Karl-Heinz Audersch, "Ich kann Nancy nicht gebrauchen," *Neues Deutschland*, November 29, 1989, 44 (281), 8.

34. "Opfer sittlicher Verwahrlosung," *Neue Zeit*, November 30, 1989 (282), 8.

35. "Verlassene Kinder gehen uns alle an," *Neue Zeit*, December 6, 1989 (287), 8.

36. Konrad Jarausch, "Realer Sozialismus als Fürsorgediktatur: zur begrifflichen Einordnung der DDR," *Historical Social Research, Supplement* 24 (2012): 249–72: and Renate Wald, *Kindheit in Der Wende—Wende Der Kindheit? Heranwachsen in Der Gesellschaft Transformation in Ostdeutschland* (Opladen: Leske & Budrich, 1998), 26.

37. Zeitungsabteilung Elterninitiative der Kombination V, "Entscheidung über uns hinweg? Kinderkrippe soll schließen," *Neues Deutschland*, January 19, 1990, 8.

38. Rosemarie K., narrative interview, November 23, 2020, Digital Archive of the HAIT.

39. "'Genauso gut wie die im Westen' Leserinnen Briefe zu Berliner Kinderbetreuung vom 11.03.91," *Berliner Zeitung*, November 3, 1991, 7.

40. Stefanie H., narrative interview, October 9, 2020, Digital Archive of the HAIT.

41. Veronika K., narrative interview, July 23, 2020, Digital Archive of the HAIT.

42. "Haben Kinderkrippen noch eine Bedeutung?" *Berliner Zeitung*, January 5, 1990, 3.

43. "Man muss wählen können, wie das Kind betreut wird," *Berliner Zeitung*, June 20, 1990, 46 (141), 7.

44. "Breite Integration behinderter Kinder schon ab Kindergarten," *Neue Zeit*, May 23, 1990, 46 (119), 3.

45. "Breite Integration behinderter Kinder schon ab Kindergarten."

46. Heike M., narrative interview, January 11, 2022, Digital Archive of the HAIT.

47. Andrea Ernst and Sabine Stampfel, *Kinder-Report: Wie Kinder in Deutschland leben* (Köln: Kiepenheuer & Witsch, 1991), 163.

48. Sabine Schulz, "Kinder machen sich stark," *Neues Deutschland*, January 25, 1990, 45 (21), 8.

49. Veronika K., narrative interview, July 23, 2020, Digital Archive of the HAIT.

50. Susanne Krispin, "Die schönsten Landschaften bleiben verwaist," *Neue Zeit*, February 8, 1991, 47 (178), 22.

51. Kathleen K., narrative interview, September 7, 2020, Digital Archive of the HAIT.

52. Leidecker, Kirchhöfer, and Güttler, *Ich weiss nicht*, 168.

53. "Auf ewig 'Ossis' und 'Wessis'?," *Deutschlandfunk*, May 24, 2023, https://www.deutsch landfunk.de/alte-neue-ostdebatte-auf-ewig-ossis-und-wessis-dlf-3deccb41-100.html, accessed October 30, 2023.

54. "Auf ewig 'Ossis' und 'Wessis'?," 147.

55. Kathleen K., narrative interview, September 7, 2020, Digital Archive of the HAIT.

56. Christiane M., narrative interview, January 22, 2022, Digital Archive of the HAIT.

BIBLIOGRAPHY

Audersch, Karl-Heinz. "Ich kann Nancy nicht gebrauchen." *Neues Deutschland*, November 29, 1989, 44 (281).

"Auf ewig 'Ossis' und 'Wessis'?" *Deutschlandfunk*, May 24, 2023. https://www.deutschland funk.de/alte-neue-ostdebatte-auf-ewig-ossis-und-wessis-dlf-3deccb41-100.html, accessed October 30, 2023.

Blankenburgh, Else. "Jugendliche Erfahrungen der Wendezeit." *Neue Zeit*, April 18, 1991.

Blaschke, Rosi. "Kinder Können Nicht Wählen." *Neues Deutschland*, March 14, 1990, 45.

"Breite Integration behinderter Kinder schon ab Kindergarten." *Neue Zeit*, May 23, 1990, 46.

Brückweh, Kerstin, and Clemens Villinger. *Die lange Geschichte der "Wende": Geschichtswissenschaft im Dialog.* Berlin: Ch. Links Verlag, 2020.

Crew, David F. "Alltagsgeschichte: A New Social History 'From Below'?" *Central European History* 22, no. 3/4 (1989): 394–407.

Die Generation der Wendezeit: Erfolgreich, nüchtern und enttäuscht. Working Paper 49 of the SFB 186 at Bremen University 1998, http://www.sfb186.uni-bremen.de/download/paper49.pdf.

"Einheit Kann Für Kinder Negative Folgen Haben." *Berliner Zeitung,* October 15, 1990, 46.

Ernst, Andrea, and Sabine Stampfel. *Kinder-Report: Wie Kinder in Deutschland leben.* Köln: Kiepenheuer & Witsch, 1991.

Haag, Hanna. "Nachwendekinder zwischen Familiengedächtnis und öffentlichem DDR-Diskurs." In *Ostdeutsche Erinnerngsdiskurse nach 1989: Narrative Kultureller Identität,* vol. 1, edited by Elisa Goudin-Steinmann and Carola Hähnel-Mesnard, 59–78. Berlin: Fank & Timme, 2013.

"Haben Kinderkrippen noch eine Bedeutung?" *Berliner Zeitung,* January 5, 1990, 3.

Hensel, Jana. *Zonenkinder.* Reinbek: Rowohlt, 2004.

Hess, Pamela. "Was bleibt von Der DDR? Erinnerungen Verbinden Wendekinder." In *Die Generation Der Wendekinder: Elaboration Eines Forschungsfeldes,* edited by Adriana Lettrari, Christian Nestler, and Nadja Troi-Boeck, 71–86. Wiesbaden: Springer, 2016.

Jarausch, Konrad. "Realer Sozialismus als Fürsorgediktatur: zur begrifflichen Einordnung der DDR." *Historical Social Research, Supplement,* 24 (2012): 249–72.

Jones, Sara. "(Extra)Ordinary Life: The Rhetoric of Representing the Socialist Everyday after Unification." *German Politics & Society* 33, no. 1/2 (2015): 119–34.

Klessmann, Christoph. *Arbeiter im "Arbeiterstaat" DDR: deutsche Traditionen, sowjetisches Modell, westdeutsches Magnetfeld (1945 bis 1971).* Bonn: Dietz, 2007.

Krispin, Susanne. "Die schönsten Landschaften bleiben verwaist." *Neue Zeit,* February 8, 1991, 47 (178), 22.

Leidecker, Gudrun, Dieter Kirchhöfer, and Dieter Güttler. *Ich weiss nicht, ob ich froh sein soll: Kinder erleben die Wende.* Stuttgart: Metzler, 1991.

Maaz, Joachim, and Lydia Heller. "'Wir Sollten Reden!'—Mutter, Vater, Staat, Kind." In *Wie War Das Für Euch? Die Dritte Generation Ost Im Gespräch Mit Ihren Eltern,* edited by Judith Enders, Mandy Schulze, and Bianca Ely, 11–27. Berlin: Ch. Links Verlag, 2016.

"Man muss wählen können, wie das kind betreut wird." *Berliner Zeitung,* June 20, 1990, 46 (141), 7.

Nichelmann, Johannes. *Nachwendekinder: Die DDR, unsere Eltern und das große Schweigen.* Sonderausgabe für die Zentrale für politische Bildung. Berlin: Zentrale für politische Bildung, 2019.

"Nur noch 'Praktisches' für meine Kinder." *Berliner Zeitung,* March 2, 1990, 11.

"Opfer sittlicher Verwahrlosung." *Neue Zeit,* November 30, 1989 (282), 8.

Rennefanz, Sabine. *Eisenkinder: Die Stille Wut Der Wendegeneration.* München: Luchterhand, 2013.

Rusch, Regina. *Plötzlich ist alles ganz anders: Kinder schreiben über unser Land.* Frankfurt am Main: Eichborn Verlag, 1992.

Schulz, Sabine. "Kinder machen sich stark." *Neues Deutschland,* January 25, 1990, 45 (21), 8.

Skulski, Gudrun. "Gefahren für Kinder?" *Neue Zeit,* January 13, 1990, 46.

"Verlassene Kinder gehen uns alle an." *Neue Zeit*, December 6, 1989 (287), 8.

Wald, Renate. *Kindheit in Der Wende—Wende Der Kindheit? Heranwachsen in Der Gesellschaft Transformation in Ostdeutschland*. Opladen: Leske & Budrich, 1998.

Yurchak, Alexei. *Everything Was Forever, Until It Was No More: The Last Soviet Generation*. Princeton, NJ: Princeton University Press, 2013.

Zeitungsabteilung Elterninitiative der Kombination V. "Entscheidung über uns hinweg? Kinderkrippe soll schließen." *Neues Deutschland*, January 19, 1990, 8.

Zimmermann, Anne. "'Kinder brauchen eine Zukunft' (Leserbrief 11-jährige Schülerin)." *Neues Deutschland*, December 15, 1989, 44 (295), 4.

13

OUT OF SIGHT BUT NOT OUT OF MIND

The Romanian Diaspora and Politics at Home

SERGIU GHERGHINA AND RALUCA FARCAS

INTRODUCTION

THERE ARE MANY INSTANCES IN WHICH MIGRANTS LIVE IN TWO WORLDS: in their country of residence and in their country of origin. The transnational ties between migrants and their home countries are often investigated through the lenses of economic (remittances) or social (contacts) relations.[1] The political involvement of migrants in their home country, meanwhile, has received considerably less coverage, with most studies addressing voting in elections organized at home. Much of this research examines migrants' support for specific parties, their motivations for turnout and political mobilization, or issues related to a broader sense of local (in the country of residence) or national (relative to the country of origin) identity. Nevertheless, we know relatively little about the broader impact of migrants on political life back home. This chapter analyzes Romanian migrants' participation in political life in their home country. Romania is a particularly compelling case for such an analysis given its extensive share of labor migrants (both temporary and permanent)—one of the largest among European Union (EU) countries over the last two decades.[2] In 2015–16, the Romanian diaspora was the fifth largest in the world and the largest in the EU in relation to the total population of the country, with 17 percent of native-born Romanians living abroad.[3] When seasonal workers, who leave temporarily to work in construction and agriculture, are included in this figure the percentage reaches 20 percent.[4] As Romanians abroad have the right to vote in Romanian elections, either physically in their country of residence or, since 2016, by mail, they possess the potential to significantly influence the political process. Meanwhile, the Romanian state engages with diaspora communities by supporting institutions, programs, and policies aimed at preserving specific ethnic ties.[5] As part of these initiatives, the Romanian diaspora is represented in the Romanian Parliament by four deputies and two senators.[6] These designated seats for the diaspora may explain electoral mobilization among migrants and why all (parliamentary) political parties encourage the diaspora population to vote.

In this chapter, we examine Romanian migrants' influence on politics in their home country, focusing particularly on national elections and popular mobilization. We illustrate how migrant participation in Romanian politics reflects the diaspora's commitment to democracy and postsocialist transformation more generally. The diaspora's participation in elections decisively influenced the results of two presidential elections, while their engagement in protests contributed to the antigovernment movements that emerged in Romania in the 2010s. Such active political participation is a sign of national belonging beyond borders. We focus on the period between 2008—a year after Romania's accession to the EU and the first year in which Romanians abroad were represented in the national legislature of their home country—and 2020, when the most recent parliamentary elections occurred. While many contributions in this volume discuss the continuities between socialism and postsocialism, this chapter presents a story of rupture from the socialist period, when migration was limited; mobilization was, with a few exceptions, state-orchestrated; and people's engagement in politics was restricted to voting for a single party.

The analysis draws on primary and secondary data, including an original survey conducted by the authors among 1,839 Romanian migrants in January 2018.[7] The secondary data is taken from electoral databases, media reports, and previous studies on the electoral behavior of Romanian migrants.[8] The media reports include interviews with migrants and should be considered illustrative rather than representative of migrant opinions. The information based on media reports is used to triangulate the information from other sources.

WHEN AND WHY DID THEY LEAVE? THE GROWTH OF THE ROMANIAN DIASPORA

Official data on Romanian migrants is unavailable as registration is not compulsory in the EU countries where many of them reside. Estimates of the Romanian diaspora range from four to six million out of a total population of roughly 22.5 million (in the mid-1990s, when migration rates were low). Romanian migration between 1990 and 2020 can be divided into three waves. First, there was temporary migration during the 1990s, driven by Romania's economic instability and low wages. During the first decade of the transition, uneven and erratic privatization led to high unemployment and low standards of living, and migrants, typically male, sought work abroad to support their families in Romania.[9] The second wave of migration started in the early 2000s and coincided with the onset of Romania's negotiations for EU accession. As the latter was supposed to occur in 2004, visa requirements were lifted a couple years before that date. The visa-free regime marked an explosion in Romanian migration: between 2000 and 2010, the estimated number of migrants tripled compared with the first wave.[10] In 2009 and 2010, roughly one quarter of Romanian households had at least one family member that migrated.[11] Most of these migrants settled in Italy and Spain, home to existing Romanian diaspora communities.[12] This wave included seasonal, temporary, and permanent migrants as well as skilled laborers and white-collar professionals, particularly medical professionals, producing significant shortages in the Romanian health care system.[13] The third wave started around the financial crisis of 2008 and was characterized by larger numbers of labor migrants (both high- and low-skilled). Meanwhile, the majority of Romanians who were already abroad during the financial crisis did not return home.[14] After 2010, the number of highly educated individuals leaving Romania increased dramatically, with many university students choosing to complete their education and seek work abroad.[15]

In explaining their reasons for emigrating, Romanian migrants identify high levels of corruption and lack of career opportunities. In a 2018 survey with migrants, 81 percent of the respondents claimed that corruption influenced their decision to leave the country. Meanwhile, nearly 76 percent claimed that lack of career opportunities prompted them to leave Romania. Low or insufficient wages/salaries were mentioned by 63 percent of those interviewed, while a desire to reunite with family was mentioned by 35 percent. Such findings are reflected in an interview with a Romanian migrant living in Sweden:

Sweden is the country of politicians without benefits and immunity. That's why I'm here and that's how Sweden was imprinted in my memory! Most likely I will not return to Romania as more than a tourist. . . . Basically, due to corruption and indifference, I left Romania. I feel that the taxes I pay to the Swedish state are also reflected in the quality of life that I and those around me have here. Like me, there are millions of Romanians who have gone to foreign countries, who may never return to Romania.[16]

POLITICAL ENGAGEMENT

Romanian migrants participate in politics, including voting and protests, in their country of origin because they hope to change the conditions that forced them to leave in the first place. As a Romanian who currently lives in Spain explained in an interview for *TimpOnline.Ro*, which covers contemporary events in Romania:

> If we changed the whole government, many of us would return home. . . . If we changed this whole government, maybe, maybe. . . . I know that Romanians don't go to the polls. That's why politicians take advantage of the fact that they've given us free rein to go abroad and they go and buy the old people's votes with a bucket. That's it![17]

Another Romanian, who lives in Belgium, claimed that concern about changes to the judiciary prompted his participation in protests in Romania in 2018.

> Romania is a few decades behind the level of Western societies and that is why I believe the current government, through the legal measures aimed at the Judiciary, does nothing but return Romania to the path it started in 1989. Yes, it is an act of contempt, of protest, but, at the same time, it is also an act of protection. For family reasons (my wife has a family in Romania), I must go to the country from time to time. I don't want to be unpleasantly surprised, to be questioned or even arrested for expressing my anti-government views on social media.[18]

Much of the research on migrants' political participation in their home countries focuses on electoral and voting behavior.[19] Determinants of voter turnout among diaspora populations range from the quality of democracy in their country of residence to integration policies to diaspora characteristics to limited opportunities for political involvement in the country of residence.[20] In addition to voting, diaspora populations engage politically in their country of origin by joining political parties, supporting political campaigns (often through financial contributions), and taking part in protests or demonstrations.[21] Earlier studies have analyzed the extent to which the migrant populations' size, the proximity of the election, the quality of democracy in the country of residence, and links between the country of origin and country of residence, along with institutional, socioeconomic, and political variables, influence Romanians' participation in elections back home.[22]

Romanian migrants' motivation for voting is rooted in effecting political change at home.[23] Many Romanians left the country due to poor economic and social conditions, driven largely by high levels of corruption and low levels of government performance.

The party in government at the time of migration often influenced people's decision to leave, as they blamed it for the poor conditions in the country. Considered from this perspective, voting could be a means of punishing those responsible for their departure and for rewarding those who instill hope. In addition to voting themselves, Romanian migrants seek to influence the voting behavior of relatives and friends. A study examining the Romanian legislative and presidential elections in 2012, 2014, and 2016 showed that migrants who are invested in electoral outcomes try to persuade family members to vote for a particular party.[24]

Research on the relationship between the Romanian diaspora and political parties in Romania indicates ties between institutions in the country and people beyond borders.[25] However, the recognition of the diaspora in party statutes does not always determine the political commitment of migrants, the new parties being more effective in determining the participation of the diaspora through informal and online interaction.[26] Another study indicates the relevance of two other determinants of the electoral participation of Romanian migrants: the degree of involvement in the local community and the type of relationship with citizens in the residence countries.[27]

CHANGING THE ELECTORAL OUTCOME: REALITY VS. MYTH

Romanians abroad played an important role in the presidential elections of 2009 and 2014, exerting a direct influence on the outcome.[28] In 2009, the incumbent president, Traian Băsescu, then a member of the Partidul Democrat Liberal (PDL; Democratic Liberal Party), competed in a second round against Mircea Geoană, the leader of the main opposition party, Partidul Social Democrat (PSD; Social Democratic Party, a successor to the Romanian Communist Party). In those elections, 10.6 million people participated, including 150,000 diaspora Romanians.[29] While Geoană led in Romania by about 15,000 votes, Băsescu led in the diaspora by 115,000 votes (as opposed to 31,000 for Geoană), enabling Băsescu to secure victory. Although the results were accepted by most of the Romanian population, supporters and party leaders of the Social Democrats criticized them, and the PSD's executive committee argued that the diaspora's vote should count less than the vote of those living in Romania.[30]

The 2014 elections, when PSD prime minister Victor Ponta ran against Klaus Iohannis, then mayor of Sibiu and member of the Partidul Național Liberal (PNL; National Liberal Party), yielded a similar pattern. In the first round Ponta secured 40 percent of the vote, while Iohannis secured 30 percent (with a turnout of roughly 53 percent of the electorate); however, Ponta only managed to secure 15 percent of the diaspora vote, while Iohannis received over 50 percent. Iohannis's support among the diaspora population, while impressive, was in fact an underestimation as major irregularities in voting procedures at diaspora polling stations were soon discovered. As the PSD has historically fared poorly among diaspora voters and because elections in the diaspora are organized by the Romanian embassies and coordinated by the Ministry of Foreign Affairs, enabling the prime minister to directly influence them, Ponta, aiming for victory, had sought to repress voter turnout in the diaspora.[31] He did this by limiting the number of available polling stations in major cities, forcing people to wait hours to vote. Throughout Germany, France, Italy, Spain, and the United Kingdom—all countries with large Romanian diasporas—only a handful of polling stations were open. For example, in Germany only five polling stations were open (in Bonn, Berlin, Hamburg, Munich, and Stuttgart), and because many temporary migrants lived considerable distances from these cities, they had to travel hundreds of kilometers to vote. As a result, many Romanian migrants were discouraged from voting or were unable to vote, and, in the end, only 130,000 in the diaspora voted.

In response to this discovery, protests erupted in diaspora communities and in Romania between the first and second rounds, with protesters demanding additional polling stations, staff, and extended voting time. While the government promised additional polling stations for the second round, this did not happen, and voters in the diaspora encouraged relatives and friends in Romania to vote against Ponta. In the end, of the nearly 315,000 diaspora residents who voted, approximately 90 percent supported Iohannis. Securing an additional two million voters in the second round, Iohannis won the election by one million votes.[32]

The diaspora usually votes against the PSD, charging it with corruption and holding it responsible for the mass migrations from Romania over the last two decades. Instead, diaspora voters typically choose centrist parties such as the Liberal Democrats (PDL) in 2008, the National Liberals (PNL) in 2016, and the Save Romania Union (USR) in 2016 and 2020, though it has also supported nationalist parties, such as the People's Party (PP-DD) in 2012 and the far-right Alliance for Romanian Unity (AUR) in 2020, which subsequently gained seats in Parliament.[33] That said, diaspora support for AUR was not significantly higher than it had been for other parties, such as Save Romania Union–Freedom, Unity and Solidarity Party (USR PLUS), and Băsescu's People's Movement Party (PMP), and was thus not a determining factor in securing parliamentary seats (of those who voted for AUR, only 11.5 percent were from the diaspora). Meanwhile, the National Liberals (PNL) pulled a smaller share of the diaspora vote than usual (see Figure 13.1).[34] Typically, the diaspora vote diverges from the vote in Romania, reflected in the fact that the PSD has won the national vote on a continuous basis in Romania since 2000, receiving 15 percent or less of the diaspora vote.

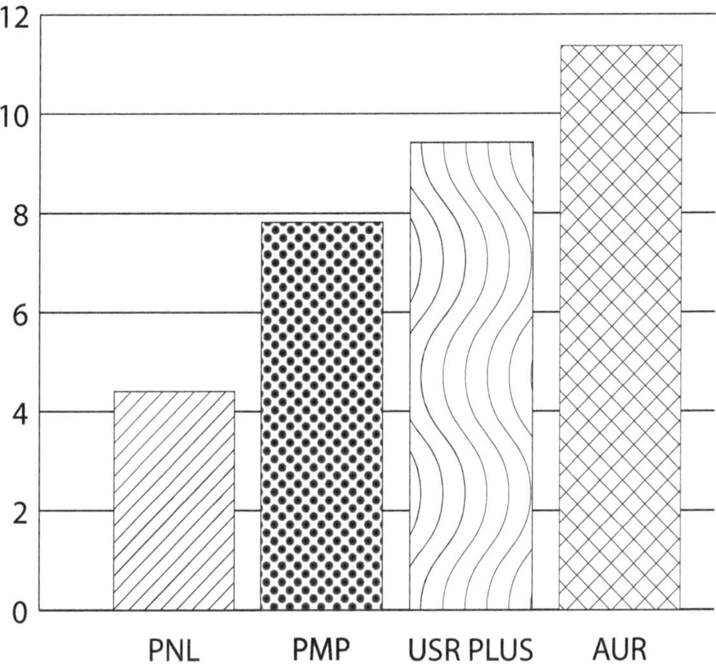

Figure 13.1. Percentage of Party Votes in the Diaspora Relative to the Total Votes Received, 2020.

MIGRANTS AND PROTEST

As in other East European countries, Romania was characterized by large waves of protests between 2010 and 2020, some of which involved the diaspora. These included the aforementioned protests in 2014, in response to efforts by Ponta to restrict diaspora voting, who claimed that the Ministry of Foreign Affairs was responsible for such poor organization and refused to amend legislation to supplement polling stations.[35] Instead, as discussed above, marginal and insufficient measures were taken to improve the situation. In response, Romanians in the diaspora engaged in ad hoc protests in front of polling stations in Great Britain, Germany, Austria, Belgium, and Italy and launched an online mobilization campaign asking relatives and friends in Romania to vote against Ponta.

Ponta's refusal to extend voting time in the diaspora by two hours intensified this mobilization. Protests were organized by the Federation of Romanian Associations in Europe (FADERE) "due to the lack of response from the Ministry of Foreign Affairs following the countless requests made by Romanians in the diaspora to regulate the issue of voting in the second round of the presidential elections." The protest appealed to all those "who were wronged and dissatisfied with the organization of elections in the diaspora to appear in front of embassies at a joint and peaceful event."[36]

The largest protests, however, occurred in 2017 in response to the PSD-led government's efforts to amend the justice and criminal codes.[37] These changes threatened to potentially subordinate justice to politics, undermining the rule of law in Romania.[38] The Romanian diaspora responded by mobilizing against these measures. A migrant from Munich explained to journalists from an independent online newspaper her decision to get involved in the following manner: "[When] laws are being prepared to— to spare the corrupt from prison and to allow them to steal without being punished up to a certain amount and to completely forgive their deed, not just to lift their punishment, then I felt that we must stop this roller coaster."[39] Meanwhile, a Romanian from Zurich claimed he protested for the same reason he did in University Square in 1990, when students and professors mobilized against the election of former communist elites to the presidency and parliament:

> The National Anticorruption Directorate (DNA) and the Attorney General are being attacked without a real basis, they are trying to empty the meaning of abuse of office by defining an arbitrary threshold, the conflict of interests for relatives is decriminalized . . . the current government is not focused on fulfilling electoral promises, but has the undeclared but visible goal of rescuing corrupt people from prison.

He further elaborated that, as a Romanian citizen, he had,

> the duty to go to the polls and choose the best option, and if it does not exist, then the lesser evil; the duty to support and strengthen democratic society. I also believe that we must not miss the opportunity to vote, even if we do not immediately see change for the better in our vote. I believe again that it is important to take a civil and firm attitude: we no longer have the time and reason to tolerate what is not tolerable as a public attitude. The solution will come from a change of attitude to each one and not through the "magic" character or party.[40]

While the protests of 2014 and 2017 were carried out by the Romanian diaspora in their countries of residence, many returned to Romania in August 2018 to the "Diaspora at Home" protests. These protests were driven by several factors. First, there was a general dissatisfaction with PSD governance and the party's continuous attempt to tamper with the judicial process. Second, the government had dismissed the chief prosecutor of the National Anticorruption Directorate (DNA), Laura Codruța Kövesi, because of her effectiveness in prosecuting public officials for corruption, many of whom belonged to the PSD.[41] Third, the PSD leader, Liviu Dragnea, was appointed president of the Chamber of Deputies in the Romanian Parliament despite pending convictions.[42] On August 10, 2018, approximately 100,000 people who had returned from the diaspora started protesting in front of the government building (on Victoria Square) in Bucharest against the PSD government. The protests became violent, as radical groups joined and instigated violence, prompting an aggressive reaction from police that ended with the injury of over 400 people.[43] In addition, water cannons and tear gas were used to evacuate participants. Simultaneously, as a sign of solidarity, a series of protests with hundreds of participants took place in cities throughout the country: Cluj-Napoca, Timișoara, Iași, Sibiu, Brașov. Dragnea claimed that the diaspora rally was political given that several members from opposition parties were present at the protests.[44]

The Romanian migrants protesting in Bucharest demanded the government's resignation on the basis of incompetence and the removal from public office of all officials suspected of corruption and criminal acts. As one diaspora protester asserted in an interview given to a TV station supporting liberal values:

> I have been in Austria for a year. Unfortunately, I had to resign from my job to protest. There are still jobs, but a protest like this only happens once in a lifetime.... We do not come to occupy the country, we come to bring real democracy, from the West, not from the East. There is no democracy in Eastern Europe.[45]

Another protester explained, "We want to bring down the Government, we have no other claims, this is no longer possible. Possibly early elections, later.... Changes to the laws of justice, law 303, 304, amendment of abuse of office, these attacks on the National Anticorruption Directorate that show that these rulers are afraid of what they did."[46] Other voices among the diaspora asserted that they wanted to see the government replaced, noting in their statements to an international press agency: "Almost all of the public sector is malfunctioning, it must be changed completely and replaced with capable people," or "We want to come home but with the current ruling of the country it is not possible, we want change for the better and a future for our children, that is why we are protesting. We want to change this government and make it better."[47] Several migrants explained that they chose to get involved in the protests for "political transparency, a modern education system [based on meritocracy and recognized worldwide], a modern medical system [again based on meritocracy and with free services for patients], and a well-developed infrastructure," as well as "to eliminate corruption in the country, to eliminate bureaucracy in Romanian consulates/embassies, to introduce electronic voting."[48] Others echoed such sentiments, claiming that Romanians needed "modern roads and schools [and] above all, to not have to pay bribes to the left and right."[49] In general, many migrants claimed that their involvement in the protests was rooted in a commitment to democratic ideals and to have "laws that protect citizens, not politicians."[50]

Many protesters wanted to see a reform of the system because they hoped to move back to Romania at some point. As one migrant noted, "I will return when we have a government with which we can talk, that has the interests of the citizen (in mind). I would like to get involved in certain areas where I could help Romania's development, because Romania can be a normal country. Because we have capable people."[51] In light of the disappointing nature of democracy in Romania, a protester from Germany argued that political participation was essential because "it is a trap to believe that anything we do doesn't change anything. Honest people need to have a say, and that's why they're getting involved."[52] In addition to engaging in protests, they argued in interviews with journalists from an independent news agency that it was important to vote:

> I think there are enough political options on the ballot. Even if some say there is nothing to vote for, I think one should always vote. Ultimately, the vote can be given to new political parties that have a plan for Romania's future. If they do not keep their promises, in the next election the stamp will end up in another box on the ballot. But the vote must be cast.[53]

Romanian migrants who participated in the 2018 protests were motivated by three factors: first, a general belief that the political situation in the country can change and it will become a place to which they can return. Because many left the country due to low wages, corruption, and poor institutional performance, they emphasized the rule of law and the need for properly functioning institutions. Second, their emphasis on the rule of law demonstrates migrants' commitment to the democratic values and ideals that characterized street protests in 1989—and the anticommunist protests in 1990. This underscores continuities in popular understandings of democracy and the practices that are mobilized (i.e., protests) to defend it. Third, many hope to counteract broader populist efforts, particularly as expressed by the PSD.

More generally, this protest culture is animated by a desire for political stability, civil liberties, fairness, and justice, illustrating the salience of 1989. Continuities are also reflected in the type of discourses used to describe poorly performing elites and state institutions. One of these is the reference to corruption, which was an accepted practice in 1989 since it was part of the old regime. In protests involving the diaspora, corruption is considered one of the major problems in the country and the main reason why many Romanians left. Moreover, people's political and social demands have become more complex, with specific demands for state modernization and democratic consolidation, as opposed to demands three decades ago about the establishment of basic institutions.

MIGRANTS' INFLUENCE ON FRIENDS AND FAMILY

The events surrounding the 2014 presidential elections indicate that the Romanian diaspora has the potential to impact the political choices of those at home. Communication between migrants abroad and their home communities continues to be strong and frequent. A survey conducted by the authors with Romanians in the diaspora asked about interactions with friends and family during the 2012 and 2016 national legislative elections and the 2014 presidential election. Roughly one-third of respondents claimed to have engaged in such discussions during the 2012 elections and more than one-half did so during the 2014 elections, a share that is also relatively stable for the 2016 legislative elections. Meanwhile, in the 2012 elections, slightly more than 10 percent of respondents claimed that they had sought to influence their friends and relatives, a number that rose to one-fourth in the 2014 and 2016 elections. This indicates that the percentage of citizens living abroad who proactively seek to make an impact on the voting behavior of friends and family is increasing. Such influence is not unidirectional as there are also instances in which friends and families of Romanians abroad seek to influence the latter's voting behavior. The data show that roughly 8 percent in 2012 and slightly more than 13 percent in 2014 and 2016 acknowledged that they received specific suggestions from individuals in their home country about how they should vote. These findings point to a complex interaction between the Romanians in the diaspora and those at home (see Figure 13.2).

In the 2014 presidential election, Romanians voted and protested together, irrespective of their location in the country or abroad. This is reflected in slogans such as "solidarity with those in the diaspora." Through continuous communication of Romanians with relatives and friends in the diaspora, certain cultural models of voting are formed.[54] In the 2014 presidential election, a poll indicated that 42 percent of respondents had a family member abroad and 12 percent were advised by members of the diaspora to vote for a particular candidate. Moreover, 20 percent were decisively influenced in their choice of candidate.[55] An interview with a Romanian migrant in the United States conducted by a journalist from an independent news agency reveals how migrants mobilize and convince those at home:

Interactions Between the Romanian Diaspora and Communities at Home

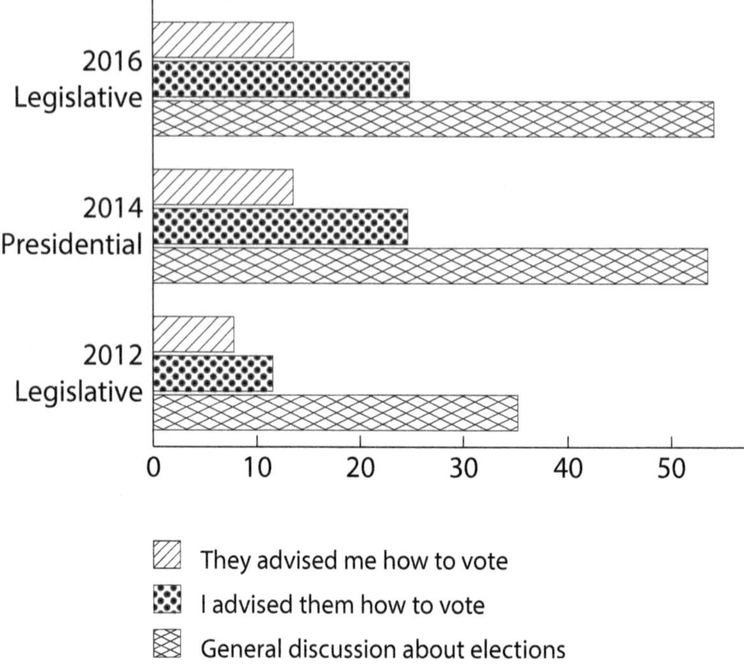

Figure 13.2. Interactions between the Romanian Diaspora and Communities at Home.

A phone call, an email, or a Skype chat is more convincing than any fake news on Romanian television. When it became clear to Romanians in the diaspora that the government was trying to restrict their right to vote, an unprecedented campaign to mobilize those in the country began. In addition to using the internet, relatives, friends, acquaintances, and neighbors were called to persuade them to vote in a certain way. It is believed that millions of phone calls were made to Romania between the two rounds. Everyone was aware that each vote was important and that Romania's direction and future depended on that vote. To understand the phenomenon on a larger scale, in Los Angeles it was discovered that Ponta admitted his defeat a little after 1 pm (11 pm in Romania), but, nevertheless, Romanians continued to go to the polls and stand in line to vote. They voted until 9 o'clock in the evening, that is, 7 in the morning in Romania![56]

CONCLUSIONS

This chapter analyzed the impact of Romanian migrants on the political life of their home country with respect to election outcomes, protests, and influence on voting behavior. The findings illustrate that on two occasions the diaspora changed the electoral fate of presidential elections: once directly in 2009 and once indirectly in 2014. Both times they supported candidates opposing the PSD, which enjoys limited popularity among the Romanian diaspora. In spite of increasing voter turnout in the diaspora, their recent voting behavior (in 2020) did not result in a change of electoral results at the national level. Unlike in 2009, the voting preferences of the diaspora are now more in line with those living in Romania. In addition to voting, the diaspora has been actively involved in two major protests, with important consequences for domestic politics. The one in 2014 determined the outcome of the presidential election, while the one in 2018 divided Romanian society between those supportive of the diaspora's choice to return to Romania to protest the government and those opposed to it. Our analysis also reveals that Romanian migrants increasingly engage in political discussions with their friends and relatives at home. In the 2014 and 2016 elections, more than half of the respondents surveyed indicated they had initiated such discussions. However, it seems that only a minority of migrants actively seek to persuade others to vote in a certain way. At the same time, some members of the diaspora claimed that friends and relatives back home tried to influence their voting behavior.

These findings indicate that Romanian migrants have an impact on the political life of their home country, especially when antidemocratic, populist, and even authoritarian tendencies are exhibited by political elites. Such participation is rooted in a sense of belonging and continued interest in what happens back home. Thus, while their departure from Romania signifies a physical rupture, their commitment to defending democracy (in the form of voting and protesting) illustrates continuity with their previous behaviors, as well as larger political mobilizations since December 1989. The first of such mobilizations was triggered by circumstances in the diaspora itself, specifically the voting "irregularities" (i.e., insufficient polling stations, long queues, and insufficient time for voting) that they experienced throughout Europe. Government efforts to undermine the diaspora's democratic rights underscored authoritarian tendencies in the country more generally, sparking protests in Romania and abroad. Such transnational mobilization set the stage for subsequent mobilizations in 2017 and 2018, also against the PSD. In addition to popular mobilization, migrants engage in political discussions with friends and family back home in an effort to influence voting behavior—with varied results since 2012. These findings suggest that the Romanian diaspora is reactive to the political developments in their home country and seeks to address the problems it is facing. As one Romanian migrant emphasized, "[I feel] far from the country, but I am always thinking about home."

NOTES

1. Luin Goldring, "Family and Collective Remittances to Mexico: A Multi-Dimensional Typology," *Development and Change* 35, no. 4 (2004): 799–840; Christian Dustmann and Josep Mestres, "Remittances and temporary migration," *Journal of Development Economics* 92, no. 1 (2010): 62–70; Susanne Wessendorf, "'Roots Migrants': Transnationalism and 'Return' among Second-Generation Italians in Switzerland," *Journal of Ethnic and Migration Studies* 33, no. 7 (2007): 1083–1102; and Jørgen Carling and Marta Bivand Erdal, "Return Migration and Transnationalism: How Are the Two Connected?," *International Migration* 52, no. 6 (2014): 2–12.

2. Andrei Dospinescu and Giuseppe Russo, *Romania: Systematic Country Diagnostic* (World Bank Group, 2018), http://documents.worldbank.org/curated/en/2104 81530907970911/pdf/128064-SCD-PUBLIC-P160439-RomaniaSCDBackground NoteMigration.pdf.

3. In this chapter we use the term "diaspora" to refer to communities of migrants with the same country of origin living abroad. OCED, "Talent Abroad: A Review of Romanian Emigrants" (Paris: OCED Publishing, 2019), https://www.oecd.org/fr/publications /talent-abroad-a-review-of-romanian-emigrants-bac53150-en.htm.

4. Cristian Stefanescu, "Romanians find their future abroad without forgetting home," *Deutsche Welle*, August 9, 2019, https://www.dw.com/en/romanians-find-their-future -abroad-without-forgetting-home/a-49972293.

5. Myra A. Waterbury, "Caught between nationalism and transnationalism: How Central and East European states respond to East–West emigration," *International Political Science Review* 39, no. 3 (2018): 338–52.

6. In the 2020–2024 parliamentary term, these seats are held by Valentin Făgărăşian (National Liberal Party), Iulian Ştefan Lorincz and Simina Tulbure (both from Save Romania Union), and Boris Volosatîi (Alliance for the Union of Romanians) in the Chamber of Deputies, and by Viorel Badea (National Liberal Party) and Radu Mihail (Save Romania Union) in the Senate.

7. Details about this survey are available in Sergiu Gherghina and Aurelian Plopeanu, "Who Wishes to Return? Ties to Home Country among the Romanian Migrants," *Nationalities Papers* 48, no. 5 (2020): 876–90.

8. Code for Romania, "Website Rezultate Vot (Website Vote Results)," 2021, https://rezult atevot.ro/elections/112/results.

9. Dumitru Sandu, *Temporary Stay Abroad: Romanians' Economic Migration: 1990–2006* (Bucharest: Open Society Foundation, 2006).

10. Dospinescu and Russo, *Romania: Systematic Country Diagnostic.*

11. Sofia Stănculescu and Manuela Stoiciu, *Impactul Crizei Economice Asupra Migratiei Fortei de Munca Din Romania* (Bucharest: Paideia, 2012).

12. Tim Elrick and Oana Ciobanu, "Migration networks and policy impacts: Insights from Romanian-Spanish migrations," *Global Networks* 9, no. 1 (2009): 100–16.

13. Dospinescu and Russo, *Romania: Systematic Country Diagnostic.*

14. Gherghina and Plopeanu, "Who Wishes to Return?"

15. Dospinescu and Russo, *Romania: Systematic Country Diagnostic.*

16. Andreas Eugensson, "Suedezii contra corupției din România: Cum am organizat un protest în Suedia în semn de solidaritate cu Piața Victoriei din București," *Republica*, 2017.

17. Cristiana Sabău, "Încep Să Plece Românii Din Străinătate: Salariul Minim de Aici Îl Câștigăm În Spania În Trei Zile," *TimpOnline.Ro*, 2017.

18. Chihaia Dumitru, "Doamna consul m-a întrebat care e motivul real pentru care renunț la cetățenie. I-am spus că nu o să-i sune bine. După care mi-a zis: Este ilegal acest motiv, nu putem scrie așa ceva". Interviu cu un fost român, *Republica*, 2018.

19. Sergiu Gherghina and Huan-Kai Tseng, "Voting home or abroad? Comparing migrants' electoral participation in countries of origin and of residence," *Nationalities Papers* 44, no. 3 (2016): 456–72.

20. Liza Mügge et al., "Migrant votes 'here' and 'there': Transnational electoral behavior of Turks in the Netherlands," *Migration Studies* 9, no. 3 (2021): 400–22; Luis Eduardo Guarnizo, Alejandro Portes, and William Haller, "Assimilation and Transnationalism: Determinants of Transnational Political Action among Contemporary Migrants," *American Journal of Sociology* 108, no. 6 (2003): 1211–48; Anar K. Ahmadov and Gwendolyn Sasse, "Empowering to engage with the homeland: Do migration experience and environment foster political remittances?" *Comparative Migration Studies* 4, no. 1 (2016): 1–25; and Katia Pilati and Barbara Herman, "Comparing engagement by migrants in domestic and in country-of-origin political activities across European cities," *Acta Politica* 55, no. 1 (2020): 103–29.

21. Luis E. Guarnizo and Ali R. Chaudhary, "Determinants of transnational political engagement among Dominican and Colombian migrants in Southern Europe," *IMI Working Papers Series*, vol. 82 (Oxford, 2014).

22. Irina Ciornei and Eva Ostergaard-Nielsen, "ST 5 emigration and turnout: Determinants of non-resident citizen electoral mobilization in home country legislative elections," paper presented at the Congress of the French Association of Political Science, 2015, 1–19.

23. Davide Bertelli et al., *Migrant Political Engagement and Voting from Abroad: Insights from Interviews with Polish and Romanian Migrants in Barcelona and Oslo* (Oslo: Peace Research Institute Oslo [PRIO], 2021).

24. Marius Grad, Sergiu Gherghina, and Adrian Ivan, "Migrants and their families in the home country: A bi-directional influence on voting behaviour," *Southeast European and Black Sea Studies* 20, no. 3 (2020): 393–410.

25. Gabriela Borz, "Political Parties and Diaspora: A Case Study of Romanian Parties'

Involvement Abroad," *Parliamentary Affairs* 73, no. 4 (2020): 901–17, https://doi
.org/10.1093/pa/gsaa044; Sergiu Gherghina and Sorina Soare, "Vote-Seeking among
Non-Resident Citizens: How Romanian Parties Form Organisations Abroad," *Representation* 59, no. 1 (2023): 423–39.

26. Borz, "Political Parties and Diaspora."

27. Gherghina and Tseng, "Voting Home or Abroad?"

28. In Romania the president is elected in a two-round system for a term of five years. The
runoff is held between the two competitors with the top results from the first round.

29. Code for Romania, "Website Rezultate Vot."

30. Adrian Năstase, "Alegeri prezidentiale la final: Primele observatii," *Personal Blog*,
2009, https://nastase.wordpress.com/2009/12/08/alegeri-prezidentiale-la-final
-primele-observatii/.

31. Sergiu Gherghina, "The Romanian presidential election, November 2014," *Electoral
Studies* 38 (2015): 109–14.

32. In the 2009 and 2019 presidential elections, the turnout in the second round was higher
than in the first round but the difference was not comparable to that of 2014.

33. AUR secured 23 percent of the diaspora vote in 2020. Vladimir Bortun, "Romanian
legislative elections in the diaspora: Record participation and the emergence of the
nationalist vote," *MIGRADEMO Blog Posts*, 2020, https://migrademo.eu/romanian
-legislative-elections-in-the-diaspora-record-participation-and-the-emergence-of-the
-nationalist-vote/; and Magdalena Ulceluse, "How the Romanian diaspora helped put a new far-right party on the political map," *EUROPP—European Politics and Policy*, 2020, https://blogs.lse.ac.uk/europpblog/2020/12/17
/how-the-romanian-diaspora-helped-put-a-new-far-right-party-on-the-political-map/.

34. Code for Romania, "Website Rezultate Vot."

35. "Mitinguri în tară și în Capitală: Aproximativ 10.000 de oameni au manifestat pentru prelungirea votului în diaspora," *Mediafax*, 2014; Gherghina, "The
Romanian presidential election, November 2014"; "Thousands protest in Romania ahead of presidential run-off vote," *Reuters*, 2015; and Andrei Schwartz,
"Romania rocked by protests ahead of presidential election runoff," *Euractiv*,
November 10, 2014, https://www.euractiv.com/section/central-europe/news
/romania-rocked-by-protests-ahead-of-presidential-election-runoff/.

36. "Romanii din Europa, proteste in fata ambasadelor—Ne cer si noua sa iesim in strada,"
Ziare.Com, 2014.

37. "Parlamentul a adoptat codul de procedură penală: LISTA amendamentelor," *Digi24*,
2018, "Parchetul general: 21 de articole modificate din codul penal ar fi neconstituționale," *Digi24*, 2018.

38. Kit Gillet, "Violence Erupts as Tens of Thousands Protest Corruption in Romania,"

New York Times, August 10, 2018; "50.000 de oameni au protestat în Piaţa Victoriei: Jandarmii au intervenit cu gaze şi spray lacrimogen: 440 de răniţi," *Stirileprotv,* 2018.

39. Andreea Ghinea, "Romani din diaspora care #rezista de peste 170 de zile: 'Pana la alegeri oamenii vor creste. starea de trezire ii va molipsi,'" *Ziare.Com*, 2017.

40. Ghinea, "Romani din diaspora care #rezista de peste 170 de zile."

41. "Tudorel Toader: Declanşez procedura de revocare din funcţie a procurorului-şef al DNA," *Digi24*, 2018. In 2019, Kövesi was elected as the first European chief prosecutor.

42. "Dragnea, condamnat la 3 ani şi 6 luni de închisoare cu executare," *Digi24*, 2018. The PSD leader Liviu Dragnea was imprisoned in May 2019 in the aftermath of the elections for the European Parliament in Romania.

43. "Anti-government protest in Romania turns violent," *Reuters*, August 10, 2018, https://www.reuters.com/article/us-romania-protests-idUSKBN1KV1YO.

44. Matei Alexandru, "Înjurăturile Politicienilor la adresa diasporei şi atitudinile ostile faţă de românii plecaţi la muncă în străinătate," *G4Media*, 2018; "Dragnea: Mitingul diasporei este politic: Îmi exprim speranţa că vor fi proteste paşnice," *Stirileprotv*, 2018.

45. "Românca plecată în austria care şi-a dat demisia ca să vină la protestul de azi," *Digi24*, August 2018.

46. "Sute de români se întorc în ţară pentru mitingul diasporei," *Digi24*, August 2018.

47. "Anti-government protest in Romania turns violent," and "Mitingul Diasporei, susţinut şi în marile oraşe din ţară: zeci de mii de oameni au protestat la cluj, iaşi, sibiu, timişoara sau braşov," *HotNews.Ro*, August 2018.

48. Anca Olteanu, "Povestile celor care se intorc, dar nu râman: Diaspora la protest in Romania," *Wall-Street.Ro*, 2018.

49. "Romanian police clash with anti-government protesters," *BBC News*, August 2018.

50. "Ce scrie presa internationala despre protestul diasporei de la bucuresti: Un protest anti-PSD din romania se termina in violenta," *Wall-Street.Ro*, 2018.

51. "Sute de români se întorc în ţară pentru mitingul diasporei."

52. Ciprian Apetrei, "Ce a cautat Diaspora la protest? Tara Lor, batjocorita si furata de unii care nu o respecta," *Ziare.Com*, August 2018.

53. Magda Gradinaru, "Plecat de 20 de ani din tara, fizicianul Cristian Presura explica de ce vine la protestul din 10 august," *Ziare.Com*, August 2018.

54. Dumitru Sandu, "Două Românii şi o diasporă?" *Contributors.Ro*, 2014.

55. "Studiu IRES: Generaţia Facebook şi convergenţa media au dus la victoria lui Klaus Iohannis," *Mediafax*, 2014.

56. Camelia Badea, "Cum se vede din SUA infrangerea lui Ponta in alegerile prezidentiale," *Ziare.Com*, 2014.

BIBLIOGRAPHY

Ahmadov, Anar K., and Gwendolyn Sasse. "Empowering to Engage with the Homeland: Do Migration Experience and Environment Foster Political Remittances?" *Comparative Migration Studies* 4, no. 1 (2016): 1–25.

Alexandru, Matei. "Înjurăturile Politicienilor La Adresa Diasporei Și Atitudinile Ostile Față de Românii Plecați La Muncă În Străinătate." *G4Media*, 2018.

Apetrei, Ciprian. "Ce a Cautat Diaspora La Protest? Tara Lor, Batjocorita Si Furata de Unii Care Nu o Respecta." *Ziare.Com*, August 2018.

Badea, Camelia. "Cum Se Vede Din SUA Infrangerea Lui Ponta in Alegerile Prezidentiale." *Ziare.Com*, 2014.

BBC News. "Romanian Police Clash with Anti-Government Protesters." August 2018.

Bertelli, Davide, Marta Bivand Erdal, Kacper Szulecki, Anatolie Cosciug, Angelina Kussy, Gabriella Mikiewicz, and Corina Tulbure. *Migrant Political Engagement and Voting from Abroad. Insights from Interviews with Polish and Romanian Migrants in Barcelona and Oslo*. Oslo: Peace Research Institute Oslo (PRIO), 2021.

Bortun, Vladimir. "Romanian Legislative Elections in the Diaspora: Record Participation and the Emergence of the Nationalist Vote." *MIGRADEMO Blog Posts*, 2020. https://migrademo.eu /romanian-legislative-elections-in-the-diaspora-record-participation-and-the-emergence-of -the-nationalist-vote/.

Borz, Gabriela. "Political Parties and Diaspora: A Case Study of Romanian Parties' Involvement Abroad." *Parliamentary Affairs* 73, no. 4 (2020): 901–17. https://doi.org/10.1093 /pa/gsaa044.

Carling, Jørgen, and Marta Bivand Erdal. "Return Migration and Transnationalism: How Are the Two Connected?" *International Migration* 52, no. 6 (2014): 2–12.

Ciornei, Irina, and Eva Ostergaard-Nielsen. "ST 5 Emigration and Turnout: Determinants of Non-Resident Citizen Electoral Mobilization in Home Country Legislative Elections," paper presented at the Congress of the French Association of Political Science, 2015, 1–19.

Code for Romania. "Website Rezultate Vot (Website Vote Results)," 2021. https://rezultatevot .ro/elections/112/results.

Digi24. "Dragnea, Condamnat La 3 Ani Și 6 Luni de Închisoare Cu Executare." 2018.

Digi24. "Parchetul General: 21 de Articole Modificate Din Codul Penal Ar Fi Neconstituționale." 2018.

Digi24. "Parlamentul a Adoptat Codul de Procedură Penală. LISTA Amendamentelor." 2018.

Digi24. "Românca Plecată În Austria Care Și-a Dat Demisia ca Să Vină La Protestul de Azi." August 2018.

Digi24. "Sute de Români Se Întorc În Țară Pentru Mitingul Diasporei." August 2018.

Digi24. "Tudorel Toader: Declanșez Procedura de Revocare Din Funcție a Procurorului-Șef Al DNA." 2018.

Dospinescu, Andrei, and Giuseppe Russo. *Romania: Systematic Country Diagnostic.* World Bank Group, 2018. http://documents.worldbank.org/curated/en/210481530907970911 /pdf/128064-SCD-PUBLIC-P160439-RomaniaSCDBackgroundNoteMigration.pdf.

Dumitru, Chihaia. "Doamna Consul M-a Întrebat Care e Motivul Real Pentru Care Renunț La Cetățenie. I-Am Spus Că Nu o Să-i Sune Bine. După Care Mi-a Zis: Este Ilegal Acest Motiv, Nu Putem Scrie Așa Ceva. Interviu Cu Un Fost Român." *Republica,* 2018.

Dustmann, Christian, and Josep Mestres. "Remittances and Temporary Migration." *Journal of Development Economics* 92, no. 1 (2010): 62–70.

Elrick, Tim, and Oana Ciobanu. "Migration Networks and Policy Impacts: Insights from Romanian-Spanish Migrations." *Global Networks* 9, no. 1 (2009): 100–16.

Eugensson, Andreas. "Suedezii Contra Corupției Din România: Cum Am Organizat Un Protest În Suedia În Semn de Solidaritate Cu Piața Victoriei Din București." *Republica,* 2017.

Gherghina, Sergiu. "The Romanian Presidential Election, November 2014." *Electoral Studies* 38 (2015): 109–14.

Gherghina, Sergiu, and Aurelian Plopeanu. "Who Wishes to Return? Ties to Home Country among the Romanian Migrants." *Nationalities Papers* 48, no. 5 (2020): 876–90.

Gherghina, Sergiu, and Sorina Soare. "Vote-Seeking Among Non-Resident Citizens: How Romanian Parties Form Organisations Abroad." *Representation* 59, no. 1 (2023): 423–39.

Gherghina, Sergiu, and Huan-Kai Tseng. "Voting Home or Abroad? Comparing Migrants' Electoral Participation in Countries of Origin and of Residence." *Nationalities Papers* 44, no. 3 (2016): 456–72.

Ghinea, Andreea. "Romani Din Diaspora Care #rezista de Peste 170 de Zile. 'Pana La Alegeri Oamenii Vor Creste. Starea de Trezire Ii va Molipsi.'" *Ziare.Com,* 2017.

Gillet, Kit. "Violence Erupts as Tens of Thousands Protest Corruption in Romania." *New York Times,* August 10, 2018.

Goldring, Luin. "Family and Collective Remittances to Mexico: A Multi-Dimensional Typology." *Development and Change* 35, no. 4 (2004): 799–840.

Grad, Marius, Sergiu Gherghina, and Adrian Ivan. "Migrants and Their Families in the Home Country: A Bi-Directional Influence on Voting Behaviour." *Southeast European and Black Sea Studies* 20, no. 3 (2020): 393–410.

Gradinaru, Magda. "Plecat de 20 de Ani Din Tara, Fizicianul Cristian Presura Explica de Ce Vine La Protestul Din 10 August." *Ziare.Com,* August 2018.

Guarnizo, Luis E., and Ali R. Chaudhary. "Determinants of Transnational Political Engagement among Dominican and Colombian Migrants in Southern Europe." *IMI Working Papers Series,* vol. 82. Oxford, 2014.

Guarnizo, Luis Eduardo, Alejandro Portes, and William Haller. "Assimilation and Transnationalism: Determinants of Transnational Political Action among Contemporary Migrants." *American Journal of Sociology* 108, no. 6 (2003): 1211–48.

HotNews.ro. "Mitingul Diasporei, Susţinut Şi În Marile Oraşe Din Ţară: Zeci de Mii de Oameni Au Protestat La Cluj, Iaşi, Sibiu, Timişoara Sau Braşov." August 2018.

Mediafax. "Mitinguri În Ţară Şi În Capitală. Aproximativ 10.000 de Oameni Au Manifestat Pentru Prelungirea Votului În Diaspora." 2014.

Mediafax. "Studiu IRES: Generaţia Facebook Şi Convergenţa Media Au Dus La Victoria Lui Klaus Iohannis." 2014.

Mügge, Liza, Maria Kranendonk, Floris Vermeulen, and Nermin Aydemir. "Migrant Votes 'Here' and 'There': Transnational Electoral Behavior of Turks in the Netherlands." *Migration Studies* 9, no. 3 (2021): 400–22.

Năstase, Adrian. "Alegeri Prezidentiale La Final: Primele Observatii." *Personal Blog*, 2009. https://nastase.wordpress.com/2009/12/08/alegeri-prezidentiale-la-final-primele-observatii/.

Olteanu, Anca. "Povestile Celor Care Se Intorc, Dar Nu Raman: Diaspora La Protest in Romania." *Wall-Street.Ro*, 2018.

Pilati, Katia, and Barbara Herman. "Comparing Engagement by Migrants in Domestic and in Country-of-Origin Political Activities across European Cities." *Acta Politica* 55, no. 1 (2020): 103–29.

Reuters. "Anti-Government Protest in Romania Turns Violent." August 10, 2018. https://www.reuters.com/article/us-romania-protests-idUSKBN1KV1YO.

Reuters. "Thousands Protest in Romania Ahead of Presidential Run-off Vote." 2015.

Sabău, Cristiana. "Încep Să Plece Românii Din Străinătate: Salariul Minim de Aici Îl Câştigăm În Spania În Trei Zile." *TimpOnline.Ro*, 2017.

Sandu, Dumitru. "Două Românii Şi o Diasporă?" *Contributors.Ro*, 2014.

Sandu, Dumitru. *Temporary Stay Abroad: Romanians' Economic Migration: 1990–2006*. Bucharest: Open Society Foundation, 2006.

Schwartz, Andrei. "Romania Rocked by Protests Ahead of Presidential Election Runoff." Euractiv, 2014.

Stănculescu, Sofia, and Manuela Stoiciu. *Impactul Crizei Economice Asupra Migratiei Fortei de Munca Din Romania*. Bucharest: Paideia, 2012.

Stefanescu, Cristian. "Romanians Find Their Future Abroad without Forgetting Home." *Deutsche Welle*, August 9, 2019. https://www.dw.com/en/romanians-find-their-future-abroad-without-forgetting-home/a-49972293.

Stirileprotv. "50.000 de Oameni Au Protestat În Piaţa Victoriei. Jandarmii Au Intervenit Cu Gaze Şi Spray Lacrimogen: 440 de Răniţi." 2018.

Stirileprotv. "Dragnea: Mitingul Diasporei Este Politic: Îmi Exprim Speranţa Că Vor Fi Proteste Paşnice." 2018.

Ulceluse, Magdalena. "How the Romanian Diaspora Helped Put a New Far-Right Party on the Political Map." *EUROPP—European Politics and Policy*, 2020. https://blogs.lse.ac.uk/europpblog/2020/12/17/how-the-romanian-diaspora-helped-put-a-new-far-right-party-on-the-political-map/.

Wall-Street.ro. "Ce Scrie Presa Internationala Despre Protestul Diasporei de La Bucuresti: Un Protest Anti-PSD Din Romania Se Termina in Violenta." 2018.

Waterbury, Myra A. "Caught between Nationalism and Transnationalism: How Central and East European States Respond to East–West Emigration." *International Political Science Review* 39, no. 3 (2018): 338–52.

Wessendorf, Susanne. "'Roots Migrants': Transnationalism and 'Return' among Second-Generation Italians in Switzerland." *Journal of Ethnic and Migration Studies* 33, no. 7 (2007): 1083–1102.

Ziare.com. "Romanii Din Europa, Proteste in Fata Ambasadelor—Ne Cer Si Noua Sa Iesim in Strada." 2014.

CONTRIBUTORS

EDITORS

Jill Massino, PhD, is associate professor of history at UNC Charlotte, where she teaches courses on modern European and comparative history. Her research examines gender, citizenship, and everyday life in socialist and postsocialist Romania. An oral historian, she is interested in the relationship between individual, collective, and state representations of the past, particularly in the context of one-party states. She has published numerous articles and books, including *Gender Politics and Everyday Life in State Socialist Eastern and Central Europe* (co-edited with Shana Penn; 2009) and *Ambiguous Transitions: Gender, the State, and Everyday Life in Socialist and Postsocialist Romania* (2019).

Markus Wien, PhD, is professor of European history at the American University in Bulgaria. His publications include *Market and Modernization: German-Bulgarian Economic Relations 1918–1944 and Their Conceptual Foundations* (2007); "Selektive Wissensimporte: Die Beispieldörfer des Mitteleuropäischen Wirtschaftstags im Kontext des bulgarischen landwirtschaftlichen Ausbildungswesens," in Carola Sachse, ed., *"Mitteleuropa' und 'Südosteuropa' als Planungsraum: Wirtschafts- und kulturpolitische Expertisen im Zeitalter der Weltkriege"* (2010); and "Zwischen Bauerndiktatur und Königsrepublik: Verfassungsfragen in Bulgarien 1918–2005," in Bernd Braun, ed., *Es lebe die Republik: Der Erste Weltkrieg und das Ende der Monarchien in Deutschland und Europa* (2021).

AUTHORS

Raia Apostolova, PhD, is an assistant professor in sociology at the Institute of Philosophy and Sociology at the Bulgarian Academy of Sciences. Her current research explores the formation and disintegration of migration regimes in the socialist and early postsocialist periods.

Corina Doboş, PhD, is senior researcher at the National Institute for the Study of Totalitarianism (Romanian Academy) and researcher and associated lecturer in History at the University of Bucharest. From 2018 to 2020 she was PI of the research project "Crafting Demographic Knowledge in the 20th Century: Population and Development in an Eastern European Periphery" (DEMOECRO). Her research interests include: the history of science, history of medicine, population theories and policies in the twentieth century, expert knowledge formation, social history, and global history.

Raluca Farcas is a PhD candidate in the Department of International Studies and Contemporary History at Babes-Bolyai University in Cluj, Romania. Her research focuses on political leadership, political participation, and security studies.

Annina Gagyiova, PhD, is a historian specializing in socialist Hungary. She currently holds a postdoctoral position at the Czech Academy of Sciences in Prague, Czech Republic. Her research interests include the history of everyday life, consumption, and expertise in state-socialist Central Eastern Europe.

Sergiu Gherghina is an associate professor of Comparative Politics in the Department of Politics, University of Glasgow. His research interests lie in party politics, legislative and voting behavior, democratization, and the use of direct democracy.

Till Hilmar received his PhD in sociology from Yale University and is a postdoctoral researcher in the Department of Sociology at the University of Vienna. His research interests include cultural and political sociology, post-1989 transformations, and text-as-data. His book *Deserved: Economic Memories after the Fall of the Iron Curtain* (2023) examines popular experiences of the East German and Czech transformations after 1989.

Sándor Horváth, PhD, is Senior Research Fellow and Head of the Department for Contemporary History at the Institute of History, Research Centre for the Humanities, Budapest. He is the author of *Stalinism Reloaded: Everyday Life in Stalin-City, Hungary* (2017) and *Children of Communism: Politicizing Youth Revolt in Communist Budapest in the 1960s* (2022). He is also founding editor of the *Hungarian Historical Review*.

Luciana M. Jinga, PhD, is a researcher at the Institute for the Investigation of Communist Crimes and the Memory of the Romanian Exile in Bucharest, Romania. Her research examines the evolution and characteristics of communist regimes in Central and Eastern Europe, with a specific focus on gender, traumatic childhood, and humanitarian aid.

Friederike Kind-Kovacs, PhD, is a Senior Researcher at the Hannah Arendt Institute for the Study of Totalitarianism in Dresden, Germany, and director of the research association Voluntarism and Care Organization during Transformation. Her research interests include the history of East and Southeast Europe, the history of media and culture during the Cold War, and everyday life and opposition in real existing socialism.

Ondrej Klípa, PhD, is assistant professor in the Department of Russian and East European Studies at Charles University, Prague. His research focuses on state socialism, nationalism, migration, and ethnic minorities.

Agnieszka Kościańska is professor in the Department of Ethnology and Cultural Anthropology at the University of Warsaw. She is the author and (co)editor of several volumes on gender and sexuality, including *Gender, Pleasure and Violence: The Construction of Expert Knowledge of Sexuality in Poland* (2021) and *To See a Moose: The History of Polish Sex Education* (2021).

Victor Petrov is an assistant professor of history at the University of Tennessee, Knoxville. He received his PhD in 2017 from Columbia University. His research focuses on the modern Balkans, the Cold War, and histories of technologies and alternative modernities. He is the author of *Balkan Cyberia: Cold War Computing, Bulgarian Modernization, and the Information Age behind the Iron Curtain* (2023).

Hadley Z. Renkin, PhD, is an associate professor in the Department of Gender Studies at Central European University, Vienna, Austria. His research focuses on sexual politics, citizenship, and belonging in Hungary and Eastern Europe, as well as on the politics of historical entanglements of science and sexuality.

Cristofer Scarboro is a professor of history at King's College in Wilkes-Barre, Pennsylvania. He is the author of *The Late Socialist Good Life in Bulgaria: Meaning and Living in a Permanent Present Tense* (2011) and co-editor of *The Socialist Good Life: Desire, Development, and Standards of Living in Eastern Europe* (2020).

Beatrice Scutaru, PhD, is an assistant professor of European history at the School of History and Geography at Dublin City University. She specializes in East European migration and diaspora populations and the history of childhood.

Joanna Wawrzyniak is associate professor in sociology and director of the Center for Research on Social Memory at the University of Warsaw. She is vice-chair of the EU COST Action "Slow Memory: Transformative Practices for Times of Uneven and Accelerating Change."

INDEX

Printed in the USA
CPSIA information can be obtained
at www.ICGtesting.com
CBHW051237181024
16053CB00010B/1046